Accountability for Violations of International Humanitarian Law

International criminal adjudication, together with the prosecution and appropriate punishment of offenders at a national level, remains the most effective means of enforcing international humanitarian law. This book considers the various issues emanating from present-day breaches of norms of international humanitarian law (IHL) and at how impunity for such breaches can be tackled.

Honouring the work of Timothy McCormack, Professor of International Law at the University of Melbourne and a world renowned expert on international humanitarian law, contributors to the book explore the interplay between the rules governing accountability for violations of IHL and other areas of law that impact on the prosecution of war crimes, including international criminal law, human rights law, arms control law, constitutional law and national criminal law.

In providing a contemporary consideration of the various issues emerging from present-day breaches of norms of IHL, especially in light of growing interest in 'fragmentation' and 'normative pluralism', this book will be of great use and interest to students and researchers in public international law, international law, and conflict studies.

Jadranka Petrovic is a Lecturer at the Department of Business Law and Taxation, Faculty of Business and Economics, Monash University, Australia.

Routledge Research in the Law of Armed Conflict

Available titles in this series include:

Accountability for Violations of International Humanitarian Law

Essays in Honour of Tim McCormack

Edited by Jadranka Petrovic

Routledge
Taylor & Francis Group

LONDON AND NEW YORK

First published 2016
by Routledge
2 Park Square, Milton Park, Abingdon, Oxon, OX14 4RN

and by Routledge
711 Third Avenue, New York, NY 10017

Routledge is an imprint of the Taylor & Francis Group, an informa business

British Library Cataloguing in Publication Data
A catalogue record for this book is available from the British Library

Library of Congress Cataloging-in-Publication Data
A catalog record has been requested for this book

ISBN: 978-1-138-02526-4 (hbk)
ISBN: 978-1-315-76955-4 (ebk)

Typeset in Baskerville by
Florence Production Ltd, Stoodleigh, Devon

Printed and bound in Great Britain by
TJ International Ltd, Padstow, Cornwall

Contents

Contributors

Bryan Cavanagh, Squadron Leader, joined the Royal Australian Air Force as a sponsored undergraduate in 2001. He has served in a variety of roles during his career, including in the Directorate of Military Justice, Headquarters 92 Wing (Maritime Patrol), Headquarters 324 Combat Support Squadron (based in Malaysia), and Headquarters 81 Wing (Air Combat). Squadron Leader Cavanagh has deployed on a number of occasions, most recently as an embedded legal adviser within the International Security Assistance Forces based in Kabul, providing advice on targeting operations. He holds a BA/LLB from the Queensland University of Technology and a Masters of Military Law from the Australian National University.

Andrew Coleman (Dr) is a Senior Lecturer in law at the Monash Business School, Monash University, Melbourne, Australia. He completed his PhD in 2008 at the Asia Pacific Centre for Military Law, the University of Melbourne, where he examined the role of the International Court of Justice in resolving claims for self-determination. Andrew has published in the area of public international law, in particular, national sovereignty, the right to democracy, globalisation and self-determination. His most recent publications include: 'International Law's Vanity – "Westphalian" Meets "Eastphalian" Sovereignty – China in Globalised World' (2013) 3(2) *Asian Journal of International Law* 237 (a co-authored article with Dr Jackson Maogoto); 'The Right to Self-Determination: Can It Lapse?' (2014) 5(1) *Journal of Philosophy of International Law* 6; 'Changing the Guard – the Price of Democracy: Lessons from the Arab Spring on Constitutionalism' in Carlo Panara and Gary Wilson (eds), *The Arab Spring New Patterns for Democracy and International Law* (Brill, 2013) 1 (a co-authored book chapter with Dr Jackson Maogoto); *Resolving Self-Determination Claims* (Routledge, 2013); and 'The Arab Spring's Constitutional Indigestion: Has Democracy Failed in the Middle East?' (2014) 35 *Liverpool Law Review* 105 (a co-authored article with Dr Jackson Maogoto).

Helen Durham (Dr) is Director of International Law and Policy at the International Committee of the Red Cross (ICRC) and was previously Director of International Law and Strategy at the Australian Red Cross. She is admitted as a Barrister and Solicitor of the Supreme Court of Victoria and is a Senior Fellow at Melbourne Law School. Helen has a Doctorate of Juridical Science from Melbourne Law School with a focus on International Humanitarian Law (IHL) and International Criminal Law. She has been involved in a range of field operations with the ICRC (in the Pacific and South Asia) as well as being part of the delegation to the negotiations for the *International Criminal Court* in Rome and New York. Helen spent time as Director of Research for the Asia Pacific Centre for Military Law and is widely published on IHL-related matters.

Sarah Finnin (Dr) graduated with a BA/LLB (Hons) from the University of Melbourne in 2006 and a PhD in Law in 2011. Her thesis, on accessorial liability under Article 25(3)(b) and (c) of the *Rome Statute*, was published in 2012 by Brill, Martinus Nijhoff Publishers. Sarah has worked as a Researcher at the Asia Pacific Centre for Military Law and as a Researcher for Major Michael 'Dan' Mori, military-appointed defence counsel to David Hicks. She was the Senior Associate to Justice Lex Lasry of the Supreme Court of Victoria from 2007 to 2009 and a Prosecutor with the Northern Territory Office of the Director of Public Prosecutions in Alice Springs from 2011 to 2013.

Ian Henderson (Dr), Group Captain, AM, PhD, joined the Royal Australian Air Force in July 1990. He has served in various legal positions at the tactical, operational and strategic level. He has deployed on three occasions: East Timor (1999), Afghanistan (2002) and the Middle East (2003) where he was the senior Australian legal officer in the Combined Air Operations Centre. He holds a BSc and LLB from Monash University, a LLM and PhD from the University of Melbourne, and he was made a member of the Order of Australia (Military Division) in 2011 'for exceptional service in the field of military law'. Along with various book chapters and journal articles on military operations law, he is the author of *The Contemporary Law of Targeting: Military Objectives, Proportionality and Precautions in Attack under Additional Protocol I* (Martinus Nijhoff, 2009).

Rebecca Hughes is a lawyer with the Northern Land Council, Darwin, Australia, where her practice focuses on indigenous land rights, native title, mining, environment and property law. After completing an LLB (Hons), BA and DML (French) at the University of Melbourne in 2008, Rebecca practiced as a lawyer at Ashurst Australia (formerly Blake Dawson), Telstra and the Northern Australian Aboriginal Justice Agency. She has also completed a GDLP. During her studies at the Melbourne Law School, Rebecca worked as a researcher at the Asia Pacific Centre for Military Law. In 2008, Rebecca was an Editor of the *Melbourne Journal of International Law*. She was also member of the University of Melbourne's Jessup Moot team in 2007 where she had the honour of being coached by Professor Tim McCormack.

Michelle Lesh (Dr) holds a BA/LLB (Hons) from Monash University (2006) and a PhD from the University of Melbourne (2012). She was a Post-Doctoral

Fellow at the Hebrew University of Jerusalem (2013). Her publications include: 'A Critical Discussion of the Second Turkel Report and How it Engages with the Duty to Investigate under International Law', *The Yearbook of International Humanitarian Law* (2013); 'Interplay as regards Conduct of Hostilities', in Jann Kleffner and Erika de Wet (eds), *Convergence and Conflicts of Human Rights and International Humanitarian Law in Military Operations* (Pretoria University Law Press, 2014); 'The Israeli Military Justice System and the Turkel Report', in Alison Duxbury and Matthew Groves (eds), *Military Justice in the Modern Age* (Cambridge University Press, forthcoming 2015); 'Accountability for Targeted Killing Operations: International Humanitarian Law, International Human Rights Law and the Relevance of the Principle of Proportionality', in Jadranka Petrovic (ed.), *Accountability for Violations of IHL: Essays in Honour of Tim McCormack* (Routledge, forthcoming 2015). She is currently working on a monograph entitled *Israel's Policy of Targeted Killing and International Humanitarian Law*. Dr Lesh's research interests include international humanitarian law, international human rights law and the interaction between these bodies of law. Her work in this field has included being a foreign law clerk for Chief Justice Barak (Ret.) at Israel's Supreme Court at the time he worked on the Target Killing case, an assistant editor of the Correspondent's Reports of the *Yearbook of International Humanitarian Law*, a research assistant for Phase II of the Turkel Commission of Enquiry into Israel's Processes for Investigating Alleged Violations of the Law of Armed Conflict, and human rights officer at UN Office for the High Commissioner for Human Rights.

Jackson Nyamuya Maogoto (Dr) holds a Bachelor of Laws with First Class Honours from Moi University (Kenya); three postgraduate degrees from the University of Cambridge (Masters in Law with Honours), University of Technology Sydney (Masters in Law) and The University of Melbourne (Doctorate in Law). Jackson is currently a Senior Lecturer in International Law at the University of Manchester. Jackson has published extensively in his fields of teaching and research interest. He is the author of seven books, several book chapters and more than three dozen refereed articles in general and specialist journals.

Eve Massingham is an International Humanitarian Law (IHL) Officer with the Australian Red Cross and a PhD candidate with the School of Law at the University of Queensland. As a British Council Chevening Scholar at King's College London, Eve completed a Master of Laws focusing on IHL and international law on the use of force. Eve also holds a Master of International Development, Bachelor of Laws (Hons) and Graduate Diploma of Legal Practice. She is admitted as a solicitor of the Supreme Courts of Queensland and New South Wales and the High Court of Australia. Eve has worked in private legal practice, as an Associate to a Federal Court Judge, as an Army Reserve Officer and as an intern with the Office of the Prosecutor of the International Criminal Court. She is published on IHL-related matters.

Vasko Nastevski (Dr) completed his PhD (2011) under the auspices of the Asia Pacific Centre for Military Law in the Melbourne Law School at the University of Melbourne. He also completed a Master of Public and International Law (2004) at the same institution. Dr Nastevski has contributed to various individual research projects relating to International Criminal Law and International Humanitarian Law and has provided advice to different media outlets on these subjects. Dr Nastevski has also published chapters on International Human Rights Law. His research has been significantly inspired by Professor Tim McCormack, especially the topic of his chapter contributed to this book.

Jadranka Petrovic (Dr) is a Melbourne Law School graduate. In addition to her degrees in law (doctoral, masters and bachelor), she has also completed a number of non-degree-based courses, both at postgraduate and undergraduate level, in law and in other disciplines at The University of Melbourne and other institutions. She currently teaches and researches in International Law at Monash University. Her research interests include various areas of International Law, including International Humanitarian Law and International Criminal Law. She is the author of *The Old Bridge of Mostar and Increasing Respect for Cultural Property in Armed Conflict* (Brill, Martinus Nijhoff Publishers, 2013). Her other work has also been published by some of the world's most prestigious publishers. Jadranka's professional membership includes the Australian Law Teachers Association, the Australian and New Zealand Society of International Law and the International Law Association. She also serves on the Editorial Board of the *Journal of Philosophy of International Law*.

Sophie Rigney is a PhD candidate at the University of Melbourne Law School, Australia. Between 2009 and 2011, she worked in Defence at the *ICTY*, including as Case Manager and Legal Assistant for the defence of Lahi Brahimaj, in the retrial of Ramush Haradinaj, Idriz Balaj and Lahi Brahimaj; and as a Legal Assistant for the Standby Counsel in the case of Radovan Karadžic. She holds first-class honours degrees in both Law and Political Science from the University of Tasmania. Her research examines the links between fairness, the rights of the accused and trial procedure in International Criminal Law.

Dale Stephens (Dr) CSM spent 20 years as a legal officer in the Royal Australian Navy. In February 2013, Captain Stephens RAN transferred to the Navy Reserve and took up a full-time position as an Associate Professor at The University of Adelaide Law School. His operational deployments include East Timor in 1999 and 2000 and Iraq in 2005 and 2008. In 2004, Dr Stephens completed a Master of Laws degree at Harvard University Law School and taught at the US Naval War College in Newport, Rhode Island during the 2004/2005 academic year. In February 2014 he completed his Doctor of Juridical Science (SJD) at Harvard Law School. His dissertation topic was 'Lawfare or Law Fair? The Role of Law in Military Decision Making'.

Phoebe Wynn-Pope (Dr) is Director of International Humanitarian Law and Movement Relations at the Australian Red Cross and a Fellow at the Asia Pacific Centre for Military Law at the University of Melbourne. She has 25 years' experience in the humanitarian sector and has worked in complex humanitarian emergencies and conflict zones throughout Africa, the Middle East and Europe including many of the major humanitarian emergencies of the 1990s: Bosnia and Herzegovina, Somalia, Rwanda and Iran/Iraq following the first Gulf War. Following this experience Phoebe returned to Australia to undertake a PhD in International Law, focusing on the role of the international community when confronting war crimes, crimes against humanity and genocide. Most recently, Phoebe was a founding Director of the Humanitarian Advisory Group where her work focused on the protection of civilians in armed conflict.

Acknowledgements

My fellow contributors and I dedicate this book to Professor Tim McCormack to thank him for his outstanding supervision of our theses at the Melbourne Law School and enriching our lives in various other ways, and to express our deepest respect for his extraordinary intellectual and unique human qualities. Professor McCormack has taken genuine personal interest in each of us as individuals, not only guiding us as an academic, patiently and skilfully, but also as a friend and mentor, walking beside us consistently and unreservedly over the years. We will be forever appreciative of his scholarship, support and kindness.

Although this book is edited by one person, who accepts full responsibility for errors and infelicities of style, others have also played an important part in its production.

First I wish to thank Professor McCormack for providing me with all the information I needed in the course of editing this book, and also each of the contributors to this book for their willingness to contribute their chapters and, as with any edited book, to sacrifice the time and effort required not only to produce those very chapters but also to meet the other various demands that a project such as this requires behind the scenes. The contributors have formed an exceptionally harmonious and dedicated team. I have been privileged to be part of it.

I note with deep sadness the passing of our colleague, Dr Paul Muggleton, on 15 December 2013. Dr Muggleton was a passionate scholar of International Humanitarian Law. Despite being keenly interested in honouring Professor McCormack through this collection, his illness prevented him from joining the project. He will be sorely missed and will remain part of this book in spirit.

I am indebted to my distinguished publisher – Routledge – without whose support and enthusiasm this collection of essays ultimately would not have been completed. In particular, I would like to acknowledge Routledge's Editorial Board for their consistent support, Katie Carpenter for her interest in my research generally, the anonymous referees for their most constructive comments and suggestions at the initial stage in the development of the book, and Mark Sapwell with whom I have closely collaborated throughout the process and who has been the most wonderful guide, armed with patience, knowledge, efficiency and understanding, the last of which has been especially precious wherever I, as an editor, faced a stumbling block. I am also very much grateful to Ashlie Jackman at Routledge, and Jennifer Hinchliffe, Amy Wheeler and the rest of the Florence Production team for their wonderful work.

My special thanks go to the Asia Pacific Centre for Military Law at the Melbourne Law School – above all to Bruce 'Ossie' Oswald for his encouragement and Cathy Hutton for her help with, *inter alia*, getting in contact with all the individuals required in relation to this book.

I am equally grateful to my dear friends and colleagues Rebecca Hughes and Peggy Law who have generously volunteered their time and skills to see various components of this project realised by making themselves available on my, always, short notice, when I was most pressed with time. I remain deeply obliged to both of them. I am just as appreciative of Rosie Bacher's assistance with proofreading footnotes in some of the chapters in this book and of Dragan's and Sasha's technical aid in the final stage of the project (when my computer, printer and other indispensible equipment started to disobey me, one after the other).

List of abbreviations

AAAS	American Association for the Advancement of Science
ABiH	Army of Bosnia and Herzegovina
ADF	Australian Defence Force
AFRC	Armed Forces Revolutionary Council
AINA	Assyrian International News Agency
API	*Additional Protocol I (Protocol I Additional to the Geneva Conventions of 12 August 1949)*
APII	*Additional Protocol II (Protocol II Additional to the Geneva Conventions of 12 August 1949)*
APSA	Association for the Protection of Syrian Archaeology
CCL No. 10	*Control Council Law No. 10*
Common Art 1	Article 1, common to all four *Geneva Conventions of 1949* and Article 1(1) of *Additional Protocols I and III to the Geneva Conventions of 1949*
DHA	Department for Humanitarian Affairs (established by UNGA)
DPP	Director of Public Prosecutions
FEC	Far Eastern Commission
FDLR	*Forces Démocratiques pour la Libération du Rwanda – Forces Combattantes Abacunguzi*
FPLC	*Forces Patriotiques pour la Libération du Congo*
GA Res	United Nations General Assembly Resolution
GCI	*1949 Geneva Convention I*
GCII	*1949 Geneva Convention II*
GCIII	*1949 Geneva Convention III*
GCIV	*1949 Geneva Convention IV*
HRC	Human Rights Committee
HREOC	Human Rights and Equal Opportunity Commission
HVO	Croat Defence Council [*Hrvatsko Vijeće Obrane*]
IAC	International armed conflict
IACHR	Inter-American Commission on Human Rights
ICC	International Criminal Court
ICJ	International Court of Justice

ICL	International Criminal Law
ICOM	International Council of Museums
ICRC	International Committee of the Red Cross
ICTR	International Criminal Tribunal for Rwanda
ICTY	International Criminal Tribunal for the former Yugoslavia
IDF	Israel Defense Force
IHL	International Humanitarian Law
IHRL	International Human Rights Law
IHT	*International Herald Tribune*
ILC	International Law Commission
ILM	*International Legal Materials*
IMT	International Military Tribunal (Nuremberg)
IMTFE	International Military Tribunal for the Far East
IS	Islamic State
ISIL	Islamic State of Iraq and the Levant
ISIS	Islamic State of Iraq and Syria
JSCOT	Joint Standing Committee on Treaties
LOAC	Law of armed conflict
MAG	Military Advocate General
NATO	North Atlantic Treaty Organization
NGOs	Non-governmental organisations
NIAC	Non-international armed conflict
OKW	German Armed Forces High Command
OTP	Office of the Prosecutor of the International Criminal Court
PISG	(Interim) Provisional Institutions of Self-Government (in Kosovo)
PRC	People's Republic of China
ROE	Rules of engagement
SCAP	Supreme Commander for the Allied Powers
SC Res	United Nations Security Council Resolution
SDC	Supreme Defence Council
SFRY	Socialist Federal Republic of Yugoslavia
SRK	Sarajevo Romanija Corps of the Army of the Republika Srpska
Syria	Syrian Arab Republic
UDI	(Kosovo) Unilateral Declaration of Independence
UK	United Kingdom
UN	United Nations
UN Doc	United Nations Document
UNESCO	United Nations Educational, Scientific and Cultural Organization
UNITAR	United Nations Institute for Training and Research
UNOCHA	UN Office for the Coordination of Humanitarian Affairs
UNOSAT	Operational Satellite Application Programme

UNRWA	United Nations Relief and Works Agency for Palestine Refugees in the Near East
UNSG	United Nations Secretary-General
UNTS	*United Nations Treaty Series*
UNWCC	United Nations War Crimes Commission
UPC	*Union des Patriotes Congolais*
US	United States of America
USSR	Union of Soviet Socialist Republics
VCLT	*Vienna Convention on the Law of Treaties 1969 (Vienna Convention)*
WWI	World War One
WWII	World War Two

Foreword

I am delighted to be a part of this tribute to one of Australia's finest contributors to international law and his role in the progress towards its better enforcement, adherence and understanding. Tim McCormack is not only a good friend but he is also someone Australia and the world should know more about and should celebrate. The challenge that has confronted those who wish to advance the cause of international law has been to find the marriage between meaningful constraints that will have some chance of practical application. Tim, uncommonly in the academic sphere, has actively pursued a deeper understanding and relationship with those who are at the coalface of these issues and 'reflective practitioners'. This has informed his support for international tribunal processes, his role in helping to create the *International Criminal Court (ICC)*, his involvement in the design of and participation in training for the military and his prolific efforts to interpret and promote understanding of the law.

This project is in many ways a perfect tribute to Tim and his work. It deals with the challenges presented to International Humanitarian Law (IHL) by the proliferation of non-international armed conflicts and the issues that have emerged in the era of the international enforcement of the law that has been ushered in by the introduction of the ICC. Insurgencies and internal conflicts are often conducted by forces whose very objective is to generate the kind of terror that they believe will result from specifically and deliberately violating the fundamental standards that IHL represents. This has been well illustrated by the conflicts in Syria and Iraq and the barbaric actions of both the Syrian Government in its use of chemical weapons against its own people and the depraved tactics of Daesh in Syria, Iraq and Libya.

Tim has long engaged in the dialogue around the problems presented to the ADF and the international community in this respect. This work will constitute an excellent contribution to that effort and in helping to resolve the dilemmas of enforcement and accountability for the standards we are attempting to set. There is no more important work in this field than ending the impunity that often has been associated with internal conflicts.

The ADF has been intimately associated with these issues throughout the history of its deployments since Somalia in 1993. In that operation we were confronted with the need to reconstitute the rule of law and good governance.

A major aspect of this was dealing with figures who had committed horrendous genocidal crimes in the civil war that gripped the country. We were able to use the guidance contained in IHL to assist with implementing a sound approach to this dilemma, which included establishing a proper detainee handling regime and facilitating the trial of the most serious of the war crimes suspects, the war lord Gutaale. This experience led me to fully appreciate what the ICC could contribute as, had that option been available to us, we could have removed Gutaale from Somalia and had him dealt with in a process that did not have the death penalty as an outcome. There was no way that he could have been held securely in Somalia and the possibility of him being able to continue on his genocidal way was too great a risk for people of the Bay region that he had predated upon.

This experience significantly informed the way that we operated in Timor Leste during the INTERFET/UNTAET operations in 1999 and the reprised intervention in 2006, creating a public security and detainee management system that was able to withstand scrutiny and that could dovetail with UN systems and ultimately an indigenous Timorese capacity.

The problems encountered in Timor Leste were to be amplified tenfold when we found ourselves operating in Iraq in 2003. Again there was the combined dilemma of establishing public security, dealing with the atrocities of the Saddam Hussein regime, fighting a counter-insurgency campaign and establishing the rule of law and good governance. The many mistakes of that time have been documented to a large degree but it was clearly one of the fundamental flaws of the operation that these issues had not been properly catered for in the preparatory planning.

This was a situation in which the *Fourth Geneva Convention* applied without question and its provisions and related supporting laws in the Hague Regulations and *Additional Protocol I*, as well as commentaries on aspects of the law of occupation, were of great assistance. There were, nevertheless, many contestable areas that suggested the need for a re-evaluation of political and regulatory issues associated with the management of transitions to indigenous sovereign government and the extent of the occupying power's authority, such as in relation to economic management.

Other problems arising from contemporary operations relate to the increasing automation and remote management of the battlespace. This includes the remote targeting of threats across borders in the grey area between law enforcement and armed conflict. Increasingly, public expectations of targeting have become much more intolerant of collateral damage and civilian casualties than the law has previously accepted. This has in fact often had a positive effect, particularly in counter-insurgency environments, where it is not possible to kill your way to success and where the emphasis ought to be on complementary social, economic and political strategies.

As ever the challenge is to ensure that the law can answer these dilemmas and make the decision process for those put in the position of having to resolve life or death calls as straightforward as possible. That is a challenge Tim McCormack has always understood and accepted, and this book continues in the Australian tradition of which Tim has been such a prominent exemplar.

Colonel, The Honourable Dr Michael Kelly AM,
Former Australian Minister for Defence Material

1 Introduction

Jadranka Petrovic

I. Professor Tim McCormack: biographical note

Professor Tim McCormack was born in Launceston and grew up in Burnie, Tasmania, Australia. He is a graduate of the University of Tasmania (LLB Hons 1982) and of Monash University (PhD 1990). His thesis considered the question of self-defence in international law in the context of Israel's bombing of the Iraqi nuclear reactor. He was the first Australian recipient of the Golda Meir Postdoctoral Fellowship to the Hebrew University of Jerusalem in 1988. Together with his wife, he spent twelve months in Israel and studied on the Ulpan Program. In 2003, he was awarded a University of Tasmania Foundation 'Outstanding Graduate' Award.

A. Australian appointments and awards

Professor McCormack is currently a Professor of Law at the Melbourne Law School and an Adjunct Professor of Law at the University of Tasmania Law School. He is a leading international authority on International Humanitarian Law (IHL) and International Criminal Law (ICL). He is the Law of Armed Conflict Expert Adviser to the Australian Defence Force Director of Military Prosecutions in Canberra and a Director of World Vision Australia. He is also a member of the Advisory Board of the Centre for Jewish History and Culture at the Faculty of Arts, The University of Melbourne; a founding member of the Tim Hawkins Memorial Scholarship Selection Committee at the University of Tasmania; and a member of the Selection Committee for the Golda Meir Postdoctoral Fellowship, Australian Friends of the Hebrew University of Jerusalem.

Professor McCormack was the Foundation Australian Red Cross Professor of International Humanitarian Law (1996–2010) at the Melbourne Law School and also the Foundation Director of the Asia Pacific Centre for Military Law (2001–2010) – a collaborative initiative (established in 2001) between the Melbourne Law School and the Australian Defence Force Legal Service.

From 1991 until 1994, Professor McCormack was a member of the Australian Red Cross Society National Committee on IHL, and from 1999 until 2002 he was a National Vice-President of the Australian Red Cross and chaired the Australian Red Cross National Advisory Committee on IHL (1994–2002). In 2001 he was awarded the Australian Red Cross Medal for outstanding volunteer service to the organisation. In 2014, he was also awarded the Australian Red Cross Distinguished Service Medal for more than 20 years of voluntary commitment to the promotion of the understanding of, and respect for, International Humanitarian Law.

His other past national appointments include a Deputy Chair of the Australian Foreign Minister's National Consultative Committee on International Security Issues, a founding member of the Foreign Minister's National Consultative Group on Bio-Security Issues, a member of the Australian Foreign Minister's National Consultative Committee on Peace and Disarmament, an expert on the Law of War providing advice to Major David McLure and Major Jonathan Hyde for the defence of SGT J and LCPL D before the Australian Military Court Martial in Sydney, and a member of the 'Safeguarding Australia' expert sub-committee to advise on the development of the Department of Education, Science and Training's National Collaborative Research Infrastructure Strategy (NCRIS) for the distribution of $540 million over 5 years for major research infrastructure capabilities.

Professor McCormack has participated in Australian Government delegations to multilateral treaty negotiations in New York, Geneva, The Hague and Rome. He provides expert international legal advice to various Australian Government departments and has delivered conference papers all over the world.

In 2005, Professor McCormack was awarded the President of the Law Institute of Victoria's *Pro Bono* Award (in recognition of the provision of IHL and ICL advice to Major Dan Mori, US Military Defence Counsel for David Hicks), which was followed by the University of Melbourne Vice-Chancellor's Knowledge Transfer Commendation (for the provision of IHL and ICL advice to Major Dan Mori, US Military Defence Counsel for David Hicks). In 2008, Professor McCormack received the Law Institute of Victoria's Paul Baker Award for his 'sustained outstanding contribution to international humanitarian and human rights law through publication, teaching and public advocacy', and in 2010 he was appointed a Fellow of the Australian Academy of Law.

B. International appointments and awards

Professor McCormack has developed an international reputation for his expertise in IHL and in ICL. In 2010, Professor McCormack was appointed the Special Adviser on IHL to the Prosecutor of the International Criminal Court in The Hague.

He is also a founding member of the Council of Advisors to the Global Institute for the Prevention of Aggression and a founding member of the Advisory Board of the International Criminal Court Moot Court Competition at the Grotius Centre for International Legal Studies at Leiden University in

The Hague, as well as a member of the international advisory boards of a number of academic institutions in Israel, Germany and Sweden.

In June 2011, Professor McCormack was appointed by the Government of Israel as one of two international observers for Phase 2 of the Turkel Commission of Enquiry into Israel's processes for investigation of alleged violations of IHL. The Final Report of the Commission, including its recommendations, was presented to Prime Minister Netanyahu in February 2013. From 2003–2007 he was the Expert Consultant on the Law of War to the Defence Team for David Hicks for trial by US Military Commission. In that capacity Professor McCormack travelled to Guántanamo Bay to attend the US Military Commission proceedings against David Hicks in March 2007. From 2002–2006, Professor McCormack acted as *amicus curiae* on international law matters to the judges of Trial Chamber III of the *International Criminal Tribunal for the former Yugoslavia (ICTY)* in The Hague for the trial of Slobodan Milošević.

In 1999, Professor McCormack was awarded the Dutch Foreign Ministry Centenary of the 1899 First Hague Peace Conference Medal for contributions to the conduct of the centenary celebrations at the Peace Palace in The Hague.

Professor McCormack is the general editor (with Christopher Greenwood of the London School of Economics) of the world's first academic book series dedicated to IHL (with Martinus Nijhoff Publishers in Leiden) and has recently co-edited the thirtieth volume of the series (his seventh book) – *Beyond Victor's Justice: The Tokyo Trial Revisited*. From 2005–2010 Professor McCormack was editor-in-chief of the prestigious international journal – the *Yearbook on International Humanitarian Law* (published by the Asser Press in The Hague).

Professor McCormack has also served on the advisory boards of a number of other prestigious journals. He is a founding member of the Board of Advisors of the journal *International Law Studies*, US Naval War College, Newport, Rhode Island, and a founding member of the Advisory Board of the *Journal of Philosophy of International Law*, as well as a member of the editorial advisory board of several other leading international and Australian academic journals, including the *International Criminal Law Review*, Martinus Nijhoff Publishers, Leiden, the *Journal of Conflict and Security Law*, Oxford University Press, Oxford, *New Zealand Armed Forces Law Review*, Armed Forces' Law Association of New Zealand, Auckland, the *Melbourne Journal of International Law*, The University of Melbourne and honorary editor of the *Jurnal Hukum Humaniter*, Centre for International Humanitarian and Human Rights Law, Trisakti University Law School, Jakarta.

C. Teaching and research

Professor McCormack has taught various graduate and undergraduate courses in several Australian law schools (the University of Melbourne, the University of Tasmania, Monash University, Australian National University and Wollongong University) and internationally (the University of Virginia, Auckland and Jerusalem). Recently he has also been awarded a Fullbright Senior

Scholarship to take up the position of Charles H Stockton Distinguished Scholar-in-Residence at the US Naval War College in Newport, Rhode Island, and has also been appointed Visiting Professor at Harvard Law School for the Winter Term (January 2016).

Professor McCormack has been involved with the Law School at the University of Melbourne for more than 20 years. During that time he has held a number of positions, including a Director of Studies, Graduate Program in Military Law and an Associate Dean for Research. At the Melbourne Law School, Professor McCormack spearheaded the teaching of IHL in the Masters programme many years ago – Australia's first graduate coursework specialisation in this field – and his teaching continues to be informed by his active and varied experiences in the field. He also developed an internationally unique specialist coursework graduate programme in Military Law at the Melbourne Law School.

Additionally, Professor McCormack has regularly lectured to graduate recruits in the Department of Foreign Affairs and Trade (DFAT) and to Australian Defence Force (ADF) officers. In particular, he has been heavily involved in the teaching of Military Operations Law (with a significant IHL component) to ADF Legal Officers as well as to legal officers, operators and planning staff from other militaries in the Asia Pacific Region. In these roles Professor McCormack has contributed to the development of a culture of respect for the Rule of Law in the ADF and among regional militaries.

Professor McCormack's current research interests include investigation and prosecution of international crimes, Australia's war crimes trials 1945–1951, and new weapons technologies and challenges for International Humanitarian Law. His research has been supported by a number of highly competitive research grants over the years (including Australian Research Council Linkage Grants, an Australia Research Council Discovery Grant and an Australian Defence Science Technology Organisation (DSTO) Grant).

Professor McCormack is the author of numerous books and book chapters and articles, book reviews and other contributions to refeed journals. The list of his voluminous consultancy reports, published conference proceedings and other publications is equally impressive.

II. Professor Tim McCormack: select bibliography

Books (authored and edited)

Fitzpatrick, G, McCormack, T and Morris, N (eds), *Australia's War Crimes Trials 1945–51* (Martinus Nijhoff Publishers, forthcoming)

Liivoja, R and McCormack, T (eds), *Routledge Handbook on the Law of Armed Conflict* (Routledge, forthcoming)

Tanaka, Y, McCormack, T and Simpson, G (eds), *Beyond Victors' Justice: The Tokyo Trial Revisited* (Martinus Nijhoff Publishers, 2011)

Blumenthal, DA and McCormack, TLH (eds), *The Legacy of Nuremberg: Institutionalised Vengeance or Civilising Influence?* (Martinus Nijhoff Publishers, 2008)

McCormack, TLH and Saunders, CA (eds), *Sir Ninian Stephen: A Tribute* (Melbourne University Press, 2007)

McCormack, TLH, Tilbury, M and Triggs, GT (eds), *A Century of War and Peace: Asia-Pacific Perspectives on the Centenary of the 1899 Hague Peace Conference* (Kluwer Law International, 2001)

Durham, H and McCormack, TLH (eds), *The Changing Face of Conflict and the Efficacy of International Humanitarian Law* (Kluwer Law International, 1999)

McCormack, TLH and Simpson, GJ (eds), *The Law of War Crimes: National and International Approaches* (Kluwer Law International, 1997)

McCormack, TLH, *Self-Defence in International Law: The Israeli Raid on the Iraqi Nuclear Reactor* (Magnes Press with St. Martin's Press, 1996)

Chapters in books

Dwyer, C and McCormack, T, 'Characterisation of the Conflict' in R Liivoja and T McCormack (eds), *Handbook on the Law of Armed Conflict* (Routledge, forthcoming 2015)

Liivoja, R, Mathews, R and McCormack, T, 'The Challenges of New Weapons Technologies' in R Liivoja and T McCormack (eds), *Handbook on the Law of Armed Conflict* (Routledge, forthcoming 2015)

McCormack, T, 'Jurisdiction' in G Fitzpatrick, T McCormack and N Morris (eds), *Australia's War Crimes Trials 1945–51* (Martinus Nijhoff Publishers, forthcoming 2015)

McCormack, T, 'Who's Afraid of the International Criminal Court?' in R Gaita and G Simpson (eds), *Who's Afraid of International Law?* (University of Western Australia Press, in press, 2014)

McCormack, T and Morris, N, 'Were the Trials Fair?' in G Fitzpatrick, T McCormack and N Morris (eds), *Australia's War Crimes Trials 1945–51* (Martinus Nijhoff Publishers, forthcoming 2015)

McCormack, T and Morris, N, 'Why Australian Trials?' in G Fitzpatrick, T McCormack and N Morris (eds), *Australia's War Crimes Trials 1945–51* (Martinus Nijhoff Publishers, forthcoming 2015)

McCormack, T and Liivoja, R, 'Australia: Regulating Private Military and Security Companies' in C Dekker and M Sossai (eds), *Multilevel Regulation of Military and Security Outsourcing: The Interplay between International, European and Domestic Norms* (Hart Publishing, 2012) 507

Finnin, S and McCormack, T, 'Tokyo's Continuing Relevance' in Y Tanaka, T McCormack and G Simpson (eds), *Beyond Victors' Justice: The Tokyo Trial Revisited* (Martinus Nijhoff Publishers, 2011) 353

McCormack, T and Oswald, BM, 'The Maintenance of Law and Order in Military Operations' in TD Gill and D Fleck (eds), *The Handbook of the International Law of Military Operations* (Oxford University Press, 2010) 445

McCormack, TLH, 'War Crimes' in V Tomaselli and I Wenzler (eds), *World at Risk: A Global Issues Sourcebook* (CQ Press, 2nd edn, 2010) 568

Durham, H and McCormack, TLH, 'Aerial Bombardment of Civilians: The Current International Legal Framework' in Y Tanaka and MB Young (eds), *Bombing Civilians: A Twentieth-Century History* (The New Press, 2009) 215

Kelly, MJ and McCormack, TLH, 'Contributions of the Nuremberg Trial to the Subsequent Development of International Law' in DA Blumenthal and TLH McCormack (eds), *The Legacy of Nuremberg: Institutionalised Vengeance or Civilising Influence?* (Martinus Nijhoff Publishers, 2008) 101

McCormack, TLH and Mtharu, P, 'Cluster Munitions, Proportionality and the Foreseeability of Civilian Damage' in O Engdahl and P Wrange (eds), *Law at War: The Law as It was and the Law as It should Be: Liber Amicorum Ove Bring* (Martinus Nijhoff Publishers, 2008) 191

McCormack, TLH, 'International Peace Envoy' in TLH McCormack and CA Saunders (eds), *Sir Ninian Stephen: A Tribute* (Melbourne University Press, 2007) 214

McCormack, TLH, 'An Australian Perspective on the ICRC Customary Law Study' in AM Helm (ed.), *The Law of War in the 21st Century: Weaponry and the Use of Force* (Naval War College Newport, 2006) 81

McCormack, TLH, 'Self-Defence in International Criminal Law' in H Abtahi and G Boas (eds), *The Dynamics of International Criminal Justice: Essays in Honour of Judge Sir Richard May* (Martinus Nijhoff Publishers, 2006) 231

Howard, J and McCormack, TLH, 'Australia' in B Brandon and M du Plessis (eds), *The Prosecution of International Crimes: A Practical Guide to the Prosecution of ICC Crimes in Commonwealth States* (Commonwealth Secretariat, London, 2005) 127

McCormack, TLH, 'Use of Force' in S Blay, R Piotrowicz and B Martin Tsamenyi (eds), *Public International Law: An Australian Perspective* (Oxford University Press, 2nd edn, 2005) 223

McCormack, TLH, 'The Importance of Effective Enforcement of International Humanitarian Law' in L Ljinzaad, J van Sambeek and B Tahzib-Lie (eds), *Making the Voice of Humanity Heard: Essays on Humanitarian Assistance and International Humanitarian Law in Honour of HRH Princess Margriet of The Netherlands* (Martinus Nijhoff Publishers, 2004) 319

McCormack, TLH, 'Crimes against Humanity' in D McGoldrick, P Rowe and E Donnelly (eds), *The Permanent International Criminal Court: Legal and Policy Issues* (Hart Publishing, 2004) 179

Kelly, MJ and McCormack, TLH, 'International and Regional Action with Regard to Conflicts in Multicultural Societies' in R Blindenbacher and A Koller (eds), *Federalism in a Changing World – Learning from Each Other* (McGill-Queen's University Press, 2003) 278

McCormack, TLH, 'Their Atrocities and Our Misdemeanours: The Reticence of States to Try Their Own Nationals for International Crimes' in M Lattimer and P Sands (eds), *Justice for Crimes against Humanity* (Hart Publishing, 2003) 107

McCormack, TLH, 'Reply to Louise Arbour' in C Saunders and K Le Roy (eds), *The Rule of Law* (The Federation Press, Sydney, 2003) 136

McCormack, TLH, 'Australia's Legislation for the Implementation of the *Rome Statute*' in M Neuner (ed.), *National Legislation Incorporating International Crimes: Approaches of Civil and Common Law Countries* (Berliner Wissenschafts-Verlag, Berlin, 2003) 65

McCormack, TLH, 'War Crimes' in V Tomaselli and S Matanovic (eds), *World at Risk: A Global Issues Sourcebook* (CQ Press, Washington DC, 2002) 585

Mathews, RJ and McCormack, TLH, 'The Relationship between International Humanitarian Law and Arms Control' in H Durham and TLH McCormack (eds), *The Changing Face of Conflict and the Efficacy of International Humanitarian Law* (Kluwer Law International, 1999) 65

Mathews, RJ and McCormack, TLH, 'Australian Security, Weapons of Mass Destruction and International Law' in A Bergin and S Scott (eds), *International Law and Australian Security* (Australian Defence Studies Centre, Canberra, 1997) 125

McCormack, TLH, 'Use of Force' in S Blay, R Piotrowicz and B Martin Tsamenyi (eds), *Public International Law: An Australian Perspective* (Oxford University Press, 1997) 238

McCormack, TLH and Simpson, GJ, 'Achieving the Promise of Nuremberg: A New International Criminal Law Regime?' in TLH McCormack and GJ Simpson (eds), *The Law of War Crimes: National and International Approaches* (Kluwer Law International, 1997) 229

McCormack, TLH, 'From Sun Tzu to the Sixth Committee: The Evolution of an International Criminal Law Regime' in TLH McCormack and GJ Simpson (eds), *The Law of War Crimes: National and International Approaches* (Kluwer Law International, 1997) 31

Mathews, RJ and McCormack, TLH, 'Verification of the Chemical Weapons Convention: National Implementation Requirements' in JB Poole and R Guthrie (eds), *Verification 1995: Arms Control, Peacekeeping and the Environment* (Westview Press, 1995) 180

McCormack, TLH, 'The Use of Force' in H Reicher (ed.), *Australian International Law: Cases and Materials* (Law Book Co Sydney, 1995) 1028

McCormack, TLH and Reicher, H, 'International Legal Personality' in H Reicher (ed.), *Australian International Law: Cases and Materials* (Law Book Co Sydney, 1995) 116

Articles in refereed journals

McCormack, T and McFarland, T, 'Mind the Gap: Can Developers of Autonomous Weapons Systems be Liable for War Crimes?' (2014) 90 *International Law Studies* 361

Liivoja, R and McCormack, T, 'Law in the Virtual Battlespace: The Tallinn Manual and the *Jus in Bello*' (2012) 15 *Yearbook of International Humanitarian Law* 45

Hagger, M and McCormack, T, 'Regulating the Use of Unmanned Combat Vehicles: Are General Principles of International Humanitarian Law Sufficient?' (2011) 21 *Journal of Law, Information and Science* (hard-copy in press www.jlisjournal.org/).

McCormack, T, 'Why Consider Legal Challenges for International Policing?' (2011) 15 *Journal of International Peacekeeping* 1

McCormack, T, 'The Contribution of the International Criminal Court to Increasing Respect for International Humanitarian Law' (2009) 27 *University of Tasmania Law Review* 22

McCormack, TLH, 'David Hicks and the Charade of Guantánamo Bay' (2007) 8 *Melbourne Journal of International Law* 273

Boas, G and McCormack, TLH, 'Learning the Lessons of the Milošević Trial' (2006) 9 *Yearbook of International Humanitarian Law* 65

Dunworth, T, Mathews, RJ and McCormack, TLH, 'National Implementation of the Biological Weapons Convention' (2006) 11 *Journal of Conflict and Security Law* 93

McCormack, TLH, 'Sixty Years From Nuremberg: What Progress for International Criminal Law?' (2005) 1 *Jurnul Hukum Humaniter* (*Humanitarian Law Journal* – in Bahasa)

1–20; the same article is also published (with the mutual agreement of both journals) in (2005) 5 *New Zealand Armed Forces Law Review* 1

Kelly, MJ, McCormack, TLH, Muggleton, P and Oswald, BM, 'Legal Aspects of Australia's Involvement in the International Force for East Timor' (2001) 83 *International Review of the Red Cross* 101

McCormack, TLH, 'What's in an Emblem?: Humanitarian Assistance Under Any Other Banner Would be as Comforting' (2000) 1 *Melbourne Journal of International Law* 175

Doherty, KL and McCormack, TLH, 'Complementarity as a Catalyst for Comprehensive Domestic Penal Legislation' (1999) 5 *University of California, Davis Journal of International Law and Policy* 147

Mathews, RJ and McCormack, TLH, 'The Influence of Humanitarian Principles in the Negotiation of Arms Control Regimes' (1999) 81 *International Review of the Red Cross* 331

McCormack, TLH and Robertson, S, 'Jurisdictional Aspects of the *Rome Statute* for a New International Criminal Court' (1999) 23 *Melbourne University Law Review* 635

McCormack, TLH and Simpson, GJ, 'Simulating Multilateral Treaty Making in the Teaching of the Law of International Organisations' (1999) 8 *Legal Education Review* 61

McCormack, TLH, 'The "Sandline Affair": Papua New Guinea Resorts to Mercenarism to End the Bougainville Conflict' (1998) 1 *Yearbook of International Humanitarian Law* 292

McCormack, TLH, 'From Solferino to Sarajevo: A Continuing Role for International Humanitarian Law?' (1997) 21 *Melbourne University Law Review* 621

McCormack, TLH, 'Selective Reaction to Atrocity: War Crimes and the Development of International Criminal Law' (1997) 60 *Albany Law Review* 681

McCormack, TLH, 'A *Non-Liquet* on Nuclear Weapons: The ICJ Avoids the Application of General Principles of International Humanitarian Law' (1997) 316 *International Review of the Red Cross* 76

McCormack, TLH, 'An Introduction to Treaties: What They Are and Where to Find Them' (1996) 4 *Australian Law Librarian* 265

Mathews, RJ and McCormack, TLH, 'The Resolution of Disputes Under the Chemical Weapons Convention' (1995) 16 *Contemporary Security Policy* 396

Mathews, RJ and McCormack, TLH, 'Entry into Force of the Chemical Weapons Convention: National Requirements and Prospective Timetable' (1995) 26 *Security Dialogue* 93

McCormack, TLH and Simpson, GJ, 'A New International Criminal Law Regime?: The Sixth Committee Debates The International Law Commission's Draft Statute for an International Criminal Court' (1995) XLII *Netherlands International Law Review* 177

McCormack, TLH and Simpson, GJ, 'The International Law Commission's Draft Code of Crimes Against the Peace and Security of Mankind: An Appraisal of the Substantive Provisions' (1994) 5 *Criminal Law Forum* 1

Letts, M, Mathews RJ, McCormack, TLH and Moraitis, C, 'The Conclusion of the Chemical Weapons Convention: An Australian Perspective' (1993) 14 *Arms Control* 311

McCormack, TLH, 'Some Australian Contributions to Chemical Weapons Non-Proliferation and Disarmament' (1992) 14 *Australian Yearbook of International Law* 157

McCormack, TLH, 'Anticipatory Self-Defence in the Legislative History of the U.N. Charter' (1991) 25 *Israel Law Review* 1

McCormack, TLH, 'HV Evatt at San Francisco: A Lasting Contribution to International Law' (1990–91) 13 *Australian Yearbook of International Law* 92

McCormack, TLH, 'International Law and the Use of Chemical Weapons in the Gulf War' (1990–91) 21 *California Western International Law Journal* 1

Book reviews in refereed journals

McCormack, TLH on Cassese A, Gaeta, P and Jones, JRWD (eds), 'The *Rome Statute of the International Criminal Court*: A Commentary' (2003) 4 *Melbourne Journal of International Law* 341

McCormack, TLH on Sassòli, M and Bouvier, A, 'How Does Law Protect in War?: Cases, Documents and Teaching Materials on Contemporary Practice in International Humanitarian Law' (2002) 50 *Netherlands International Law Review* 291

McCormack, TLH on Meron, T, 'War Crimes Law Comes of Age' (2000) XLVII *Netherlands International Law Review* 97

McCormack, TLH on Weiss, TG (ed.), 'The United Nations and Civil Wars' (1999) 11 *Pacifica Review* 329

McCormack, TLH on Bassiouni, MC and Manikas, P (eds), 'The Law of the International Criminal Tribunal for the Former Yugoslavia' (1998) XLV *Netherlands International Law Review* 435

McCormack, TLH on Dinstein, Y and Tabory, M (eds), 'War Crimes in International Law' (1998) 18 *Australian Yearbook of International Law* 107

McCormack, TLH on White, NG, 'The Law of International Organisations' (1998) 347 *The Round Table: The Commonwealth Journal of International Affairs* 383

McCormack, TLH on Bassiouni, MC, 'Crimes Against Humanity in International Law' (1996) 17 *Australian Yearbook of International Law* 266

McCormack, TLH on Woodliffe, J, 'The Peacetime Use of Foreign Military Installations under Modern International Law' (1994) 15 *Australian Yearbook of International Law* 321

McCormack, TLH on Janis, MW (ed.), 'The Influence of Religion on the Development of International Law' (1993) 21 *International Journal of Legal Information* 86

McCormack, TLH on Cassese, A, 'Human Rights in a Changing World' (1992) 18 *Melbourne University Law Review* 493

McCormack, TLH on Lapidoth, R and Hirsch, M (eds), 'The Arab-Israeli Conflict and its Resolution: Selected Documents' (1992) 14 *Australian Yearbook of International Law* 316

McCormack, TLH on Butler, WE (ed.), 'The Non-Use of Force in International Law' (1991) 18 *International Journal of Legal Information* 225

McCormack, TLH on Meyrowitz, E, 'Regulation of Nuclear Weapons: The Relevance of International Law' (1991) 19 *International Journal of Legal Information* 147

McCormack, TLH on Bustelo, MR and Alston, P (eds), 'Whose New World Order: What Role for the United Nations?' (1988/89) 12 *Australian Yearbook of International Law* 303

Editing of refereed journals

McCormack, T, Guest Editor, Symposium Issue on 'Legal Challenges for International Policing' in (2011) 15 *Journal of International Peacekeeping* (Issues No 1 and 2)

McCormack, T, Correspondents' Reports Editor (2010) 13 *Yearbook of International Humanitarian Law*

McCormack, T, General Editor and McCormack, T and Kleffner, J co-Managing Editors (2009) 12 *Yearbook of International Humanitarian Law*

McCormack, T, General Editor (2008) 11 *Yearbook of International Humanitarian Law*

McCormack, T, General Editor (2007) 10 *Yearbook of International Humanitarian Law*

McCormack, T, General Editor (2006) 9 *Yearbook of International Humanitarian Law*

McCormack, T, General Editor (2005) 8 *Yearbook of International Humanitarian Law*

McCormack, T, General Editor (2004) 7 *Yearbook of International Humanitarian Law*
McCormack, T, General Editor (2003) 6 *Yearbook of International Humanitarian Law*

Other contributions to refereed journals

McCormack, TLH, 'Australia' in 'Correspondents' Reports' (2003) 6 *Yearbook of International Humanitarian Law* 453
McCormack, TLH, 'Australia' in 'Correspondents' Reports' (2002) 5 *Yearbook of International Humanitarian Law* 431
McCormack, TLH, 'Australia' in 'Correspondents' Reports' (2001) 4 *Yearbook of International Humanitarian Law* 440
McCormack, TLH, 'Australia' in 'Correspondents' Reports' (2000) 3 *Yearbook of International Humanitarian Law* 414
McCormack, TLH, 'Solomon Islands' in 'Correspondents' Reports' (2000) 3 *Yearbook of International Humanitarian Law* 577
McCormack, TLH, 'Australia' in 'Correspondents' Reports' (1999) 2 *Yearbook of International Humanitarian Law* 329
McCormack, TLH, 'New Zealand' in 'Correspondents' Reports' (1999) 2 *Yearbook of International Humanitarian Law* 393
McCormack, TLH, 'Australia' in 'Correspondents' Reports' (1998) 1 *Yearbook of International Humanitarian Law* 407
McCormack, TLH, 'Papua New Guinea' in 'Correspondents' Reports' (1998) 1 *Yearbook of International Humanitarian Law* 488

Consultancy reports

McCormack, T, 'Australian Law and Practice Relevant to Investigation and Prosecution of LOAC Violations', The Public Commission to Examine the Maritime Incident of 31 May 2010: The Turkel Commission Second Report, *Israel's Mechanisms for Examining and Investigating Complaints and Claims of Violations of the Laws of Armed Conflict According to International Law* (February 2013) 643
McCormack, T, 'US Civil Liability for Providing Material Support to a Terrorist Organisation', prepared for World Vision Australia (20 March 2012)
McCormack, T, 'Opinion on Possible Challenges to the Extradition Request: Sri Lanka – United Arab Emirates', prepared for Robert Stary and Associates, Melbourne (15 July 2011)
McCormack, TLH and Mtharu, P, *Expected Civilian Damage and the Proportionality Equation*, presented to the Review Conference of the 1980 Certain Conventional Weapons Convention, United Nations, Geneva (November 2006)
McCormack, TLH, Finnin, S and Mtharu, P, *International Humanitarian Law and Explosive Remnants of War: Report on States Parties' Responses to the Questionnaire*, presented to the Group of Governmental Experts' Working Group on Explosive Remnants of War of the States Parties to the 1980 Certain Conventional Weapons Convention, United Nations, Geneva (March 2006)
McCormack, TLH, *Prosecutor v Slobodan Milošević, 'Amicus Curiae's* Reply to Prosecution Submission in Response to Trial Chamber's Preliminary Order on *Amicus Curiae* Observations *Proprio Motu* on the Desirability of Submissions on the Alternative Bases of Individual Criminal Responsibility Alleged in the Case and on the Issue of Trials *In Absentia*' (14 June 2005)

McCormack, TLH, *Prosecutor v Slobodan Milošević*, *'Amicus Curiae* Observations *Proprio Motu* on the Desirability of Submissions on the Alternative Bases of Individual Criminal Responsibility Alleged in the Case and on Trials *In Absentia*', Case No. IT-02–54-T (25 April 2005)

McCormack, TLH and Clarke, B, 'Aspects of the Jurisdiction *Ratione Materiae* of the Military Commission for the Proposed Trial of David Hicks', filed as an Expert Opinion in the Motions Phase of Proceedings Against David Hicks, Guantánamo Bay (November 2004)

McCormack, TLH, *Prosecutor v Slobodan Milošević*, *'Amicus Curiae* Observations *Proprio Motu* on Relevant Issues of International Law', Case No. IT-02–54-T (25 August 2004)

McCormack, TLH, 'Conspiracy and Criminal Organizations in Post-World War II War Crimes Trials', Expert Opinion for Major Michael Mori, Counsel for David Hicks (17 June 2004)

McCormack, TLH, *Prosecutor v Slobodan Milošević*, *'Amicus Curiae* Submissions on Self-Defence as it Arises in the Bosnia-Herzegovina Part of the Case as Stipulated in the Order of the Chamber to the *Amicus* of 23 July 2003', Case No. IT-02–54-T (1 March 2004)

McCormack, TLH, *Prosecutor v Slobodan Milošević*, *'Amicus Curiae* Submissions on Self-Defence as it Arises in the Croatia Part of the Case as Stipulated in the Order of the Chamber to the *Amicus* of 23 July 2003', Case No. IT-02–54-T (11 February 2004)

McCormack, TLH, 'Duress as a Defence to the Perpetration of a War Crime or Crime Against Humanity', Clothier Anderson and Associates, Melbourne (February 2004)

McCormack, TLH, *Prosecutor v Slobodan Milošević*, *'Amicus Curiae* Submissions on Self-Defence as it Arises in the Kosovo Part of the Case as Stipulated in Part (a) of the Order of the Chamber to the *Amicus* of 11 December 2002', Case No. IT-02–54-T (30 October 2003)

McCormack, TLH, *Prosecutor v Slobodan Milošević*, *'Amicus Curiae* Observations *Proprio Motu* on Relevant Issues of International Law', Case No. IT-02–54-T (21 July 2003)

McCormack, TLH, *Prosecutor v Slobodan Milošević*, *'Amicus Curiae* Submissions on the Law of Self-Defence as Stipulated in Parts (b) and (c) of the Order of the Chamber to the *Amicus* of 11 December 2002', Case No. IT-02–54-T (14 July 2003)

McCormack, TLH, 'International Law Aspects in Extradition Proceedings against Konrads Kalejs', Expert Opinion for the Commonwealth Director of Public Prosecutions, Melbourne (March 2001)

McCormack, TLH, 'War Crimes in Internal Armed Conflicts and Elements of a Crime against Humanity', Department of Immigration and Multicultural Affairs, Canberra (November 1999)

McCormack, TLH, 'Complicity in, or Aiding and Abetting, War Crimes or Crimes against Humanity', Erskine Rodan and Associates, Melbourne (March 1998)

McCormack, TLH, 'National Implementation of International Humanitarian Law Instruments in South Pacific Island States', International Committee of the Red Cross, Geneva (February 1998)

McCormack, TLH, 'NPT, SPNFZ and CWC: Facilitating Action by Vanuatu', Department of Foreign Affairs and Trade, Canberra (April 1995)

McCormack, TLH, 'Chemical Weapons Regional Initiative Visit to South Pacific Capitals', Department of Foreign Affairs and Trade, Canberra (June 1994)

Mathews, RJ and McCormack, TLH, 'Illustrative Model Legislation for the Implementation of the Chemical Weapons Convention Into Domestic Law: Text and

Explanatory Memorandum', Department of Foreign Affairs and Trade, Canberra, September 1993, 1–36 (subsequently tabled at the Preparatory Commission for the Chemical Weapons Convention in The Hague as a Working Paper: Doc. No. PC-IV/A/WP.10) (23 September 1993)

McCormack, TLH and Simpson, GJ, 'The Draft Code of Crimes against the Peace and Security of Mankind: An Analysis of the Relationship Between the Draft Code's Specific Crimes and Existing International Law', Legal Office, Department of Foreign Affairs and Trade, Canberra (November 1992)

McCormack, TLH, 'Towards a Chemical Weapons Convention: Australian Perspectives on the Outstanding Issues to Implementation', Department of Foreign Affairs and Trade, Canberra (November 1991)

Published conference proceedings

Dunworth, T, Mathews, RJ and McCormack, TLH, 'National Implementation of the Biological Weapons Convention', in RJ Mathews (ed.), *Proceedings of the Biological Weapons Convention Regional Workshop*, Melbourne Law School, 21–25 February 2005, Asia Pacific Centre for Military Law (2005) 69

McCormack, TLH, 'General Obligations under the Biological Weapons Convention', in RJ Mathews (ed.), *Proceedings of the Biological Weapons Convention Regional Workshop*, Melbourne Law School, 21–25 February 2005, Asia Pacific Centre for Military Law (2005) 26

Kelly, MJ and McCormack, TLH, 'International and Regional Action With Regard to Conflicts in Multicultural Societies', *Federalism in a Changing World: Learning From Each Other*, Conference Reader for the International Conference on Federalism, St Gallen, 27–30 August 2002, 363

McCormack, TLH, 'National Implementing Legislation for the Chemical Weapons Convention', *Proceedings of the Regional Seminar on National Implementation of the Chemical Weapons Convention,* Jakarta, 28–30 November 1994, Provisional Technical Secretariat of the Organisation for the Prohibition of Chemical Weapons Occasional Paper No 9, 95

Mathews, RJ and McCormack, TLH, 'Disputes Between the Inspected State Party and the Inspection Team', *Hague Academy of International Law Colloquium on the Chemical Weapons Convention*, The Hague, 24–26 November 1994, 509

McCormack, TLH, 'New Standards in the Monitoring of Multilateral Arms Control and Disarmament Treaties', *Proceedings of the Second Annual Meeting of the Australian and New Zealand Society of International Law*, ANU, Canberra, 27–29 May 1994, 18

McCormack, TLH, 'National Implementing Legislation for the Chemical Weapons Convention', *Proceedings of the Regional Seminar on National Implementation of the Chemical Weapons Convention*, Bangkok, 9–10 May 1994, Provisional Technical Secretariat of the Organisation for the Prohibition of Chemical Weapons Occasional Paper No 4, 123

McCormack, TLH, 'The Australian Approach to National Implementation of the Chemical Weapons Convention', *Proceedings of the 88th Annual Meeting of the American Society of International Law*, Washington DC, 5–8 April 1994, 233

McCormack, TLH, 'Australia: National Implementation of the Chemical Weapons Convention', *Proceedings of the Seminar on National Implementation*, The Hague, 18 December 1993, Provisional Technical Secretariat of the Organisation for the Prohibition of Chemical Weapons Occasional Paper No 2, 149

McCormack, TLH, 'The United Nations Draft Code of Crimes Against the Peace and Security of Mankind: An Appraisal of the Substantive Provisions', *Proceedings of the First Annual Meeting of the Australian and New Zealand Society of International Law*, ANU, Canberra, 28–30 May 1993, 36

McCormack, TLH, 'International Legal Issues for the Implementation of the Chemical Weapons Convention', *Proceedings of the Chemical Weapons Regional Initiative Seminar*, 31 March 1993–2 April 1993, Part 5, 1

McCormack, TLH, 'What Does it Mean to Become an Original Signatory to the Chemical Weapons Convention?', *Proceedings of the Chemical Weapons Regional Initiative Seminar*, Sydney, 21–23 June 1992, 107

McCormack, TLH, 'Some Australian Initiatives in Chemical Weapons Non-Proliferation and Disarmament' (1992) *Proceedings of the Annual International Law Weekend*, ANU, Canberra, 15–17 May 1992, 132

McCormack, TLH, 'Some Implications from the Iraq-Kuwait Situation for the Law Governing the Use of Force' (1991) *Proceedings of the Annual International Law Weekend*, ANU, Canberra, 10–12 May 1991, 125

Other publications

McCormack, T, 'Kony 2012 and the ICC', *Crosslight*, April 2012, No 220, 12

McCormack, T, 'Bringing Warlords to Justice', *Herald Sun*, Briefed: The Law Blog, 21 March 2012 http://blogs.news.com.au/heraldsun/law/index.php/heraldsun/comments/bringing_warlords_to_justice/

McCormack, T, 'Crimes of War Get Lost in Law Limbo', *The Age*, 20 July 2011, 17

McCormack, T, 'Commandos Finally Get Justice as Afghan Charges Dismissed', *The Age*, 25 May 2011, 17

McCormack, T, 'The Importance of Effective Enforcement of International Humanitarian Law' (2010) 18 *International Humanitarian Law Magazine*, symposium issue on Punishing War Crimes: International Criminal Tribunals, Australian Red Cross, 3

McCormack, T, 'The Need for Protection' (2010) 17 *International Humanitarian Law Magazine*, symposium issue on Protection for Humanitarian Workers, Australian Red Cross, 22

McCormack, T, 'Negotiating the Geneva Conventions and Contributing to International Humanitarian Law' (2009) 16 *International Humanitarian Law Magazine*, symposium issue on the 60th Anniversary of the Geneva Conventions, Australian Red Cross, 14

McCormack, T, 'Guantanamo's Closure is Just the Beginning: The Future for Detainees Raises Questions About Australia's Role', *The Age*, 2 February 2009, 13

McCormack, TLH, 'A Sorry Tale of Torture', book review of Mamdouh Habib with Julia Collingwood, *My Story: The Tale of a Terrorist Who Wasn't*, in *The Age*, 15 November 2008, A2, 27

McCormack, TLH, 'Lest We Forget the Criminal Atrocities of War', *The Age*, 10 November 2008, 11

McCormack, TLH, 'Taking on the Tyrants: The International Criminal Court May Have Some Failings but it has Generated a Worldwide Change in Attitude', *The Age*, 16 July 2008, 11

McCormack, TLH, 'Bush Loses, Freedom Reigns: The US Supreme Court's Decision is a Victory for the Rule of Law', *The Age*, 16 June 2008, 15

McCormack, TLH, 'Trials of International Criminal Law', book review of Gerry Simpson, *Law, War and Crime: War Crimes Trials and the Reinvention of International Law*, in *The Age*, 19 January 2008, A2, 20

McCormack, TLH, 'A Shameful Episode: The Howard Government's Behaviour in the Hicks Affair Will Forever Remain a Blight on Australia', *The Age*, 29 December 2007, 19

McCormack, TLH, 'March 2007: Ideal Time to Push for Lenient Deal for Hicks', *Melbourne University Magazine*, August 2007, 15

McCormack, TLH, 'Why I Was Happy to Assist David Hicks', *The Melbourne Anglican*, June 2007, 17

McCormack, TLH, 'Trial of David Hicks Was a Political Fix by Two Governments', *The Age*, 21 May 2007, 13

McCormack, TLH, 'Remembering a Vietnam Digger' (2007) 44 *Tasmania 40° South*, 48

McCormack, TLH, 'Hope Riddled With Flaws', book review of Adam LeBor, *Complicity With Evil: The United Nations in the Age of Modern Genocide* and James Traub, *The Best Intentions: Kofi Annan and the UN in the Era of American Power*, in *The Age*, 03 February 2007, A2, 23

McCormack, TLH, 'Sixty Years From Nuremberg: What Progress for International Criminal Law?' (2006) 4 *Victorian Institute of Forensic Medicine Review* 8–15 (this article is the same as that published in the refereed journals (2005) 1 *Jurnul Hukum Humaniter (Humanitarian Law Journal* – in Bahasa) 1 and in (2005) 5 *New Zealand Armed Forces Law Review* 1 and was published in the *VIFM Review* with the mutual consent of the editors of both refereed journals)

McCormack, TLH, 'Nuremberg's Lessons for Guantanamo', *The Age*, 22 November 2005, 15

McCormack, TLH, 'David Hicks: A Case of Guilt by Association?', *The Age*, 12 June 2004, Insight, 9

McCormack, TLH, 'Blix Delivers His Case for Truth', book review of Hans Blix, *Disarming Iraq: The Search for Weapons of Mass Destruction*, in *The Age*, 15 May 2004, Review, 6

McCormack, TLH, 'Strengthening Regional Enforcement of International Criminal Law Post-September 11', Melbourne Institute of Asian Languages and Societies Asia Policy Paper Series, No 2, May 2003, 1

McCormack, TLH, 'The New International Criminal Court' (2001) 10 *Res Publica* 1

Mathews, RJ and McCormack, TLH, 'Entry into Force of the Chemical Weapons Convention: Activities and Prospective Timetable' (1994) 25 *Chemical Weapons Convention Bulletin* 1

McCormack, TLH and Simpson, GJ, 'Grand Days Revisited?: An International Criminal Court for the Twenty-First Century' (1994) 22 *International Law News* 17

McCormack, TLH, 'International Custody Disputes: International Legal Aspects' (1992) 16 *International Law News* 18

McCormack, TLH, 'Asia-Pacific Economic Co-operation: A Leading Forum for Regional Economic Development' (1992) 1(2) *LawAsia Comparative Constitutional Law Newsletter* 7

McCormack, TLH, 'Banning Chemical Weapons: Australia's Continuing Contribution', *Australia/Israel Review*, 21 April 1992, 8 (also published, with the permission of the editors of both journals in (1992) 15 *International Law News* 14)

McCormack, TLH, 'Australia's Ratification of the U.N. Convention on the Rights of the Child' (September 1991) *International Law News* 9

McCormack, TLH, 'Rabta Burns and the World Breathes Easy', *Canberra Times*, 17 April 1990, 8

McCormack, TLH, 'Chemical-Weapons Ban Draws Nigh', *Canberra Times*, 23 February 1990, 9

McCormack, TLH, 'Iraqi Rocket Launching Boosts Weapons Fear', *Canberra Times*, 8 January 1990, 9

McCormack, TLH, 'Ambitious Bush Bends Law in Ambush of Panama', *Canberra Times*, 30 December 1989, 8

McCormack, TLH, 'The Iraqi Kurds: Forgotten Victims', *Australia/Israel Review*, 11 July 1989, 8

McCormack, TLH, 'Chemical Weapons and the Right of Pre-Emptive Self-Defence', *Australia/Israel Review*, 14 April 1989, 8

III. Professor Tim McCormack: research higher degree work in IHL

Professor Tim McCormack is one of the most eminent international authorities on IHL and enforcement of the violations of that law, as well as the prosecution of war crimes. He has been involved for more than 20 years in these areas of International Law – 'teaching about it, writing about it and publicly advocating it',[1] as he has put it.

At the Melbourne Law School, Professor McCormack has established one of the world's strongest concentrations of research higher degree work in IHL. Student numbers in PhD, Masters and Juris Doctor programmes are now spectacularly high. In Professor McCormack's view 'there is no need to convince students that they ought to be interested [in this area of law]. They *are* interested. They are signing up in numbers.'[2]

This high level of student interest is also demonstrated by the fact that Professor McCormack is currently supervising nine doctoral students. Since 1995, another twenty-two doctoral students whose theses he has supervised or co-supervised have already graduated. The list of topics and principal issues considered in their theses is impressive:

- Askin, Kelly, 'Rape as an International War Crime';
- Boas, Gideon, 'Trying Former Heads of State and Senior Officials for War Crimes: Lessons in Complex Litigation from the Milošević Trial';
- Burke, Roisin, 'Sexual Exploitation and Abuse by UN Military Contingents: Moving Beyond the Current *Status Quo* and Responsibility under International Law';
- Carell, Michael, 'Australia's Prosecution of Japanese War Criminals: Stimuli and Constraints';
- Clarke, Ben, 'Occupation, Resistance and the Law: Was Armed Resistance to the Occupation of Iraq Justified under International Law?';
- Coleman, Andrew, 'The Role of the International Court of Justice and Self-Determination';
- Durham, Helen, 'Role of NGOs in the Proceedings of an International Criminal Court';
- Duxbury, Alison, 'The Participation of States in International Organisations: The Role of Human Rights and Democracy';
- Finnin, Sarah, 'Elements of Accessorial Modes of Liability: Articles 25(3)(b) and (c) of the Rome Statute of the International Criminal Court';
- Henderson, Ian, 'Targeting During Armed Conflict: A Legal Analysis';
- Ladan, Abdul Muyassir, 'The Exclusive Economic Zone and the Practice of African States';

---

1 'ICC Position "An Honour" Says Prof Tim McCormack', The Melbourne Newsroom (3 March 2010) http://newsroom.melbourne.edu/studio/ep-69.
2 Ibid.

- Lesh, Michelle, 'Inside the Scope of the Law?: Israel's Policy of Targeted Killing and International Humanitarian Law';
- Maogoto, Jackson, 'Influence of Political Constraints on the Development of International Criminal Law';
- McDougall, Carrie, 'Prosecuting the Accumulated Evil of the Whole: Defining an "Act of Aggression" for the Purposes of the Rome Statute of the International Criminal Court';
- Millar, Hayli, 'Accountability for Gross Violations of Human Rights in the Aftermath of Armed Conflict';
- Muggleton, Paul, 'The International Crime of Aggression';
- Nastevski, Vasko, 'The Enactment of War Crimes Legislation in Australia Without Offending the Prohibition on Retrospective Legislation';
- Oswald, Bruce, 'The Application of International Law to United Nations and Regional Peace Operations';
- Petrovic, Jadranka, 'The Old Bridge of Mostar and Increasing Respect for Cultural Property in Armed Conflict';
- Schlesinger, Nicole, 'An Exploration of Extralegal Factors Influencing the Development of the Law of the International Criminal Tribunals for the Former Yugoslavia and Rwanda';
- Taylor, Savitri, 'Australia's Implementation of its Refugee Convention Obligation of Non-Refoulement'; and
- Wynn-Pope, Phoebe, 'The Responsibility to Protect against Crimes against Humanity and Genocide: Effective Operationalisation of the Principle'.

Professor McCormack has additionally supervised nine LLM theses (completed between 1992 and 2008) and six MA students (who graduated between 1999 and 2000):

- Agan, Maris, 'Territorial Sovereignty and the Spratly Islands Dispute';
- Boas, Gideon, 'Australian Practice in International Humanitarian Law';
- Bourke, Paul, 'Prospects for an International Criminal Court';
- Dewar, Scott, 'The Concept of International Human Responsibilities Alongside Rights';
- Dixon, Julia, 'Lessons from the Chemical Weapons Convention for Other Arms Control Regimes';
- Goldner, Anthony, 'International Responses to Genocide';
- Irving, James, 'Australia's Counter-Terrorism Laws and Freedom of Speech';
- Martin, Lester, 'Whither Taiwan?: The International Legal Status of Taiwan';
- Olney, Darren, 'Effectiveness of the World Bank';
- Perton, Victor, MP, 'Human Rights and the New World Order';
- Siourthas, Jenny, 'Towards Asia-Pacific Union: A Comparative Analysis of the Asia-Pacific Economic Cooperation Process and other Initiatives for Cooperation in the Asia-Pacific Region';
- Stephens, Dale, 'Use of Force and International Law in East Timor';

- Storey, Sarah, 'International Humanitarian Law and Failed States';
- Stylianou, Helen, 'Strengthening the International Atomic Energy Agency's Inspection Regime'; and
- Vitakoudis, Andrew, 'International Legal Status of the International Olympic Committee'.

But why are so many students interested in IHL and in Professor McCormack's supervision in particular?

In the 50 years following the establishment of the first *ad hoc* international criminal tribunals in response to atrocities committed during World War II, namely the Nuremberg International Military Tribunal and the Tokyo International Military Tribunal,[3] the international criminal justice system seemed to be in a state of hibernation. This dormant state of international criminal justice[4] has changed dramatically around the end of the twentieth century. Emerging from the outrage of the international community to the events that took place in the territory of the former Yugoslavia following the dissolution of that State, and in Rwanda in the 1990s, *ad hoc* international criminal tribunals were established by the United Nations Security Council resolutions in 1993 and 1994 respectively.[5] Since then, there has been a spectacular proliferation of international criminal tribunals,[6] which has culminated in the establishment

3 The Nuremberg International Military Tribunal [IMT] and the Tokyo International Military Tribunal for the Far East [IMTFE] established in 1945 and 1946 respectively.

4 For discussion on the question of the failure to provide accountability see, eg, M Cherif Bassiouni, 'Accountability for Violations of International Humanitarian Law and Other Serious Violations of Human Rights' in Bassiouni, *Post-Conflict Justice* (Ardsley Transnational Publishers, 2002), 383, 384–6 (observing that since WWII, in sharp contrast to the decline of international armed conflict, the number of non-international armed conflicts has dramatically increased, which has resulted in massive violations of International Humanitarian and Human Rights Law, and noting that during the twentieth century over 170 million civilian deaths have resulted as a consequence of non-international armed conflicts and the abuses by repressive governments, compared with an estimated 33 million military casualties (since WWII alone, in more than 250 non-international armed conflicts and situations which include the abuses by repressive governments, an estimated 86 million people died), and arguing that inadequate prosecutions at either the national or international level have occurred, which is, in his view, due to justice being 'all too frequently bartered away for political settlements'. Ibid 386).

5 See, UN Security Council resolution on establishment of an international criminal tribunal for the former Yugoslavia and adoption of the *Statute* of the Tribunal, UN Security Council Res 827 of 25 May 1993, UN SCOR, 48th sess, 3217th mtg. The *Statute* is contained in UN Doc S/25704, annex (1993) and attached to the *Report of the Secretary-General Pursuant to Paragraph 2 of Security Council Resolution 808 [ICTY]*; UN Security Council resolution on establishment of an international criminal tribunal for Rwanda, UN Security Council Res 955 (1994) of 8 November 1994, UN Doc. S/RES/955 (1994) [ICTR].

6 In addition to the two *ad hoc* international criminal tribunals and the permanent *International Criminal Court [ICC]* another development in international criminal justice mechanisms has marked the era of 'proliferation of international criminal justice', namely, establishment of the so-called 'hybrid' or mixed national-international and internationalised criminal tribunals. Such

of the permanent *International Criminal Court (ICC)*[7] which has the unique capacity to challenge impunity for atrocities,[8] wherever committed and irrespective of whether that be during the time of armed conflict or, as the case may be, in peace time.

As the former *ICTY* Judge Patricia Wald observed in reference to the *ICTY*, 'a phenomenal body of jurisprudence that brings life to the abstract precepts of international law'[9] has been developed by these international criminal justice mechanisms. Despite many imperfections, international criminal adjudication is now an indispensable method for redressing wartime atrocities. In an era where IHL is still better known for its violations than for when it is upheld, as Professor McCormack succinctly puts it, 'this particular body of law is literally a matter of life and death'[10] – that is, 'when the law is observed in conflict fewer people die and when it is violated many more people die'.[11] Accordingly, this international criminal adjudication, together with the prosecution and appropriate punishment of offenders at a national level, remains 'the most effective means of enforcing International Humanitarian Law'.[12]

Students are interested in this area of International Law and in various aspects of the phenomenon of international criminal justice, and there is no better way of exploring the intricacies of these fascinating and indispensible areas of law than with a scholar who has dedicated his career to improving understanding of and respect for norms that, *inter alia*, protect the most vulnerable in an armed conflict, and ensuring that where there is a failure to obey such norms, that they are properly enforced.

In addition to his intellectual command, his infectious passion for International Law and justice, and his skills in academic guidance, it is also Professor McCormack's human warmth and his unconditional support for his students and colleagues, which makes students opt for his supervision. Professor

---

tribunals were established in East Timor, Kosovo, Bosnia and Herzegovina, Sierra Leone, Cambodia, Iraq and Lebanon. See, eg, Sarah Williams, *Hybrid and Internationalised Criminal Tribunals: Selected Jurisdictional Issues* (Bloomsbury Publishing, 2012).

7 The ICC was established by the *Rome Statute* which was adopted on 17 July 1998 by the United Nations Diplomatic Conference of Plenipotentiaries. Four years later, after sixty States ratified this treaty, it came into force. UN Doc A/CONF.183/9 opened for signature 17 July 1998, 2187 UNTS 3 (entered into force 1 July 2002).

8 Karl Quinn, 'Kony Video Puts ICC in Spotlight', *National* 13 March 2012 www.smh.com.au/national/kony-video-puts-icc-in-spotlight-20120312-luwd0.h....

9 Patricia Wald, 'UN Should Stay the Course in The Hague' *The Korea Herald* 10 November 2007, [5] http://listserve.buffalo.edu/archives/justwatch-l.html.

10 'Professor Tim McCormack Honoured for Work with Australian Red Cross' 21 November 2014, Melbourne Law School www.law.unimelb.edu.au/melbourne-law-school/newd-and-event/news-and-ev... ['Professor Tim McCormack Honoured'].

11 Ibid.

12 See, Antonio Cassese, 'On the Current Trends towards Criminal Prosecution and Punishment of Breaches of International Humanitarian Law' (1998) 9 *European Journal of International Law* 1, 10.

McCormack has assisted many students by suggesting job opportunities both during their candidature as well as after graduation, by exposing the students to the academic community through involvement in publications and conferences, and by providing the students with contacts from his broad network. His patience and support when students face personal hardship, and his concern to ensure that students do not suffer social isolation during their candidature, are but only a few examples of how Professor McCormack supports his students.

My fellow contributors to this book and I will always remember fondly the time spent at the Asia Pacific Centre for Military Law at the Melbourne Law School, the invaluable hours of conversation with Professor McCormack about thesis-related issues, as well as other academic matters, the regular, weekly morning teas at this centre, organised by Professor McCormack to which he invited a number of world-leading scholars, including Professor Frits Kalshoven and Professor Michael Schmitt, from whose visits students benefited immensely. And how could we forget the cakes, chocolates and all the other delicious food which Professor McCormack bought personally for such gatherings? Not to mention his kind invitations to numerous prestigious functions held at the Melbourne Law School, the Supreme Court of Victoria and elsewhere, as well as the after-class drinks and delicious lunches also organised by him, all of which we could have only dreamt about prior to undertaking our studies with him.

Although enrolments in his classes and supervision are always high Professor McCormack respects each student as an individual, and also acts as a friend – always ready to listen and support. Professor McCormack's teaching methods in and beyond the classroom have inspired many and have certainly had lots to do with this and many other contributors' decision to pursue academia, or other work, in the field of IHL and ICL.

This collection of essays is a heartfelt thank you to Professor McCormack, born of a deep gratitude and respect for his scholarship and his friendship; a man whose academic career has been shaped by a continued commitment to increasing understanding of and respect for IHL[13] and providing constant help to others. The rewarding collaboration between the fourteen contributors has resulted in a book comprising twelve chapters. Each of these is written by one or more of Professor McCormack's students, which is what, among other factors, makes this volume unique. Nine chapters have been written solely by Professor McCormack's higher degree by research students. Three chapters have been co-authored. All three leading authors of such chapters are Professor McCormack's former doctoral students, and while the co-authors have not yet had the privilege of undertaking a thesis under Professor McCormack's supervision, they have had the honour of interacting with him in other capacities for a number of years.

---

13 'Professor Tim McCormack Honoured', above n 10.

This book provides a contemporary consideration of various issues emerging from present-day breaches of norms of IHL and of how impunity for such breaches can be tackled. The book is particularly concerned with the interplay between the rules governing accountability for violations of IHL and those of other areas of law, including ICL, Human Rights Law, general principles of International Law and national Criminal Law, that impact on the prosecution of war crimes. The chapters are integrated around the central theme of accountability for violations of IHL. They carefully examine different aspects of this topic such as the role of international courts and tribunals, the conception of crimes and culpability, the procedural rights of the accused, as well as issues concerning the national experience of conducting war crimes trials. Other challenges to determining accountability for violations of IHL, including cultural factors, the interaction between the rules of IHL and the rules of International Human Rights Law in the context of investigations into targeted killing operations, the role of the International Court of Justice in protecting humanitarian values, questions of humanitarian assistance, and, finally, questions in relation to the use of World Heritage List sites and other cultural property for military purposes in a specific context are also explored.

Jackson Nyamuya Maogoto provides a fascinating overview of the development of international tribunals in the twentieth century. The primary pivot of his chapter is discussion of the extension of jurisdictional bases that circumvented aspects of statist based criminal jurisdiction through international courts and tribunals. Maogoto focuses on the concept of sovereign immunity while extending universal jurisdiction into the sphere of national criminal jurisdiction through the framework of international crimes. Maogoto's discussion revolves around three pathways that form the basis of the substantive development: the Nuremberg and Tokyo International Military Tribunals and the notion of sovereign appropriation following unconditional surrender; the *ad hoc* International Criminal Tribunals for the former Yugoslavia and Rwanda and primacy on the basis of the Security Council's 'police' power; and the permanent ICC, which in some ways seeks to balance the two polar and historic positions (primacy and usurpation of sovereignty by the international community and concession to the continuing primacy of national criminal jurisdiction). Maogoto paints 'a qualitative shift from State supremacy to an ethical vision in which human values ultimately prevail over State rights where the two are in conflict' and points to a concomitant 'shift in authority from States to the international community'.

Sarah Finnin's chapter is centred on ordering the commission of a crime, a well-recognised mode of liability under IHL whose elements have been developed in detail in the jurisprudence of the post-World War II military tribunals and more recently the *ad hoc* International Criminal Tribunals for the former Yugoslavia and Rwanda. Now that the first cases of ordering the commission of international crimes are coming before the ICC, Finnin's focus on the case of Sylvestre Mudacumura makes her chapter a timely and important contribution to the area of accountability for violations of IHL. Finnin engages in the elements for ordering outlined in the 2012 decision issuing an arrest warrant and in doing so highlights the similarities and differences between the approach taken by *ad hoc* tribunals and the ICC's approach in *Mudacumura* to liability for ordering. Finnin also questions the basis for, and appropriateness of, the 'direct effect' test adopted for establishing the necessary link between the accused's conduct and the substantive crime.

Ian Henderson's and Bryan Cavanagh's chapter examines the relationship between the criminal law concept of individual self-defence and the law of armed conflict. By limiting itself to use of force to protect individuals against bodily harm, the chapter looks at the questions of how and whether the international law relating to the conduct of hostilities in armed conflict, particularly targeting law, is affected by the 'defence' of self-defence under both domestic and international criminal law. The chapter focuses on two jurisdictions applicable to an Australian military member: the Australian federal jurisdiction under the *Criminal Code Act 1995* (Cth) and the *Rome Statute of the International Criminal Court*, arguing that the discussion relevant to these two jurisdictions can be transposed and re-analysed for other jurisdictions. Henderson and Cavanagh underline the distinction between the use of force in the exercise of the combatant's privilege and the use of force in self-defence and observe that the 'battlefield is not the place for legal niceties and nuances'. The combatant's privilege is in essence a licence to kill or wound enemy combatants and destroy enemy military objectives (as they define it) and when force is used in the exercise of this privilege the governing legal regime is the law of armed conflict. Conversely, when force is used in self-defence, the governing legal regime is criminal law. Henderson and Cavanagh argue that the law of armed conflict is most suited to the use of force on the battlefield and that the law of self-defence is best left for non-combat operations.

Michelle Lesh takes up the issue of targeted killing operations, which has assumed increasing relevance in International Law. Her chapter notes that the primary purpose of investigating targeted killings is to create accountability for potential violations of the law. In assessing when accountability measures are necessary, the chapter examines the duty to investigate and the principle of proportionality. By pointing to the primacy of the principle of accountability in IHL and International Human Rights Law, the chapter focuses on the interaction of these rules in the context of investigations into targeted operations. Lesh observes that the growing use of drone attacks and other forms of targeted killings, particularly in non-international armed conflicts, where the geographical boundaries of conflict are often challenged and where attacks are regularly operated remotely, renders the two legal frameworks potentially applicable when questions of accountability are at issue. She argues that there are strong policy and humanitarian reasons to impose constraints on targeted killings and that these require that every targeted killing should be investigated.

Phoebe Wynn-Pope examines the concept of humanitarian assistance in the context of the ongoing Syrian conflict. This chapter draws attention to the poignancy of this conflict in which approximately 100,000 civilians have been killed since hostilities began in 2011, and which resulted in humanitarian disaster of catastrophic proportions, leaving more than 9.5 million people in need of assistance, and creating more than 2.5 million refugees and more than 6.5 million internally displaced people. Wynn-Pope considers the obligations on parties to a conflict to provide for the needs of the civilian population and to allow access to humanitarian agencies providing assistance. She contends that the international community has been ineffective in the face of severe human suffering in Syria where humanitarian access has been particularly restricted. She also reviews and considers the impact of the United Nations Security Council Resolution 2139 of 22 February 2014 demanding humanitarian access and explores the question of whether the denial of humanitarian assistance is judiciable at the ICC.

By focusing on the same conflict, but on different subject matter, Jadranka Petrovic and Rebecca Hughes examine the normative implications of the belligerent use of the World Heritage List sites and other immovable cultural property for military purposes in the present day Syria. Petrovic and Hughes highlight the magnitude of the Syrian cultural disaster, caused, *inter alia*, by the use of the ancient sites by the military on all sides to the conflict and argue that despite the universal value of cultural property, relevant instruments of neither IHL nor ICL adequately address the question of the use of cultural property for military purposes, which in the Syrian context may result in allowing those in control of cultural property, and who expose it to destruction or damage, to walk away with impunity. Since cultural property is precious, not just locally, but also across borders and across generations, Petrovic and Hughes urge that its protection must be a matter of high priority for the international community and call for the criminalisation of any use of cultural property for military purposes.

Dale Stephens' chapter examines the significance of the growth of ICL and its superimposition of particularised thresholds for criminal liability over traditional understanding of the law of armed conflict. Stephens argues that while the genre of ICL is rightly heralded as a successful enterprise, there is inevitably something lost in such a manoeuvre. He asks whether the rise of ICL has witnessed the arrival of a more accountable age, or whether the conduct of military operations in times of armed conflict responds more faithfully to tenets of restraint from post-modernist influences, and argues that, while not without significant potential, the emergence of ICL, and the evolving jurisprudence of the various tribunals and courts dealing with military operational matters, has not provided any kind of decisive accountability mechanism for the 'normal' conduct of warfare, particularly in the context of targeting. Stephens concludes that although this may be disappointing on one level, on the other it may be an entirely predictable outcome given the social goals of ICL.

Sophie Rigney's chapter concerns the procedural rules governing disclosure of information at the ICC. She argues that the way that disclosure of information is undertaken at this court is permitting an environment where the rights of the accused are not given full respect. Rigney undertakes a doctrinal analysis of recent *ICC* case law to examine the links between disclosure rules, the concept of fairness and the procedural rights of the accused, revealing an emerging trend of non-disclosure of material held by both the prosecutor and the victims. She notes that disclosure obligations operate to ensure the principle of equality of arms. Consequently, the emerging trend of non-disclosure of exculpatory material may pose a particular challenge for the full and proper adherence to the requirement of disclosure. Rigney characterises this as 'a fracturing between the rules of procedure, the rights of the accused, and perhaps the fairness of the trial'. In her view, since ICC trials are integral to accountability for violations of IHL and ICL, this fracturing warrants close attention.

Vasko Nastevski looks at the Australian experience of war crimes trials since the end of World War II. He surveys war crimes legislation adopted in Australia since 1945, largely reflecting international developments to bring accountability for international crimes. Nastevski stresses that the approach taken has been piecemeal and underpinned by historical attitudes proclaiming instinctive confidence in the domestic legal system, resulting in legislative gaps that simply do not cover many of the allegations of war criminals residing in Australia. In Nastevski's opinion Australia's experience in bringing to justice war criminals is disappointing: 'Whilst there seems to be acceptance of Australia's role participating in an articulation of some international conscience through international multilateral treaties ... at the same time, Australia's attitude is derisory of international law's utility for domestic implementation.' He argues for the necessity of enacting comprehensive war crimes legislation to provide an adequate legislative basis for the prosecution of alleged war criminals in Australia, thereby ensuring nobody is excused from facing justice in this State.

Andrew Coleman's chapter concerns the role of the International Court of Justice in regulating IHL. The chapter highlights the lack of attention in scholarly writing to this particular role of this court. The chapter observes that although IHL clearly falls within this court's jurisdiction, many doubts have been raised by commentators in view of the recent and heavily criticised *Bosnian Genocide Case* and the subsequent *Kosovo Opinion*. Colman argues that the Court's decisions in these two cases have rather promoted the idea of prevention of IHL violations by 'establishing a code of conduct that promotes people's rights, and international humanitarian values over antiquated notions of sovereignty and States' rights'. Colman concludes that the International Court of Justice can make, and has already made, a major contribution to protecting international humanitarian values and IHL.

While acknowledging the importance of international criminal adjudication in enforcement of IHL, Helen Durham and Eve Massingham emphasise the equal relevance of other broader cultural and social factors that encourage compliance with IHL. They remind us that the *1949 Geneva Conventions* set out a range of accountability mechanisms, including the obligation to disseminate the texts of the *Conventions* and the obligations on States to take precautions against the effects of attacks. By noting that many of these obligations apply before, during and after armed conflict they stress that these positive actions are vitally important for preventing violations occurring in the first place. Durham and Massingham argue that accountability involves more than prosecutions and that a wider examination not just of legal normative obligations, but also ways to find connections to ideas of a culture of accountability is increasingly important. Accountability through social pressure and shame is one such example. They conclude that '[i]f we are to continue to strive for Gustav Moynier's vision of each State being "ultimately the best guardian of the limits it has itself imposed" we need to be multi-focused and multi-disciplined – prosecuting, educating, connecting, implementing and finding new ways to inspire accountability'.

The chapters described above highlight the indivisibility of IHL from various other areas of law. All of them provide thought-provoking approaches to an array of issues emanating from the present-day breaches of IHL. The chapters are grouped together by the shared belief that those breaches have to be addressed for the benefit of the entire international community – a belief inspired by the grandeur of an academic who has, among many other notable achievements, been instrumental in introducing the authors of this collection to the intricacies and sensitivities of this field.

2 Taming Westphalian sovereignty

International penal process and the expansion of universal jurisdiction

Jackson Nyamuya Maogoto[1]

I. Introduction

The modern independent nation-state was founded upon a reverence of sovereignty emanated from the *Peace of Westphalia* of 1648, which ended the wars of religion between the Protestant and Catholic States. The treaty completed a process that began towards the end of the Middle Ages, which focused upon the establishment of single overriding authorities in the growing national areas of Europe. Westphalian sovereignty enshrined the internal and external autonomy of the State.[2] The accompanying sovereign tenets of political independence and territorial supremacy established the State's freedom of action and unlimited use of power internally, forbidding an exercise of jurisdiction by any State over issues and individuals within another State's territorial boundaries, thus precluding external interference and unsolicited intervention. Consistently reinforced by early international law, internal and external supremacy of the State strengthened the importance of complete autonomy of the sovereign State in managing its own internal affairs and its international capacity to determine the nature of its obligations.[3] Importantly among sovereign prerogatives reserved to the State was the decision on when to go to war and how to wage war. The legal framework governing conduct in war was largely based on non-binding theoretical treatises of publicists and the slow accretions of customary restraints derived from State practice.

As the modern international system continued to develop, multilateralism found its voice in the nineteenth century with efforts to increase the level of

1 LL.B (Hons) (Moi), LL.M (Hons) (Cantab), Ph.D (Melb), GCertPPT (UoN). Senior Lecturer, School of Law, University of Manchester (UK). The author is honoured to contribute this chapter. Professor Tim McCormack was more than simply his doctoral supervisor. He is and remains that unique combination of scholar, gentleman and mentor.

The views expressed in this chapter are those of the author alone and do not necessarily reflect the views of the University of Manchester.

2 Jackson N Maogoto, *State Sovereignty and International Criminal Law: Versailles to Rome* (Transnational Publishers, 2003) 1.

3 Ibid.

voluntary compliance and to hold States responsible to the international community for violations of certain international obligations in the conduct of war. However, unilateral political or military retaliation continued to be the main vehicles through which States were censured for offensive conduct. It was the failure of this informal international enforcement mechanism during the 1870 Franco–Prussian War[4] that led Gustave Moynier to present a proposal to the International Committee of the Red Cross, calling for the establishment by treaty of an international tribunal to enforce laws of war and other humanitarian norms on 3 April 1872.[5]

Until Moynier suggested the establishment of an international criminal court, almost all trials for violations of the laws of war were by *ad hoc* tribunals constituted by one of the belligerents – usually the victor – rather than by ordinary courts or by any form of supranational tribunal or court. So long as the warring sides observed the requisite formalities that limited use of force, there was no talk of war crimes. The general perception of the time was that since crimes during war were committed by persons under the command of a sovereign in violation of rules of engagement, punishment after the conflict was the preserve of national military courts in keeping in tune with the notion of sovereignty and the paramountcy of sovereign immunity. Rarely were soldiers punished for wartime atrocity especially in light of the fact that traditionally, peace treaties which concluded wars almost always contained general amnesties.[6] The notion of war as a sovereign prerogative simply did not lend itself to the concept of individualised war guilt considering the absolute immunity that attached to the actions of a State and its officials. Unsurprisingly, Moynier's proposal was received coldly by international scholars and governments of the day. Not only was it considered radically revolutionary, it simply ran counter to recognised principles of international law of the time.

About three decades after Moynier's proposal, technological and industrial advances which pointed to a major change in the face of warfare led to the epochal Hague Peace Conferences.[7] The elevation of inter-State and regional relations into international relations in the context of an international legal system

---

4   For details, see Michael Howard, *Franco-Prussian War: The German Invasion of France 1870–1871* (Macmillan & Co, 1962); AJP Taylor, *The Struggle for Mastery in Europe 1848–1918* (Oxford University Press, 1954) 206–217.

5   The proposal was published in the *Bulletin international des Societes de secours aux militaires blesses* (the predecessor of the International Review of the Red Cross), under the title: *Note sur la Creation d'une Instituition Judiciaire Internationale Propre a Prevenir et a Reprimer les Belowctions a la Convention de Geneve*. For a text of the draft convention, see Christopher Keith Hall, 'The First Proposal for a Permanent International Criminal Court', *International Review of the Red Cross* No 322 (March, 1998) 72–4.

6   Howard Ball, *Prosecuting War Crimes and Genocide: The Twentieth Century Experience* (University Press of Kansas, 1999) 14.

7   James B Scott (ed.), *Texts of the Peace Conferences at The Hague, 1899 and 1907* (Ginn & Co, 1908); James B Scott (ed.), *The Reports to The Hague Conferences of 1899 and 1907* (Clarendon Press,

was marked by the adoption of the *Hague Conventions* of 1899 and 1907 which sought to codify universal rules and norms regarding warfare binding on State Parties and also opened the doors to an era of arms control.[8] Laws regulating the means and methods of warfare drafted at the two Hague Conferences formed the bedrock of modern laws of war, and are generally considered by international law scholars to be a significant achievement in the effort to humanise war through law. The Hague Conferences[9] and their movement towards pacific settlement of disputes marked the beginning of the attempts to restrain the State's uncontrolled power by limiting the right of war both as an instrument of law and as a legally recognised means for the changing of legal rights.[10] Equally important, the conferences resulted in the codification of certain actions in wartime as war crimes and also gave birth to a fundamental principle that the individual, irrespective of nationality, had rights and duties inherent in human nature and was both a subject and a member of an international community heralding the concept of universal rights.

This chapter considers 'international' tribunals in the twentieth century. The primary pivot of this chapter will be a discussion of the extension of jurisdictional bases that circumvented aspects of statist based criminal jurisdiction through international courts and tribunals. Focus will be on the role of international courts and tribunals in contributing to limitations in the scope of sovereign immunity while extending universal jurisdiction into the sphere of national criminal jurisdiction through the framework of international crimes. Three pathways will form the basis of the substantive development. First, the International Military Tribunals (IMTs) and the notion of sovereign appropriation following unconditional surrender. Second, the *ad hoc* international criminal tribunals and primacy on the basis of the Security Council's police power. Third, the *International Criminal Court (ICC)*, which in some ways seeks to balance the two polar and historic positions (primacy and usurpation of sovereignty by the international community and concession to the continuing primacy of national criminal jurisdiction).

II. World War I: sowing the seeds of challenge to State sovereignty

World War I witnessed one of the largest military mobilisations in history, with the Allied Powers mobilising over 40 million soldiers and the Central Powers

---

1917).

8 For a listing and brief commentary on the major conventions in the Hague Law regime, see M Cherif Bassiouni, *International Crimes: Digest/Index of International Instruments 1815–1985* (Oceana Publications, 1986). See also European Law Students Association, *Handbook on the International Criminal Court* (1997) 41–4. The *Hague Conventions* can also be accessed via the ICRC website www.icrc.org/eng/resources/.

9 See the *Hague Conventions of 1899 and 1907 on the Pacific Settlement of Disputes*. See Scott, *Texts of the Peace Conferences at The Hague, 1899 and 1907*, above n 7.

10 Hersch Lauterpacht (ed.), *Oppenheim's International Law: Disputes, War and Neutrality* (Longman,

mobilising close to 20 million soldiers. Four years later, with the Armistice in force, the war came to an abrupt halt. The smoke cleared slowly and the devastation of cities, the loss of life, mangled bodies and scattered families lay revealed. The facts of the death, destruction and the financial cost of the war staggered the 'civilised' world.[11] Unbridled German and Turkish conduct during the war promoted civil and political outrage in Europe and America, prompting calls at the end of the war for trials of political leaders and military personnel in both countries. The 'iron curtain' of Westphalian sovereignty was the primary objection advanced by both Germany and Turkey, against Allied calls for the establishment of international tribunals to try the officials and personnel of these countries implicated in wartime atrocities. Both nations, in light of these international efforts, strongly advocated against such a move arguing that sovereignty over territory and authority over nationals, a sacrosanct principle of international law, was threatened if the proposed supranational tribunals proceeded.

The Paris Peace Conference was the centre point of post-World War I efforts to not only redefine international relations, but also to resolve Europe's prevalent militarism and imperialism through a series of negotiated treaties. The Paris Peace Conference's activities were extensive, attempting to resolve virtually all points of concern at the international level, from redrawing boundaries, granting mandates and crafting reparations bills to dismantling empires through the recognition of nations as independent States.[12] In settling upon the peace terms, it was not possible wholly to ignore the responsibility of those who were deemed to have first drawn the sword and therefore might be held accountable for the horror that ensued. Importantly, the Paris Peace Conference within whose framework the issue of judicial accountability for the atrocities was discussed, established the Allied Commission on the Responsibility of the War and on the Enforcement of Penalties (Allied Commission).[13] The Allied Commission's

---

1952) vol II, 179.

11 For war costs at a glance, see Charles F Horne, *The Great Events of the War* (National Alumni, 1923) vol II; Harold Elk Straubing (ed.), *The Last Magnificent War and Eyewitness Accounts of World War I* (Paragon House, 1989) 402–3.

12 For the work of the Paris Peace Conference, see, eg, Sir Harold George Nicolson, *Peacemaking* (Houghton Mifflin Co, 1933); Ray Stannard Baker, *Woodrow Wilson and World Settlement* (Doubleday, Page & Co, 1922) 3 vols; Arthur Walworth, *Wilson and His Peacemakers: American Diplomacy at the Paris Peace Conference 1919* (Norton and Co, 1986); Arthur Walworth, *America's Moment: 1918* (Norton and Co, 1918).

13 The Commission was comprised of two members from each of the five Great Powers: the United States of America, the British Empire, France, Italy and Japan. The additional States composing the Allied and Associated Powers were Belgium, Bolivia, Brazil, China, Cuba, Czechoslovakia, Ecuador, Greece, Guatemala, Haiti, the Hedjaz, Honduras, Liberia, Nicaragua, Panama, Peru, Poland, Portugal, Romania, the Serb-Croat-Slovene State, Siam and Uruguay. Carnegie Endowment for International Peace, *The Treaties of Peace 1919–1923* (1924) 3. The additional States, having a special interest in the matter, met and decided that Belgium, Greece, Poland, Romania and Serbia should each name a representative to the Commission as well. Commission on the Responsibility of the Authors of the War and on Enforcement of Penalties, 'Report Presented to the Preliminary Peace Conference, 29 March

mandate was to investigate and report on the responsibility of those who had initiated the war and those who had violated the laws and customs of war in order to prosecute them.[14] This Allied Commission, after intensive and extensive deliberations, subsequently recommended both the insertion of penal provisions in the two main peace treaties negotiated between the two principal war crimes perpetrators (Germany and Turkey) and the victorious Allies, and the establishment of international tribunals to secure judicial accountability for wartime atrocities of the two main perpetrators.

A. The Allies' failure to establish an international penal process

1. The Peace Treaty of Versailles and the German National Trials

The Allied Commission completed its report in 1920 and submitted a list of 20,000 alleged German war criminals[15] who were to be tried by a supranational Allied tribunal – a radical innovation that sought to extend the ambit of universal jurisdiction by subsuming the national penal process. The dispensation with State consent arguably heralded the birth in a practical manner of the idea that an international criminal tribunal could have primacy over a national court.

The *Peace Treaty of Versailles*[16] signified the resolve of the international community to hold those accused of violations of the laws and customs of war personally liable. The 'public arraignment' of the Kaiser for offences against morality and the sanctity of treaties was particularly significant. It was a step towards the abrogation of sovereign immunity and the imposition of international criminal liability upon governmental leaders. However by 1922, 3 years after the signing of the *Peace Treaty of Versailles* the Allied governments still had not formed the tribunals they had committed themselves to establish in Articles 228 and 229 of the Treaty.[17] In a bid to pacify advocates for justice, instead of establishing a supranational tribunal, as provided for in Article 228 of the *Peace Treaty of Versailles*,[18] the Allied Governments requested that Germany prosecute the individuals identified by the Allied Commission. This meant that instead of setting up an international tribunal, Germany would conduct the prosecutions of a limited number of war criminals before the Supreme Court of Germany (*Reichsgericht*) in Leipzig.

1919' (1920) 14 *American Journal of International Law* 95, 96.

14   Ibid.

15   M Cherif Bassiouni, 'Combating Impunity for International Crimes' (2000) 71 *University of Colorado Law Review* 409, 413.

16   Treaty of Peace Between the Allied and Associated Powers and Germany (Peace Treaty of Versailles), concluded at Versailles, 28 June 1919, 2 Bevans 43.

17   Ibid.

Despite the initial list of 20,000 alleged German war criminals being drastically scaled back to 895, the outcome of the Leipzig proceedings was dismal by any standard of retributive justice.[19] Out of a total of 895 cases, 850 suspects were summarily struck out. Of the forty-five remaining defendants, only twelve trials were held; half resulted in acquittals and half in convictions with light sentences.[20] 'The German public showed indignation that German judges could be found to sentence the war criminals and the press brought all possible pressure to bear on the Court.'[21] In the face of the popular domestic exaltation of defendants, and significantly their benign treatment by the German Supreme Court, the Allies appointed an Allied Commission of Jurists to examine the effect of the popular response on the proceedings. The Commission of Jurists unanimously recommended to the Supreme Council that the Leipzig trials be suspended and the remaining defendants be tried before Allied courts but the Commission's recommendations failed to yield the desired results.[22] The Allies had moved on, preoccupied with matters of geopolitical considerations rather than international justice.

2 Peace Treaty of Sevres and the Turkish National Trials

When Turkey signed the Armistice on 30 October 1918, she lay at the mercy of the European Allies. Winston Churchill (who was the British Minister of Munitions as the Armistice came into force) described Turkey as being 'under the spell of defeat, and of deserved defeat.'[23] The Allies, pursuant to their 1915 Declaration,[24] sought to initiate criminal proceedings against Turkish officials suspected of complicity in the Armenian massacres as well as war crimes but first they had to define in greater detail the crimes contained in that Declaration. This task naturally fell on the Allied Commission. The Commission took cognisance of the fact that in 1915, Turkey, an ally of Germany, killed an estimated 250,000 to 1 million Armenians as part of an alleged policy of persecution against that ethnic group.[25] Prior to the Allied Commission's work on this matter, nothing in international legal norms contemplated individual criminal responsibility under international law for public officials and others who committed crimes against their own citizens.

---

18 Ibid.
19 Maogoto, *State Sovereignty and International Criminal Law*, above n 2 at 55.
20 Ibid 54–6.
21 The United Nations War Crimes Commission, History of The United Nations War Crimes Commission and the Development of The Laws of War (1948) 51–2.
22 German War Crimes: Report of the Proceedings, British Parliamentary Papers, Cmnd 1450 (1921).
23 Winston Churchill, *The World Crisis: The Aftermath* (Macmillan, 1929) 367.
24 Declaration of France, Great Britain and Russia, 24 May 1915, quoted in Egon Schwelb, 'Crimes Against Humanity' (1946) *British Year Book of International Law* 23.

The Commission examined, among other offences, 'barbarous and illegitimate methods of warfare.' This included the category of 'offences against the laws and customs of war, and the principles of humanity,' which the French representative of the Third Sub-Commission,[26] Ferdinand Larnaude, insisted was 'absolutely' necessary to ensure human rights.[27] The Allied Commission proceeded in its investigation according to the terms of the *1907 Hague Convention (IV)*.[28] This Convention, part of the 1907 Second Hague Peace Conference package, was intended to give 'a fresh development to the humanitarian principles [towards] evolving a lofty conception of the common welfare of humanity.'[29]

Despite the objections by the US and Japan, the Commission's efforts resulted in several articles stipulating the trial and punishment of those responsible for the genocide being drafted and inserted into the *Peace Treaty of Sevres*, signed on 10 August 1920.[30] Under Article 226, the Turkish government recognised 'the right of trial and punishment by the Allied Powers, notwithstanding any proceedings or prosecution before a tribunal in Turkey.'[31] Moreover, Turkey was obligated to surrender 'all persons accused of having committed an act in violation of the laws and customs of war, who are specified either by name or by rank, office or employment which they held under Turkish authorities.'[32] Under Article 230 of the *Peace Treaty*, Turkey was further obligated to hand over to the Allied Powers the persons whose surrender may be required by the latter as being responsible for the massacres committed during the continuance of the state of war on territory, which formed part of the Turkish Empire on 1 August 1914. It was further stipulated that '[t]he Allied powers reserve to themselves the right to designate the tribunal, which shall try the persons so accused, and the Turkish Government undertakes to recognise such tribunal.'[33] As a principal legal authority on this issue declared:

25 Maogoto, *State Sovereignty and International Criminal Law*, above n 2 at 57.
26 The Allied Commission appointed three Sub-Commissions to consider the questions to be faced. The Third Sub-Commission was concerned with the responsibility for the violation of the Laws and Customs of War. See *Report of the Commission on Responsibilities of the Conference of Paris on the Violation of the Laws and Customs of War* (Carnegie Endowment for Peace, 1919).
27 Her Majesty's Stationery Office, British Foreign Office Papers (FO), FO 608/246, Proces-Verbal no 6 at 57 (folio 417) (8 March 1919); see J Read, *Atrocity Propaganda 1914–1919* (Yale University Press, 1941) 240–84.
28 Convention Respecting the Laws and Customs of War on Land, 18 October 1907, Preamble, 36 Stat 2277, 2779–80, 1 Bevans 631, 632 (*1907 Hague Convention IV*).
29 United Nations War Crimes Commission, History of the United Nations Commission and the Development of Laws of War (1948) 24.
30 *Peace Treaty of Sevres*, 10 August 1920, reprinted in Treaty of Peace Between the Allied Powers and Turkey, 15 *American Journal of International Law* 179 (Supp No 1921).
31 Ibid 180.
32 Ibid 180–1.
33 Ibid 181.

[T]he provisions of Article 230 of the *Peace Treaty of Sevres* were obviously intended to cover, in conformity with the Allied note of 1915 [the 24 May 1915 Allied Declaration] offences which had been committed on Turkish territory against persons of Turkish citizenship, though of Armenian . . . race.[34]

Subsequently, disagreements, feuds and rivalries among the Allies, on the one hand, and the general war-weariness among the peoples they represented, on the other, helped undermine the Allies' unity in the establishment of a supranational tribunal to secure international justice. Yielding to the pressures of an ascendant nationalist political elite that moved to fill the vacuum in Turkey, the Allies abjectly discarded the two-year-old *Peace Treaty of Sevres*,[35] which was the basis of the prosecution and punishment of the authors and participants in the Armenian genocide and other war crimes with the signing of the *Peace Treaty of Lausanne* in 1923.[36] This Treaty expunged all references to one of the most heinous undertakings under the cover of the war – Armenian massacres (and, indeed, to Armenia itself) – thus codifying impunity and frustrating the quest for international justice. However it is of significance that the momentum of the *Peace Treaty of Sevres* contributed in delivering a measure of justice through a series of domestic trials.[37] Prosecutions by Turkish courts relied on the *Ottoman Penal Code and Military Code*[38] while drawing strongly on international norms relating to the Laws of War as then existing. These resulted in a series of indictments, verdicts and sentences – an extraordinary but unheralded milestone.[39]

III. World War II: anchoring the erosion of State sovereignty

Global in scope, World War II pitted a fascist coalition striving for world supremacy – Germany, Japan and Italy – against an unlikely 'grand alliance' of Great Powers[40] who united to prevent the hegemonic goals of the Axis Powers. The world witnessed some of the worst atrocities in the history of civilised

34 United Nations War Crimes Commission, above n 29 at 45.
35 *Peace Treaty of Sevres*, 10 August 1920, reprinted in Treaty of Peace Between the Allied Powers and Turkey, 15 *American Journal of International Law* 179 (Supp No 1921).
36 *Peace Treaty of Lausanne*, 24 July 1923, reprinted in Treaty with Turkey and Other Instruments Signed at Lausanne 24 July 1923, 18 *American Journal of International Law* 1 (Supp No 1924).
37 These targeted: (1) the members of Ittihad's Central Committee; (2) wartime Cabinet Ministers; (3) a host of provincial governors; and (4) high ranking military officers.
38 Adnan Guriz, 'Sources of Turkish Law' in Tugrul Ansay and Don Wallace, Jr (eds), *Introduction to Turkish Law* (Kluwer Law International, 1996) 10.
39 For an explication, see generally Jackson N Maogoto, 'Reading the Shadows of History – The Bridges between Turkish and Ethiopian "Internationalised" Domestic Crime Trials' in Gerry J Simpson and Kevin J Heller (eds), *Untold Stories: Hidden Histories of War Crimes Trials* (Oxford University Press, 2013).
40 The United Kingdom, the United States, France and the USSR.

humankind, perpetrated against both soldiers and civilians. Germany and Japan stood out as their army command not only allowed their armies to conduct the war with merciless and unrelenting harshness, but demanded deliberate brutality in dealing with the enemy as a means of ensuring victory and extinguishing resistance in occupied territory. The cruel and unsparing nature of the war was the end result of a combination of modern technology and the total disregard for legal and moral standards. The Axis Powers were not alone in the violation of the laws of war; the Allied troops committed violations too but the sheer extent and magnitude of the Axis crimes eclipsed and overshadowed those by the victorious Allies. In any event, losing the war that Germany had initiated and Japan had spread did leave the victorious Allies on a moral ground of sorts.

The atrocities of World War II compelled the need for international prosecutions after an Allied victory. In 1942 as the war raged on, the Allied Powers signed the *St James Declaration*,[41] establishing the United Nations War Crimes Commission (UNWCC). About 2 years after the establishment of the UNWCC, on 1 November 1943, the Allied heads of state, Franklin Delano Roosevelt, Winston Churchill and Joseph Stalin, issued the *Moscow Declaration*[42] which aimed at reaffirming the intention of the Allies to try officials and personnel of the Axis Powers for various atrocities in violation of laws of war. The UNWCC activities were the first comprehensive attempt to unravel the factual complexity of the undeniably horrible crimes committed by the German Nazi regime and the marauding Japanese forces in Asia. That the crimes were cruel and inhuman to a degree not previously known to humanity was exceptionally well documented by the Nazis themselves.[43] Millions of innocent civilians were murdered as part of a systematic cold-blooded plan or series of plans.[44] Both Major Axis Powers carried out crimes against Allied soldiers and

---

41 The St James Declaration, 13 January 1942, reprinted in Punishment for War Crimes: The Inter-Allied Declaration Signed at St James's Palace, London, on 13 January 1942, and Relative Documents (Inter-above n 29 at 89–92. The Declaration of St James was the first step leading to the establishment of the International Military Tribunal at Nuremberg.

42 Statement Signed by President Roosevelt, Prime Minister Churchill and Premier Stalin Regarding Atrocities (*The Moscow Declaration*), *The Times* (London) (UK) 3 November 1946 reprinted in US Government Printing Office, *Report of Robert H Jackson, United States Representative to the International Conference on Military Trials* (1949) 11–12.

43 See International Military Tribunal, *Trial of The Major War Criminals Before The International Military Tribunal* (1946–1949) (1949–1953) (25 vols) vol 1, 22–2 (documents in evidence at Nuremberg); Office of United States Chief of Counsel For The Prosecution of Axis Criminality, *Nazi Conspiracy and Aggression* (1946) (ten volumes of German documents collected by the American and British staffs at Nuremberg); see also R Conot, *Justice at Nuremberg* (Harper & Row, 1983) 24–5 (describing the daunting task of assimilating the wealth of German documents available to the Tribunal); Robert H Jackson, *The Nuremberg Case* (Knopf, 1947) 433 ('In preparation for the trial over 100,000 captured German documents were screened or examined.').

44 See The Judgment, International Military Tribunal, vol 1, ibid 224–6; vol 2, ibid 192, 200–01; vol 3, ibid 401–03; vol 8, ibid 216; vol 19, ibid 537. The Judgment is also reproduced in volume 22 ibid 171.

terrorised the populations of the countries they occupied. Human beings were used for medical experiments in which pain, suffering and death were the expected results, entire towns were destroyed, their inhabitants murdered and the buildings razed to the ground. Though the list of crimes was virtually endless, it was important to collect and collate hard evidence relating to these crimes for the purpose of criminal trials.

A. The London Conference on Military Tribunals

1. The International Military Tribunal at Nuremberg

While the UNWCC was collecting evidence, the four Major Allied Powers had to reach a decision with respect to the prosecution and punishment of war criminals, particularly the leaders of the Nazi regime, as called for by the *Moscow Declaration* signed in 1943 by Churchill, Roosevelt and Stalin.[45] In the relatively short span of time from June until August of 1945, representatives of the United Kingdom, the Free French, the Union of Soviet Socialist Republics (USSR), and the United States negotiated, drafted and signed the *Treaty of London*.[46] The drafters were faced with the arduous task of defining the crimes for which the defendants would be prosecuted. The *Nuremberg Charter* ultimately provided in Article 6 for the prosecution of the following substantive crimes: (a) crimes against peace; (b) war crimes; and (c) crimes against humanity.[47]

The controversy regarding the law to be applied at the trial began with the intended inclusion of the charge of 'crimes against peace'. The contestation surrounding this charge essentially mirrored the earlier internal concerns within the American administration at the end of World War I, that waging aggressive war was an unprecedented charge. Justice Jackson, the representative of the United States at the London Conference, prevailed in his view that the limiting phrase should not be included as the prohibition against aggression is universal and could also be applied against all other States.[48] The United States had thus changed its position from that of post-World War I by accepting that war of aggression had become a crime under international law. In the end, a compromise was reached whereby the *Charter* used language stating that the

---

45 *Declaration on Security (The Moscow Declaration)*, 9 United States Department of State Bulletin (1943) 308, reprinted in (1944) 8 *American Journal of International Law* 5.

46 The *Treaty of London* includes both the Agreement by the Government of the United States of America, the Provisional Government of the French Republic, the Government of the United Kingdom of Great Britain and Northern Ireland, and the Government of the Union of Soviet Socialist Republics, for the Prosecution and Punishment of the Major War Criminals of the European Axis and the Charter of the International Military Tribunal [*Nuremberg Charter*] 8 August 1945, 58 Stat 1544, EAS No 472, 82 UNTS 280 reprinted in International Military Tribunal, vol 1, ibid 10.

47 Ibid Article 6.

48 See *Report of Robert H Jackson*, above n 42 at vii–viii.

purpose of the Tribunal was to prosecute crimes of the Axis, while the specific definitions of crimes within the *Charter* made no reference to any particular government.

The easiest category of crimes to define was 'war crimes'.[49] War crimes in Article 6(b) included customary law as identified, *inter alia*, by reference to the *1907 Hague Convention IV*[50] and conventional law as evidenced in the 1929 *Geneva Convention Relative to the Treatment of Prisoners of War*.[51] The Charter further provided that '[t]he official position of defendants, whether as heads of state or responsible officials in Government departments, shall not be considered as freeing them from responsibility or mitigating punishment.'[52] Further, '[t]he fact that [an individual] acted pursuant to [superior orders] shall not free him from responsibility, but may be considered in mitigation of punishment.'[53] The rejection of the superior orders defence, a key defence enshrined in most of the military manuals of the time[54] deserves comment as it struck directly at the standing of national law within the international arena. Though the rejection of this defence in the drafting of the *Nuremberg Charter* was heavily criticised, the rejection was of necessity based on the presumption of an applicable legal order outside of and beyond the nation-state, a further affirmation of the efficacy and validity of international law as a system capable of articulating legal principles and norms applicable within the statal sphere. This rejection of an almost universally accepted defence in the national sphere was an important sign of transformation of the Westphalian paradigm. It further cemented the fact that the Nuremberg Tribunal was not simply an occupation court trying violations of local law but an international body trying violations of international norms.[55]

A more difficult legal issue was whether 'crimes against humanity' under Article 6(c) existed under a combination of sources of international law, namely

---

49   *Nuremberg Charter*, above n 46, Art 6(b) (c) (amended by the protocol of 6 October 1945).

50   *1907 Hague Convention IV*.

51   The 1929 *Geneva Convention Relative to the Treatment of Prisoners of War*, 27 July 1929, 118 LNTS 343, 47 Stat. 2021, 2 Bevans 932.

52   *Nuremberg Charter*, above n 46 at 12 (Art 7).

53   Ibid 12 (Art 8).

54   Lassa Oppenheim, *International Law: A Treatise (War)* (Longmans, Green and Co, 1st edn 1906) vol II, 264–5. The *British Manual of Military Law*, No 443 (1914) relied upon Oppenheim in its formulation. Oppenheim's recognition of the defence remained in the first five editions up to 1940, when it changed to become the basis for the *Nuremberg Charter's* Article 8 which denied the defence. *US Department of the Army Field Manual: The Law of Land Warfare* (1940) 27–10 (1940) reflected the same position in § 345(1). On 15 November 1944, a revision of § 345(1) limited, but retained, a qualified defence. But see *US Department of the Army Field Manual: The Law of Land Warfare* (1956) 27–10. For a historical evaluation of the question, see Leslie C Green, 'Superior Orders and Command Responsibility' (1989) 27 *Canadian Year Book of International Law* 167; Major William H Parks, 'Command Responsibility for War Crimes' (1973) 62 *Military Law Review* 1.

55   Fred L Morrison, 'The Significance of Nuremberg for Modern International Law' (1995) 149 *Military Law Review* 207, 212–13.

conventions, custom and general principles of law.[56] Because 'crimes against humanity' had not been a part of treaty law, the Allies needed to avoid a rigid interpretation of the principles of legality in order to avoid enacting *ex post facto* legislation that could be successfully challenged in court. The rationale for 'crimes against humanity' was predicated on a theory of the jurisdictional extension of war crimes. The reasoning was that war crimes applied to certain protected persons in time of war between belligerent States, and 'crimes against humanity' merely extended the same 'war crimes' proscriptions to the same categories of protected persons, provided those acts were linked to the initiation and conduct of war.[57] The inclusion of Article 6(c) was ground breaking as it meant Germans could be prosecuted for killing German Jews who were, because of their nationality, outside the protection of laws of war. In other words, their persecution could be caught in the wider net cast by international norms. The inclusion of crimes against humanity, a concept that had been firmly rejected by the United States and Japan at the end of World War I, was quite an innovation in international law. This is not to say that murder or extermination of peoples was allowed before that. That prohibition was, however, only a prohibition provided for by national law. The international community did not deal with it, out of respect for national sovereignty. The novelty consisted in the fact that such acts were now considered international crimes, and that, by the recognition of the 'crime against humanity', national sovereignty was restricted in its *internal* aspects just as national sovereignty was restricted by the crime against peace in its *external* aspects.

Of the twenty-two high profile defendants who appeared before the Nuremberg IMT, eleven were given the death penalty, three were acquitted, three were given life imprisonment and four were given sentences of imprisonment ranging from 10 to 20 years. Subsequent to the *Nuremberg Charter* the Allies passed *Control Council Law No. 10 (CCL No. 10)*[58] patterned after the *Nuremberg Charter*. It provided the legal basis for the Allies to prosecute alleged German war criminals in their respective zones of occupation.[59] *CCL No. 10*

---

56 M Cherif Bassiouni, *Crimes against Humanity in International Criminal Law* (Brill, Martinus Nijhoff, 2nd revised edn, 1999) 18; Egon Schwelb, 'Crimes against Humanity' (1946) 23 *British Year Book of International Law* 178.

57 See Bassiouni, *Crimes against Humanity*, ibid 18–47; M Cherif Bassiouni, 'International Law and the Holocaust' (1979) 9 *California Western International Law Journal* 201. See also Leila Sadat Wexler, 'The Interpretation of the Nuremberg Principles by the French Court of Cassation' (1994) 32 *Columbia Journal of Transnational Law* 289; Schwelb, 'Crimes against Humanity', ibid.

58 *Allied Control Council Law No 10, Punishment of Persons Guilty of War Crimes, Crimes Against Peace and Against Humanity*, 20 December 1945, Official Gazette of the Control Council for Germany, No. 3, Berlin, 31 January 1946 [hereinafter '*CCL No 10*'], reprinted in Benjamin B Ferencz, *An International Criminal Court, a Step Toward World Peace: A Documentary History and Analysis* (Oceana Publications, 1980) 488.

59 Ibid.

authorised the four key zone commanders[60] to set up tribunals for the punishment of war crimes, crimes against peace and crimes against humanity. Prosecutions in the Allied zones of occupation under the auspices of *CCL No. 10* were more in the nature of domestic as opposed to international prosecutions premised on Allies exercising sovereign power over Germany as a result of the country's unconditional surrender.[61]

2 The International Military Tribunal for the Far East at Tokyo

The history of the Tokyo Trials began with the establishment of the Far Eastern Commission (FEC). With the unconditional surrender of Japan, control over occupational matters in the Far East rested with General Douglas Macarthur, a United States army general appointed as the Supreme Commander for the Allied Powers (SCAP). On 19 January 1946, General Macarthur, in his capacity as the SCAP for the Pacific Theatre, and on behalf of the Far Eastern Commission (FEC), established the International Military Tribunal for the Far East (Tokyo Tribunal) through a general military order.[62]

The *Tokyo Charter*[63] followed the broad outline of the Big Four agreement in London that had established the Nuremberg Tribunal. Like the *Nuremberg Charter*, it provided for the prosecution and punishment of those accused of committing 'crimes against peace', 'war crimes' and 'crimes against humanity'.[64] The respective instruments are substantially the same, with a few exceptions. One such exception is that Article 5(c) of the *Tokyo Charter* provided that persecution on political and racial grounds constituted 'crimes against humanity', whereas Article 6(c) of the *Nuremberg Charter* included religious grounds as well. Such an inclusion was necessary in the *Nuremberg Charter* because of the Holocaust against the Jewish people.[65] Also with respect to 'crimes against humanity', the *Nuremberg Charter* provided that 'inhumane acts committed against any civilian population' were subject to prosecution. The *Tokyo Charter* eliminated the phrase 'against

60   France, Great Britain, Union of Soviet Socialist Republics and United States of America.

61   In the British Zone, military tribunals tried 937 persons, acquitted 260, and sentenced 230 to death. In the United Stated [US] Zone, 177 persons were tried by military tribunals, twenty-four were sentenced to death, thirty-five acquitted. In the French Zone, military courts tried 2,107 people, condemned 104 to death, acquitted 404, and gave 1,235 shorter prison terms. The Union of Soviet Socialist Republics [USSR] did not hold such trials in its zone of occupation, but instead tried Nazi military personnel in the USSR for atrocities committed against civilians during Germany's occupation of their territory.

62   Special Proclamation by the Supreme Commander for the Allied Powers at Tokyo, 19 January 1946, TIAS No. 1589, 4 Bevans 20; Charter dated 19 January 1946, 4 Bevans 21; Amended Charter dated 26 April 1946, 4 Bevans 27, 28 [*Tokyo Charter*].

63   US Department of State, *Trial of the Japanese War Criminals* (1946) 39–44.

64   *Nuremberg Charter*, above n 46; *Tokyo Charter*, above n 62.

65   See M Cherif Bassiouni, 'International Law and the Holocaust' (1979) 9 *California Western International Law Journal* 202; Bassiouni, *Crimes against Humanity*, above n 56 at 34.

any civilian population' from Article 5(c), thereby expanding the class of persons beyond civilians only. The definition was broadened to: 'to make punishment possible for large-scale killing of military personnel in an unlawful war'.[66]

Twenty-eight Japanese military and political leaders were charged with 'Class A crimes', and more than 5,700 Japanese nationals were charged with 'Class B' and 'C' crimes. Class A defendants (major political and civilian leaders) faced the Tokyo IMT. Class B and C defendants faced national prosecutions in domestic courts/tribunals that spanned countries and continents: Great Britain, France, the Netherlands and the United States to Australia, China and the Philippines.[67]

B. Sovereignty constrained: the Nuremberg and Tokyo principles

Important principles were articulated at the post-World War II international trials. These principles are commonly referred to as the Nuremberg Principles owing to the fact that they were first laid down by the Nuremberg Tribunal which handed down its judgment as the Tokyo Trials were commencing. The Tokyo Trial served to re-affirm many of these principles. The decisions of 1945–1946 erased any lingering doubts about the illegality of aggressive war, affirmed the emergence of international human rights law, abrogated sovereign immunity and imposed individual criminal liability on government leaders, officials and personnel. Importantly, shortly after the Nuremberg decision, the United Nations General Assembly, in a unanimous resolution, affirmed the Nuremberg principles as accepted principles of international criminal law.[68]

1. Internationalisation of the individual

The concept that international law should take into account the rights and duties of individuals was not a position generally accepted as a part of international law immediately prior to Nuremberg. At that time, international law dealt with the rights and duties of States and applied only to interactions and conflicts among States.[69] There is, however, evidence that individual rights were a

---

66 BVA Roling, *The Tokyo Trial and Beyond: Reflections of a Peacemonger* (Polity Press, 1993) 3. See also BVA Roling, 'The Nuremberg and Tokyo Trials in Retrospect' in M Cherif Bassiouni and Ved P Nanda (eds), *A Treatise on International Criminal Law* (Charles C Thomas Publisher, 1973) 590.

67 Over 2,200 trials were held outside of Japan against 5,600 Japanese nationals and Japanese collaborators accused of various crimes. More than 4,400 were convicted and about 1,000 were sentenced to death. See generally Meirion Harries and Susan Harries, *Soldiers of the Sun: The Rise and Fall of the Imperial Japanese Army Paperback* (Random House, 1994).

68 Affirmation of the Principles of International Law recognised in the Charter of the Nuremberg Tribunal, GA Res 95(1), UN GAOR, 1st sess, UN Doc A/236 (1947) at 188.

69 American Law Institute, *Restatement of the Law, Foreign Relations Law of the United States* (1986) Part III at 144–5 (Introductory Note).

concern of international law in the eighteenth century,[70] but this interest faded in the nineteenth and twentieth centuries as the statist concept of international law gained popularity. Nuremberg revived the commitment to protect individual rights. Once again, it was primarily normative concerns that reinforced this concept into international law.

The Nuremberg Tribunal in holding agents of State decision-making personally responsible for crimes against peace, war crimes and crimes against humanity affirmed that these transgressions were not only international legal wrongs, but wrongs punishable through the ascription of personal responsibility by criminal law sanctions. The message of Nuremberg echoed later at Tokyo was clear; those who authorised and committed crimes against peace, war crimes and other humanitarian crimes would be personally responsible for those crimes and would be made to suffer the consequences of their conduct. To hold the perpetrators of these proscribed forms of conduct accountable signified that terrible things could not be done to individuals without a resulting meaningful international sense of responsibility. This infusion of morals and concern for individual rights into international law launched the modern doctrine of international human rights law.

2. Externalising the State and its sovereignty

Nuremberg and Tokyo represented practical manifestations of the authority of the international community under international law to question, assess and pass judgment on the internal activities and laws of the State. In holding that the local municipal law of the sovereign State of Germany provided no cover for individuals who had violated international rules governing the conduct of warfare, Nuremberg upheld the notion that a State was bound by international law even when its government had chosen not to be so bound. If we view the operational state of international criminal law as constitutionally allocated to sovereign States by custom, practice and treaty law, then Nuremberg was an important constitutional allocation of competence to the international community and away from the sovereign nation-state. This is the accurate juridical position which Nuremberg (and Tokyo) occupied in the global constitutive process. The Nuremberg tribunal confronted the dualism between sovereign versus personal responsibility directly: '[h]e who violates the laws of war cannot obtain immunity while acting in pursuance of the authority of the State if the State in authorising action moves outside its competence under international law.'[71]

---

70 See generally Louis B Sohn, 'The New International Law: Protection of the Rights of the Individual rather than States' (1982) 32 *American University Law Review* 12 (tracing the concerns of international law with the rights of the individual from Nuremberg through 1982).

71 See Katherine B Fite, *The Nürnberg Judgment, A Summary* (US Government Printing Office, 1947).

3 Supranational jurisdiction for international law violations

Universal jurisdiction allows any nation to prosecute offenders for certain crimes even when the prosecuting nation lacks a traditional nexus with either the crime, the alleged offender or the victim. Courts developed this doctrine centuries ago to address piracy and later extended it to cover slave trading.[72] The pirate and slave trader were deemed *hostis generis humanis* – the enemy of all people. The progressive trends in certain judicial opinions as well as legal writings in the interwar period buoyed by post-World War I efforts at international criminal accountability contributed in paving the way for the Nuremberg and Tokyo tribunals. The milestone was that universal jurisdiction was extended to cover several offences other than the traditional piracy and slave trading. The doctrine was expanded to include crimes against peace, war crimes and crimes against humanity. Universal jurisdiction was a vital legacy of Nuremberg. Until Nuremberg and Tokyo, it was only national courts that would prosecute criminals for crimes committed in a particular country provided that there existed either a territorial or nationality nexus.

IV. 1945–1990: sovereignty and international criminal justice – backward and forward

The post-World War II era was a period in which the freedom and independence of the State in law-making was subjected to limitations by international law in respect of certain international interests. What had been unthinkable before World War II became commonplace. The dozens of human rights and humanitarian instruments adopted after the post-World War II trials were based on the premise that sovereign States are not free to abuse their own citizens with impunity. These instruments were designed to reinforce the legacy of the IMTs as a continuous rather than sporadic epoch of international law's progress. In essence, the protection of human rights against the depredations of national governments – even their own governments – became the focus of much of the development of international law following Nuremberg and Tokyo. This proliferation of international legal instruments protecting the rights of individuals without examination of their nationality or their connection to another State formed a sharp break with the past as they sought to limit the State's law-making competence. Besides demonstrating that legal values arising from international law impose obligations directly on the State, these instruments and their progeny are a sign that the citizen is not subject only to the dictates of the national sovereign but a subject of the dictates of international law as well.

---

72 For a concise but detailed discussion of the history of universal jurisdiction and its contemporary practice, see M Cherif Bassiouni, 'Universal Jurisdiction for International Crimes: Historical Perspectives and Contemporary Practice' (2001) 42 *Virginia Journal of International Law* 81.

Even as international human rights and humanitarian law instruments marked the important steps by international law to limit sovereignty, the Cold War was to tie the issue of sovereignty to ideological and revolutionary agendas. The world experienced the third struggle for hegemonic domination of the twentieth century hot on the heels of the conclusion of the second. The USSR increasingly saw the notion of 'restriction of sovereignty' and the conceptions of 'common interest' and 'common good' as nothing more than a diplomatic screen hiding the avaricious and predatory aims of the imperialist Powers.[73] The effect of this position was to strengthen sovereignty considerations as the UN became a ground for cultivating the agenda of nationalism brought to the fore with the appearance of the 'Third World' as a force in the years after World War II. With sovereignty viewed as a vital element of global international society, the power politics of the Cold War era served to curtail the expected benefits from the limitation of sovereignty articulated at the post-World War II trials. The Cold War had two paradoxical aspects and was an era of mixed blessings for international law. While tremendous advances were made in propagating and perpetuating the Nuremberg and Tokyo legacy through the codification and broadening of international criminal law, East–West rivalries effectively prevented any efforts at enforcement at the international level. In this era, it was in domestic courts that most of the international jurisprudence was developed.

V. The 1990s: sovereignty in retreat, international penal process in ascendance

The end of the Cold War, which paralysed the United Nations from its inception, was a cause for celebration and hope. Following the historic Security Council Summit Meeting of January 1992, the then Secretary-General of the United Nations, Boutros Boutros-Ghali, spoke of a growing conviction 'among nations large and small, that an opportunity has been regained to achieve the great objectives of the *UN Charter* – a United Nations capable of maintaining international peace and security, of securing justice and human rights and of promoting, in the words of the *Charter*, "social progress and better standards of life in larger freedom"'.[74] This bold and idealistic statement did not however reflect the international reality of the moment. While Western leaders were still congratulating themselves over the end of communism and the fall of the Soviet empire, the security structure that helped bring about those events had begun to come apart. Less than 2 years after the fall of the Berlin Wall, the structure

---

73 See, eg, IE Korovin, 'Respect for Sovereignty: An Unchanging Principle of Soviet Foreign Policy' (1956) *International Affairs* (Moscow) 11, 32, 37–9.

74 Report of the Secretary-General on the Work of the Organisation, UN GAOR, 47th sess, UN Doc A/47/277, S/24111 (1992) 3.

of international law was under threat and appeared to be crumbling. The Balkans had erupted into a theatre of war and Rwanda's genocidal conflagration was in the making. It took a war in Europe (Croatia in 1991) to stir public interest. The war in Bosnia-Herzegovina (1992) and the Rwandan genocide (1994)[75] amplified the alarm bell, though it had been sounded a good deal earlier in January 1991 with the overthrow of Somalia's President Siad Barre.[76]

The two *ad hoc* international criminal tribunals established in the 1990s were meant to minimise the peripheral deterioration in the international rule of law. While it is arguable that the *ad hoc* tribunals were first and foremost, the by-products of international realpolitik born out of a political desire to redeem the international community's conscience rather than the primary commitment of the international community to guarantee international justice, the two tribunals also established the beginning of a new pattern in the genuine international implementation of international criminal law and the move back to the international model inaugurated at Nuremberg. In the Cold War era, national prosecutions boldly supplanted this model.

A. The ICTFY: international justice erodes State sovereignty

In an unprecedented decision, the International Tribunal for the Prosecution of Persons Responsible for Serious Violations of International Humanitarian Law Committed in the Territory of the Former Yugoslavia Since 1991 (ICTFY) was established by the United Nations Security Council in May 1993[77] by the Security Council as an enforcement measure pursuant to Chapter VII of the *UN Charter*.[78] Its creation was essentially prompted by three considerations. First, by 1993, it had become obvious that the parties to the Yugoslav conflict

---

75 Roy Gutman and David Reiff (eds), *Crimes of War: What the Public Should Know* (Norton and Co, 1999) 50–6, 230–5, 312–15.

76 Fighting between various Somali factions and clans resulted in widespread death and destruction causing a dire need for emergency humanitarian assistance. See, eg, *The Situation in Somalia: Report of the Secretary-General*, UN SCOR, 47th sess, UN Doc S/23829/Add 1 (1992) at 7, 9, 11, 13; *The Situation in Somalia: Report of the Secretary-General*, UN SCOR, 47th sess, UN Doc S/23693 (1992) at 4.

77 See SC Res 808, UN SCOR, 48th sess, 3175th mtg, UN Doc S/RES/808 (1993) at 2 (SC Res 808) (requesting a report on how such a Tribunal might be established). See also Security Council Resolution on Establishing an International Tribunal for the Prosecution of Persons Responsible for Serious Violations of International Humanitarian Law Committed in the Territory of the Former Yugoslavia, SC Res 827, UN SCOR, 48th sess, 3217th mtg, UN Doc S/RES/827 (1993) at 2 (SC Res 827) (creating the Tribunal).

78 Chapter VII of the *UN Charter* allows the United Nations to use military force and act in areas otherwise reserved to the domestic jurisdiction of States. United Nations operations in Iraq, Somalia and Haiti were all authorised under Chapter VII. See SC Res 678, UN SCOR, 45th sess, Res and Dec, UN Doc S/INF/46 (1990) at 27; SC Res 794, UN SCOR, 47th sess, Res and Dec, UN Doc S/INF/48 (1992) at 63; SC Res 841, UN SCOR, 48th sess, Res and Dec, UN Doc S/INF/49 (1993) at 119.

were unwilling, and in the case of Bosnia and Herzegovina unable, to bring to justice persons responsible for the egregious crimes that were taking place. Second, by establishing the Tribunal, the Security Council hoped to deflect criticism for its reluctance to take more decisive action to stop the bloodshed in the former Yugoslavia. Third, the Tribunal was intended to meet the crucial goal of deterrence with the possibility of arrest, prosecution and punishment signalling an intention to curb impunity and discourage criminality. Not without controversy, the international community, with the Security Council at its helm, decided that the establishment of an international tribunal empowered to prosecute persons responsible for serious violations of international humanitarian law committed in the territory of the former Yugoslavia since 1991 was a worthy precedent to set, worthy even to the extent of subjugating the sovereignty of the States involved.

For such a striking move as the creation of an international criminal tribunal established under the auspices of the UN, there was surprisingly little objection within the larger international community. Although several countries offered draft statutes that differed in jurisdictional scope and other powers, only one State actually denied the power of the Security Council to establish a tribunal at all. Unsurprisingly, this was the Federal Republic of Yugoslavia, which argued that its state sovereignty would be unacceptably violated by the establishment of an international tribunal that held the prejudicial goal of prosecuting Serbs.[79] Yugoslavia stated that while it 'considers that all perpetrators of war crimes committed in the territory of the former Yugoslavia should be prosecuted and punished',[80] this was the proper mandate for national, as opposed to international, laws and tribunals. The Federal Republic of Yugoslavia further challenged the mandate of the Security Council to establish the Tribunal, drawing on the fact that neither the *UN Charter* generally, nor Chapter VII specifically, grant power to the Security Council to create tribunals as a means of maintaining international peace and security.[81] Further, the Federal Republic of Yugoslavia also made a wide appeal to the international community, drawing on the principles of sovereignty and dignity cherished by all States.[82]

The international community was presented with a difficult choice. It could either rigidly uphold the sanctity of State sovereignty, even at the risk of allowing horrific acts of war to go untried and unpunished, or it could undermine State sovereignty in a move that clearly overrode the wishes of the States most closely involved by creating an international criminal tribunal – one that would demand the extradition of those States' nationals for public trial, make incursions into

---

79 See Letter Dated 19 May 1993 From the Charge D'Affaires of the Permanent Mission of Yugoslavia (Serbia and Montenegro) to the United Nations Addressed to the Secretary-General, UN Doc A/48/170-S/25801 (1993) (Yugoslav Letter), 6, 10.

80 Ibid 3.

81 Ibid 6–9.

82 Ibid 10.

their demarcated territories for the exact purpose of collecting evidence by which to prosecute their nationals, exhume their mass grave sites, and deepen a sense of subjugation within those States already angered by a perceived prejudice against them.[83]

The specific provisions of the *ICTFY Statute* reflect the influence of the *Nuremberg Charter*. The Tribunal has subject matter jurisdiction over four categories of crimes: (1) grave breaches of the 1949 *Geneva Conventions*; (2) other violations of the laws and customs of war; (3) genocide; and (4) crimes against humanity.[84] Significantly, the *ICTFY Statute* affirmed certain major components of international humanitarian law as customary law, including those rules establishing personal criminal responsibility for violations and breaches of these norms. The principle of individual criminal responsibility for the commission of these crimes formed the cornerstone of the Tribunal's operation.[85] The Tribunal's jurisdiction over the above-mentioned crimes is not exclusive, as national courts may also try indicted war criminals.[86] Nevertheless, the Tribunal retains primacy over national courts and may step into the national judicial proceedings at any time to take over the trial.[87]

States' obligations under the *ICTFY Statute* and its *Rules of Procedure and Evidence* extend not only to executing arrest warrants but to producing evidence and taking testimony as well. In some countries, existing law was adequate to provide this type of assistance to the Tribunal. However, for most States their statist-based domestic law frameworks on criminal justice were not suited to this novel vertical structure that transcended the State. Many countries (voluntarily or through various forms of international pressure) were to subsequently pass

---

83 Anne Bodley, 'Weakening the Principle of Sovereignty in International Law: The International Criminal Tribunal for the Former Yugoslavia' (1999) 31 *New York University Journal of International Law and Politics* 417, 439.

84 The *Statute* and the *Rules of Procedure and Evidence of the Tribunal* are reprinted in *International Criminal Tribunal for the former Yugoslavia, Basic Documents/Documents de Référence* (1995) Arts 2–5. For a detailed commentary on the ICTFY's subject matter jurisdiction, see John RWD Jones, *The Practice of the International Criminal Tribunals for the Former Yugoslavia and Rwanda* (Martinus Nijhoff, 1998) 7–60; Virginia Morris and Michael Scharf, *An Insider's Guide to the International Criminal Tribunal for the Former Yugoslavia: A Documentary Analysis* (2 vols) (Transnational Publishers, 1995) vol I, 61–88; Sean D Murphy, 'Progress and Jurisprudence of the International Criminal Tribunal for the Former Yugoslavia' (1999) 93 *American Journal of International Law* 57, 65–71.

85 Ibid Article 7 (setting forth the scope for who can be held criminally liable). For a detailed discussion of Article 7 in the ICTFY jurisprudence, see Jones, ibid at 62–72; Morris and Scharf, *An Insider's Guide*, ibid at 91–115 (discussing who is liable, what defences are available and when immunity may be granted); Murphy, 'Progress and Jurisprudence', above ibid at 71–2.

86 Ibid Articles 9–10.

87 ICTFY Statute, ibid Article 9; First Annual Report of the International Tribunal for the Prosecution of Persons Responsible for Serious Violations of International Humanitarian Law Committed in the Territory of the Former Yugoslavia Since 1991, UN GAOR, 49th sess, pt 1, 11–14, UN Docs A/49/342, S/1994/1007 (14 November 1994) www.un.org/icty/rapportan/first-94.htm pt 2, 89.

implementing legislation to facilitate cooperation. The International Tribunal's significant coercive powers to investigate, demand extradition and prosecute, with States prevailed upon to render judicial assistance, was a landmark substantial incursion into the sovereignty of the States.

B. The ICTR: consolidating the advances of international justice

The *International Criminal Tribunal for Rwanda (ICTR)* created in 1994 grew out of the response of the UN human rights system to the Rwandan tragedy. Parallel to the efforts within the UN human rights system, the government of Rwanda that came to power by toppling the genocidal regime made a request to the UN Security Council for assistance to bring those responsible for the genocide to justice.[88] The *ICTR* was mandated to 'prosecute persons responsible for serious violations of international humanitarian law committed in the territory of Rwanda and Rwandan citizens responsible for such violations committed in the territory of neighbouring States, between 1 January 1994 and 31 December 1994.'[89]

Though Article 1 of the *ICTR Statute* limits the *ICTR*'s temporal jurisdiction to the year 1994 only,[90] the Article also states that the *ICTR* 'shall have the power to prosecute persons responsible for serious violations of international humanitarian law committed in the territory of Rwanda and Rwandan citizens responsible for such violations committed in the territory of neighbouring States'.[91] By granting the *ICTR* the competence to prosecute Rwandans who allegedly committed certain crimes abroad, the Security Council added a new dimension to the humanitarian law of non-international armed conflict. Consequently, the Statute granted the *ICTR* both personal and territorial jurisdiction in Rwanda as well as limited personal and territorial jurisdiction in surrounding States. Under the *ICTR Statute* the Court possesses 'primacy over national courts of all states', such that it may formally request national courts to defer to its competence.[92] Rwanda formally requested the creation of a tribunal, and thereby voluntarily surrendered some of its jurisdiction to the Security Council's judicial creation. By contrast, according to the Statute, Rwanda's neighbours must surrender some of their jurisdiction to the *ICTR* without choice.[93]

---

88 Letter dated 28 September 1994 from the Permanent Representative of Rwanda Addressed to the President of the Security Council, UNSCOR, 49th sess, UN Doc S/1994/1115 (1994) 4.

89 The *Statute of the International Tribunal for Rwanda* is set out as an annex to SC Res 955, UN SCOR, 49th Year, 3453D mtg, UN Doc S/RES/955 (1994).

90 Ibid.

91 Ibid at 1.

92 Ibid Article 8(2).

93 Ibid Articles 7–8.

Article 2 of the *ICTR Statute*[94] replicates Articles 2 and 3 of the *Genocide Convention*.[95] Similar to the *1949 Geneva Conventions*, the *Genocide Convention* obligates States Parties to enact the legislation necessary to provide effective penalties for persons guilty of genocide.[96] Article 3, 'Crimes against humanity', of the *ICTR Statute*[97] resembled Article 6(c) of the *Nuremberg Charter*.[98] Employing the Nuremberg concept of crimes against humanity in Rwanda constitutes an important legal development. The *Nuremberg Charter* was established to prosecute 'war criminals',[99] and it explicitly defined crimes against humanity as specified inhumane acts[100] but linked the crimes to war. Article 4 empowered the *ICTR* to prosecute persons committing, or ordering to be committed, serious violations of Article 3 Common to the *Geneva Conventions of 1949* and of the *Additional Protocol II* thereto of 1977.[101] Until the *ICTR*'s establishment, it was generally accepted that neither Common Article 3 nor *Additional Protocol II* provided a basis for universal jurisdiction and that in the international arena, they constituted an uncertain basis for individual criminal responsibility.[102] The extension by the *ICTR Statute* of international penal responsibility to persons guilty of non-grave breaches in non-international armed conflict was a development of enormous normative importance.[103]

By specifying in Article 28 of the Tribunal's Statute that States shall cooperate with the *ICTR* and comply without undue delay with any request for assistance, including the arrest or detention of persons and the surrender of the accused to the *ICTR*,[104] the UN Security Council, through its creation of the *ICTR*, added a compulsory arrest and surrender requirement to acts that the *Geneva Conventions* and *Additional Protocol II* had previously conceptualised as being governed by domestic discretion and thus beyond both the *aut dedere aut judicare* obligation and external penal action. This explicit extension of the concept of criminality to Common Article 3 and *Additional Protocol II* in the *ICTR Statute* represents another important development of international humanitarian law that further contributes to the diminution of State sovereignty through limitation of State discretion in favour of broadening international penal power.

Closely related to the issue of primacy is the broader obligation of States to comply with requests from the Tribunal for the arrest or detention of persons.

---

94 Ibid Article 2.
95 *Convention on the Prevention and Punishment of the Crime of Genocide* [*Genocide Convention*], adopted 9 December 1948, GA Res 260 A (III), 78 UNTS 227, 280 (entered into force 12 January 1951)
96 Ibid Article 5.
97 *Statute of the International Criminal Tribunal for Rwanda* [*ICTR Statute*], Security Council Resolution 955, 8 November 1994, Art 3.
98 *Nuremberg Charter* Article 6(c).
99 Ibid Article 6.
100 Ibid Article 6(c).
101 *ICTR Statute*, above n 97, Art 4.
102 Theodor Meron, *War Crimes Law Comes of Age* (Oxford University Press, 1998) 235.
103 Ibid.
104 *ICTR Statute*, above n 97, Art 28.

The *ICTR Statute* provides that '[s]tates shall comply without undue delay with any request for assistance or an order issued by a Trial Chamber, including, but not limited to . . . the arrest or detention of persons'.[105] This closely parallels the language of the Security Council decision creating the ICTFY, which refers to the 'obligation of states to comply with requests for assistance or orders issued by a Trial Chamber under Article 29 of the Statute'.[106]

C. The International Criminal Court: challenges and concessions to sovereignty

The project to establish an international criminal court, commenced in the aftermath of World War I, was geared to cement the legacy of the IMTs through the establishment of a permanent international penal institution. However the Cold War set in shortly thereafter resulting in the project waxing and waning within the UN system. Practical realisation remained stymied. Finally in the 1990s, after more than four decades of fruitless wrangling, the project of establishing an international criminal court finally took on added impetus in the face of the various episodes of systematic and widespread bloodshed alluded to above.

Re-energised efforts by the UN General Assembly saw requests to the International Law Commission (ILC) to prepare a report on international criminal jurisdiction in 1989. This progressed further with the consideration of the 1991 Draft Code of Crimes 2 years later.[107] Subsequently, the 1994 ILC Draft Statute formed the basis on which the General Assembly established the *Ad Hoc* Committee on the Establishment of an International Criminal Court.[108] In quick succession the following year, the Preparatory Committee for the Establishment of an International Criminal Court was inaugurated.[109] The Preparatory Committee's Report was submitted to the General Assembly's 51st session on 28 October 1996, with a recommendation that the General Assembly extend the Preparatory Committee's term with a specific mandate to negotiate proposals with a view to producing a consolidated text of a Convention, Statute and annexed instruments by 1998.[110] It was envisaged that the draft instruments would be considered by a plenipotentiary conference, as in fact eventually

---

105   *ICTFY Statute* Article 29.
106   Resolution 827, at 4.
107   *Report of the International Law Commission*, UN GAOR, 46th sess, Supp No 10, UN Doc A/46/10 (1991) at 198.
108   *Report of the Ad Hoc Committee on the Establishment of an International Criminal Court*, UN GAOR, 50th sess, Supp No 22, UN Doc A/50/22.
109   GA Res 50/46, UN GAOR, 50th sess, UN Doc A/RES/50/46 (1995). See also, Summary of the Proceedings of the Preparatory Committee on the Establishment of an International Criminal Court, UN GAOR, 50th sess, Supp No 22, UN Doc A/50/22 (1995).
110   Ibid.

happened leading to the adoption of the *Rome Statute* for a permanent *International Criminal Court (ICC)* in the summer of 1998.[111] As a matter of process, the making of the *Rome Statute* was extraordinary. Not only was the *Statute* voted on by States, thereby erasing any illusions one may have held about the continuing relevance of absolute paradigms of sovereignty in modern times, but the law made by the Statute extends to the entire world in cases involving referrals by the Security Council under Chapter VII.[112] Essentially, the ICC will directly or indirectly affect all members of the international community.

The *Rome Statute* has four organs: the Presidency, the Judiciary (which is composed of three divisions: Appeals, Trial and Pre-Trial Divisions), the Office of the Prosecutor and the Registry.[113] The Statute provides that the judges are all to be elected as full-time members of the Court,[114] and that the Prosecutor, Deputy Prosecutors,[115] and Registrar[116] shall also serve on a full-time basis. The Statute also expressly addresses the need for continuing oversight by the States Parties by establishing an Assembly of States Parties and providing rules for its organisation and operation.

The *Rome Statute* grants broad powers to the Prosecutor's Office.[117] Article 15 of the *Rome Statute* provides that the Prosecutor of the court 'may initiate investigations *proprio motu* on the basis of information on crimes within the jurisdiction of the Court'.[118] Thus, the ICC Prosecutor may, on his/her own initiative, launch investigations and indict individuals for crimes within the ICC's jurisdiction. The prosecutor may investigate alleged crimes based on the referral of the UN Security Council, State Parties, victims or any other reliable source.[119] The Prosecutor determines the reliability of the source, as 'he or she deems appropriate'.[120] With the authority to initiate investigations on his/her own initiative, the ICC Prosecutor is an effective inquisitor with the authority to use his/her office in different States and regions of the world wherever any matters

---

111 *Rome Statute of the International Criminal Court [Rome Statute]*, UN Doc A/CONF 183/9 reprinted in 37 ILM 999.

112 *Rome Statute* Article 13.

113 Ibid Article 34.

114 Ibid Article 35(1). There is a provision permitting the Presidency to reduce Judges' terms if the workload so warrants. Ibid Article 35(3). Article 40(3) adds that judges 'required to serve on a full-time basis shall not engage in any other occupation of a professional nature.' Ibid Article 40(3).

115 Ibid Article 42(2).

116 Ibid Article 43(5).

117 'Is a UN International Criminal Court in the US National Interest?: Hearing before the Subcommittee on International Operations of the Senate Committee on Foreign Relations', 105th Cong 1, 29 (1998) at 26–8 (testimony of Ambassador David J Scheffer) (acknowledging the powers and limitations of the Office of the Prosecutor). Prosecutors with any semblance of independence are currently disfavoured in the United States.

118 *Rome Statute*, above n 111, Art 15.

119 Ibid.

120 Ibid.

of concern to the Court arise without being unduly shackled by national sovereignty concerns in matters that warrant his/her attention.

The geographic scope of the Court's jurisdiction, *ratione loci*, varies depending on the mechanism by which the case comes to the Court. In the event that the Security Council refers the matter, jurisdiction covers the territory of every State in the world, whether or not the State in question is a party to the Statute.[121] In cases involving a Security Council referral, the Statute's scope is unbounded by geography. Referrals from the Security Council are founded upon the Council's powers to address issues of international peace and security as outlined in Article 39 of the *UN Charter*.

If the matter is referred by a State Party or initiated *proprio motu* by the Prosecutor, however, the Court's jurisdiction is more restricted but still extensive. In such instances, jurisdiction extends to the territory of a non-State Party only if that State consents to the jurisdiction of the Court, irrespective of whether the acts were committed in the territory of the consenting State or the accused is a national of the consenting State.[122] Thus this regime additionally gives the ICC jurisdiction over the citizens of non-States Parties, allowing the ICC to exercise its jurisdiction in certain circumstances within the territory of non-States Parties.[123]

An intriguing aspect of the *Rome Statute*, which underscores its nature as a constitutive document, is that it combines jurisdiction to prescribe, to adjudicate and to enforce the all-in-one instrument. It is perhaps the implementation and implications of the jurisdictional theories of the Statute that are its most revolutionary features.[124] Through a rather extraordinary process, these three jurisdictional categories classically known to international law have been transformed from norms.[125] The move has been to determine rules that establish under what conditions the States Parties to the Statute, may prescribe international rules of conduct, may adjudicate breaches of those rules and may enforce those adjudications.

The *Rome Statute* reflects the practical experience of the international community in the Yugoslavia and Rwanda Tribunals in several important ways, and no doubt represents an improvement over its predecessors. Yet in one respect the ICC will do no better, and may not even equal, its sister institutions, for it will operate not on the basis of primacy jurisdiction, but subject to the principle of complementarity. Both the Preamble to the *Statute* and Article 1 express a

---

121   Ibid.
122   Ibid Articles 4(2), 12(2).
123   Ibid.
124   Leila Nadya Sadat and S Richard Carden, 'The New International Criminal Court: An Uneasy Revolution' (2000) 88 *Georgetown Law Journal* 38, 406.
125   Rosalyn Higgins, *Problems and Process: International Law and How We Use It* (Clarendon Press, 1994) 56.

fundamental principle of the *Rome Statute*: that the Court is to be 'complementary' to national criminal jurisdictions.[126] Analysis of the Articles on admissibility demonstrates that complementarity does not mean 'concurrent' jurisdiction. Under Article 17, the Court may exercise jurisdiction only if: (1) national jurisdictions are 'unwilling or genuinely unable' to exercise jurisdiction; (2) the crime is of sufficient gravity; and (3) the person has not already been tried for the conduct on which the complaint is based.[127]

International cooperation and judicial assistance as set out in the *Rome Statute* is at the very heart of the ultimate effectiveness of the Court by placing an affirmative obligation on States.[128] Criminal prosecution is inherently tied to notions of national sovereignty and the control over persons and territory which are fundamental to that notion. Articles 86 and 88 form the foundation of the obligation on States Parties to cooperate with the ICC. According to Article 86, 'States Parties shall, in accordance with the provisions of this Statute, cooperate fully with the Court in its investigation and prosecution of crimes within the jurisdiction of the Court.'[129] This general requirement is supplemented by further articles of the *Rome Statute* and the ICC's *Rules of Procedure and Evidence*[130] that govern specific aspects of cooperation in such contexts as the arrest and surrender of individuals and the collection of evidence. Article 88 obliges States to adopt domestic laws to facilitate cooperation with the ICC.[131] The obligation on States Parties to arrest and surrender accused is found in several articles of the *Rome Statute*. The general Article 86 obligation to 'cooperate fully with the Court in its investigation and prosecution of crimes'[132] is supplemented by Article 89, which specifically addresses 'surrender of persons to the Court'.[133] Under Article 89(1), the Court can transmit a request for the arrest and surrender of a person, together with material supporting that request,[134] to a State on the territory of which that person may be found. The Statute is clear as to the obligation of States Parties upon receiving such a request: they must comply.[135]

---

126 *Rome Statute*, preamble and Article 1.
127 Ibid Article 17(1).
128 Ibid. Part 9 contains the provisions on the nature and type of international cooperation and judicial assistance by States.
129 Ibid Article 86.
130 *Rules of Procedure and Evidence*, UN Doc PCNICC/2000/1/Add.1 (2 November 2000).
131 See *Rome Statute*, above n 110, Art 88. Article 88 provides that 'States Parties shall ensure that there are procedures available under their national law for all of the forms of cooperation which are specified under this Part'.
132 Ibid Article 86.
133 Ibid Article 89.
134 Ibid Articles 89(1) and 91.
135 Ibid Article 89(1) ('States Parties shall, in accordance with the provisions of this Part and the procedure under their national law, comply with requests for arrest and surrender.').

VI. Conclusion

The new balance achieved between the jurisdiction of national courts and that of the international criminal tribunals marks the end of an era when the exercise of criminal jurisdiction fell within the unfettered prerogatives of the sovereign State. Although hardcore realists still cling to the notion that States are supreme, reality points to the fact that international law norms have developed rules whose aim is to modulate the behaviour of States. This implies violation of, or intrusion upon, State authority. International penal process has already significantly contributed to a diminution of the overall concept of sovereignty. The significance of the international penal process and its accompanying tenet of international justice reflects an evolution in the perception of sovereignty heralding a qualitative shift from State supremacy to an ethical vision in which human values ultimately prevail over State rights where the two are in conflict.

The international penal process represents a shift in authority from States to the international community. Sovereignty has been chipped away, both from the outside and from within, as the concept of an international penal process has been increasingly recognised as trumping the right of States to hold sole rights in the exercise of certain prerogatives. We can conceive of any reconceptualisation of sovereignty as moving both downward (inward) from the State incorporating both human and 'peoples' rights and upward (outward) from the State as we look for ways to respond to the need to protect these rights within a global framework as well as respond to the increasing permeability of borders. The notion of international justice now points towards a sphere that, though controlled by States, is ineffaceably external to power.

3 Liability for ordering the commission of international crimes

Sarah Finnin[1]

I. Introduction

Holding individuals liable for ordering subordinates to engage in conduct that violates international humanitarian law is an important mechanism for ensuring accountability for such violations. Ordering has long been recognised as a mode of liability under international humanitarian law. *Control Council Law No 10*, which governed the subsequent trials of war criminals in post-war occupied Germany, provided that a person who ordered the commission of a crime was an accessory, and would be deemed to have committed such crime.[2] The High Contracting Parties of the *1949 Geneva Conventions* undertook to enact legislation necessary to provide effective penal sanctions for persons 'committing, *or ordering* to be committed' any of the grave breaches of those Conventions.[3] Liability for ordering was explicitly included in Articles 7(1) and 6(1) of the *Statutes for the International Criminal Tribunals for the former Yugoslavia* (*ICTY*) and *Rwanda* (*ICTR*)

1 This chapter is derived from the author's previous publication: Sarah Finnin, *Elements of Accessorial Modes of Liability: Article 25(3)(b) and (c) of the Rome Statute of the International Criminal Court* (Martinus Nijhoff, 2012). The views expressed herein are those of the author alone and do not necessarily reflect the views of the *International Criminal Tribunal for the former Yugoslavia* or the United Nations in general. The author is grateful to Matthew Cross for his comments on an earlier draft of this chapter.
2 *Control Council Law No 10: Punishment of Persons Guilty of War Crimes, Crimes against Peace and against Humanity*, signed 20 December 1945, Article II(2)(b) in Official Gazette of the Control Council for Germany, No 3, Berlin, 31 January 1946, 50.
3 *Geneva Convention for the Amelioration of the Condition of the Wounded and Sick in Armed Forces in the Field*, opened for signature 12 August 1949, 75 UNTS 31 (entered into force 21 October 1950) Article 49 (emphasis added); *Geneva Convention for the Amelioration of the Condition of Wounded, Sick and Shipwrecked Members of Armed Forces at Sea*, opened for signature 12 August 1949, 75 UNTS 85 (entered into force 21 October 1950) Article 50 (emphasis added); *Geneva Convention Relative to the Treatment of Prisoners of War*, opened for signature 12 August 1949, 75 UNTS 135 (entered into force 21 October 1950) Article 129 (emphasis added); *Geneva Convention Relative to the Protection of Civilian Persons in Time of War*, opened for signature 12 August 1949, 75 UNTS 287 (entered into force 21 October 1950) Article 146 (emphasis added) [collectively *1949 Geneva Conventions*].

(collectively *ad hoc* Tribunals) respectively,[4] and has been developed in the jurisprudence of those and other tribunals.

Article 25(3)(b) of the *Rome Statute of the International Criminal Court* (ICC)[5] also recognises ordering as a mode of liability. In 2012, Pre-Trial Chamber II issued the first decision in which a chamber examined the elements of ordering under that provision in any detail.[6] The case, arising out of the Situation in the Democratic Republic of the Congo, concerns Sylvestre Mudacumura, the alleged supreme commander of the military wing of the *Forces Démocratiques pour la Libération du Rwanda – Forces Combattantes Abacunguzi* (FDLR).[7] The application for a warrant of arrest accused Mudacumura of issuing an order to FDLR troops in 2009 to create a humanitarian catastrophe in the Kivus by attacking civilians and ensuring the implementation of that order.[8] The Office of the Prosecutor (OTP) sought an arrest warrant for Mudacumura for war crimes and crimes against humanity on the basis of ordering under Article 25(3)(b) (as an alternative to liability as a principal perpetrator under Article 25(3)(a)). Having found that there were no reasonable grounds to believe that a common plan existed for the purposes of Article 25(3)(a), the Chamber proceeded to outline the elements of ordering as a mode of liability.[9]

In addition to the *Mudacumura Case*, the OTP is pursuing liability for ordering under Article 25(3)(b) as an alternative to liability as a principal perpetrator in a handful of other cases.[10] For example, the *Ntaganda Case* also arises out of the Situation in the Democratic Republic of the Congo. Bosco Ntaganda was a key military operations commander in the *Forces Patriotiques pour la Libération du Congo* (FPLC), the military wing of the *Union des Patriotes Congolais* (UPC), whose troops (together with Hema civilian supporters) allegedly carried out a widespread and systematic attack against the civilian population of Ituri in 2002

4   *Statute of the International Criminal Tribunal for the former Yugoslavia*, adopted 25 May 1993, annexed to SC Res 827 (1993), UN Doc S/RES/827 (25 May 1993); *Statute of the International Criminal Tribunal for Rwanda*, adopted 8 November 1994, annexed to SC Res 955 (1994), UN Doc S/RES/955 (8 November 1994).

5   *Rome Statute of the International Criminal Court*, opened for signature 17 July 1998, 2187 UNTS 3 (entered into force 1 July 2002) [*Rome Statute*].

6   *Prosecutor v Sylvestre Mudacumura (Decision on the Prosecutor's Application under Article 58)* (*International Criminal Court, Pre-Trial Chamber II*, Case No ICC-01/04-01/12, 13 July 2012) [62] [*Mudacumura Arrest Warrant Decision*]. A warrant for arrest was also issued for Dominic Ongwen on the basis of ordering in 2005. See *Situation in Uganda (Warrant of Arrest for Dominic Ongwen)* (International Criminal Court, Pre-Trial Chamber II, Case No ICC/02/04, 8 July 2005) [30].

7   *Prosecutor v Sylvestre Mudacumura (Second Public Redacted Version of Prosecution's Application under Article 58)* (*International Criminal Court, Pre-Trial Chamber II*, Case No ICC-01/04, 4 July 2012) [4], [24] [*Mudacumura Arrest Warrant Application*].

8   Ibid [4], [17].

9   *Mudacumura Arrest Warrant Decision* at [62]–[63].

10 In addition to the *Ntaganda* and *Ruto Cases* discussed below, ordering is also a mode of liability under consideration in the *Gbagbo and Blé Goudé Case*. See *Prosecutor v Laurent Gbagbo (Decision on the Confirmation of Charges against Laurent Gbagbo)* (International Criminal Court, Pre-Trial Chamber I, Case No ICC-02/11-01/11, 12 June 2014) [242]–[251]; *Prosecutor v Charles Blé Goudé (Decision on the Confirmation of Charges against Charles Blé Goudé)* (International Criminal Court, Pre-Trial Chamber I, Case No ICC-02/11-02/11, 11 December 2014) [159]–[166]. See also

and 2003.[11] It is alleged that he directly participated in attacks 'by commanding troops   in the field, giving orders before and during attacks and actively participating in combat'.[12] In June 2014, Pre-Trial Chamber II confirmed charges against Ntaganda on the basis of ordering, as an alternative to liability as a direct perpetrator and/or indirect co-perpetrator under Article 25(3)(a).[13]

A third case, *Ruto*, arises out of the Situation in the Republic of Kenya. William Samoei Ruto was at the head of the 'Network', a group based on existing Kalenjin tribal structures which allegedly cultivated anti-Kikuyu sentiment and planned and implemented attacks during the 2007 post-election violence in the Rift Valley province of Kenya.[14] Prior to the commencement of the trial in September 2013, the OTP requested that the Trial Chamber give notice under Regulation 55(1) of the Regulations of the Court[15] that the form of individual criminal responsibility pleaded with respect to Ruto might be subject to legal recharacterisation in the course of the proceedings.[16] While the Pre-Trial Chamber confirmed the charges against Ruto on the theory of indirect co-perpetration under Article 25(3)(a), the OTP argued that Ruto's criminal responsibility could equally be characterised as ordering under Article 25(3)(b) (among other forms of liability).[17]

As this chapter will discuss, the approach taken to ordering in these first cases before the ICC bears a close resemblance to that developed in the jurisprudence of the *ad hoc* Tribunals. For example, just like the jurisprudence of the *ad hoc* Tribunals, current ICC jurisprudence requires proof that the accused held a position of authority with respect to the principal perpetrator. In addition, both

---

Prosecutor v Laurent Gbagbo and Charles Blé Goudé (Decision on Prosecution Requests to Join the Cases and Related Matters) (International Criminal Court, Trial Chamber I, Case Nos ICC-02/11-01/11 and ICC-02/11-02/11, 11 March 2015).

11 *Prosecutor v Bosco Ntaganda (Updated Document Containing the Charges)* (*International Criminal Court, Pre-Trial Chamber I*, Case No ICC-01/04-02/06, 16 February 2015) [1], [5]–[6] [*Ntaganda DCC*].

12 Ibid [6].

13 *Prosecutor v Bosco Ntaganda (Decision Pursuant to Article 61(7)(a) and (b) of the Rome Statute on the Charges of the Prosecutor against Bosco Ntaganda)* (*International Criminal Court, Pre-Trial Chamber II*, Case No ICC-01/04-02/06) (*Ntaganda Confirmation* Decision).

14 See, eg, *Prosecutor v William Samoei Ruto and Joshua Arap Sang (Prosecution's Updated Pre-Trial Brief)* (*International Criminal Court, Trial Chamber V(A)*, Case No ICC-01/09-01/11, 9 September 2013) [18], [24], [28].

15 Regulation 55 authorises the Trial Chamber to modify the legal characterisation of facts provided certain conditions are met, thereby enabling a conviction for a different crime, or on the basis of a different mode of liability, than that originally charged.

16 *Prosecutor v William Samoei Ruto and Joshua Arap Sang (Prosecution's Submissions on the Law of Indirect Co-perpetration under Article 25(3)(a) of the Statute and Application for Notice to Be Given under Regulation 55(2) with respect to William Samoei Ruto's Individual Criminal Responsibility)* (*International Criminal Court, Trial Chamber V*, Case No ICC-01/09-01/11, 3 July 2012) [24] [*Ruto Recharacterisation Application*].

17 *Ruto Recharacterisation Application* at [29]. The OTP also submitted that Ruto's criminal responsibility could be characterised as soliciting or inducing under Article 25(3)(b), aiding, abetting or otherwise assisting under Article 25(3)(c), or contributing to the commission of a crime by a group of persons acting with a common purpose under Article 25(3)(d).

the *ad hoc* Tribunals and the ICC extend liability for ordering to cases where the accused orders the principal perpetrator to engage in *lawful* conduct which results in the commission or attempted commission of a crime. However, there are some important differences. First, the test for causation departs somewhat from the earlier jurisprudence. Second, the application of Article 30 of the *Rome Statute* results in a more stringent mental element than that imposed by the law that governs the *ad hoc* Tribunals. This chapter will analyse the similarities and differences in approach, and will reflect on the future of this mode of liability at the ICC.

II. The elements of ordering

The term 'orders' is not defined in Article 25 of the *Rome Statute*. In addition, while the material and mental elements of the substantive crimes under the jurisdiction of the Court were elaborated by the Preparatory Commission in the Elements of Crimes, no such element-by-element list was prepared for the modes of liability under Article 25. Rather, the task of determining what elements must be established with respect to each mode of liability has been left to the Court to determine through the application of Article 25 to specific cases. Pre-Trial Chamber II in *Mudacumura* was the first chamber of the Court to undertake this task with respect to ordering.

Pre-Trial Chamber II accepted the position taken by Pre-Trial Chamber I in the *Katanga* and *Lubanga* cases that ordering 'is a form of accessorial liability'.[18] 'Taking note' of the jurisprudence of the *ad hoc* Tribunals as a source of applicable law under Article 21(1)(b) of the *Rome Statute*, it stated:

> the Chamber considers that, to be responsible under Article 25(3)(b) of the Statute it must be established that: (a) the person is in a position of authority, (b) the person instructs another person in any form to either: (i) commit a crime which in fact occurs or is attempted or (ii) perform an act or omission in the execution of which a crime is carried out, (c) the order had a direct effect on the commission or attempted commission of the crime, and (d) the person is at least aware that the crime will be committed in the ordinary course of events as a consequence of the execution or implementation of the order. The person can give the order through an intermediary and need not give the order directly to the physical perpetrator.[19]

---

18 *Mudacumura Arrest Warrant Decision* at [63], citing *Prosecutor v Germain Katanga and Mathieu Ngudjolo Chui* (*Decision on the Confirmation of Charges*) (*International Criminal Court, Pre-Trial Chamber I*, Case No ICC-01/04-01/07, 30 September 2008) at [517] and *Prosecutor v Thomas Lubanga Dyilo* (*Decision on Confirmation of Charges*) (*International Criminal Court, Pre-Trial Chamber I*, Case No ICC/01/04-01/06, 29 January 2007) [320]–[321] [*Lubanga Confirmation Decision*]. Cf *Prosecutor v Milan Milutinović, Nikola Šainović, Dragoljub Ojdanić, Nebojša Pavković, Vladimir Lazarević and Sreten Lukić* (*Judgment*) (*International Criminal Tribunal for the former Yugoslavia, Trial Chamber III*, Case No IT-05-87, 26 February 2009) vol 1, [181].

19 *Mudacumura Arrest Warrant Decision* at [63]. See also *Ntaganda Confirmation Decision* at [145].

The following sections of this chapter will compare this approach to that taken under the jurisprudence of the *ad hoc* Tribunals.

A. Instructing another person in any form

As quoted above, Pre-Trial Chamber II in *Mudacumura* required proof that the accused 'instruct[ed] another person in any form'.[20] In support of this finding, the Chamber cited the case of *Kamuhanda*, where the *ICTR* Appeals Chamber found that '[t]here is no requirement that an order be given in writing or in any particular form'.[21] The *ad hoc* Tribunals have also held that an order can be explicit or implicit.[22] For example, Mudacumura's orders to carry out so-called resupply or '*ravitaillement*' operations – which the OTP argued was a euphemism for pillaging operations during which FDLR troops forcefully robbed the local population of their personal property and committed other crimes[23] – would constitute orders to pillage.

The Pre-Trial Chamber in *Mudacumura* also followed the approach taken by various *ICTY* Trial Chambers by accepting that an accused 'can give the order through an intermediary and need not give the order directly to the physical perpetrator'.[24] Thus an individual who gives an order, and relies on other individuals for its transmittal through the chain of command and for its implementation, may be criminally liable for any resulting crime provided the other elements of ordering are satisfied.[25]

20 Ibid.
21 Ibid citing *Prosecutor v Jean de Dieu Kamuhanda (Judgment)* (*International Criminal Tribunal for Rwanda, Appeals Chamber*, Case No ICTR-99-54A, 19 September 2005) [76] [*Kamuhanda Appeals Judgment*].
22 *Prosecutor v Tihomir Blaškić (Judgment)* (*International Criminal Tribunal for the former Yugoslavia, Trial Chamber I*, Case No IT-95-14, 3 March 2000) [281] [*Blaškić Trial Judgment*]; *Prosecutor v Mladen Naletilić, aka 'Tuta', and Vinko Martinović, aka 'Štela' (Judgment)* (*International Criminal Tribunal for the former Yugoslavia, Trial Chamber I*, Case No IT-98-34, 31 March 2003) [61]. This may mean that the order need not be worded in such a way that literal compliance is required. This was the position taken in the post-WWII *Hostage* case, where the US Nuremberg Military Tribunal held that it was immaterial whether an order distributed by the accused List was 'mandatory or directory'. The fact that it *authorised* the killing of hostages to an extent not permitted by international law was determinative: *United States v Wilhelm List et al. (Judgment)*, Case No 7 in *Trials of War Criminals before the Nuernberg Military Tribunals under Control Council No 10, Nuernberg, October 1946–April 1949* (US Government Printing Office, 1950) vol XI, 1230, 1269 (*Hostage*). See also *Prosecutor v Bosco Ntaganda (Transcript of Confirmation Hearing)* (*International Criminal Court, Pre-Trial Chamber I*, Case No ICC-01/04-02/06, 12 February 2014) 17 [*Ntaganda Confirmation Transcript*] (referring to evidence of 'implied orders to destroy property').
23 *Mudacumura Arrest Warrant Application* at [17].
24 *Mudacumura Arrest Warrant Decision* at [63], citing *Prosecutor v Vlastimir Đorđević (Judgment)* (*International Criminal Tribunal for the former Yugoslavia, Trial Chamber II*, Case No IT-05-87/1, 23 February 2011) [1871] [*Đorđević Trial Judgment*], *Prosecutor v Dario Kordić and Mario Čerkez (Judgment)* (*International Criminal Tribunal for the former Yugoslavia, Trial Chamber III*, Case No IT-95-14/2, 26 February 2001) [388] [*Kordić Trial Judgment*], and *Blaškić Trial Judgment* at [282].
25 See, eg, *Blaškić Trial Judgment* at [282]. See also *Ntaganda Confirmation Transcript* at 17, where the OTP referred to evidence that Ntaganda's orders were reissued by his subordinate commanders who repeated them to the troops.

More detailed definitions of the concept of an order have been provided by commentators. For example, Bantekas defines an order as 'a demand for action or omission, written or oral, addressed either to a specific individual or unknown recipients, which compels its addressees to implement the demanded action or omission'.[26] In the context of Article 33 of the *Rome Statute*,[27] Triffterer defines an order as 'all oral or written or otherwise expressed demands, addressing a certain person or groups of persons individually or by describing their functions, for instance as local military commanders, to behave in a specific way, whether by acting or omitting [to act] . . . any sort of communication between a superior and a subordinated person whatsoever is sufficient'.[28] Based on these definitions, it appears that an 'order' may cover both directions in the narrow sense (ie, an instruction addressed to a specific individual or individuals, requiring action on one occasion or in relation to an isolated matter),[29] as well as general directions (for example, a statute which requires a certain class of individuals to act in a particular way in an established set of circumstances).

An example of a general direction is the Commando Order issued during WWII. This written order was issued by Hitler and distributed to all commanders of the German armed forces. It stated that all Allied commandos encountered by German forces were 'to be slaughtered to the last man', even if they were prepared to give themselves up. The legality of this order was considered in the *High Command Case*, in which the US Nuremberg Military Tribunal found that it represented a clear violation of the laws of war.[30] A more recent example is the *ICTY* case of *Dragomir Milošević*, which concerned crimes committed during the siege of Sarajevo. In that case, the Trial Chamber found Milošević responsible for ordering Sarajevo Romanija Corps (SRK) troops under his command to engage in a campaign of continuous sniping and shelling of the

---

26 Ilias Bantekas, *Principles of Direct and Superior Responsibility in International Humanitarian Law* (Manchester University Press, 2002) 50.

27 Article 33 of the *Rome Statute* provides a 'defence' of superior orders in situations where a war crime has been committed by a subordinate who was under a legal obligation to obey orders of the government or a superior, provided that other conditions are met.

28 Otto Triffterer, 'Article 33: Superior Orders and Prescription of Law' in Otto Triffterer (ed.), *Commentary on the Rome Statute of the International Criminal Court: Observers' Notes, Article by Article* (Hart, 2nd edn, 2008) 915, 923.

29 For an example of a direction in the narrow sense, see the post-WWII case of *Buck: Trial of Karl Buck and Ten Others* (British Military Court, Wuppertal, Germany, 6–10 May 1946), Case No 29 in United Nations War Crimes Commission, *Law Reports of Trials of War Criminals* (His Majesty's Stationery Office, 1948) vol 5, 39 [*Buck*]. This case, which was heard by a British Military Court, involved an oral order given by the accused to his subordinates to have specific prisoners of war shot.

30 *United States v Wilhelm von Leeb et al. (Judgment)*, Case No 12 in *Trials of War Criminals before the Nuernberg Military Tribunals under Control Council No 10, Nuernberg, October 1946–April 1949* (US Government Printing Office, 1950) vol XI, 462, 525–7 [*High Command*].

civilian population of Sarajevo.[31] The Appeals Chamber found no error, '[i]n principle', with an approach which did not involve analysing whether Milošević ordered *every sniping or shelling incident*, but 'rather concluded that those incidents could only take place if ordered by him in the framework of a *campaign* directed against the civilian population of Sarajevo'.[32] However, the Chamber underlined that such a 'general approach' required 'great caution'.[33] On the facts of the case, the Appeals Chamber was not satisfied that the Trial Chamber had established beyond reasonable doubt that Milošević had instructed his troops to perform the campaign of sniping and shelling as a whole.[34]

Therefore, based on previous jurisprudence, it appears that general orders may be sufficient to establish liability provided that the evidence is capable of supporting the necessary inferences to prove the elements of ordering beyond reasonable doubt. Based on the limited material available to the public at this stage of the proceedings, some of the orders relied upon in *Mudacumura* appear to be general or standing orders. For example, Pre-Trial Chamber II found reasonable grounds to believe that in early 2009 'a *general* order to create a humanitarian catastrophe was issued', as well as 'a *general* order to pillage civilian property in order to sustain the FDLR's military efforts'.[35] According to the application for an arrest warrant, Mudacumura's order to attack civilians was transmitted to all FDLR commanders and read out to the troops in the field.[36] It allegedly 'identified the primary target as the civilian population' and directed combatants 'to treat civilians as enemies and traitors and to make them "suffer"'.[37] The order to pillage 'directed the troops to pillage civilian property and burn down entire villages to create a tide of refugees and ensure that civilians . . . could never return'.[38]

Similarly, the *Ntaganda Case* may be partly based on general orders. In its submissions during the confirmation hearing, the OTP argued that there were

---

31 In doing so, the Trial Chamber had not relied on any evidence that would identify a specific order issued by Milošević with respect to the campaign of shelling and sniping as such. Rather, it relied on the nature of the campaign carried out in the context of a tight command structure to conclude that the sniping and shelling of the civilian population could only have been carried out on Milošević's instructions and orders: *Dragomir Milošević (Judgment)* (*International Criminal Tribunal for the former Yugoslavia, Appeals Chamber*, Case No IT-98-29/1-A, 12 November 2009) [267] [*Milošević Appeals Judgment*].

32 *Milošević Appeals Judgment* at [265] (emphasis added).

33 Ibid.

34 Ibid [267].

35 *Mudacumura Arrest Warrant Decision* at [65] (emphases added). See also *Mudacumura Arrest Warrant Application* at [4], [23] (alleging that Mudacumura transmitted an order to FDLR troops to create a humanitarian catastrophe in the Kivus through attacks on civilians, which remained in place throughout the period relevant to the application).

36 *Mudacumura Arrest Warrant Application* at [17].

37 Ibid.

38 Ibid. The OTP also relied upon orders to engage in so-called resupply or '*ravitaillement*' operations to establish that he issued orders to pillage.

substantial grounds to believe Ntaganda 'issued standing orders or general instructions as to how his troops should behave during the hostilities', including standing orders 'to attack and displace civilians, to kill and pillage and destroy property'. The crimes committed by his troops during the operations in Banyali-Kilo and Walendu-Djatsi collectivités allegedly flow from these standing orders, among others.[39]

The allegations regarding general orders given by both Mudacumura and Ntaganda, if proven, would most likely overcome the 'great caution' required by the *Milošević* Appeals Chamber, particularly given that they are supported by evidence that both Mudacumura and Ntaganda also gave specific orders.[40] Indeed, the OTP alleged during the confirmation hearing that Bosco Ntaganda frequently met with his subordinate commanders at the battlefront to provide further direction in accordance with those general orders.[41]

B. Authority to order

Pre-Trial Chamber II in *Mudacumura* required proof that the accused was 'in a position of authority'.[42] Again, this is consistent with the approach taken by the *ad hoc* Tribunals, which have defined ordering broadly as involving a person in a position of authority using that authority to order another person, who is subject to that authority, to commit a crime.[43] This definition seems to have been taken from the commentary to the International Law Commission's 1996 Draft Code of Crimes against the Peace and Security of Mankind, which also envisaged ordering as applying to an individual 'who is in a position of authority and uses his authority to compel another individual to commit a crime'.[44]

The requirement that the accused have the authority to give orders to the principal perpetrator is what sets ordering apart from soliciting or inducing.[45]

---

39 *Ntaganda Confirmation Transcript* at 11, 15, 20.
40 Pre-Trial Chamber II also found that there was evidence Mudacumura 'specifically gave prior approval' for two particular incidents (being the attacks on Mianga and Busurungi), during which there were reasonable grounds to believe that FDLR units committed murder, mutilation, cruel treatment, rape, torture, destruction of property and pillaging: *Mudacumura Arrest Warrant Decision* at [39]–[40], [42]–[47], [49]–[54], [65]. In addition to his standing orders, the OTP submitted that there were substantial grounds to believe that Ntaganda gave specific orders to target individual civilians, property and protected objects and to recruit and use children under the age of 15 years to participate actively in hostilities: *Ntaganda Confirmation Transcript* at 19–21. See also *Ntaganda Confirmation Decision* at [148].
41 *Ntaganda Confirmation Transcript* at 18.
42 *Mudacumura Arrest Warrant Decision* at [63].
43 See, eg, *Prosecutor v Dario Kordić and Mario Čerkez (Judgment) (International Criminal Tribunal for the former Yugoslavia, Appeals Chamber*, Case No IT-95-14/2, 17 December 2004) [28] [*Kordić Appeals Judgment*]; *Prosecutor v André Ntagerura, Emmanuel Bagambiki and Samuel Imanishimwe (Judgment) (International Criminal Tribunal for Rwanda Appeals Chamber*, Case No ICTR-99-46-A, 7 July 2006) [365].
44 International Law Commission, 'Draft Code of Crimes against the Peace and Security of Mankind with Commentaries' (1996), reprinted in (1996) II(2) *Yearbook of the International Law Commission* 17, 20.
45 See *Đorđević Trial Judgment* at [1871] (with respect to 'instigating').

Without it, the inclusion of the term 'ordering' in Article 25(3)(b) would be superfluous, as such conduct could be sufficiently dealt with as 'soliciting or inducing' under that sub-paragraph. It is therefore appropriate, in my view, that the Court maintain this requirement. The appropriateness of such a requirement is also supported by Article 33 of the *Rome Statute*, which deals with the 'defence' of obedience to superior orders. That provision applies to similar factual scenarios as those which may come before the ICC as cases of 'ordering': while Article 25(3)(b) criminalises the *ordering* of a crime, Article 33 excuses the commission of a crime *pursuant to an order* in certain limited circumstances. The application of Article 33 is limited to cases where the recipient of the order is under a legal obligation to obey the order given.[46] This suggests that the individual who gives the order must have some (legal) authority to give orders to the recipient. While the limitation in Article 33 is not directly applicable to Article 25(3)(b), the reference to ordering in Article 25(3)(b) should be interpreted consistently with Article 33 insofar as it is possible to do so.

If the Court were to adopt a requirement that the accused possess the authority to give orders, the following questions would have to be addressed: (i) what is the character of the authority to order; and (ii) what is meant by a person in a position of authority and a person who is subject to that authority?

With respect to the character of the authority, the *ad hoc* Tribunals have stated that the authority to order may be formal (*de jure*) or informal (*de facto*),[47] and according to the *ICTR* may even be of a purely temporary nature.[48] As for the relationship between the person in a position of authority and the person subject to that authority, initially the Trial Chambers of the *ad hoc* Tribunals appeared to require the existence of a superior–subordinate relationship between them.[49] However, in *Kordić*, the Prosecution submitted before Trial Chamber III of the *ICTY* that in addition to orders given by regular military commanders, orders of superiors or commanders of 'irregular' bodies such as paramilitary forces or special units would also fall within the scope of 'ordering', despite there being no formal superior–subordinate command structure.[50] The Trial Chamber, following the Prosecution's argument, departed from earlier judgments of the *ad hoc* Tribunals and held that 'no formal superior–subordinate relationship is

---

46 In addition, Article 33 applies only to orders to commit war crimes that are not manifestly unlawful, in circumstances where the person did not know the order was unlawful.

47 See, eg, *Prosecutor v Laurent Semanza (Judgment)* (*International Criminal Tribunal for Rwanda, Appeals Chamber*, Case No ICTR-97-20, 20 May 2005) [363] [*Semanza Appeals Judgment*]; *Milošević Appeals Judgment* at [290].

48 See, eg, *Semanza Appeals Judgment* at [363].

49 In the *ICTR*, see, eg, *Prosecutor v Jean-Paul Akayesu (Judgment)* (*International Criminal Tribunal for Rwanda, Trial Chamber I*, Case No ICTR-96-4, 2 September 1998) [483]. In the *ICTY*, the *Blaškić* Trial Chamber appeared to accept the Prosecution submission that ordering 'implies a superior–subordinate relationship between the person who orders and the one who carries it out': *Blaškić Trial Judgment* at [268].

50 *Kordić Trial Judgment* at [382].

required for a finding of "ordering" so long as it is demonstrated that the accused possessed the authority to order'.[51] This position was followed by other Trial Chambers of the *ICTY* and was later confirmed by the Appeals Chamber in the *Kordić Appeals Judgment*.[52] In the *ICTR*, some Trial Chambers continued to require that a superior–subordinate relationship be proven, until the Appeals Chamber formally brought the *ICTR* jurisprudence into line with that of the *ICTY* in *Semanza* in 2005.[53]

Therefore, the *ad hoc* Tribunals have not viewed the relationship between the person giving the order and the person executing it as being the same as that which exists in cases of superior responsibility, which requires a superior–subordinate relationship.[54] However, while the existence of a superior–subordinate relationship is not *required*, it may be *sufficient* to establish the presence of the necessary authority to order. Thus, while a superior will have the necessary authority to order with respect to his subordinates, this is not the only relationship in which such authority to order can exist.

So in what other relationships will the necessary authority to order arise? According to the *ad hoc* Tribunals, whether the position of authority has been shown to exist is a question of fact, to be determined in light of the circumstances of the case.[55] It may be reasonably inferred,[56] for example, from the fact that the order was obeyed.[57] In *Gacumbitsi*, the *ICTR* Trial Chamber highlighted some of the circumstances which may be relevant to the question of whether there is sufficient authority to order, in the absence of proof of a formal superior–subordinate relationship. These included the accused's 'social, economic, political or administrative standing' and even 'his abiding moral principles'.[58] Similarly, in *Semanza*, the *ICTR* Appeals Chamber viewed the accused's influence in the community – based on factors such as his previous service as *bourgmestre*, his prior good works, his political position, his connections with high governmental officials and his wealth[59] – as amounting to authority to order.[60] The result is

---

51 Ibid at [388].

52 *Kordić Appeals Judgment* at [28].

53 *Semanza Appeals Judgment* at [361]–[364].

54 See, eg, *Prosecutor v Zejnil Delalić, Zdravko Mucić, Hazim Delić and Esad Landžo ('Čelebići') (Judgment)* (*International Criminal Tribunal for the former Yugoslavia, Trial Chamber II*, Case No IT-96-21, 16 November 1998) [346]. Nor is it required that the person giving the order exercise 'effective control' (ie, the material ability to prevent or punish criminal conduct) over the person carrying it out. See, *Semanza Appeals Judgment* at [202].

55 See, eg, *Blaškić Trial Judgment* at [281].

56 See, eg, *Prosecutor v Radoslav Brđanin (Judgment)* (*International Criminal Tribunal for the former Yugoslavia, Trial Chamber II*, Case No IT-99-36, 1 September 2004) [270].

57 See, eg, *Prosecutor v Jean de Dieu Kamuhanda (Judgment)* (*International Criminal Tribunal for Rwanda, Trial Chamber II*, Case No ICTR-99-54, 22 January 2004) [594].

58 *Prosecutor v Sylvestre Gacumbitsi (Judgment)* (*International Criminal Tribunal for Rwanda, Trial Chamber III*, Case No ICTR-01-64, 17 June 2004) [282].

59 See *Prosecutor v Laurent Semanza (Judgment)* (*International Criminal Tribunal for Rwanda, Trial Chamber III*, Case No ICTR-97-20, 15 May 2003) [411]–[419].

60 *Semanza Appeals Judgment* at [363].

an incredibly broad and flexible test for establishing whether an individual has authority to give orders to another person, which has the potential to encompass many cases which might be more appropriately classified as cases of soliciting or inducing.

In my view, the better approach would be that which appears to have been followed in two trial judgments of the *ad hoc* Tribunals, which have required that the person giving the order have the authority to issue *binding* orders to the alleged principal perpetrator.[61] These judgments have not clarified the meaning of the term 'binding', but it could be taken to mean that the orderer must have the authority to issue orders which are *enforceable* by virtue of some legal, administrative or disciplinary regime. Taking the example raised in *Kordić* of 'irregular' bodies such as paramilitary forces or special units, such bodies would only fulfil this proposed test if it could be shown that there existed some internal disciplinary system or structure which could ensure compliance with orders given by 'superiors' to 'subordinates' within that body.[62]

However, such a test should not be applied too strictly. Whether an individual has such authority would be a question of fact, to be determined by examining the way in which the particular regime functioned *in practice* at the time the alleged order was given. The judgment of the US Nuremberg Military Tribunal in the post-WWII *High Command Case* provides an example of how this test should be applied in practice. There, the Tribunal was not so much concerned with *legal* or *formal* authority to order, but rather with *factual* or *practical* authority to order. When considering whether the accused Reinecke could be held responsible for ordering the commission of crimes, the Tribunal stated:

> We are not concerned in this case with the fact that the defendant did not have direct command authority or disciplinary authority over the personnel of [prisoner of war] camps or units of the army. He issued the over-all directives in the name of the OKW and the Commander in Chief of the OKW, with which they were *compelled to comply*.[63]

---

61 *Prosecutor v Pavle Strugar (Judgment)* (*International Criminal Tribunal for the former Yugoslavia, Trial Chamber II*, Case No IT-01-42, 31 January 2005) [331] [*Strugar Trial Judgment*]. See also *Prosecutor v Tharcisse Muvunyi (Judgment)* (*International Criminal Tribunal for Rwanda, Trial Chamber II*, Case No ICTR-00-55, 12 September 2006) [467].

62 This would be similar to the requirement under Article 43(1) of *Additional Protocol I* that the armed forces of a Party to an international armed conflict (whether regular or irregular forces, such as members of resistance or guerrilla groups) be 'subject to an internal disciplinary system' which shall enforce compliance with the rules of international law applicable in armed conflict in order to be regarded as combatants who have the right to participate directly in hostilities: *Protocol Additional to the Geneva Conventions of 12 August 1949 and Relating to the Protection of Victims of International Armed Conflicts*, opened for signature 12 December 1977, 1125 UNTS 3 (entered into force 7 December 1978).

63 *High Command* at 651 (emphasis added). The Tribunal noted (at 651) that orders issued by Reinecke were *binding* upon subordinate units to whom they were directed.

And further,

> This Tribunal is not concerned with fine formalities or divisions of authority. The evidence establishes overwhelmingly the over-all control and supervision of the defendant Reinecke as to prisoners of war under the supreme authority of the OKW and his power over prisoner of war camps and prisoner of war affairs. The evidence shows that he exercised that authority by issuing orders . . . [64]

Thus, while Reinecke did not have formal command over the individuals he ordered to perform criminal acts, the fact that the system within which he functioned ensured compliance with his directives was a sufficient basis to ground liability.

This proposed test would not require that the individual giving the order possess the authority to issue the *precise* order given, nor would it require that the legal, administrative or disciplinary regime would in fact enforce the precise order given. It would be unlikely that such a test could ever be satisfied, given that a regime would rarely provide authority for, and enforce, an order to engage in conduct which would constitute a crime. Such an order would likely be considered *ultra vires*, or outside the authority of the person who gave it, and therefore unenforceable. Rather, to satisfy this proposed test it would simply need to be shown that the individual possessed authority to issue enforceable orders in the abstract. Whether the precise order given was within that authority, and therefore enforceable, would be immaterial. Similarly, it would not need to be established that the manner in which the regime enforced orders was legal; for example, a body that ensures the implementation of orders given by superiors through violence or intimidation would also qualify.

While similar to the requirement of organisational control currently required for liability as an indirect perpetrator under Article 25(3)(a), the type of control required under this proposed test is lower. Nevertheless, as Judge Van den Wyngaert has argued, evidence relating to organisational control will be relevant, as 'the authority required for ordering liability will also often be exercised within the structure of an organisation'.[65]

In *Mudacumura*, the OTP submitted in its application for a warrant of arrest that Mudacumura, as the supreme commander of the FDLR military wing, 'had the authority to issue orders and enforce their execution'.[66] Pre-Trial Chamber II found reasonable grounds to believe that Mudacumura acted in a position of

---

64 Ibid 653–4.

65 *Prosecutor v Mathieu Ngudjolo Chui (Judgment pursuant to Article 74 of the Statute: Concurring Opinion of Judge Van den Wyngaert) (International Criminal Court, Trial Chamber II,* Case No ICC-01/04-02/12, 18 December 2012) [56].

66 *Mudacumura Arrest Warrant Application* at [24].

authority throughout the relevant time period.[67] It accepted that he was the 'top military commander of the FDLR', which was a 'large, well organised organisation [with] a clear hierarchical structure' within which compliance with Mudacumura's orders was 'required'.[68] Mudacumura 'had control over his forces and authority over recruiting, promoting, removing and disciplining them'.[69] In support of this finding, the Chamber cited evidence that Mudacumura took efforts to prevent soldiers from demobilising, to authorise their marriage and to control the information they received from the outside world or even from within the FDLR.[70]

Similarly, in the *Ntaganda Case*, the OTP argued in support of its case for confirmation under Article 25(3)(b) that Ntaganda held a position of 'influence' as Deputy Chief of Staff in charge of operations in the UPC/FPLC, with 'command authority' over the troops.[71] Elsewhere in the Document Containing the Charges, it is alleged that Ntaganda 'had effective command and control' over the troops, 'who were organised, hierarchical, well-equipped and well-trained' with a 'functioning command structure'.[72] He had the power to 'appoint, promote, demote, remove and punish commanders and soldiers, or to recommend that such measures be taken'.[73] He had the power to instruct commanders and soldiers, deploy or withdraw troops and to ensure his subordinates complied with his orders.[74]

In *Ruto*, in support of its application for notice to be given of the possibility of legal recharacterisation, the OTP cited evidence that Ruto was the designated leader of the Network, which was under 'responsible command' and had an 'established hierarchy'.[75] It alleged that Ruto 'exercised his control over the [Network] and its supporters in a manner that assured that his orders were carried out' through both a payment mechanism and a punishment mechanism.[76] Specifically, the localised level of subordinates who were responsible for specific geographical areas ensured compliance with Ruto's orders in their respective areas by paying direct perpetrators and by threatening punishment in case of insubordination.[77]

---

67 *Mudacumura Arrest Warrant Decision* at [64].
68 Ibid.
69 Ibid.
70 Ibid.
71 *Ntaganda DCC* at [134]. See also *Ntaganda Confirmation Transcript* at 14; *Ntaganda Confirmation Decision* at [120], [147].
72 *Ntaganda DCC* at [7], [172]. See also *Ntaganda Confirmation Decision* at [119].
73 *Ntaganda DCC* at [172]. See also *Ntaganda Confirmation Decision* at [120], [147], [149].
74 *Ntaganda DCC* at [172]. See also *Ntaganda Confirmation Decision* at [120].
75 *Ruto Recharacterisation Application* at [30].
76 *Prosecutor v William Samoei Ruto and Joshua Arap Sang (Prosecution Filing in Compliance with the Chamber's 'Order Regarding Applications for Notice of Possibility of Variation of Legal Characterisation') (International Criminal Court, Trial Chamber V(A), Case No ICC-01/09-01/11-943, 17 September 2012), Annex A.*
77 Ibid.

The approach to these cases is consistent with the proposed test outlined above, that authority to order must involve the authority to issue orders which are enforceable by virtue of some legal, administrative or disciplinary regime. Both Mudacumura and Ntaganda are alleged to have acted within a hierarchical and functioning command structure, which gave them authority to discipline and remove their troops. Ruto's Network, while *ad hoc* and of a different character to the FDLR and the UPC/FPLC, is also hierarchical and allegedly ensures compliance with orders through reward and punishment.

C. The nature of the act ordered

Pre-Trial Chamber II in *Mudacumura* held that responsibility under Article 25(3)(b) will arise where it is established that the accused instructed another person to 'either: (i) commit a crime which in fact occurs or is attempted or (ii) perform an act or omission in the execution of which a crime is carried out'.[78] Thus, the accused need not order the principal perpetrator to engage in an act that actually *constitutes* a crime under the jurisdiction of the Court. It is sufficient that he has ordered his subordinates to engage in an act that could *result* in the commission of such a crime. Again, this is consistent with the jurisprudence of the *ad hoc* Tribunals. In *Blaškić*, the *ICTY* Appeals Chamber 'created' these two alternatives,[79] whereby an individual may be found liable for ordering either (i) criminal conduct; or (ii) a (lawful) act or omission, where he is aware of the substantial likelihood that a crime will be committed in the realisation of that act or omission.[80]

As Boas, Bischoff and Reid note, the case of *Strugar* before the *ICTY* demonstrates the effect of these alternative elements.[81] Pavle Strugar was a commander in the Yugoslav People's Army. On 5 December 1991 he ordered his troops to engage in a lawful attack on Croatian defensive positions stationed on Mount Srđ, which overlooked Dubrovnik. In the course of that lawful attack, his forces engaged in deliberate and indiscriminate shelling of the Old Town of Dubrovnik. The Trial Chamber found that the shelling constituted the crime

---

78   *Mudacumura Arrest Warrant Decision* at [63], citing *Prosecutor v François Karera (Judgment)* (*International Criminal Tribunal for Rwanda, Appeals Chamber*, Case No ICTR-01-74, 2 February 2009) [211] and *Prosecutor v Ferdinand Nahimana, Jean-Bosco Barayagwiza and Hassan Ngeze (Judgment)* (*International Criminal Tribunal for Rwanda, Appeals Chamber*, Case No ICTR-99-52, 28 November 2007) [481].

79   Gideon Boas, James Bischoff and Natalie Reid, *International Criminal Law Practitioner Library Volume 1: Forms of Responsibility in International Criminal Law* (Cambridge University Press, 2007) 353, discussing *Kordić Appeals Judgment*.

80   See, eg, *Prosecutor v Tihomir Blaškić (Judgment)* (*International Criminal Tribunal for the former Yugoslavia, Appeals Chamber*, Case No IT-95-14, 29 July 2004) [42].

81   Boas, Bischoff and Reid, above n 79, 353.

of devastation not justified by military necessity.[82] In addition, because the Old Town was a UN World Cultural Heritage site, this shelling also amounted to the crime of destruction of cultural property.[83] There was no evidence that Strugar had ordered the unlawful shelling of the Old Town.[84] Rather, Strugar had ordered the *lawful* attack on Croatian defensive positions and had left the detailed planning of the attack to his subordinates.

The issue before the *ICTY* was whether Strugar could still be found guilty on the basis of ordering, even though he had not *specifically* ordered his forces to engage in unlawful shelling. The Trial Chamber held that he could, so long as it could be proven that Strugar had been aware of a substantial likelihood that his forces would engage in unlawful shelling during the lawful attack.[85] However, on the facts before it, the Chamber was not satisfied that Strugar had had such awareness. Rather, it found that he was only aware of the 'possibility' that his forces would 'resort to deliberate and indiscriminate shelling' of Dubrovnik.[86] Therefore, Strugar was not found liable for the unlawful shelling of the Old Town of Dubrovnik on the basis of ordering. Nevertheless, according to Boas, Bischoff and Reid, the Chamber 'clearly implied' that he would have been convicted on this basis had he been aware of the substantial likelihood that criminal shelling would occur, even though he did not specifically order any criminal activities.[87]

The 'creation' of these alternatives occurs through the application of the relevant mental element. Under the law governing the *ICTY*, the mental element for ordering is awareness of a substantial likelihood that a result will occur (something akin to recklessness under common law or *dolus eventualis* under civil law). However, Article 30 of the *Rome Statute* does not incorporate this standard. Rather, Article 30(2)(b) requires awareness that the consequence 'will occur in the ordinary course of events'.[88] While there has been some disagreement among both academics and Pre-Trial and Trial Chambers as to whether the language 'will occur in the ordinary course of events' covers cases which would

---

82 *Strugar Trial Judgment* at [330].

83 Ibid [327], [330].

84 Ibid [338], [345].

85 Ibid [346].

86 Ibid [347].

87 Boas, Bischoff and Reid, above n 79, 353.

88 If, however, the Court were to treat the nature of the ordered act as a circumstance element (ie, as an element which qualifies the conduct element), the relevant mental element under Article 30(3) would be awareness that the circumstance exists. Thus, it would be necessary to prove that the accused was aware that a crime *would* be committed as a consequence of the execution or implementation of the order (not just that it would be committed *in the ordinary course of events*), which is a higher standard than that set in *Mudacumura*: Finnin, *Elements*, above n 1, 27–30, 59–60, 173–5, 189–90.

fall in the categories of recklessness or *dolus eventualis*,[89] the issue appears to have been settled by the Appeals Chamber, which held in *Lubanga* that this language conveys '*virtual* certainty'.[90] It seems, therefore, that the language of Article 30(2)(b) sets a more demanding standard than the law governing the *ICTY*.

Applying the language of Article 30(2)(b), Pre-Trial Chamber II in *Mudacumura* found that the accused must be 'at least aware that the crime will be committed in the ordinary course of events as a consequence of the execution or implementation of the order'.[91] Thus, it issued an arrest warrant in part on the basis that there was evidence that he 'specifically gave prior approval' for the attacks on Mianga and Busurungi, during which there were reasonable gounds to believe that FDLR units committed murder, mutilation, cruel treatment, rape, torture, destruction of property and pillaging.[92] The Chamber found reasonable grounds to believe that Mudacumura was 'at least aware that by issuing said orders, crimes would be committed in the ordinary course of events as a consequence of the execution of his orders'.[93] It was not required to go further, to determine whether there were also reasonable grounds to believe that the attacks on Mianga and Busurungi were themselves unlawful.

D. Causation

For an individual to be held criminally responsible and be liable to punishment for ordering the commission or attempted commission of a crime, a crime must actually occur or be attempted.[94] This is clear from the language of Article 25(3)(b). In addition, according to the Pre-Trial Chamber in *Mudacumura*, the order given by the accused must have 'a direct effect on the commission or attempted commission of the crime'.[95] This suggests a causal link between the conduct of the accused (ie, the giving of the instruction) and the commission or attempted commission of the crime by the principal perpetrator.

---

89   See, eg, Sarah Finnin, 'Mental Elements under Article 30 of the Rome Statute of the International Criminal Court: A Comparative Analysis' (2012) 61 *International and Comparative Law Quarterly* 325, 344–9; Finnin, *Elements*, above n 1, 166–73.

90   See *Prosecutor v Thomas Lubanga Dyilo (Judgment on the appeal of Mr Thomas Lubanga Dyilo against his conviction) (International Criminal Court, Appeals Chamber,* Case No ICC/01/04-01/06 A 5, 1 December 2014) [447].

91   *Mudacumura Arrest Warrant Decision* at [63].

92   Ibid [39]–[40], [42]–[47], [49]–[54], [65].

93   Ibid [67].

94   Ibid [63].

95   Ibid.

While the *Rome Statute* does not contain a provision regarding causation,[96] most commentators agree that such a requirement is implicit (at least with respect to commission liability).[97] Whether such a requirement is necessary in the case of accessorial liability is unclear. There is nothing in the text of Article 25(3)(b) to suggest that the accused's conduct needs to have any effect on the commission or attempted commission of the substantive crime by the principal perpetrator, so long as that crime occurs or is attempted. However, to allow for liability to arise where the accused's conduct has no impact whatsoever would be to establish inchoate liability, rather than accessorial liability. While the negotiators of the *Rome Statute* clearly intended to establish inchoate liability for direct and public incitement to commit genocide (Article 25(3)(e)) and attempt (Article 25(3)(f)), no such intention can be discerned with respect to Article 25(3)(b).

The basis for Pre-Trial Chamber II's 'direct effect' test for establishing this causal link is not identified in the *Mudacumura Decision*. It may have been drawn from the jurisprudence of the *ad hoc* Tribunals, which have at different times

---

96 A draft provision on *actus reus* prepared by the Preparatory Committee in 1997 stated that '[a] person is only criminally responsible under this Statute for committing a crime if the harm required for the commission of the crime is *caused by* and [accountable] [attributable] to his or her act or omission': *Decisions Taken by the Preparatory Committee at its Session Held from 11–21 February 1997*, UN Doc A/AC.249/1997/L.5 (12 March 1997) Annex II: Report of the Working Group on General Principles of Criminal Law and Penalties, Article G(3) (emphasis added). Paragraph (3) was placed in square brackets because some delegations thought that a provision on causation was not necessary: at n 22. An identical provision was adopted by the Preparatory Committee in its Draft Statute of 1998: *Report of the Preparatory Committee on the Establishment of an International Criminal Court*, UN Doc A/Conf.183/2/Add.1 (14 April 1998) Addendum: Part One: Draft Statute for the International Criminal Court, Article 28(3). Again, paragraph (3) was placed in square brackets: at n 16. See also Edward Wise, 'General Principles of Criminal Law' (1998) 13*ter Nouvelles Études Pénales: Model Draft Statute for the International Criminal Court Based on the Preparatory Committee's Text to the Diplomatic Conference, Rome, June 15–July 17 1998* 39, 49. The provision on *actus reus* was dropped at the Rome Diplomatic Conference: see Roger Clark, 'Drafting a General Part to a Penal Code: Some Thoughts Inspired by the Negotiations on the Rome Statute of the International Criminal Court and by the Court's First Substantive Law Discussion in the *Lubanga Dyilo* Confirmation Proceedings' (2008) 19 *Criminal Law Forum* 519, 522–3.

97 As Werle notes, the causation requirement arises implicitly out of Article 30 (Article 30(2)(b) refers to *causing* a consequence): Gerhard Werle, *Principles of International Criminal Law* (TMC Asser Press, 2nd edn, 2009) 144–5. See also Otto Triffterer, 'The New International Criminal Law: Its General Principles Establishing Individual Responsibility' in Kalliopi Koufa (ed.), *The New International Criminal Law* (Sakkoulas Publications, 2003) 639, 692; Kevin Heller, 'The Rome Statute of the International Criminal Court' in Kevin Heller and Markus Dubber (eds), *The Handbook of Comparative Criminal Law* (Stanford University Press, 2010) 593, 605; Roger Clark, 'The Mental Element in International Criminal Law: The Rome Statute of the International Criminal Court and the Elements of Offences' (2001) 12 *Criminal Law Forum* 291, 304 (n 42).

applied a 'direct and substantial effect' test,[98] or a 'substantial contribution' test.[99] However, there is no basis for the application of such a test in the wording of Article 25(3)(b). Unlike Article 25(3)(e), which provides for '*direct* and public incitement to commit genocide', no such qualification applies to ordering. Pre-Trial Chamber II's attempt to read a direct effect requirement into the wording of Article 25(3)(b) therefore goes against general principles of treaty interpretation, which require that a treaty be interpreted in good faith in accordance with the ordinary meaning to be given to its terms in their context (including the wording of surrounding provisions).[100]

The meaning of the 'direct effect' test for establishing this causal link is also not identified in the *Mudacumura Decision*. The use of the term 'direct' clearly does not refer to a direct link between the accused and the principal perpetrator, as the Pre-Trial Chamber expressly stated that the accused can give the order through an intermediary. It also does not appear to refer to a direct link between the terms of the order and the commission of the crime, because it is sufficient to prove that the accused merely ordered the performance of an otherwise lawful act or omission *in the execution of which* a crime was carried out. Thus, the use of the term 'direct' does not appear to correspond to its conventional meaning, which entails an absence of deviation, reflexion, interference, interruption, intervening agency or intermediaries.[101] So on what basis does one distinguish between a direct and indirect effect on the commission or attempted commission of a crime?

Perhaps Pre-Trial Chamber II was attempting, in the same manner as the *ad hoc* Tribunals, to treat the causal link as a factor of which there can be more or less. In other words, it may be an attempt to give causation 'a scalar quality', by treating it as 'a matter of continuous variation, as opposed to a binary, black and white sort of relationship'.[102] The use of the term 'direct' may therefore be simply an attempt to *quantify* the causal link.[103] 'Direct' is not the most appropriate term in the context of accessorial liability, however, where the effect of the

---

98   See, eg, *Prosecutor v Augustin Ndindiliyimana, François-Xavier Nzuwonemeye and Innocent Sagahutu* (*Judgment*) (*International Criminal Tribunal for Rwanda, Appeals Chamber*, Case No ICTR-00-56-A, 27 February 2014) [365].

99   See, eg, *Prosecutor v Ljube Boškoski and Johan Tarčulovski* (*Judgment*) (*International Criminal Tribunal for the former Yugoslavia, Appeals Chamber*, Case No IT-04-82, 19 May 2010) [160].

100   *Vienna Convention on the Law of Treaties*, opened for signature 23 May 1969, 1155 UNTS 331 (entered into force 27 January 1980) Article 31(1); Richard Gardiner, *Treaty Interpretation* (Oxford University Press, 2010) 177–8.

101   See, eg, Michael Proffitt, *Oxford English Dictionary Online* (December 2013) Oxford University Press www.oed.com.

102   Michael Moore, 'Causing, Aiding, and the Superfluity of Accomplice Liability' (2008) 156 *University of Pennsylvania Law Review* 395, 421.

103   Ibid.

accused's conduct is by its very nature indirect as it operates through the actions of a third party (the principal perpetrator). A better approach may have been to use a quantifying word which focuses more on the *extent* to which the accused's conduct has made a contribution to the commission or attempted commission of the crime, rather than its *character* (for example, 'significant' or 'substantial'). While these alternatives may be justifiably described as vague, circular and subjective,[104] this weakness can also be viewed as their strength. It allows the test for a causal link to 'handle the infinite number of circumstances where the issue of causation can arise'.[105]

Furthermore, while it is true that no bright line separates a 'substantial' or 'significant' effect from an 'insubstantial' or 'insignificant' one, international judges are frequently required to draw distinctions based on subjective criteria. For example, they must decide whether certain harms can be considered 'serious bodily or mental harm' for the purposes of the definition of genocide or 'great suffering' for the purposes of war crimes,[106] and whether certain forms of sexual violence are of 'comparable gravity' to rape, sexual slavery, enforced prostitution or enforced sterilisation,[107] just to name a couple of examples.

III. Conclusion

The lack of any guidance from the States Parties or the Preparatory Commission with respect to the interpretation of Article 25 has led to it becoming among the most debated provisions of the *Rome Statute*. As there is limited appellate jurisprudence analysing Article 25, fundamental differences of opinion have arisen among the Chambers of the Court (and academics) with respect to both the structure of Article 25 as a whole and the elements of particular modes of liability set out therein. The *Mudacumura Decision* of Pre-Trial Chamber II has given us our first glimpse at how the Court will treat ordering as a mode of liability under Article 25(3)(b) of the *Rome Statute*.

104　See, eg, Michael Moore, *Causation and Responsibility: An Essay in Law, Morals, and Metaphysics* (Oxford University Press, 2010) 88 (admitting that the 'substantial factor' test is 'circular and vague'); Joshua Dressler, 'Reforming Complicity Law: Trivial Assistance as a Lesser Offense?' (2008) 5 *Ohio State Journal of Criminal Law* 427, 448 (conceding that 'substantial' is an 'imprecise term'); Model Penal Code § 2.04(3) cmt at 31 (American Law Institute, Tentative Draft No 1, 1953) (conceding 'the vagueness of "substantially facilitates"'); Joshua Dressler, 'Reassessing the Theoretical Underpinnings of Accomplice Liability: New Solutions to an Old Problem' (1985) 37 *Hastings Law Journal* 91, 122 (addressing the criticism that the 'substantial participation' test is 'too subjective').

105　Stanley Yeo, 'Blamable Causation' (2000) 24 *Criminal Law Journal* 144, 147.

106　See *Rome Statute* Article 6(b), 8(2)(a)(iii).

107　See *Rome Statute* Article 7(1)(g).

The elements of ordering adopted by Pre-Trial Chamber II closely resemble those developed in the jurisprudence of the *ad hoc* Tribunals, particularly with respect to the conduct of the accused and the requirement that the accused be in a position of authority with respect to the principal perpetrator. While the terms of Article 30 regarding mental elements have required some modification to the approach of the *ad hoc* Tribunals, Pre-Trial Chamber II has also maintained the alternative elements adopted by those Tribunals with respect to the nature of the act in which the principal perpetrator is ordered to engage. Thus, an accused will be held liable for ordering not only criminal conduct *per se* but also lawful conduct, which results in the commission of a crime by virtue of the manner in which the order is implemented.

The Court may wish to consider adopting a test for establishing authority to order which, in a manner similar to Article 33 of the *Rome Statute*, would require proof of authority to issue orders which are enforceable by virtue of some legal, administrative or disciplinary regime. While stricter than the test adopted by the *ad hoc* Tribunals, such a test would most likely still cover the factual scenarios presented by the *Mudacumura, Ntaganda* and *Ruto* cases and would ensure that liability for ordering is reserved for cases that deserve that label. Finally, the test adopted by Pre-Trial Chamber II to establish the causal link between the accused's conduct and the commission or attempted commission of the crime should be reconsidered. The imposition of a 'direct effect' test goes against general principles of treaty interpretation and is an inappropriate measure for causation in the context of accessorial liability, which by its very nature is indirect. Putting aside the test for causation, the *Mudacumura Decision* provides a good starting point for the development of the Court's jurisprudence with respect to ordering as a mode of liability.

4 Military members claiming self-defence during armed conflict

Often misguided and unhelpful

Ian Henderson and Bryan Cavanagh[1]

I. Introduction

The principal legal regime governing the use of force by military members during an armed conflict is the law of armed conflict (LOAC), which dictates who and what the military can attack and what means and methods can be employed when doing so. These rules reflect a balance between the principles of military necessity and humanity.[2] Potentially upsetting the balance afforded by LOAC is an apparent trend towards relying on self-defence under criminal law as a justification for the use of force during armed conflicts.[3] One possible cause for this trend is a combination of restrictive rules relating to the use of offensive force in counter-insurgency operations, combined with an emphasis on the paramount nature of the 'inherent right of self-defence' in the military training and doctrine of some States. The problem with this trend is that due to the interaction between the law of self-defence and the combatant's privilege, self-defence has a narrower application on the battlefield than is generally understood.

As a criminal law concept, self-defence cannot be meaningfully discussed in isolation from the jurisdiction in which it operates as the law varies from jurisdiction to jurisdiction. Two jurisdictions applicable to an Australian military member are examined in this chapter: (1) the Australian federal jurisdiction

---

1 This chapter was written in the authors' personal capacities and does not necessarily represent the views of the Australian Government or the Australian Department of Defence.
2 Michael Schmitt, 'Military Necessity and Humanity in International Humanitarian Law: Preserving the Delicate Balance' (2009–2010) 50 *Virginia Journal of International Law* 795.
3 For the purpose of this chapter, 'self-defence' refers to an individual person's response to a threat of injury or death to themselves or another person (what is sometimes termed 'individual self-defence'), 'national self-defence' refers to the right of a State to respond to an armed attack; and 'unit self-defence' refers to situations where a military unit uses force in response to a threat to that unit or another military unit.

under the *Criminal Code Act 1995* (Cth) (*Australian Criminal Code*),[4] and (2) the *Rome Statute of the International Criminal Court*.[5] While this chapter uses these two jurisdictions, the discussion can be transposed and re-analysed for other jurisdictions. For reasons of brevity and to focus on the core issues, the following discussion of self-defence is limited to use of force to protect individuals against bodily harm.

II. Self-defence – different concepts

Self-defence is not a unitary concept, but rather has different legal and operational meanings. It is vital to distinguish between the different meanings and always ask in what context the term 'self-defence' is being used.

A. Distinguishing the different types of self-defence

The *Charter of the United Nations* Article 51 and customary international law[6] allow a State to act in self-defence against an armed attack. Article 51 uses the term 'the inherent right of individual or collective self-defence'. This is the concept of national self-defence. In this context the word 'individual' refers to an

---

4 Section 10.4 'Self-defence'
   (1) A person is not criminally responsible for an offence if he or she carries out the conduct constituting the offence in self-defence.
   (2) A person carries out conduct in self-defence if and only if he or she believes the conduct is necessary:
   (a) to defend himself or herself or another person;
   . . .
   and the conduct is a reasonable response in the circumstances as he or she perceives them.
   . . .
   (4) This section does not apply if:
   (a) the person is responding to lawful conduct; and
   (b) he or she knew that the conduct was lawful.
   However, conduct is not lawful merely because the person carrying it out is not criminally responsible for it.
5 *Rome Statute of the International Criminal Court*, opened for signature 17 July 1998, 2187 UNTS 3 (entered into force 1 July 2002) (*Rome Statute*) Article 31 'Grounds for excluding criminal responsibility':
   1. In addition to other grounds for excluding criminal responsibility provided for in this Statute, a person shall not be criminally responsible if, at the time of that person's conduct:
   . . .
   (c) The person acts reasonably to defend himself or herself or another person . . . against an imminent and unlawful use of force in a manner proportionate to the degree of danger to the person or the other person or property protected. The fact that the person was involved in a defensive operation conducted by forces shall not in itself constitute a ground for excluding criminal responsibility under this sub-paragraph.
6 *Military and Paramilitary Activities in and against Nicaragua (Nicaragua v United States of America)* (Merits)[1986] ICJ Rep 14 [176].

individual State, as opposed to where States act collectively. This type of self-defence is generally not relevant to a person's individual criminal liability for acts connected with an armed conflict. The use of the word 'inherent' in Article 51 when discussing a State's right of self-defence may be a source of confusion as to whether an individual also has an inherent right of self-defence. This point is discussed below.

Like the separation between the *jus in bello* and the *jus ad bellum*, the criminal defence of self-defence operates independently of the legal basis for the use of force by a State. The *International Criminal Tribunal for the former Yugoslavia (ICTY)* has held that military operations in national self-defence do not provide a justification for serious violations of International Humanitarian Law.[7] The court noted that any argument raising individual self-defence must be assessed on its own facts and in the specific circumstances relating to each charge.[8] This legal principle is consistent with the final sentence of *Rome Statute* Article 31(1)(c), which states: 'The fact that the person was involved in a defensive operation conducted by forces shall not in itself constitute a ground for excluding criminal responsibility under this subparagraph'.

It has been suggested that a right of individual self-defence[9] and a right of unit self-defence[10] exist separately to the criminal law defence of self-defence – that is, that a person (and military unit) has an inherent right of self-defence. Briefly, unit self-defence is a term used in rules of engagement (ROE). It can be defined as 'the right of unit commanders to defend their unit [such as a platoon or ship], or other units of their nation, and other specified units against hostile acts or hostile intent'.[11] In some militaries, along with being described as a right, it is also described as an obligation.[12] In other words, a commander is positively required to act in unit self-defence and can be held accountable for not doing so.

7　*Prosecutor v Kordić and Čerkez (Judgment) (International Criminal Tribunal for the former Yugoslavia, Trial Chamber*, Case No IT-95-14/2-T, 26 February 2001) [452].

8　Ibid.

9　The issue of whether self-defence exists as a human right is addressed in 'Final report submitted by Barbara Frey, Special Rapporteur, in accordance with Sub-Commission resolution 2002/25 – Prevention of human rights violations committed with small arms and light weapons' [9] UN Doc A/HRC/Sub.1/58/27 (2006). The report concluded that self-defence is not a human right, rather self-defence is better characterised as a means of protecting the right to life and, as such, a basis for avoiding responsibility for violating the rights of another.

10　Dale Stephens, 'Rules of Engagement and the Concept of Unit Self Defence' (1998) 45 *Naval Law Review* 126, 127; Charles Trumbull IV 'The Basis of Unit Self-Defence and Implications for the Use of Force' (2012–2013) 23 *Duke Journal of Comparative and International Law* 121, 122.

11　International Institute of Humanitarian Law, *Rules of Engagement* (2009) annex D, 85 [*San Remo ROE Handbook*].

12　CJCSI 3131.01B, *US Standing Rules of Engagement*, extracted in International and Operational Law Department, Judge Advocate General's Legal Centre and School, US Army, *Operational Law Handbook* (2013) 85.

While it is beyond the scope of this chapter to examine in detail whether individual and unit self-defence exist as rights separate from the criminal law, it is important to acknowledge the concepts to avoid confusion over the use of terminology. The language used to describe these rights is the same or similar to that of the criminal law of self-defence. As noted above, the criminal law is jurisdiction specific – it is the legislation and case law of a particular jurisdiction that gives meaning to the language and concepts within that jurisdiction, not the asserted legal basis of the rights of individual and unit self-defence.

With respect to unit self-defence, while other commentators argue it has an independent legal basis,[13] it is suggested that the better approach is to view unit self-defence purely as an ROE concept (much like the term 'observed indirect fire')[14] that has underlying law and legal consequences but is not a substantive legal right in itself. Considered that way, unit self-defence can be thought of as:

a)   a form of delegated authority from the national command chain of a State to exercise a State's right of national self-defence in limited circumstances and in a constrained fashion;

b)   a reminder of the criminal law authority to act in self-defence to protect oneself and protect others;[15] and

c)   an order or command to use military force when certain 'triggers' are present.

Deconstructing unit self-defence in this way is helpful as it focuses on the legal basis for any given use of force (or non-use of force if a commander failed to act in unit self-defence) based on the jurisdiction in which the issue would be litigated.

B. Distinguishing self-defence under the criminal law from self-defence as an operational constraint

With two exceptions,[16] LOAC does not directly address self-defence – it treats all acts of violence against an adversary, including those in defence, as

---

13   Ibid; Trumbull, above n 10.

14   *San Remo ROE Handbook*, above n 11, annex D, 84–5.

15   Recalling that the criminal law concept of self-defence allows a person to not only defend him or herself, but also to defend another person where the person to be aided is in a situation where the law would allow that person to act in self-defence.

16   References to 'self-defence' can be found in the rules relating to the loss of protected status of civilian civil defence personnel and military members assigned to civil defence organisations. Such personnel can 'bear light individual weapons for the purpose of maintaining order or for self-defence' without losing their protected status. *Protocol Additional to the Geneva Conventions of 12 August 1949, and relating to the Protection of Victims of International Armed Conflicts*, opened for signature 12 December 1977, 1125 UNTS 3 (entered into force 7 December 1978) Arts 65(3) and 67(1)(d) [*Additional Protocol I*]. Similar provisions that relate to the use of arms in defence are contained in *Geneva Convention for the Amelioration of the Condition of the Wounded and Sick in Armed Forces in the Field*, opened for signature 12 August 1949, 75 UNTS 31 (entered into force 21 October 1950) [*Geneva Convention I*] and *Additional Protocol I* Article 13(2).

'attacks'.[17] LOAC provides a legal authority for such attacks and regulates their conduct.[18] However, there are various political and military considerations for limiting attacks authorised by LOAC to situations that are similar to the parameters of self-defence.

It may be that while the legal threshold of an armed conflict has been satisfied, one of the parties is still pursuing diplomatic efforts to avoid a full-scale conflict and, therefore, as a strategic consideration desires to limit combat action. At the operational level, it may be that a military commander is seeking to control where and when offensive military force is used in order to concentrate available resources on a decisive attack. Or at the tactical level, a military commander may seek to limit the situations where soldiers will fire their weapons because of the clandestine nature of the mission. In this context, self-defence can be used as a label (albeit a potentially confusing one) by command to impose an operational constraint on the use of force. In such a case 'self-defence' does not operate as a criminal defence but rather as an ROE trigger. A soldier who holds fire and does not shoot at the enemy until attacked first due to an ROE restriction to only use force in 'self-defence' is still legally operating under the LOAC paradigm and not the criminal law paradigm.

III. Situations where self-defence does not apply

Self-defence has a narrower application on the battlefield than is generally understood. First, where Person A is lawfully using force against Person B, self-defence does not as a matter of law apply to any use of counter-force by Person B. Second, if Person A is unlawfully using force against Person B, resort to a claim of self-defence is unnecessary if Person B is authorised by law to use force against Person A. Fundamental to understanding how these two points affect the application of self-defence on the battlefield is the legal concept known as the combatant's privilege.

A. The combatant's privilege

The combatant's privilege:

> is in essence a license to kill or wound enemy combatants and destroy other enemy military objectives. A privileged combatant may also cause incidental civilian casualties. A lawful combatant possessing this privilege must be given prisoner of war status . . . upon capture and immunity from criminal prosecution under the domestic law of his captor for his hostile acts that do not violate the laws and customs of war.[19]

---

17 *Additional Protocol I* Article 49.
18 Discussed in section IV of this chapter.
19 Inter-American Commission on Human Rights, *Report on Terrorism and Human Rights*, OEA/Ser. L/V/II.116 Doc 5 rev 1 corr (22 October 2002) www.cidh.oas.org/Terrorism/Eng/toc.htm [68] [IACHR].

In *United States v List* it was held that:

> It cannot be questioned that acts done in time of war under the military authority of an enemy cannot involve any criminal liability on the part of officers or soldiers if the acts are not prohibited by the conventional or customary rules of war.[20]

The main treaty provisions that support the existence of the combatant's privilege are:

a)   *Hague IV Regulations respecting the Laws and Customs of War on Land* Articles 1 and 2[21] and *Additional Protocol I* Article 43(2), which set out who may lawfully participate in hostilities; and
b)   *Geneva Convention III* provides that prisoners of war may not be sentenced 'to any penalties except those provided for in respect of members of the armed forces of the said Power who have committed the same acts'.[22]

Goldman and Tittemore explain that while

> the *1949 Geneva Conventions* and its two[23] *Additional Protocols* . . . contain no provision that expressly recognizes the immunity of such combatants from prosecution for their legitimate acts performed in the line of duty . . . this immunity mandated by customary law is inferentially recognized in Article 87 of the *Third Geneva Convention* . . . [s]ince the detaining power would not prosecute its own soldiers for their legitimate acts of war, it cannot try prisoners of war for comparable acts [either].[24]

The US Court of Appeals (Fourth Circuit) ruled on combatant status in a case concerning a resident of the United States who was being held in military detention. The defendant, al-Marri, was originally arrested and held in civilian custody in December 2001, but in June 2003 was declared an enemy combatant

---

20   *United States of America v List*, in H. Lauterpacht (ed.), *Annual Digest and Reports of Public International Law Cases: Being a Selection from the Decisions of International Courts and Tribunals and Military Courts Given During the Year 1948* (Butterworth, 1953) 632, 649 [*Hostages Trial*].

21   *Regulations respecting the Laws and Customs of War on Land, annex to Convention (IV) respecting the Laws and Customs of War on Land 1907*, signed at The Hague 18 October 1907, 3 Martens Nouveau Recueil (ser 3) 461 (entered into force 26 January 1910) [*Hague IV Regulations*].

22   *Geneva Convention Relative to the Treatment of Prisoners of War*, opened for signature 12 August 1949, 75 UNTS 135 (entered into force 21 October 1950) [*Geneva Convention III*] Article 87.

23   At the time of publication.

24   Robert Goldman and Brian Tittemore, 'Unprivileged Combatants and the Hostilities in Afghanistan: Their Status and Rights Under International Humanitarian and Human Rights Law' (American Society of International Law: Task Force on Terrorism, 2002) 3–4 www.asil.org/taskforce/goldman.pdf.

and transferred to military custody and held without trial. He filed a petition for a writ of *habeas corpus*. A plurality of the Court of Appeals held:

> While civilians are subject to trial and punishment in civilian courts for all crimes committed during wartime in the country in which they are captured and held, combatant status protects an individual from trial and punishment by the capturing nation, unless the combatant has violated the law of war.[25]

The Privy Council came to a similar finding in *The Public Prosecutor v Oie Hee Koi*,[26] a case concerning captured soldiers who had been charged and convicted under domestic law for actions directly arising out of combat action. On appeal, the majority of their Lordships advised:

> [T]hese convictions ought not to be allowed to stand. True that the language of Section 57 covers 'any person' but upon its proper construction Section 57 cannot be read so widely as to cover members of the regular Indonesian armed forces fighting as such in Malaysia in the course of what, it has been assumed, was an armed conflict between Malaysia and Indonesia. The Act is an Internal Security measure, part of the domestic law, and not directed at the military forces of a hostile power attacking Malaysia. It would be an illegitimate extension of established practice to read Section 58 as referring to members of regular forces fighting in enemy country. Members of such forces are not subject to domestic criminal law. If they were so subject they would be committing crimes from murder downwards in fighting against their enemy in the ordinary course of carrying out their recognised military duties.[27]

While the existence of the combatant's privilege, limited to a defined class of combatants[28] in an international armed conflict (IAC), is not disputed, the situation is somewhat more complex in the context of a non-international armed conflict (NIAC).[29] In a NIAC, the side opposing the government forces has no

---

25 *Al-Marri v Pucciarelli*, 534 F 3d 213 (4th Cir, 2008) n 11.

26 *The Public Prosecutor v Oie Hee Koi and others* (Malaysia) [1967] UKPC 21.

27 Ibid 9. Lord Guest and Sir Garfield Barwick dissented on this point (at 14).

28 Without going into technicalities, the combatant's privilege also extends to, among others, unincorporated militias (*Geneva Convention III* Art 4A(2)) and *levée en masse* (*Hague Regulations IV* Art 2; *Geneva Convention III* Art 4A(6)). See IACHR, above n 19, [67].

29 A NIAC is in contra-distinction to an IAC. In general, an IAC occurs between two States; whereas a NIAC occurs between a State and a non-State Party (or between two non-State Parties). See UK Ministry of Defence, *The Manual of the Law of Armed Conflict* (Oxford University Press, 2004) 1.9; Michael Schmitt, Charles Garraway and Yoram Dinstein (drafting committee), *The Manual on the Law of Non-International Armed Conflict: with Commentary* (International Institute of Humanitarian Law, 2006) 2. While that is the general position, for States Parties to *Additional Protocol I* an *international* armed conflict would exist between a State and a non-State Party where 'peoples are fighting against colonial domination and alien occupation and against racist régimes in the exercise of their right of self-determination . . . ' (*Additional Protocol I* Art 1(4)).

legal right to be participating in an armed conflict.[30]A consequence of this is that the individuals who make up the non-government forces do not have the equivalent of the combatant's privilege that applies in an IAC.[31] The idea of extending such immunity to non-government forces was raised and rejected during the drafting conferences for the *Geneva Conventions* in 1949 and the *Additional Protocols* between 1974–1977.[32] As explained by the IACHR:

> Since lawful combatant and prisoner of war status directly flow from the combatant's privilege, recognition of this privilege is limited under customary and conventional international law to situations of international armed conflict as defined under the *1949 Geneva Conventions* and *Additional Protocol I*. In contrast, a government engaged in a civil war or other kind of internal hostilities is not obliged to accord its armed opponents prisoner of war status since these dissidents do not have the combatant's privilege. Such governments therefore are free to prosecute all captured dissidents for sedition and their other violent acts.[33]

Accordingly, those individuals can be prosecuted for acts that *prima facie* comply with LOAC but nonetheless amount to domestic crimes such as murder and destruction of property.[34] This is reinforced by *Additional Protocol II* Article 6(5), which states:

30   *Al-Marri v Pucciarelli*, 534 F 3d 213 (4th Cir, 2008) 233:
   Common Article 3 and other Geneva Convention provisions applying to non-international conflicts (in contrast to those applying to international conflicts) simply do not recognise the 'legal category' of enemy combatant.
31   *R v Gul* (Appellant) [2013] UKSC 64, [50]: 'in international humanitarian law, it appears that insurgents in non-international armed conflicts do not enjoy combatant immunity'. See also Emily Crawford, *The Treatment of Combatants and Insurgents under the Law of Armed Conflict* (Oxford University Press, 2010) 78–9, quoted with approval in *Gul*.
32   Sandesh Sivakumaran, 'Re-envisaging the International Law of Internal Armed Conflict' (2011) 22(1) *European Journal of International Law* 219, 244.
33   IACHR, above n 19, [70]. Solf explains the policy reasons why governments would not wish to extend the combatant's privilege to non-State actors in a NIAC (Waldemar Solf, 'The Status of Combatants in non-International Armed Conflicts under Domestic Law and Transnational Practice' (1983) 33 *American University Law Review* 53, 59). See also International Committee of the Red Cross, *The Relevance of IHL in the Context of Terrorism* (2011) www.icrc.org/eng/resources/documents/misc/terrorism-ihl-210705.htm: In non-international armed conflict, combatant and prisoner of war status are not provided for, because States are not willing to grant members of armed opposition groups immunity from prosecution under domestic law for taking up arms.
34   International Committee of the Red Cross, above n 33:
   Members of organised armed groups are entitled to no special status under the laws of NIAC and may be prosecuted under domestic criminal law if they have taken part in hostilities.
   See also Solf, above n 33, 57–61. See generally Goldman and Tittemore, above n 24; Michael Schmitt, 'The Status of Opposition Fighters in a Non-International Armed Conflict' in Kenneth Watkin and Andrew Norris (eds), *Non-International Armed Conflict in the Twenty-first Century* (International Law Studies, vol 88, 2012) 119.

At the end of hostilities, the authorities in power shall endeavour to grant the broadest possible amnesty to persons who have participated in the armed conflict, or those deprived of their liberty for reasons related to the armed conflict, whether they are interned or detained.[35]

As Watts identifies:

However, this provision merely charges States to 'endeavour' to grant amnesty to fighters. Amnesty is by no means an international legal obligation in NIAC. Domestic law represents the far more relevant legal source for both treatment obligations and immunities if any arising from participation in NIAC.[36]

Therefore, if a member of the non-government forces shoots a member of the government forces in a manner that otherwise complies with LOAC, that person can still be prosecuted under domestic law. It is worth noting at this point that it is not a crime under international law to be an unprivileged belligerent – a member of the non-government forces does not commit a crime under international law simply by engaging in acts of hostilities against government forces. Rather:

[T]he term 'unlawful' combatant is used only to denote the fact that the person lacks the combatant's privilege and is not entitled to participate in hostilities. Mere combatancy by such persons is not tantamount to a violation of the laws and customs of war, although their specific hostile acts may qualify as such.[37]

There is no clear answer as to whether the government forces enjoy the equivalent of the combatant's privilege in a NIAC.[38] There is no treaty law on the point, nor is the issue clearly addressed in customary international law.[39]

---

35 *Protocol Additional to the Geneva Conventions of 12 August 1949, and relating to the Protection of Victims of Non-International Armed Conflicts*, opened for signature 12 December 1977, 1125 UNTS 609 (entered into force 7 December 1978) Art 6(5) [*Additional Protocol II*].

36 Sean Watts, 'Present and Future Conceptions of the Status of Government Forces in Non-International Armed Conflict' in Kenneth Watkin and Andrew Norris (eds), *Non-International Armed Conflict in the Twenty-first Century* (International Law Studies, vol 88) 145, 149. See also Crawford, above n 31, 79.

37 IACHR, above n 19, [69]. See generally Ian Henderson, 'Civilian intelligence agencies and the use of armed drones' (2010) 13 *Yearbook of International Humanitarian Law* 133, 144; Schmitt, above n 34, 121. For example, there are international and domestic crimes for targeting civilians or members of the government forces who are *hors de combat* (see *Rome Statute* Art 8(2)(c)(1) and *Australian Criminal Code* s 268.70(1).

38 Strictly speaking, there are no 'combatants' in a NIAC; hence the reference to 'government forces' and 'the *equivalent* of the combatant's privilege'.

39 Watts, above n 36, 149.

This is important for many reasons, not the least of which is that the government forces may not win the armed conflict and the new government may not be predisposed to exercise any prosecutorial discretion in favour of the now former government forces. Most commentators do not seem to address the issue one way or the other; although a few commentators do positively argue that such a privilege either does, or at least should, exist.[40] The best that can be said at the moment is that the issue remains in doubt. From here on the discussion will focus on combatants and 'combatant's privilege' in an IAC, but the discussion applies *mutatis mutandis* to members of the government forces in a NIAC.

Moving on from the *existence* of the combatant's privilege, two further questions warrant discussion. First, it is unclear whether the combatant's privilege is a personal immunity (immune from prosecution under domestic law for any acts) or a functional immunity (immune from prosecution only for those acts that can be attributed to military operations). Second, it is not certain whether the privilege applies only to foreign domestic law (eg, the Detaining Power under *Geneva Convention III* Article 87) or also to the domestic law of the military member. The answers to these two questions are fundamental to understanding how LOAC and self-defence interact in an armed conflict.

Whether the combatant's privilege is a personal immunity or a functional immunity does not appear to have been directly addressed in case law or scholarship. The relevant passage in *Oie Hee Koi* extracted above could be read either way. An inference can be drawn from *Geneva Convention III* Article 87 that the combatant's privilege is a functional immunity as the Article does not completely prohibit the prosecution of enemy combatants, but rather provides that enemy combatants can only be tried (or more accurately, sentenced) in the same circumstances as the Detaining Power's own armed forces. While *Geneva Convention III* Article 87 does not create the combatant's privilege but merely provides one manifestation of the customary international law rule in limited treaty form,[41] its wording strongly supports the view that the combatant's privilege is a functional immunity. In addition, the interpretation that the combatant's privilege is a functional immunity is consistent with the role and ambit of LOAC. Starting from the proposition that outside of armed conflict a State could try a member of a foreign State's armed forces, LOAC should (as a minimum) provide that military members cannot be prosecuted for activities conducted in furtherance of military operations. It is less apparent why LOAC should provide immunity to the actions of military members that are unrelated to the conduct of military operations.

---

40   Kenneth Watkin, 'Warriors Without Rights? Combatants, Unprivileged Belligerents, and the Struggle over Legitimacy' (Programme on Humanitarian Policy and Conflict Research, 2005) www.hpcr.org/pdfs/OccasionalPaper2.pdf, 65; Henderson, above n 37, 150–3. For a comprehensive treatment of the issue, see Watts, above n 36.
41   Goldman and Tittemore, above n 24.

If the combatant's privilege is a functional immunity, were a military member to claim that force was used in self-defence, then the proper forum for testing that assertion is a criminal court – including a criminal court of a Detaining Power. To illustrate this point, suppose a soldier of State A shoots a civilian on the territory of State A and asserts the shooting was in self-defence, the soldier could be tried in a domestic criminal court to test the assertion.[42] Now imagine it was a soldier of State B who shot the civilian in the context of ongoing armed conflict between States A and B and the soldier of State B has been captured and is being held a prisoner of war by State A. The authorities of State A investigate the killing of the civilian and the soldier of State B claims the use of force was in self-defence. In light of the first example concerning the soldier of State A, it is apparent that *Geneva Convention III* Article 87 would not prevent the trial of the soldier from State B before the courts of State A to test that assertion.

In conclusion, while certain arguments support the view that the combatant's privilege should be treated as a functional immunity and in the opinion of the authors that is the better interpretation, the matter is not beyond doubt. Regardless of which view of the law is the better view, the second issue raised above remains relevant: does the combatant's privilege also apply to a military member of State A before the domestic courts of the military member's own State?

Imagine a soldier from State A shooting a soldier from State B on the territory of State A. The soldier of State A does not claim the shooting was in self-defence but rather was a lawful act of combat. What is there to prevent a prosecutor from charging the soldier with murder? Or suppose an even more fraught but otherwise legally similar example of the soldier from State A shooting a civilian from State A on the basis that the civilian was taking a direct part in hostilities. Or finally the example of a soldier from State A in a NIAC knowingly causing incidental death to a civilian from State A while attacking either the non-State actors or other lawful objects of attack. For the purpose of these examples, assume that there are appropriate charges available and jurisdiction is otherwise available – the only issue we are concerned with is whether the combatant's privilege applies to act as a bar on prosecution in the domestic courts of a soldier's own State.

As a matter of international law, whether the combatant's privilege extends to bar prosecution of a military member under his or her own State's criminal law is currently unclear. *Geneva Convention III* Article 87 does not assist (as it is limited to the situation of prisoners of war), while *Hague IV Regulations* Article 1 and *Additional Protocol I* Article 43(2) do lend some support to the conclusion that it does so extend. The authors are unaware of any relevant statement of customary international law. As outlined below, there is some domestic State

---

42 Putting aside any domestic law issues in State A such as jurisdiction by civil or military courts over military members of State A.

practice exempting military members from the application of ordinary criminal law to actions occurring in the context of armed conflict. However, there is no indication of whether that practice is purely a domestic policy issue or was believed to be a legal requirement; and, therefore, has the necessary *opinio juris* element for customary international law purposes.

As for the domestic law position, by its very nature domestic law varies from jurisdiction to jurisdiction. While some jurisdictions have addressed this by statute,[43] others have not.[44] The fact that the ordinary criminal law might criminalise actions that would otherwise be lawful under LOAC is discussed in the 2013 report of the Council of Australian Governments, *Review of Counter Terrorism Legislation*.[45] Recommendations 6 and 7 of that report specifically address the problem that a broad definition of a 'terrorist act' would make conduct in an armed conflict criminal whether it was otherwise in accordance with LOAC. Similarly, the 2012 Declassified Annual Report of the Independent National Security Legislation Monitor notes that 'Australia's definition of terrorist act does not recognize combatant's immunity and potentially includes as unlawful action taken by parties to an armed conflict where that action is lawful under [LOAC]'.[46] Compare this to Canada, where the definition of a terrorist activity under *Criminal Code*, RSC 1985, c C-46, s 83.01:

> Does not include an act or omission that is committed during an armed conflict and that, at the time and in the place of its commission, is in accordance with customary international law or conventional international law applicable to the conflict, or the activities undertaken by military forces of a state in the exercise of their official duties, to the extent that those activities are governed by other rules of international law.

Returning to the Australian situation, what appears to be underappreciated is that it is not just terrorism offences that are of concern. For example, through the extraterritorial application of the *Defence Force Discipline Act 1982* (Cth),[47] 'ordinary' offences like murder, assault and property damage also *prima facie* apply to acts of Australian Defence Force personnel during armed conflict against the enemy and in compliance with LOAC. This is important because in dualist

---

43 For example, US Model Penal Code sub-s 3.03(2)(b).

44 Australia is one example of a country that has not provided immunity or a defence under the ordinary criminal law for acts committed as part of military operations by its military members.

45 Council of Australian Governments, Report, *Review of Counter Terrorism Legislation* (2013) www.coagctreview.gov.au/Report/Pages/default.aspx.

46 Independent National Security Legislation Monitor, *Declassified Annual Report* (2012) www.dpmc.gov.au/inslm/docs/INSLM_Annual_Report_20121220.pdf 122.

47 The *Defence Force Discipline Act 1982* (Cth) is the disciplinary legislation applicable to Australian Defence Force personnel. For operations on Australian soil, Commonwealth, State and Territory criminal law would be directly applicable, alongside the *Defence Force Discipline Act*.

States like Australia, international law rules are not automatically part of the domestic law.[48] Nor would an international law rule amount to lawful authority for the purposes of rules like *Australian Criminal Code* Section 10.5.

Examples from the United Kingdom and the United States of America further illustrate the issue. In *R v Page*,[49] the United Kingdom Courts-Martial Appeal Court heard an appeal from a conviction by court-martial of a British soldier who had been convicted of murder for the killing of an Egyptian national in Egypt. The court held, in obiter, that the common law definition of murder being an unlawful killing under the King's peace excepts from murder killing in the course of war.[50] As Liivoja notes, this does not assist with property destruction or all the other potential crimes arising from combat activities.[51] Nor would it assist where the crime of murder has been codified if the codification does not include a reference to the King's peace.

In the United States of America, *Model Penal Code* Subsection 3.03(2)(b) proposes that criminal statutes expressly recognise a public authority justification for a killing that 'occurs in the lawful conduct of war'. This section has been picked up by a number of State legislatures. In *United States v McMonagle*,[52] the appellant had been convicted by general court-martial of, *inter alia*, murder while engaged in acts inherently dangerous to others during Operation Just Cause in Panama.

An element of the offence under *Uniform Code of Military Justice* Article 118(3) (murder while engaged in an act inherently dangerous to others) is that 'the killing was unlawful'.[53] The US Court of Military Appeals held 'with respect to Article 118(3) that the killing was justified if appellant honestly and reasonably thought that he was shooting at a combatant'.[54]

What these two cases show is that for killing in the course of armed conflict not to amount to murder in a military member's own domestic law, there either needs to be a statutory provision to that effect (the US example), or for the crime of murder not to apply as a matter of common law definition or statutory construction (the UK example).

In summary, LOAC recognises a combatant's privilege for combatants in IAC that, as a matter of international law, provides immunity from criminal

---

48 With respect to treaties see *Dietrich v The Queen* (1992) 177 CLR 292. With respect to customary international law see *Chow Hung Ching and Another v The King* (1949) 77 CLR 449.

49 [1954] 1 QB 170.

50 Ibid 175.

51 Rain Liivoja, 'Divergent Approaches to Combatant's Privilege in Municipal Law' (Presented at the Conference on Investigating Operational Incidents in a Military Context: Law, Justice, Politics, Australian Centre for Military & Security Law, Australian National University, Canberra, 29 September 2012) (publication forthcoming).

52 38 MJ 53 (CMA 1993).

53 Ibid 3.

54 Ibid 9. See also Solf, above n 33, n 51 and accompanying text.

prosecution under the domestic law of an opposing belligerent State for acts that do not violate LOAC (eg, murder and property damage). It is unclear whether, as a matter of international law, the combatant's privilege applies to a combatant's own domestic law or, alternatively, whether any relevant immunities need to be found solely in the combatant's own domestic law. In a NIAC, it is clear that non-State actors do not have the equivalent of the combatant's privilege (while noting that *Additional Protocol II* Article 6(5) does encourage 'the authorities in power . . . to grant the broadest possible amnesty to persons who have participated in the armed conflict'). It is unclear whether there is the equivalent of the combatant's privilege for the government forces; although there is support among some of the commentators for concluding that there is such a privilege.

B. The combatant's privilege and the law of self-defence

Article 31(1)(c) of the *Rome Statute* provides that actions in self-defence must be in response to an unlawful use of force.[55] Similarly, the *Australian Criminal Code* subsection 10.4(4)(a) states that self-defence does not apply if a person is responding to lawful conduct.[56] As combatants have a lawful authority to attack other combatants in an IAC, an Australian combatant could not rely on self-defence as the legal justification for responding to an attack from a combatant from State B. Of course, the Australian combatant can respond to the lawful attack from the combatant from State B; however, the legal authority for doing so is LOAC.

The criminal law concept of self-defence only operates to exclude criminal liability for acts that would otherwise be unlawful. As it is a *defence*, it only operates if there is an offence. If a person is exercising the combatant's privilege, then resort to a claim of self-defence is unnecessary. Self-defence is not the appropriate legal paradigm where a combatant in the context of an IAC kills an enemy combatant who is posing an immediate threat (or a civilian who is directly participating in hostilities) as LOAC provides the appropriate legal authority to attack these categories of people.[57] As the combatant is not committing an offence, the plea of self-defence simply does not arise.

It does not matter whether the combatant knew whether the other person was an enemy combatant or a civilian taking a direct part in hostilities, as both

---

55 It would appear that there is no requirement that the person must know that the conduct to which they are responding is unlawful; however, it is suggested that the act should be objectively unlawful (Hannah Tonkin 'Defensive Force under the Rome Statute' (2005) 6 *Melbourne Journal of International Law* 86, 95).

56 And in the case of the *Australian Criminal Code*, the person must also know that the conduct was lawful (*Australian Criminal Code* s 10.4(4)(b)). One would expect that through basic LOAC training every Australian combatant would be aware that during an armed conflict combatants can lawfully attack each other.

57 See *Additional Protocol I* Article 43(2).

are lawful targets.[58] Also, it does not matter whether, in the particular circumstances of the direct participation in hostilities by the civilian outside of the context of an armed conflict, this would have amounted to conduct that would satisfy the requirements for acting in self-defence. A civilian who lays a land-mine can be attacked just as much as one who is about to activate a command-detonated mine.[59] By directly participating in hostilities, a civilian loses their protected status and LOAC provides lawful authority for a military member to attack them.[60]

It follows that if in responding to an attack during an IAC an Australian combatant acts in a way that is not authorised by LOAC and commits a war crime, then self-defence would not be available as a defence to that war crime. For example, self-defence could not be used to exclude criminal liability in the situation where, in responding to an attack from a combatant from State B, the Australian combatant employs a poisoned weapon,[61] prohibited gas[62] or other prohibited weapon.[63] However, if the combatant from State B attacked the Australian combatant with a prohibited weapon, such an attack would no longer be lawful. Therefore, the Australian combatant could claim self-defence in relation to his or her use of a prohibited weapon in response.[64]

If it is accepted that the combatant's privilege applies to government forces during a NIAC, then, if a member of the government forces is attacked by a member of the non-government forces (or a civilian taking a direct part in hostilities) resort to a claim of self-defence is also unnecessary. Again, the killings would be lawful under LOAC and should be treated as *prima facie* lawful under criminal law. Finally, self-defence would not apply to a member of the non-government forces if attacked by a member of the government forces in a NIAC as the attack by the member of the government forces would be

---

58 Space does not allow a full discussion of the situation where a civilian is attacking a combatant for reasons unrelated to the hostilities, except to say that it is the objective nature of the act that is the issue and not the subjective intent of the individual (Nils Melzer, *Interpretive Guidance on the Notion of Direct Participation in Hostilities under International Humanitarian Law* (International Committee of the Red Cross, 2009) 59).

59 The use of lethal force against a person during the act of placing a land-mine would, in all but the rarest of circumstances, not be a necessary or reasonable response in self-defence.

60 Tonkin, above n 55, 92–3, explains the issue as follows:
   In accordance with Article 21(1)(b) [of the *Rome Statute*], claims of defensive force must be considered in light of the applicable treaties and principles of international law, including the established principles of the international law of armed conflict. For example, if a protected person under the *Geneva Conventions* – such as a civilian – unlawfully uses force, that person may lose his or her status as a protected person. In such cases resort to Article 31 by the defendant would be unnecessary, as the case-in-chief would lack an essential element.

61 *Rome Statute* Article 8(2)(b)(xvii).

62 Ibid Article 8(2)(b)(xviii).

63 Ibid Article 8(2)(b)(xix).

64 Ingrid Detter, *The Law of War* (Cambridge University Press, 2nd edn, 2000) 429; Yoram Dinstein, *The Conduct of Hostilities under the Law of International Armed Conflict* (Cambridge University Press, 2nd edn, 2010) 286–7.

lawful.[65] Recalling that members of the non-government forces do not have any initial legal authority for the use of force against the member of the government armed forces,[66] and as self-defence would not be available, any use of force by the member of the non-government forces against the member of the government forces would be illegal.

IV. Contrasting the requirements of self-defence with relevant rules of LOAC

While the concept of the combatant's privilege narrows the ambit for the application of self-defence, self-defence will continue to operate side-by-side with LOAC on the battlefield. It is, therefore, important to understand how each area of the law operates and how each area potentially affects key military concepts. The following section explains and distinguishes some terms common to both branches of the law and then analyses how self-defence operates with respect to precautions in attack, a 'duty to retreat', prohibited weapons and military orders.

A. Necessary, reasonable and proportionate

Terms like or very similar to 'necessary', 'reasonable' and 'proportionate' are used in both the law of self-defence and LOAC, as well as ROE. This can cause confusion if it is not fully appreciated that each term has a distinct legal meaning depending upon the legal context in which it is used.

An act can only be said to be 'necessary' in self-defence when the act was required in the circumstances to respond to a threat. What is necessary under self-defence in the criminal law should not be confused with 'military necessity' under LOAC. 'Military necessity' is not about measuring the degree of force used in a particular circumstance. 'Military necessity' permits a belligerent, subject to the laws of war, to apply any amount and kind of force to compel the complete submission of the enemy with the least possible expenditure of time, life and money.[67] A military commander is free to impose restrictions on attacks during an armed conflict; however, it would be a mistake to impose those restrictions on the incorrect belief that LOAC requires that only necessary force be used against the enemy.

---

65 Assuming for the purposes of this example that the member of the government forces is complying with both domestic law and LOAC. If, for example, the member of the non-government forces had surrendered, it would be lawful for that person to defend against an unlawful attack.

66 In other words, unlike the situation between combatants in an IAC, there is no legal basis for members of non-government forces to 'attack' government forces in a NIAC (noting that for States Parties to *Additional Protocol I*, it is an *international* armed conflict where 'peoples are fighting against colonial domination and alien occupation and against racist régimes in the exercise of their right of self-determination' (*Additional Protocol I* Art 1(4)). This aspect is discussed in more detail above.

67 *Hostages Trial*, above n 20, 646.

Reasonableness provides a flexible objective standard against which the actions of a person in self-defence can be measured. Under the *Australian Criminal Code*, what is reasonable encompasses the requirement of proportionality; whereas under the *Rome Statute* proportionality is identified as a separate and additional element. There is no requirement under LOAC that attacks against enemy combatants and civilians taking a direct part in hostilities be constrained by an objective standard of reasonableness. For example, under LOAC it is permissible to attack an 18-year-old army recruit still undergoing basic training even though the attacker already has overwhelming numerical superiority.

The proportionality equation in self-defence compares the degree of danger faced by a person with his or her response. It looks at whether the degree of force used to avert the danger was excessive. Determining proportionality is not a matter of precision and cannot be reduced to a mathematical formula. Proportionality under self-defence should not be confused with the concept of proportionality under LOAC. Proportionality under LOAC does not compare the level of force used in an attack against the threat faced. A pilot flying at 20,000 feet above sea level can bomb a single soldier on the ground who is posing no direct threat to the pilot or to allied ground forces. Rather, the issue is whether any incidental civilian injury or death (and civilian property destruction – 'collateral damage') expected to be caused by an attack is excessive (ie, is not proportional) to the military advantage anticipated to be gained from the attack.[68] In other words, under LOAC the issue is about the degree and extent of harm caused to civilian *bystanders* – it is most definitely not about the degree of harm caused to the person or persons as the subject of the attack. There is no general requirement under LOAC to limit the level of force used against the enemy; and accordingly, the military principle of the use of overwhelming force to overcome the enemy is entirely consistent with LOAC.[69]

B. Precautions in attack

Under LOAC, a number of rules have been developed to provide protection to the civilian population. These include the precautions in attack set out in *Additional Protocol I* Article 57, which are accepted as customary international law in both international and non-international armed conflicts.[70] Australia has adopted the LOAC 6-Step Targeting process that reflects the requirements of Article 57. The steps are:

1. Locate and observe the potential target and its surrounding area.
2. Assess whether the target is a valid military objective and that it is otherwise unprotected from attack by LOAC.

---

68 *Additional Protocol I* Article 57(2)(b).
69 See the discussion of 'military necessity' in the *Hostages Trial*, above n 20, 646.
70 Jean-Marie Henckaerts and Louise Doswald-Beck (eds), *Customary International Humanitarian Law*, vol I (Cambridge University Press, 2005) rules 14–21.

3. Take all feasible precautions to minimise collateral damage.
4. Assess whether any expected collateral damage is proportional (ie, not excessive) to the anticipated military advantage to be gained from the attack.
5. Take such care as is appropriate in the tactical situation to release or fire the weapon to achieve the best possible chance of hitting the selected aim point.
6. Cancel or suspend the attack should it become apparent that any one of the assessments made under steps 2 or 4 is no longer valid.[71]

By expressing the requirements of Article 57 as separate steps, commanders are able to allocate responsibility for compliance to different people involved in an attack. For example, for an air to ground attack a soldier on the ground with line of sight to the intended target could be responsible for steps 1–4 and the pilot (or other aircrew member responsible for weapons release) is responsible for step 5. Step 6 would be shared between the soldier and the aircrew.

This is not the case when acting in self-defence. There is no equivalent of the LOAC 6-Step Targeting process (no legal 'division of labour') under criminal law. Rather, the person who 'pulls the trigger' will be responsible for the decision. Accordingly, he or she must personally decide whether the use of lethal force is justified in self-defence. Instead of applying the precautions in attacks set out in *Additional Protocol I* Article 57, the person will be guided by the requirements of using reasonable, necessary and proportionate force. It is unclear whether the requirement of reasonableness would extend to requiring a military member to do everything feasible to assess and minimise potential death or injury to civilians prior to acting in self-defence. Even if it could be said that these considerations are relevant to the reasonableness assessment, they are unlikely to be as effective as protecting the civilian population as the explicit requirements of *Additional Protocol I* Article 57. This is unsurprising, as the law of self-defence was not developed to specifically address these types of issues that are unique to military operations.

Conversely, it is highly likely that reasonableness under the law of self-defence imposes a higher standard of care on a military member to avoid causing *any* injury or death to civilians. There does not appear to be any reported Australian case law on this point, but the domestic law of the US clearly provides that while acting in self-defence can excuse unintentional injury or even death to a bystander,[72] self-defence does not excuse knowingly or recklessly injuring or

---

71 This LOAC 6-step targeting process reduces the key legal considerations when conducting an attack into a series of steps that can be applied by military forces to assist with complying with LOAC. The 6-step process also facilitates the allocation of responsibility, and legal accountability, where more than one individual is involved in planning and executing an attack. For further information, see Ian Henderson, *The Contemporary Law of Targeting: Military Objectives, Proportionality and Precautions in Attack under Additional Protocol I* (Martinus Nijhoff, 2009) 233–42.
72 *People v Adams*, 9 Ill App 3d 61 (1972).

killing a bystander.[73] Compare this to LOAC, which permits *expected* incidental loss of civilian life and injury to civilians (collateral damage), provided that the collateral damage is not excessive in relation to the military advantage anticipated to be gained from the attack.[74]

C. Weapons

LOAC prohibits the use of certain weapons. Under the *Rome Statute* and the *Australian Criminal Code* it is a war crime to employ poison or poisoned weapons,[75] prohibited gases,[76] or prohibited bullets.[77] In contrast, the law of self-defence does not specifically address the means of response to a threat.

In some jurisdictions, for example New Zealand, self-defence operates to exclude criminal responsibility for use of force.[78] It is an interesting question, but beyond the scope of this chapter, whether in these jurisdictions self-defence could be claimed with respect to a war crime of employing a prohibited weapon. However, under the *Australian Criminal Code* and the *Rome Statute*, there is no limitation on pleading self-defence only to use of force. Therefore, the use of a prohibited weapon would be consistent with self-defence analysed under the *Australian Criminal Code* and the *Rome Statute* provided that a person's actions were a necessary, reasonable and proportionate response to the threat.

D. Duty to Retreat

Under LOAC, there is no requirement to retreat from an attack. The position under self-defence varies from jurisdiction to jurisdiction. Leverick identifies four positions that have been adopted with respect to this issue:[79]

---

73 *Henwood v People*, 54 Colo 188 (1913) [8]:
   The defendant claimed to have fired the shots at Von Phul with the intention of striking him for the purpose of protecting his own life. If the facts justified him in so doing, his action in this respect would be lawful, but, if he did so without due caution or circumspection, taking into consideration the presence of others in the bar-room, he was not guiltless, but might be adjudged guilty of involuntary manslaughter in causing the death of [a bystander].
   See also *Annot*, 18 ALR 917 (1922) 928:
   If one, without criminal intent or design, shoots at one man, causing, as a result of carelessness, the death of another, he is guilty of manslaughter. *Ringer v State* (1905) 74 Ark. 262, 85 S.W. 410. So, one who fires a shot, when knowing that he cannot do so without hitting an innocent person, is guilty of voluntary homicide, but in determining that question, regard must be had to the circumstances under which the shot was fired. Ibid. An accused is guilty of involuntary manslaughter, where, in shooting at one carelessly and recklessly, in self-defence, he kills another. *Scott v State* (1905) 75 Ark. 142, 86 S.W. 1004.
74 *Additional Protocol I* Article 57(2)(a)(iii).
75 *Rome Statute* Article 2(a)(xvii); *Australian Criminal Code* s 268.55.
76 *Rome Statute* Article 2(a)(xviii); *Australian Criminal Code* s 268.56.
77 *Rome Statute* Article 2(a)(xix); *Australian Criminal Code* s 268.57.
78 *Crimes Act 1961* (NZ) s 48: 'Everyone is justified in using, in the defence of himself or another, such force as, in the circumstances as he believes them to be, it is reasonable to use'.
79 Fiona Leverick, *Killing in Self-Defence* (Oxford University Press, 2006) 69–75.

a) *An absolute retreat rule.* The accused must make an attempt to retreat before using force in self-defence regardless of the circumstances.

b) *A strong retreat rule.* The accused must make an attempt to retreat before using force in self-defence only if an opportunity to do so actually exists.

c) *A weak retreat rule.* Retreat is not treated as an independent variable, but rather as one factor that is taken into account in deciding whether the accused's actions were necessary or reasonable.

d) *No retreat rule.* There is no duty on the accused to take an opportunity to retreat. The victim of an attack has the right to stand their ground and meet force with force.

Both the *Australian Criminal Code*[80] and the *Rome Statute*[81] apply the weak retreat rule. The interaction between the weak retreat rule and military duty can raise difficult questions when a member is given a task that either explicitly or impliedly requires them not to retreat from a threatening situation. For example, it appears that an Australian combatant could *prima facie* plead self-defence when, contrary to orders, he or she retreated or abandoned their post in the face of the enemy during an IAC. Conversely, a court may take into account the nature of the military duties when assessing the reasonableness of the member's response if the member did not retreat.

E. Command restrictions

There is nothing in LOAC that prevents a military commander from imposing restrictions on the use of force. Such restrictions are common and are regularly promulgated through ROE. The situation under self-defence is less clear. The issue can be expressed as follows: can a commander issue an enforceable order to a soldier not to shoot in situations where the soldier would otherwise be able to shoot in self-defence? In other words, can a soldier rely on the defence of self-defence when charged with the offence of failing to comply with an order?

This issue will not arise under the *Rome Statute* as there is no offence of failing to comply with a lawful order. Under the *Australian Criminal Code*, self-defence is not limited to violent crimes. There appears to be no reason why self-defence could not be successfully pled as a defence to a charge of *Disobedience of lawful command*,[82] or *Failing to comply with a general order*[83] if the conduct by the soldier was a necessary and reasonable response to a threat.

V. Summary and conclusion

When force is used in the exercise of the combatant's privilege the governing legal regime is LOAC; when force is used in self-defence, the governing legal

---

80 Stephen Odgers, *Principles of Federal Criminal Law* (Thomson Reuters, 2nd edn, 2010) 134–6.
81 Tonkin above n 55, 104.
82 *Defence Force Discipline Act* s 27.
83 Ibid s 29.

regime is criminal law. The following table summarises how different issues are analysed when conducted under the authority of LOAC or self-defence. For the purposes of this table, the LOAC applicable in both an IAC and a NIAC will be used, while the test for self-defence under the *Australian Criminal Code* is used.

Issue	*LOAC*	*Self-Defence*
In what circumstances does the legal regime apply?	When a military member is killing or wounding the enemy.	Where a military member is subject to an unlawful use of force and is not otherwise authorised under LOAC to respond to the use of force.
Is use of lethal force permissible?	Yes, against enemy combatants, dissident armed forces, other opposition organised armed groups and civilians taking a direct part in hostilities.	Yes, but only if use of lethal force is necessary and reasonable to protect life.
Is the level of force in response to an attack measured in relation to the threat posed by the attacker?	No (eg, can attack an unarmed combatant, as long as not *hors de combat*).	Yes.
Is there a requirement to take precautions in attack, such as taking all feasible precautions to avoid/minimise collateral damage to property?	Yes.	Not explicitly – may be taken into account in assessing the reasonableness of a response.
Is it lawful to cause injury to bystanders when using force?	Yes, if the expected injury to bystanders is not excessive to the military advantage anticipated from the use of force.	Unclear, but the better view is no, where such injury was reasonably foreseeable.
Is it permissible to use weapons prohibited by LOAC?	No.	Yes, if such use is necessary and reasonable.
Is there a duty to retreat?	No.	Not as such, but whether or not retreat was an option is a factor in considering whether use of force is necessary and reasonable in the circumstances.
Required to obey lawful commands?	Yes.	No, if disobeying is necessary and reasonable.

The battlefield is not the place for legal niceties and nuances. Accordingly, doctrine and training for military members needs to be clear on the different types of self-defence and their relationship to ROE. This requires a clear understanding of the different legal bases for self-defence and the different spheres of application. As LOAC has been developed specifically for combat operations, it will often be the case that LOAC is the legal paradigm most suited to the use of force on the battlefield and the law of self-defence is best left for non-combat operations.

Where LOAC is the governing legal paradigm, States should ensure that they have enacted the combatant's privilege in domestic law for captured enemy forces and for their own military members. States should also review their disciplinary codes to harmonise the application of those laws with their own domestic law of self-defence.

5 Accountability for targeted killing operations

International humanitarian law, international human rights law and the relevance of the principle of proportionality

Michelle Lesh[1]

I. Introduction

Targeted killings are controversial. Their growing prevalence calls for clarity in this developing area of international law. One aspect that requires consideration in determining the legality of this practice is *ex post facto* investigations into such killings. The primary purpose of investigating targeted killing operations after the fact is to create accountability for potential violations of the law. In addition, it may foster attempts to minimise potential civilian harm in future attacks through having the benefit of learning from past attacks.

This chapter will discuss two areas of law relevant to assessing whether accountability measures are necessary for targeting operations. The first area that will be examined is the duty to investigate. The obligation to investigate allegations of violations tests international law, particularly in relation to a practice like targeted killing. The law on this question is underdeveloped and

1 Dr Michelle Lesh is a Golda Meir Post-Doctoral Fellow at the Hebrew University of Jerusalem. In this festschrift to Professor Tim McCormack, it seems most fitting for me to explore the topic of investigations into targeted killing operations, and to draw on the examples of the Israeli Supreme Court *Targeted Killing* case and the *Israeli Turkel Commission Report (Part II)* on the duty to investigate. My involvement in these two legal documents would not have been possible without Tim's kindness and generosity. That work in Jerusalem, our many conversations and collaborations over the years, and his finely judged understanding of the field of international humanitarian law has been invaluable in helping me to find my way through its complexities. This book reflects the fact that I am not alone in being greatly indebted to him. Lastly and most importantly, I am profoundly grateful for Tim's nourishing care for me as a person, first as his student and now in warm friendship. It is a privilege to contribute to this book in his honour.

The views expressed in this chapter are those of the author alone and do not represent any institutional position.

the treaty provisions lack clear guidance. The second area that will be examined in this chapter is the principle of proportionality and the difficulties that emerge from the inherently subjective nature of proportionality assessments. This part of the chapter will discuss whether one way of complimenting the principle is through an *ex post facto* investigation to enhance the protection of civilians during armed conflict. The norms of both international humanitarian law (IHL) and international human rights law (IHRL) are relevant to the analysis undertaken in this chapter. The growing use of drone attacks and other forms of targeted killings, particularly in non-international armed conflicts, where the geographical boundaries of conflict are often challenged and where attacks are regularly operated remotely, renders the two legal frameworks potentially applicable when questions of accountability are at issue.

II. Duty to investigate

This section will explore the duty to investigate according to IHL and IHRL, with a particular focus on targeted killings. It will begin by setting out the threshold for triggering an investigation under the two paradigms and it will then outline the manner in which investigations are conducted. The discussion that follows, especially in the second part of this section, will draw on the analysis of the *Turkel Report* because of the way it has contributed to understanding how to conduct an investigation.[2] This section will demonstrate that on the question

2 In June 2010, the Turkel Commission – a public commission of inquiry – was appointed by the Government of Israel, following the maritime incident in which the Israel Defense Forces (IDF) intercepted the Mavi Marmara, a flotilla sailing from Turkey for Gaza. Supreme Court Justice (Ret.) Jacob Turkel chaired the Commission and its members were Professor Shabtai Rosenne (until his death in September 2010), IDF General (Ret.) Amos Horev, Ambassador Reuven Merhav and Professor Miguel Deutch. In addition, international observers were appointed to the Commission: Lord David Trimble, Brigadier-General (Ret.) Kenneth Watkin (until May 2011) and Professor Tim McCormack (from June 2011). The Commission was asked to examine the legality of the blockade on Gaza and whether the actions carried out by Israel to enforce the blockade on board the Mavi Marmara were legal. These questions were addressed by the Commission in its First Report, submitted to the Government in January 2011. The Commission's mandate also included assessing Israel's mechanisms for examining and investigating violations of international law according to the laws of war. The Commission reviewed military and civilian mechanisms for investigating behaviour by the IDF, the Israel Police, the Israel Security Agency, the Israel Prison Service and the civilian echelon; and the compatibility of those accountability structures with Israel's obligations under international law. This part of the mandate formed its Second Report, which it submitted to the Government in February 2013. See, Turkel Commission, *The Public Commission to Examine the Maritime Incident of 31 May 2010. Report: Part*, January 2011, www.turkel-committee.com/files/wordocs// 870720021 1english.pdf; Turkel Commission, *The Public Commission to Examine the Maritime Incident of 31 May 2010. Second Report: Israeli's Mechanisms for Examining and Investigating Complaints and Claims of Violations of the Laws of Armed Conflict According to International Law*, February 2013, www.turkelcommittee.gov.il/files/newDoc3/The%20Turkel%20Report%20for%20website. pdf [*Turkel Commission Second Report*].

of the duty to investigate, the two legal frameworks compliment each other in some regards and are divergent in others.

A. *The grounds for triggering an investigation*

IHL is one of the normative frameworks relevant to the duty to investigate, particularly in the context of targeted killing operations occurring during an armed conflict. Treaty provisions on the duty to investigate under IHL are sparse.[3] According to Article 146 *Fourth Geneva Convention (GCIV)* Parties have a duty to actively pursue prosecution of grave breaches of the *Convention.*[4] For the purposes of targeted killing the relevant grave breaches are wilful killing and wilfully depriving a protected person of the rights of a fair and regular trial.[5] The most obvious way in which IHL deals with accountability is through criminal responsibility. This includes command responsibility,[6] superior orders and the obligation not to follow illegal orders.[7] The duty to investigate grave breaches, as laid down in *GCIV*, is further developed in Articles 85–87 *Additional Protocol I to the Geneva Conventions (API).*[8] The *Commentary on the Additional Protocols* (*Commentary*) confirms the importance of commanders in the implementation of this duty.[9] Moreover, the *Commentary* interprets the concept of a commander

---

3 A general starting point is Common Article 1 of the four *Geneva Conventions*: '[t]he High Contracting Parties undertake to respect and to ensure respect for the present Convention in all circumstances.' The obligation 'to ensure respect' has been interpreted expansively. *Geneva Convention for the Amelioration of the Condition of the Wounded and Sick in Armed Forces in the Field*, opened for signature 12 August 1949, 75 UNTS 31 (entered into force 21 October 1950) [*GCI*]; *Geneva Convention of the Amelioration of the Condition of the Wounded, Sick and Shipwrecked Members of Armed Forces at Sea*, opened for signature 12 August 1949, 75 UNTS 85 (entered into force 21 October 1950) [*GCII*]; *Geneva Convention Relative to the Treatment of Prisoners of War*, opened for signature 12 August 1949, 75 UNTS 135 (entered into force 21 October 1950) [*GCIII*]; *Geneva Convention Relative to the Protection of Civilian Persons in Time of War*, opened for signature 12 August 1949, 75 UNTS 287 (entered into force 21 October 1950) [*GCIV*] [collectively, *Geneva Conventions*]. See, also, Carlo Focarelli, 'Common Article 1 of the 1949 Geneva Conventions: A Soap Bubble?' (2010) 21 *European Journal of International Law* 125.
4 *GCIV* Articles 146–7.
5 See Jean Pictet (ed.), *The Geneva Conventions of 12 August 1949*: Commentary Published under the General Editorship of J S Pictet (1956) vol 4, Arts 147, 157.
6 *Protocol Additional to the Geneva Conventions of 12 August 1949 and relating to the Protection of Victims of International Armed Conflicts (Protocol I)*, Arts 86–7, opened for signature 8 June 1977, 1125 UNTS 3 (entered into force 7 December 1978) [*API*]. See *Prosecutor v Delalić (Judgment)* (*ICTY, Appeals Chamber*, Case No. IT-96-21-A, 20 February 2001) [182]–[199].
7 *Rome Statute of the International Criminal Court* Article 33, opened for signature 17 July 1998, 2187 UNTS 90 (entered into force 1 July 2002) (*Rome Statute*). See *Prosecutor v Erdemović (Sentencing Judgment)* (*ICTY, Trial Chamber*, Case No IT-96-22-Tbis, 5 March 1998).
8 *API* Articles 85–7.
9 Yves Sandoz, Christophe Swinarski and Bruno Zimmerman (eds), *Commentary on the Additional Protocols of 8 June 1977 to the Geneva Conventions of 12 August 1949* (Martinus Nijhoff, 1987), 1017 [3549]; Turkel Commission Second Report, above n 2, 77–9, 366–9.

broadly to include all members of the military exercising some kind of command function, no matter how junior.[10]

War crimes require investigation when there is a reasonable suspicion that they have occurred.[11] In the context of targeted killings, attacks suspected of amounting to war crimes therefore require an investigation. An investigation would be required according to IHL during an armed conflict, if the targeted individual was not a legitimate target according the definition of 'combatant' or 'civilians directly participating in hostilities';[12] or if civilians killed and injured in the course of the operation render the killing a breach of the principle of proportionality because the extent of the expected collateral damage is excessive relative to the military value of killing the targets.[13] There is support for the position that war crimes extend beyond 'grave breaches' enumerated in the treaty law (from the perspective of targeted killing: wilful killing and wilfully depriving a protected person of the rights of a fair and regular trial) to encompass 'serious violations'.[14]

IHRL is another normative framework relevant to the duty to investigate, particularly in the context of drone attacks that take place outside the context of an armed conflict or in the territory of the attacker. Although there is dispute regarding the extraterritorial application of IHRL,[15] the chapter adopts the view that IHRL does apply extraterritorially where a State exercises effective control over territory or persons.[16]

---

10 Sandoz, Swinarski and Zimmerman, above n 9, [3553].
11 Jean-Marie Henckaerts and Louise Doswald-Beck, *Customary International Humanitarian Law* (Cambridge University Press, 2005), Rule 158; *Turkel Commission Second Report*, above n 2, 73–4, 100.
12 See *GCIII* Article 4A; *API* Articles 43–4; 51(3).
13 *API* Article 51 (4), (5)(b); 57 (1), (2).
14 *Turkel Commission Second Report*, above n 2, 94–9; *Statute of the International Tribunal for the former Yugoslavia*, Article 1; *Prosecutor v Tadić* (*Decision on the Defence Motion for Interlocutory Appeal on Jurisdiction*) (*ICTY, Appeals Chamber*, Case No IT-94-1-AR72, 2 October 1995) [70]; *Rome Statute* Article 8. See Amichai Cohen and Yuval Shany, 'Beyond the Grave Breaches Regime: The Duty to Investigate Alleged Violations of International Law Governing Armed Conflict' (2011) 14 *Yearbook of International Humanitarian Law* 37, 40.
15 For an in-depth analysis of the extraterritorial application of human rights law see Noam Lubell, *Extraterritorial Use of Force Against Non-State Actors* (2010); Marko Milanović, *Extraterritorial Application of Human Rights Treaties: Law, Principles and Policy* (2011).
16 See *Legal Consequences of the Construction of a Wall in the Occupied Palestinian Territory* (Advisory Opinion) [2004] ICJ Rep 136 [109–13] [*Wall Opinion*]; Armed Activities in the Territory of the Democratic Republic of Congo (*DRC v Uganda*) [2005] ICJ Rep 7, [216–17] [*Armed Activities*]; Human Rights Committee, General Comment No. 31: The Nature of the General Legal Obligation Imposed on States Parties to the Covenant, UN Doc CCPR/C/21/Rev.1/Add.13 (26 May 2004) [10]; *McCann v UK* (1996) 21 EHRR 97, [145–8] [*McCann*]; *Coard et al. v United States of America*, IACiHR (1999) [37]; Manfred Nowak, UN Covenant on Civil and Political Rights: CCPR Commentary (2005) 41–3; Christof Heyns, Report of the Special Rapporteur on Extrajudicial, Summary or Arbitrary Executions, 68th sess, UN Doc A/68/382 (13 September 2013) [42–51]; *Turkel Commission Second Report*, above n 2, 64–5.

The obligation to investigate violations of human rights law derives from the general obligation 'to uphold and guarantee' human rights and from the right to have 'effective remedy' by a competent authority.[17] Various human rights sources have interpreted the substantive rights and the general obligation to ensure the realisation of human rights to include the obligation to investigate human rights violations. In particular, the right to life has been interpreted to require an investigation immediately following the use of lethal force in a law enforcement context.[18] The right to life has long been acknowledged as part of custom, and a duty to investigate has long been assumed to be a central part of that norm.

Under IHRL, the range of activities requiring an investigation is much wider than under IHL. Targeted killing will most likely be prohibited under this framework because IHRL is much stricter on the circumstances in which the use of lethal force is permissible. This is based on the assumption that in law enforcement situations non-lethal measures, such as arrest, are available to the relevant authorities due to their level of control over the situation and, as such, it is rare that the nature of the threat is so imminent that lethal force is considered necessary and proportionate.[19]

Therefore, the grounds for triggering an investigation depend very much on the applicable normative framework. In the context of armed conflict, the death of an uninvolved civilian during hostilities does not of itself give rise to an immediate duty to investigate, primarily because the principle of proportionality may permit for collateral damage.[20] By way of contrast, in a situation of law

---

17 See, eg, *International Covenant on Civil and Political Rights*, opened for signature 16 December 1966, 999 UNTS 171, Art 2 (entered into force 23 March 1976); *Convention against Torture and Other Cruel, Inhumane or Degrading Treatment or Punishment*, opened for signature 10 December 1984, 1465 UNTS 85, Arts 6–8 (entered into force 26 June 1987); *Basic Principles on the Use of Force and Firearms by Law Enforcement Officials* Arts 6, 11(f), 22–3 www2.ohchr.org/english/law/firearms.htm; *Principles on the Effective Prevention and Investigation of Extra-Legal, Arbitrary and Summary Executions*, ESC Res 1989/65, UN ESCOR, 15th plen mtg, UN Doc E/RES/1989/65 (24 May 1989) Arts 9, 10, 11; *Principles on the Effective Investigation and Documentation of Torture and Other Cruel, Inhumane or Degrading Treatment or Punishment*, GA Res 55/89, UN GAOR, UN Doc A/RES/55/89 (22 February 2001) annex.

18 Human Rights Committee, General Comment No. 31, above n 16, [15], [18]; Human Rights Committee, *Views: Communication No. 563/1993* (27 October 1995) [8.6] (*Bautista de Arellana v Columbia*); The European Court of Human Rights and case law similarly imply that accountability procedures are required where the inherent right to life has been violated. See, eg, *McCann*, above n 16; *Ergi v Turkey* (2001) 32 EHRR 18, [85]; *Isayeva v Russia* (2005) 41 EHRR 38, [210–11]; *Al-Skeini v UK* (ECtHR, Grand Chamber, Application No 55721/07, 7 July 2011) [163]. Other human rights tribunals have reached similar findings. See, eg, *Case of the Ituango Massacres (Judgment)* (IACtHR, Ser C, No 148, 1 July 2006); *Case of the 'Mapiripan Massacre' (Judgment)* (IACtHR, Ser C, No 134, 15 September 2005).

19 Basic Principles, above n 17; *Principles on the Effective Prevention*, above n 17, Art 1; *McCann*, above n 16 [203–14].

20 *Turkel Commission Second Report*, above n 2, 110.

enforcement the killing (or serious injury) of an individual by security forces gives rise in itself to an immediate duty to investigate, because of the *prima facie* suspicion of criminality inherent in such a situation.[21] Whether the targeted killing operation is characterised as occurring during active combat or as law enforcement will therefore influence the judgment that a reasonable suspicion of criminality has been reached and that an investigation is required.

B. How to conduct an investigation

In addition to the grounds that would trigger an investigation, an important aspect of the duty to investigate is the manner in which the investigation is conducted. In regard to that aspect of the duty there is greater convergence under the two normative frameworks. Partly because IHL has very little *lex scripta* on the processes for fulfilling the duty to investigate, the trend has been to turn to the rich jurisprudence of IHRL, which provides detail on the manner of conducting an investigation. The general principles that comprise an 'effective investigation' are those of independence, impartiality, thoroughness and effectiveness, promptness and transparency. These principles have been recognised and accepted in UN documents as well as by scholars.[22] To date, the Turkel Commission provides the deepest analysis of the principles for conducting an effective investigation. It does so by drawing largely on the jurisprudence of the European Court for Human Rights. The Commission sees 'no fundamental difference' in the principles as they apply to a law enforcement context and an armed conflict context except that the 'precise content' of the principles may differ in their application due to sensitivity to the surrounding context and circumstances.[23]

Each principle will be briefly explained to demonstrate the way in which the Commission interpreted the interaction of the paradigms in different contexts. The principle of independence broadly relates to the requirement that the

---

21 Ibid 103.
22 See, eg, The Basic Principles and Guidelines on the Right to Remedy and Reparations for Victims of Violations of International Human Rights and Serious Violations of International Humanitarian Law, (16 December 2005) UN Doc. A/RES/60/147 (2006); Human Rights in Palestine and Other Occupied Arab Territories: *Report of the United Nations Fact Finding Mission on the Gaza Conflict*, UN Doc A/HRC/12/48 (2009) [1814]; Human Rights Council, *Report of the Committee of Independent Experts in international humanitarian and human rights law to monitor and assess any domestic, legal or other proceedings undertaken by both the Government of Israel and the Palestinian side, in light of General Assembly resolution 64/245, including the independence, effectiveness, genuineness of these investigations and their conformity with international standards*, UN Doc A/HRC/15/50 (23 September 2010) [30] [*Tomuschat Report*]; Michael N Schmitt, 'Investigating Violations of International Law in Armed Conflict' (2011) 2 *Harvard National Security Journal* 31, 83; Cohen and Shany, above n 14, 60.
23 *Turkel Commission Second Report*, above n 2, 115.

investigation be both institutionally and practically independent from the event under investigation.[24] The principle of impartiality, according to the Commission, is intended to ensure that the investigation is conducted, and is perceived to be conducted, in an unbiased fashion.[25] In the context of an armed conflict, independence and impartiality are reflected in the fact that the investigation is outside the chain of command, and by ensuring that the investigator has adequate operational knowledge to perform an effective investigation.[26] The principle of effectiveness and thoroughness addresses the means for carrying out an investigation so that it achieves the purpose of uncovering the facts, while also doing justice to the conditions of armed conflict.[27] The need to avoid unreasonable delays both in the commencement and duration of an investigation is the reason for the principle of promptness.[28] The Commission divides the principle of transparency into two duties: to inform victims (and their family members) of their rights and information concerning proceedings, and to publish the findings of the investigation.[29] The Commission came to the conclusion that it is desirable the latter apply during armed conflict because of the way it can contribute to the realisation of central aspects of the duty to investigate under IHL: compliance and deterrence.[30] The emphasis the *Turkel Report* places on transparency is in line with, but does not go as far as, a number of UN reports submitted to the General Assembly only months after the Turkel Commission published its report.[31] The UN Special Rapporteur on extrajudicial, summary or arbitrary executions took a different approach to that of the Turkel Commission when he extended the right of victims to access information to armed conflict.[32] Also worth noting in this context is that the previous Special Rapporteur on extrajudicial killings, Philip Alston, has (in his academic writing) emphasised the importance of transparency to the concept of accountability and has lamented the lack of it in the context of the US practice of targeted killing conducted by the CIA.[33]

Ultimately, because the IHL investigation requirement is limited in terms of procedural detail, the IHRL general principles can be applied to situations of armed conflict without much difficulty, provided that the IHRL procedures

---

24 Ibid 118–25.
25 Ibid 125.
26 Ibid 140–1.
27 Ibid 127–31, 141–3.
28 Ibid 132–4.
29 Ibid 90–4.
30 Ibid 145.
31 Ben Emmerson, *Promotion and Protection of Human Rights and Fundamental Freedoms while Countering Terrorism* (Interim Report), 68th sess, UN Doc A/68/389 (18 September 2013) at 44–5; Heyns, above n 16 [97].
32 Heyns, above n 16, [100].
33 See Philip Alston, 'The CIA and Targeted Killings Beyond Borders' (2011) 2 *Harvard National Security Journal* 283.

do not render the investigation ineffective during an armed conflict.[34] If this is the case, the entire basis for the investigation requirement is made redundant.[35] Alston, in his capacity as Special Rapporteur, similarly stated that the effectiveness of the investigation may impose constraints on the procedures.[36] Hence, the application of the principles must be done in a manner that helps achieve the overall aim of an 'effective investigation'. In this analysis on the interaction of IHL and IHRL norms on the question of accountability for targeted killing operations, the approach of the Turkel Commission, which carefully modified the principles for an effective investigation to situations of armed conflict, is particularly relevant. The *Report's* heavy reliance on IHRL, especially concerning the question of 'how to investigate', confirms that IHRL should come into play where lack of clarity exists in IHL.[37] This is consistent with the *lex specialis* maxim, which is the generally accepted approach to navigating the IHL/IHRL interaction.[38]

C. Concluding comments on duty to investigate

The duty to investigate under IHL and IHRL provides sufficient guidance on accountability measures. Although the interaction between the two regimes is generally complementary in regards to the manner of conducting an investigation (the general principles), the grounds for triggering an investigation differ under the two frameworks. In the context of targeted killing operations, accountability measures therefore become tricky because it presumes clarity on the dominant normative framework regulating the activity. The complexity of current day conflicts, where targeted killing is a popular means of warfare, often makes it difficult to determine which normative framework regulates the specific activity.

---

34 See, eg, Kenneth Watkin, 'Controlling the Use of Force: A Role for Human Rights Norms in Contemporary Armed Conflict' (2004) 98 *American Journal of International Law* 34; Cordula Droege, 'Elective affinities? Human Rights and Humanitarian Law' (2008) 90 *International Review of the Red Cross* 542.

35 *Tomuschat Report*, above n 22, [29]. For an instructive example of the importance of 'effectiveness' see Schmitt, 'Investigating Violations', above n 22, 84.

36 See Civil and Political Rights, including the Question of Disappearances and Summary Executions: Extrajudicial, Summary or Arbitrary Executions: Report of the Special Rapporteur, Philip Alston: Addendum, UN ESCOR, UN Doc E/CN.4/2006/53/Add.1 (26 March 2006) [36].

37 *Turkel Commission Second Report*, above n 2, 68.

38 Both IHL and IHRL apply in the context of armed conflict. To the extent that IHL (the *lex specialis*) does not provide a rule, or the rule is unclear, it is appropriate to draw guidance from IHRL (the *lex generalis*). See *Armed Activities* [216]; *Wall Opinion* [106]; *Legality of the Threat or Use of Nuclear Weapons* (Advisory Opinion) [1996] ICJ Rep 226, 256 [26] [*Nuclear Weapons Opinion*]; Human Rights Committee, General Comment No 31, above n 16, [11].

III. The principle of proportionality

Another rule that is relevant when thinking about accountability more broadly is the principle of proportionality. According to IHL, proportionality plays an important role in limiting the force of an attack against an opposing party to the conflict because it focuses on minimising loss of civilian life or damage to civilian property. Targeted killings generally occur in densely populated areas, where civilians are likely to be affected by the attack. There has been, therefore growing concern for the civilian impact of such attacks. This section will begin by reflecting upon whether the principle of proportionality under IHL can be drawn upon as a source for accountability measures. In particular, it will assess whether *ex post* investigations into targeted killing operations can remedy the applicability problems that exist due to the subjective nature of proportionality. The second part of this section will explore a tension in the relationship between accountability and proportionality, which is that under IHRL proportionality does not focus primarily on the incidental damage caused by the attack, but on the nature of lethal force intended against the specific individual.[39] Different conceptions of proportionality inform IHL and IHRL. As a consequence the legal framework that regulates targeted killing appears to oscillate between these conceptions.[40] A situation has therefore emerged in which it is not at all clear how to approach targeted killings in the context of investigations.[41] The Israeli approach, particularly in the context of the *Targeted Killing Case*, will be discussed

---

39 Proportionality under IHRL assesses the risk posed by an individual in order to determine the amount of force proportionate to the threat. It allows for the use of force in the limited circumstances where necessary. ICCPR Article 4(1); Human Rights Committee, *General Comment No 29: States of Emergency (Article 4)*, UN Doc CCPR/C/21/Rev.1/Add.11 (31 August 2001) [4]; Human Rights Committee, *Views: Communication No R.11/45*, 37th sess, UN Doc A/37/40 (5 February 1979) 137 (*de Guerrero v Colombia*).

40 For discussion of the different meanings of 'proportionality' under IHL and IHRL and the implications on the legality for targeted killing operations see Larry May, 'Targeted Killings and Proportionality in Law: Two Models' (2013) 11 *Journal of International Criminal Justice* 47. See, also Amos N. Guiora, 'Targeted Killing: When Proportionality gets all out of Proportion' (2012) 45 *Case Western Reserve Journal of International* Law 235.

41 Alston, in his in-depth analysis on accountability for CIA targeted killing operations, takes the view that 'the characterization of the applicable legal regime does not *per se* affect the general argument that an appropriate level of accountability and thus transparency is required to be observed. What is appropriate will, in turn, be affected by the applicable regime'. On the face of it Alston's position need not be in tension with the one set forth in this chapter. Alston's point is that *all* investigations require the *appropriate* level of accountability and in turn transparency, regardless of the applicable framework. However, if his position is read in conjunction with his overall premise that efforts towards accountability are *always* required in order for a State to uphold its international law obligations because to do otherwise would assume de facto immunity from the constraints of international law, then it can be assumed that Alston would have little sympathy for the emphasis on the different meanings of proportionality under the two regimes as a determining factor in accountability for targeted killings. Alston, 'CIA and Targeted Killings', above n 33, 308.

as an example of a hybrid model of assessing targeted killing, where the IHRL and IHL standards of proportionality influence the investigation requirement set out in the judgment.

A. *Proportionality as a source for accountability measures*

The principle of proportionality is a key rule in IHL.[42] It attempts to give expression to the underlying premise of this body of law, which is to minimise civilian suffering while taking cognisance of military necessity.[43] This doctrine establishes a limitation on the conduct of hostilities. It requires that any expected 'collateral damage' arising from a military attack must be proportional to the military advantage anticipated.[44] The principle of precautions in attack establishes obligations in the planning of the attack. There is a duty to take 'constant care' to restrict the incidental damage caused by attacks.[45] Thus, a positive duty is placed on military commanders and those who plan and are responsible for military operations.[46] There are two ways in which accountability can be connected to, and can complement, the principle of proportionality under IHL. The first addresses interpretations of the obligation to take precautions in attack and the second attempts to provide a remedy to alleviate the problems associated with the subjective nature of the proportionality assessment.

1. Precautions in attack

The duty to take 'feasible precaution' arguably includes an investigation of potential violations of the principle of proportionality.[47] According to Cohen and Shany:

> Investigation of past incidents in which harm has occurred is arguably part of the 'constant care' which parties are expected to demonstrate in order

---

42   *API* codifies proportionality as part of *jus in bello*. See Judith Gardam, 'Proportionality and Force in International Law' (1993) 87 *American Journal of International Law* 391.

43   The principle of proportionality attempts to balance both the principle of military necessity and humanity. See Sandoz, Swinarski and Zimmerman, above n 9, [2206]; UK Ministry of Defence, *The Manual of the Law of Armed Conflict* (2004) [3]; Leslie C Green, *The Contemporary Law of Armed Conflict* (3rd edn, 2008) 389; APV Rogers, *Law on the Battlefield* (3rd edn, 2012) 21; Michael Bothe, Karl Josef Partsch and Waldemar Solf, *New Rules for Victims of Armed Conflicts: Commentary on the Two 1977 Protocols Additional to the Geneva Conventions of 1949* (1982), 309.

44   *API* Article 51 (4), (5)(b). See, also, Bothe, Partsch and Solf above n 43, 309.

45   *API* Article 57 (1). See also Article 57 (2).

46   Henckaerts and Doswald-Beck, above n 11, rule 15.

47   See, eg, Eyal Benvenisti, *Legal Opinion Submitted to the Turkel Commission*, 'The State of Israel's obligation to examine and investigate violations of the laws of war' www.turkelcommittee.com/ files/wordocs/Benvenisti_opinion.pdf.

to assess on an ongoing basis the proportionate nature of the methods and means of warfare they employ.[48]

This reading of the duty to take precautions in attack seems an appropriate reflection of the 'constant care' requirement. The word 'constant' leaves room for the possibility of expanding the duty beyond pre-attack measures to include post-attack assessments. Other interpretations of the relationship between the duty to take precautions in attack and the duty to investigate have emerged in the literature.[49]

If the duty to take precautions in attack can be legitimately interpreted to include an investigation into past incidents, then such investigations will hopefully promote the kind of attention that needs to be paid to what the decision-makers can reasonably foresee. This is made more important by the fact that generally, as noted, targeted killing operations take place in densely populated areas. In these areas civilian presence is often changing, therefore affecting the factual scenario. Investigations after the fact will ensure a more rigorous system of assessing proportionality. In this way, a legal analysis of the targeted killing occurs both before the attack is carried out and after it occurs.

2. The subjective nature of proportionality

The second way in which accountability connects to proportionality is that investigations can compensate for the ambiguity of the proportionality assessment. The subjective dimension that is essential to the principle of proportionality inevitably creates difficulty in its application. This difficulty is unavoidable. Application of the proportionality formula is often described in terms of balancing different (and often conflicting) considerations.[50] This can be seen in the way the law forbids, on the one side, civilians from being the object of an attack because they have civilian immunity, but allows, on the other, unavoidable and incidental civilian casualties that result from a lawful attack against a military objective. Judgments of proportionality require one to weigh up the factors that will determine whether or not an attack is excessive.

---

48 Cohen and Shany, above n 14, 47.

49 Margalit, for example, argues that IHRL informs the appropriate remedy for the precautions in attack violations. Alon Margalit, 'Did LOAC Take the Lead? Reassessing Israel's Targeted Killing of Salah Shehadeh and the Subsequent Calls for Criminal Accountability' (2012) 17 *Journal of Conflict & Security Law* 147, 172.

50 'Final Report to the Prosecutor by the Committee Established to review the NATO Bombing Campaign against the Federal Republic of Yugoslavia' (2000) [48] www.icty.org/x/file/About/OTP/otp_report_nato_bombing_en.pdf: '[i]t is much easier to formulate the principle of proportionality in general terms than it is to apply it to a particular set of circumstances because the comparison is often between unlike quantities and values. One cannot easily assess the value of innocent human lives as opposed to capturing a particular military objective.'

There is little consensus on whether the subjective nature of the proportionality test is its flaw or its strength. Despite criticisms of the subjective nature of proportionality,[51] many commentators (in particular those with military experience) reject introducing criteria that they believe would be rigid in their application.[52] Such criteria are unworkable (those commentators argue) because they do not allow for the flexibility inherent in the very concept of proportionality, which requires balancing conflicting objectives. In accepting that the principle of proportionality entails 'constructive ambiguity', one commentator cautioned that 'the scale should always be tilted in favour of furthering the protection of the civilian population'.[53] *Ex post* investigations are one way of achieving that 'tilt'.

Setting up an investigation after every targeted killing is a valuable way to remedy the limited concept of proportionality under IHL, which assesses the expected damage.[54] This proposal deviates from the IHL requirement that limits investigation to credible allegations of war crimes and, accordingly, the proposal is based on humanitarian reasons. The *Air and Missile Warfare Manual* explains that 'the consequences that actually flow from an attack come into play in the course of an *ex post* evaluation of whether the attacker ought reasonably to have expected the resulting collateral damage'.[55] Therefore, the IHRL requirement to investigate every use of lethal force should be strongly considered to apply to situations of active combat based on an attempt to give meaning to the principle of proportionality without suggesting that it is required by that principle. Indeed, practice seems to indicate that a number of States investigate all cases involving civilian death.[56]

51   See, eg, Antonio Cassese, 'The Prohibition of Indiscriminate Means of Warfare' in Robert J Akkerman, Peter J van Krieken and Charles O Pannenborg (eds), *Declarations on Principles: A Quest for Universal Peace* (1979) 171, 184.

52   William J Fenrick, 'The Rule of Proportionality and Protocol I in Conventional Warfare' (1982) *Military Law Review* 107, 126; Stefan Oeter, 'Methods and Means of Combat' in Dieter Fleck (ed.), *The Handbook of Humanitarian Law in Armed Conflict* (Oxford University Press, 2nd edn, 2008) 173.

53   Jason D Wright, '"Excessive" Ambiguity: Analysing and Refining the Proportionality Standard' (2012) 94 *International Review of the Red Cross* 819, 853.

54   See Gabriella Blum and Philip Heymann, 'Law and Policy of Targeted Killing' (2010) 1 *Harvard National Security Journal* 145, 159.

55   Program on Humanitarian Policy and Conflict Research at Harvard University, *Commentary on the HPCR Manual on International Law Applicable to Air and Missile Warfare* (2010) rule 14(5), 91 http://ihlresearch.org/amw/Commentary%20on%20the%20HPCR%20Manual.pdf. See also Amichai Cohen and Yuval Shany, 'A Development of Modest Proportions: The Application of the Principle of Proportionality in the *Targeted Killings* Case' (2007) 5 *Journal of International Criminal Justice* 310, 319.

56   In the *Turkel Report* comparative survey of six military justice systems, it found that in five of the countries surveyed, a factual investigation is conducted into all civilian deaths (absent of a suspicion of an offence) as a matter of policy or practice. See *Turkel Commission Second Report*, above n 2, 263.

B. The Israeli approach: the Targeted Killing Case and beyond

In December 2006 the Israeli Supreme Court ruled on the legality of Israel's policy of targeted killing (*Targeted Killing Case*). The judgment determined that targeted killings must be assessed on a case-by-case basis. It held that if the target is deemed to be legitimate in accordance with the Court's interpretation of the meaning of 'civilian directly participating in hostilities', the operation must still adhere to certain requirements in order to be permissible. One of those requirements is that a retrospective, independent investigation must occur 'regarding the precision of the identification of the target and the circumstances of the attack upon him'.[57] By requiring an investigation after *every* targeted killing, it is clear that Chief Justice (Ret.) Barak does not believe that targeted killings generally amount to war crimes: that would be inconsistent with his finding that it cannot be determined in advance that every targeted killing is legal. Therefore the likelihood of civilian deaths and injury during an otherwise legal targeted killing operation may be what motivated Barak CJ to include a requirement beyond the obligations of the chosen normative framework for assessing targeted killing (IHL). It is for this reason that one of the references used in the judgment to support this requirement was a *European Court of Human Rights Case*.[58] As with the arrest requirement, the judgment indicates the influence of IHRL on its consideration of the legality of targeted killing.

The relevance of proportionality to the investigation requirement is worth reflecting upon here. The investigation requirement is based on an institutional aspect of proportionality *stricto sensu* that exists under Israeli domestic law.[59] Proportionality under Israeli law is more akin to the IHRL concept of proportionality than the IHL principle.[60] As mentioned in the introduction to this section, proportionality is a key concept in both IHL and IHRL, yet their meanings are very different.[61]

---

57 Public Committee against Torture in Israel v Government of Israel [2006] HCJ 769/02 [*Targeted Killings* case] http://elyon1.court.gov.il/files_eng/02/690/007/a34/02007690.a34.pdf [40]. See also Separate Opinion of Chief Justice (Ret.) Beinisch.

58 *McKerr v The United Kingdom*, 34 EHRR 553, 559 (2001).

59 Cohen and Shany, 'A Development of Modest Proportions', above n 55, 312.

60 David Kretzmer, 'Rethinking the Application of IHL in Non-International Armed Conflicts' (2009) 42 *Israel Law Review* 8, 19. For a brief summary of the Israeli domestic law three-step test to proportionality see Aharon Barak, 'Proportional Effect – The Israeli Experience' (2007) 14 (on file with the author). See also Yuval Shany, 'Competing Legal Paradigms for Fighting Terror' in Orna Ben-Naftali (ed.), *International Humanitarian Law and International Human Rights Law: Pas de Deux* (2011) 26–7.

61 See Noam Lubell, 'Challenges in Applying Human Rights Law to Armed Conflict' (2005) 87 *International Review of the Red Cross* 745–6; Nils Melzer, *Targeted Killing in International Law* (2008), 359 (fn 260). Although this chapter is concerned with the meanings of proportionality under IHL and IHRL it is important to note that there are additional meanings of this principle under international law. See, Wright, above n 53, 836.

In understanding why the *Targeted Killing Case* chose to base the investigation requirement on the IHRL concept of proportionality it is necessary to refer to what the judgment says about proportionality under IHL. In the *Targeted Killing Case* Barak CJ (Ret.) explained that a balance must be achieved between conflicting values. He called this 'a value based test'.[62] Barak CJ acknowledged that 'performing [the] balance is difficult'. For that reason the law should 'proceed case by case'.[63] He recognised that there are many 'hard cases'. Barak CJ emphasised that the customary rule protecting civilians is central to the principle of proportionality.[64] Barak CJ offered no simple formula and concluded that 'despite the difficulty of that balancing, there's no choice but to perform it'.[65] Deputy Chief Justice (Ret.) Rivlin also warned that 'the decision is likely to be difficult and complex'.[66] In relation to the principle of proportionality Barak CJ makes the following subtle suggestion:

> [T]he possibility of concentrating that law into the legal category to which it belongs, while formulating a comprehensive doctrine of proportionality, as is common in the internal law of many states, should be considered. That cannot be examined in the framework of the petition before us. We shall concentrate upon the aspect of proportionality which is accepted, without exception, as relevant to the subject under discussion.[67]

Thus, while the *Targeted Killing Case* made the decision that it was beyond the scope of the judgment to propose changes to the IHL principle of proportionality, the requirements it placed on targeted killing, such as investigation and arrest, tacitly revealed its preferred approach to proportionality. The arrest requirement also reflects an aspect of the proportionality test under Israeli law (the 'less harmful measure').[68]

---

62 *Targeted Killing Case* [45].

63 Ibid 46.

64 Ibid 45; *API* Article 51(2)(III).

65 Ibid.

66 Ibid 5 (Separate Opinion of Deputy Chief Justice (Ret.) Rivlin). Rivlin devoted a large part of his concurring opinion to the principle of proportionality. The obligation upon the State to honour the lives of civilians and the principle of human dignity is integral to his discussion.

67 Ibid 44.

68 The *Targeted Killing Case*'s 'less harmful means' requirement creates even greater confusion than the investigation requirement because of the Judgment's lack of clarity in stating explicitly the body of (international) law upon which the arrest requirement was based. This has contributed to the debate surrounding the ICRC Guidance on DPH and Section IX of the Guidance ('restraints on the use of force') because the *Targeted Killing Case* was referenced as support for the position that IHL requires restraints on the use of force. Melzer, the author of the Guidance, discusses the relevance of the IHRL principle of proportionality to the 'capture v kill' debate in his book and there too he relies on the *Targeted Killings Case*'s less harmful means requirement. See Melzer, *Targeted Killing*, above n 61, 294, 286; 359 (fn 260); ICRC, *Interpretive Guidance on the Notion of Direct Participation in Hostilities under International Humanitarian Law* (2009) 81;

The investigation requirement indicates that on the one hand the *lex generalis* (the IHRL duty to investigate every death) is supplanting the *lex specialis* (the IHL duty to investigate alleged war crimes) and it therefore appears to be reversing the application of the *lex specialis* maxim. On the other hand, the requirement to investigate every targeted killing gives expression to the *lex specialis* because a retrospective investigation is a way to fill the gap in the process started by the *ex ante* proportionality assessment. The *Targeted Killing Case* combines IHL and IHRL standards in creating an obligation to investigate every targeted killing. It is for this reason that the *Targeted Killing Case*'s approach has been described as a 'mixed' or 'hybrid' model. It is a fair reading of the judgment to conclude that the requirement, based on proportionality under IHRL, to investigate every targeted killing, is implicitly motivated by dissatisfaction with the difficulties and vagueness of the IHL principle of proportionality. *Ex post* investigations will almost certainly contribute to minimising civilian harm.[69]

Larry May contends that during armed conflict proportionality is increasingly being interpreted in human rights terms and provides the example of the *Targeted Killing Case*'s less harmful means requirement (ie, arrest). May endorses the Court's approach and proposes that proportionality be understood to place restrictions on when an individual can be killed, particularly if they can be captured instead. He arrives at the conclusion that:

> Not only does proportionality concern the lives and property of civilians, as well as the natural environment, but also, it is my view that proportionality calculations must be made concerning the killing of the terrorist 'combatant'. This means that there must be a calculation (almost surely by an impartial institution) that the killing of the terrorist is not disproportionate in light of the military objective to be achieved by this death.[70]

Nils Melzer, 'Keeping the Balance between Military Necessity and Humanity: A Response to Four Critiques on the ICRC's Interpretive Guidance on the Notion of Direct Participation in Hostilities' (2010) 42 *New York Journal of International Law and Politics* 831, 898–9, 902, 903, 912. For criticism see W Hays Parks, 'Part IX of the ICRC "Direct Participation in Hostilities" Study: No Mandate, No Expertise and Legally Incorrect' (2010) 42 *International Law and Politics* 769, 793.

69 Cohen and Shany, 'A Development of Modest Proportions' above n 55, 319.

70 May, above n 40, 61. It should be noted that central to May's argument is the distinction he makes between targeted killings that follow the IHL model and those that follow the domestic law enforcement model. According to his thesis the former model is grounded in status (such as group membership) and the latter is grounded in conduct/behaviour. He argues for a hybrid approach in targeted killing cases. However, a case could be made that in the debate surrounding the meaning of 'direct participation in hostilities' the conduct/behaviour of the individual informs whether they fall into the status of 'civilians directly participating in hostilities'. If this argument is accepted then his position that the IHRL conception of proportionality should inform targeted killing assessments becomes less compelling.

What is interesting for the purposes of the relationship between proportionality and accountability is that May argues that proportionality calculations must be conducted by an 'impartial institution'.[71] He conceives this assessment to occur before the targeted killing in order to determine whether there are grounds to go ahead with the operation.[72] However, a case could be made that a similar assessment by a suitable mechanism should occur after the operation as a way to remedy the difficulties with the commander making a proportionality calculation before the fact. The importance of the mechanism being 'impartial' is connected to the subjective nature of the proportionality assessment, which can, of course, be argued either way, depending on how one interprets the term 'excessive'. It is therefore important that the assessment is made in a sober and independent manner.

1. Implementing the investigation requirement

In order to more fully understand the relevance of proportionality to investigations it is important to examine how Israel has implemented this judicial requirement. Since the *Targeted Killing Case* was handed down in 2006, there has not been public confirmation that a committee has been established to investigate every targeted killing. A 2008 *Ha'aretz* newspaper report on targeted killing found that 'a committee to examine the assassination after the fact has yet to be appointed'.[73] According to *Ha'aretz* the then Attorney General Menachem Mazuz instructed the Prime Minister that '[t]his step must be completed without further delay . . . for fear that a continued delay is liable to constitute contempt of court'.[74]

The January 2011 *Thabat Thabat Case*, however, indicates that a permanent committee has indeed been established. That case is also relevant because of its interpretation of proportionality in relation to the investigation requirement. Dr Thabat was killed by Israel in 2000.[75] In January 2002, his wife petitioned the Supreme Court to order the Attorney General to open a criminal

---

71 May does little more to elaborate on what kind of institution should carry out this assessment: 'I will not pursue the question of what would be the best institution to assess proportionality in such cases.' May, above n 40, 58.

72 'In the majority of cases some kind of judicial or quasi-judicial proceeding should precede the targeted killing.' Ibid 63.

73 Uri Blau, 'License to Kill', *Ha'aretz* (Tel Aviv), 28 November 2008, 9.

74 Ibid.

75 Thabat was a dentist with the United Nations Relief Works Agency and the Secretary of the Fatah organisation in Tul-Karem. Criticism was mounted that Thabat did not play a military role in the organisation and was a great supporter of the peace process. Israel claimed that Thabat's 'role as commander of a Tanzim cell, who instructed his people where to carry out attacks . . . removes him from the civilian category'. See, eg, Orna Ben-Naftali and Keren Michaeli, '"We Must Not Make a Scarecrow of the Law": A Legal Analysis of the Israeli Policy of Targeted Killing' (2003) 36 *Cornell International Law Journal* 234, 280.

investigation into the targeted killing of her husband. The request was suspended until after the *Targeted Killing Case* was handed down. The *Thabat Thabat Case* confirmed that there is a requirement to investigate targeted killings, as that had been established in the *Targeted Killing Case*. The 2011 judgment stated that it is necessary to conduct a thorough and retrospective investigation on a case-by-case basis to determine if a civilian taking a direct part in the hostilities, or innocent civilians, were killed or injured and whether the harm caused breached the principle of proportionality. However, it is unclear whether Chief Justice (Ret.) Beinisch was referring to the IHRL or IHL principle of proportionality.[76] In the Judge's view she obviously thought the proportionality assessment applies to both the target and the incidental damage. She did not, however, elaborate on whether she meant that the assessment must determine if the target met the anticipated military advantage in order to justify that the expected civilian casualties was not excessive; or alternatively, whether she meant that the proportionality assessment must determine the risk posed by the civilian depending on if s/he was directly participating in hostilities, as well as the potential harm to that civilian and to bystanders. Another way that her emphasis on proportionality could be interpreted is that she believes that only targeted killings that provoke a suspicion that the principle of proportionality has been breached require an investigation.

Beinisch CJ dismissed the petition in part because the petitioners failed to make use of the 'special commission' and because the Supreme Court should only hear cases after they have been reviewed by that commission. It is therefore reasonable to conclude from this judgment that such a permanent commission exists, but that its mandate has not been made public. Consequently it is unknown whether every targeted killing is investigated (as set out in the *Targeted Killing Case*) or only those that prompted a suspicion that there had been a breach of proportionality. There is equally no information about whether any disciplinary or other measures have been taken as a result of such investigations. When speculating about whether such a commission exists, it is relevant to note that although the *Targeted Killing Case* did not require its existence to be made public, the failure to do so is consistent with growing calls that forms of accountability for targeted killing operations be transparent.[77] Interestingly, however, the *Turkel Report* does not specify that accountability measures for targeted killing operations be transparent.[78]

---

76   *Tabet v Attorney-General* (2011) HCJ 474/02 (unreported, Hebrew), [10].
77   See Emmerson, above n 31; Heyns, above n 16; Alston, above n 33.
78   Targeted killing operations would arguably require a 'fact-finding assessment' created by the Commission. The Commission briefly touches on how to conduct a fact-finding assessment effectively and references some of the general principles, but transparency is not included. It emphasises that a fact-finding assessment must be conducted according to its purpose, which is to collect relevant information about the alleged incident that facilitates rather than hinders a subsequent investigation. *Turkel Commission Second Report*, above n 2, 147–8.

Prior to the *Thabat Thabat Decision*, the *Shehadeh Case*[79] is one of the only investigations into a targeted killing publicly known because the Supreme Court – in response to a petition – especially appointed it. Similar to the *Thabat Thabat Case*, the 2003 petition requesting a criminal investigation into the targeted killing of Shehadeh was suspended until the *Targeted Killing Case*. In 2007, the Court requested that the State examine the circumstances in which innocent civilians were killed during the Shehadeh operation and that, in the spirit of the instructions set out in the *Target Killing Case*, this be done by an objective body.[80] In February 2011, 3 years after the Strasberg-Cohen Commission was established and almost 9 years after the targeted killing, it submitted its report to the Prime Minister.[81] According to the eight page declassified summary of the report, the Commission found Shehadeh to be a civilian directly participating in hostilities[82] and that the attack was not disproportionate according to IHL.[83] In regard to both these findings, however, the Commission turned to IHRL language in applying IHL concepts, thereby creating confusion: '[t]he situation necessitated effective, immediate and pinpointed measures to eliminate or at least minimize the attacks'.[84] Significantly, on the question of proportionality the Commission did find the collateral damage to be excessive, however, because

79 At midnight on 22 July 2002, in the residential al-Daraj' neighbourhood in Gaza City, an Israeli fighter plane dropped a one-tonne bomb on a building to kill the leader of Hamas military wing Salah Shehadeh. It also killed fourteen bystanders, nine of whom were children, and injured more than seventy people. The bomb landed with precision, but caused a huge crater and tremendous destruction. See, eg, Amos Harel, 'Analysis: From a "Pinpoint Operation to Massive Casualties"', *Ha'aretz* (Tel Aviv), 24 July 2002 www.haaretz.com/print-edition/news/analysis-from-a-pinpoint-operation-to-massive-casualties-1.38889. See, also, Sharon Weill, 'The Targeted Killing of Salah Shehadeh: From Gaza to Madrid' (2009) 7 *Journal of International Criminal Justice* 617.

80 *Yoav Hess v Judge Advocate General* (2008) HCJ 8794/03. For English translation of the judgment see www.adh-geneva.ch/RULAC/pdf_state/HCJ-decision-8794-03-1-.pdf.

81 An unclassified summary of the report containing the main findings of the Commission was published: Ministry of Foreign Affairs, *Summary of Strasberg-Cohen Report* http://mfa.gov.il/MFA/AboutIsrael/State/Law/Pages/Salah_Shehadeh-Special_Investigatory_Commission_27-Feb-2011.aspx. The full report contains facts concerning national security and was therefore not disclosed to the public. For an analysis of the legality of the Shehadeh targeting and a critique of the Commission's report see Margalit, above n 49, 147.

82 Summary of Shehadeh investigation, above n 81, [6], [9].

83 Ibid [10], [13]–[14].

84 Ibid [6], [9]. The Commission's confusion between taking the position that the required proportionality balance was not achieved yet concluding that the operation was proportionate because it was unforeseen is repeated throughout the report: at [26]. The press did question whether the summary that was released was written by the Commission itself or the Prime Minister's Office. If the latter wrote the summary then these criticisms about confusing IHL and IHRL cannot be attributed to the Commission itself. See Barak Ravid, 'Civilian Deaths in Shehadeh hit unintentional, Committee says', *Ha'aretz* (Tel Aviv), 1 March 2001 www.haaretz.com/print-edition/news/civilian-deaths-in-shehadeh-hit-unintentional-committee-says-1.346338.

it was the result of faulty intelligence, it was not expected, and therefore did not violate IHL. Nor did it develop further its discussion of proportionality, including what was the expected collateral damage in the attack, and it also did not make a determination on whether the obligation to take feasible precautions was breached.[85] The Commission found that no criminal offence had been committed by any of those involved in the operation.[86]

The emphasis that seems to be placed on the principle of proportionality in these accountability measures, post the *Targeted Killing Case*, is echoed in the Military Advocate General (MAG) of the Israel Defense Force (IDF)'s approach to investigations. According to IHL the principle of proportionality is the determining factor in whether an investigation is required. This is reflected in the MAG's investigations into incidents occurring during Operation Pillar of Defense in November 2012.[87] Although not all operations were targeted killings, the overall approach of the MAG is nonetheless telling. In April 2013, it publicly issued an update on the investigative process. The document stated that in relation to the eighty-seven incidents that were cited as having occurred during Operation Pillar of Defense, it found no basis to open criminal investigations into approximately sixty-five incidents. Moreover, with respect to fifteen incidents, additional information was required in order to make a decision whether to open an investigation.[88] The main conclusion that the MAG's update draws about the operation as a whole relates to proportionality: 'a considerable emphasis was put on minimising collateral damage to uninvolved civilians and civilian property, beyond the requirements of the Law of Armed Conflict'.[89]

There is reason to be uneasy about the fact that in those sixty-five cases not a single investigation was opened in an operation where civilian casualties occurred. The reason for unease is compounded by the growing intolerance among public opinion for civilian casualties at war. It is worth noting that a 2013 report by the UN Special Rapporteur on Counterterrorism and Human Rights differentiated the Israeli practice of invoking the principle of proportionality to

---

85 For a critique of these aspects of the *Report* see Margalit, above n 49, 160, 167.

86 Summary of Shehadeh investigation, above n 81, [14].

87 The IDF launched Pillar of Defense in the Gaza Strip and the operation lasted eight days, until a ceasefire was reached between Israel and Hamas. According to the IDF, it attacked 1500 targets inside the Gaza Strip and Palestinian militant groups fired over 1500 rockets at Israel. Five Israeli civilians were killed from rocket fire. Statistics compiled by B'Tselem indicate that Israel killed 167 Palestinians, including at least 87 that did not take part in hostilities, 32 of whom were minors. See IDF, *Operation Pillar of Defense: Summary of Events* (22 November 2012) www.idfblog.com/2012/11/22/operation-pillar-of-defense-summary-of-events/;
Shuli Schneiderman ed., B'Tselem, *Human Rights Violations During Operation Pillar of Defense: 14–21 November 2012* (May 2013) www.btselem.org/download/201305_pillar_of_defense_operation_eng.pdf.

88 IDF, The Examination of Alleged Misconduct During Operation 'Pillar of Defense' – An Update, www.law.idf.il/SIP_STORAGE/files/4/1364.pdf.

89 Ibid.

justify civilian casualties, from the practice of the United Kingdom and the United States. The latter countries do not authorise aerial strikes even if civilian casualties would be rendered 'proportionate' because of high-value military targets.[90] The difficulties inherent in the subjective nature of proportionality would be somewhat assuaged by requiring an *ex post* investigation because this would reduce the likelihood that the subjective nature of the principle would be exploited to demonstrate that no investigation is required because there is no suspicion of criminality.

Although it is less convincing to make a case that every incident that occurred during an operation like Pillar of Defense requires an investigation, the MAG's investigative approach to this operation is revealing because of its dramatic conclusion, on the basis of the principle of proportionality, that no investigations into sixty-five incidents are required.[91] In a practice like targeted killing, however, it seems more plausible to make a case that investigations are indeed required after every targeted killing. The *Turkel Report* in fact proposes as much. The Turkel Commission introduces the concept of a 'fact-finding assessment'. It is a preliminary assessment into certain incidents where the threshold of a reasonable suspicion that would trigger an investigation of whether war crime has been committed has not been met, but where more information is required.[92] According to the Commission, clarification as to whether an investigation is needed is particularly relevant when an 'exceptional incident has occurred', one which points to facts or circumstances that might subsequently reveal the need for an investigation. The example the Commission provides of such an incident is 'civilian casualties that were not anticipated when the attack was planned'.[93] A case could be made that targeted killing operations which appear to meet the proportionality requirement, albeit with civilian casualties, would fall into this category. It is worth noting that the UN Special Rapporteur on Counter-terrorism and Human Rights welcomed the Turkel Commission's fact-finding assessment as an appropriate preliminary investigation into drone attacks.[94]

C. Concluding comments on proportionality

Applications of the principle of proportionality are controversial and there are arguments over whether there are intrinsic tensions that make such controversy

---

90 Emmerson, above n 31, at [75]. See, also, United States, Office of the President, Fact Sheet: US policy standards on the use of force in counterterrorism operations outside the United States and areas of active hostilities, 23 May 2013 www.whitehouse.gov/the-press-office/2013/05/23/fact-sheet-us-policy-standards-and-procedures-use-force-counterterrorism.

91 More generally, see Droege, above n 34, 542.

92 *Turkel Commission Second Report*, above n 2, 102–3; 106.

93 Ibid 103.

94 Heyns, above n 16, at [45]; Emmerson, above n 31, [45]. Special Rapporteur Emmerson expanded the Commission's approach to include the application of the principle of transparency to this preliminary investigation.

inescapable. A margin of appreciation is deliberately built into the law. This necessarily creates lack of clarity in the law. The subjective nature of the principle means that it can be exploited.

A brief survey of the Israeli practice shows that investigations do not occur after every targeted killing and that the subjective nature of the principle of proportionality is generally relied on to justify the claim that because there is no reason to suspect a breach of IHL there is no requirement to investigate. This contrasts with Israeli legal documents such as the *Targeted Killing Case* and the *Turkel Report*, which advocate a more rigorous approach to accountability. Thus, it appears that the relevant Israeli institutions have interpreted the *Targeted Killing Case* as saying that an investigation is required only when there is a suspicion that proportionality has been breached. This is in line with a strictly IHL reading of the duty to investigate (ie, where there is a reasonable suspicion of a war crime). Like all legal documents, the judgment is open to various valid interpretations; however, it is regrettable that the judgment's attempt to combine IHL and IHRL standards in its investigation requirement has not been adopted in practice.[95]

IV. Conclusion

Accountability for targeted killing operations requires greater clarity about the duty to investigate under international law. This duty, in its current developing stage, can be understood as imposing an obligation on States to conduct an 'effective investigation' in cases of a reasonable suspicion of violations of international law.[96] Such investigations must adhere to the standards of independence, impartiality, effectiveness and thoroughness, promptness and transparency.

From the perspective of the legality of targeted killings, it seems clear that targeted killing operations and drone attacks that occur in the context of an armed conflict, where the target was not a legitimate target for attack, or where the number of civilians killed as a result of the attack was excessive according to the rule on proportionality, then an investigation is required because there is a reasonable suspicion that a war crime has been committed. Where there is no reasonable suspicion of a war crime, then an argument could be made that a 'fact-finding assessment' (proposed by the Turkel Commission) is required because of the exceptional nature of such an operation, which, more often than

---

95 One of the main reasons Alston cautions against the often-made suggestion that the US should follow the Israeli approach is that: 'a major problem in this regard lies in the gap that separates that court's normative framework from the practice that has followed in supposedly implementing it.' Alston, above n 33, 411. See, also 415–16.

96 In the context of targeted killing, under IHL, alleged war crimes and other 'serious violations' require an investigation. Under IHRL, every death and serious injury requires an immediate investigation.

not, occurs in areas densely populated with civilians. Targeted killing operations that occur in the context of a law enforcement situation automatically require an investigation because of the suspected criminality under IHRL that any lethal use of force poses.

Often, however, it is difficult to determine the dominant normative framework in targeted killing operations. The way in which some of those killings are remotely operated and orchestrated raises political and moral questions that severely test the adequacy of the both legal frameworks to current realities. Civilian deaths are the predictable and constant consequence of targeted killings. Those deaths are the most important part of moral, legal and political realities. If, as seems to be the case, the law does not afford civilians sufficient protections in the changed conditions of warfare, then there are strong humanitarian reasons to impose constraints on targeted killings, even if, as things stand, many of them are not strictly unlawful. To do so would be to support the idea that every targeted killing should be investigated.

6 Humanitarian access in international humanitarian law

The case of Syria and Security Council Resolution 2139 (2014)

Phoebe Wynn-Pope[1]

I. Introduction

Twenty years ago the fastest genocide in history took place and, as the world watched on, 800,000 Tutsis were hunted down, targeted and killed as a part of a systematic process of elimination. Just a year later, in 1995, 8000 men and boys in Srebrenica were killed in the worst massacre in Europe since World War II. These events have had a profound effect on how the international community approaches its response to armed conflict. By the end of the 1990s the United Nations Security Council had identified the *protection of civilians in armed conflict* as a thematic concern.[2] Two years later the seminal *Responsibility to Protect Report* was published.[3] This report noted that while it was the responsibility of a State to safeguard and protect its population, when a State was failing to protect its own people, the international community had a responsibility to do so. At the World Summit in 2005 the international community unanimously agreed that there was a responsibility for the international community to help protect populations, wherever they are, from four international crimes: genocide, crimes against humanity, war crimes and ethnic cleansing.[4]

---

1 Dr Phoebe Wynn-Pope is Director of International Humanitarian Law at the Australian Red Cross, and a Fellow at the Asia Pacific Centre for Military Law, University of Melbourne. I would like to thank Professor Tim McCormack who has provided me with unmeasured and generous help and guidance. It has been a great honour and privilege to study with him. The views expressed in this chapter are exclusively mine and do not represent any institutional position. I would like to acknowledge the assistance of Fauve Kurnadi in the preparation of this chapter.

2 Phoebe Wynn-Pope, *Evolution of the Protection of Civilians in Armed Conflict* (February 2013) Oxfam Australia and Australian Civil-Military Centre www.oxfam.org.au/2013/05/research-for-protection/ and http://acmc.gov.au/in-search-of-common-ground-protection-of-civilians-in-armed-conflict/.

3 The International Commission on Intervention and State Sovereignty, *The Responsibility to Protect: Research, Bibliography, Background* (December 2001) International Coalition for the Responsibility to Protect http://responsibilitytoprotect.org/index.php/publications.

4 *2005 World Summit Outcome*, GA Res 60/1, 60th sess, UN Doc A/Res/60/1 (24 October 2005).

Despite increasing recognition of the collective responsibility of the international community to protect civilians caught up in situations of armed conflict, to date the international community has been ineffective in the face of severe human suffering in Syria. There may have been little opportunity to provide physical protection to the people of Syria, but at a minimum, when protection fails, the provision of effective humanitarian assistance should be available. However, access to the civilian population in Syria has been limited at best, and reports of widespread malnutrition, limited and restricted access to healthcare, and general deprivation have been alarming despite a Security Council resolution demanding the facilitation and expansion of humanitarian relief operations.[5]

This chapter will explore the effectiveness of international humanitarian law obligations on States and parties to a conflict in providing humanitarian assistance, or allowing humanitarian organisations access to civilian populations in both international and non-international armed conflict as a critical function in the protection of civilians. This will be done in three sections. The first section will seek to identify the right to humanitarian assistance in armed conflict through the framework of international humanitarian law. The second section will review the current situation in Syria, the UN Security Council's response to the humanitarian crisis through UN Security Council Resolution 2139,[6] and the subsequent implementation of that resolution. The third section will consider whether the denial of humanitarian assistance may be considered a war crime and the implications that the lack of humanitarian access to the Syrian population has for humanitarian action in the future.

II. Humanitarian access in international humanitarian law

A. The nature of humanitarian assistance

The nature of humanitarian assistance offered and provided for in international humanitarian law is contextually based in the development of humanitarian practice. In 1991, the UN General Assembly established the Department for Humanitarian Affairs (DHA) (now the UN Office for the Coordination of Humanitarian Affairs – UNOCHA) and tasked it with coordinating the UN's efforts to provide humanitarian assistance in times of crisis.[7] The General Assembly resolution establishing the DHA borrowed from the fundamental

---

5 *United Nations Security Council Resolution*, SC Res 2139, 7116th mtg, UN Doc S/RES/2139 (22 February 2014), 4 (SC Resolution 2139, UN Doc S/RES/2139).

6 Ibid.

7 Strengthening of the coordination of humanitarian emergency assistance of the United Nations GA Res 46, 78th plen mtg, UN Doc A/RES/46/182 (19 December 1991) (GA Resolution 46, UN Doc A/RES/46/182).

principles of the Red Cross and Red Crescent Movement,[8] and noted that '[h]umanitarian assistance must be provided in accordance with the principles of humanity, neutrality and impartiality'.[9]

This resolution helps us to understand the nature of humanitarian action today. It also contributes to a picture of what constitutes 'humanitarian assistance' and 'relief' in the context of armed conflict where international humanitarian law applies. At the United Nations, a call for humanitarian access and protection for humanitarian actors seeking to provide assistance in times of armed conflict is often accompanied by a requirement for the delivery of such assistance to be consistent with the 'humanitarian principles'.

These three principles of humanity, neutrality and impartiality, each of which are given definition in the *Statutes of the International Red Cross and Red Crescent Movement*, form the basis of all humanitarian action. 'Humanity' relates to the humanitarian imperative and the need to alleviate and redress human suffering wherever it is found.[10] The General Assembly resolution, consistent with the protections offered in international humanitarian law, draws particular attention to vulnerable groups such as children, women and the elderly, and ensures that the dignity and rights of all people should be both respected and protected. 'Neutrality' demands that any humanitarian assistance be provided without engaging in hostilities or taking sides in controversies of a 'political, racial, religious or ideological nature'.[11] This principle is strictly adhered to by the Red Cross and Red Crescent Movement, which is mandated and bound by international humanitarian law. However, it is a principle increasingly difficult for many multi-mandate human rights-based humanitarian organisations to maintain in light of their own organisational standards. In Afghanistan, after the fall of the Taliban, Fiona Terry noted:

[I]n the euphoric period following the ousting of the Taliban regime, they [international NGOs] uncritically accepted the 'post-conflict' and 'stabilization' discourses that designated an end to the need for humanitarian assistance, and hence the principles that guided them. The overwhelming majority embraced a role in 'post conflict' reconstruction and development efforts, and joined the political project to extend the government's legitimacy throughout the country. A neutral approach was deemed 'impossible', 'old fashioned', and even morally contestable in these new conflicts, and the integrated political – military – 'humanitarian' approach to state-building was embraced as the way of the future.[12]

---

8 Hugo Slim, 'Relief Agencies and Moral Standing in War: Principles of Neutrality, Impartiality and Solidarity' (1997) 7(4) *Development in Practice* 342.
9 *GA Resolution* 46, UN Doc A/RES/46/182.
10 *Statutes of the International Red Cross and Red Crescent Movement* (adopted by the 25th International Conference of the Red Cross at Geneva in 1986, amended in 1995 and 2006), preamble.
11 Ibid.
12 Fiona Terry, 'The International Committee of the Red Cross in Afghanistan: Reasserting the Neutrality of Humanitarian Action' (2011) 93(881) *International Review of the Red Cross*, 176.

Discussion and debate around the role of neutrality, humanitarian assistance and the role of NGOs in stabilisation and post-conflict development programmes raged and remained unresolved in the humanitarian community.[13] The question of neutrality remains difficult and, where agencies have been perceived to lose their neutrality, it is possible they may also lose access. This occurred in Darfur after the *ICC* indicted President Al-Bashir for war crimes and crimes against humanity.[14] Accused of bearing witness for the ICC, 13 of the largest aid agencies working in Darfur were expelled and operations suspended.

The third key humanitarian principle, 'impartiality', requires humanitarian assistance to be provided on the basis of need without discriminating as to 'nationality, race, religious beliefs, class or political opinions'.[15] Priority must be given to those in most immediate distress.

These three principles provide the basis of humanitarian action both at the United Nations and in the broader humanitarian community, and offer a measure of transparency and accountability for humanitarian assistance wherever it may take place. The principles also provide a clear understanding for the type of work that is considered humanitarian assistance in the context of this chapter.

1. The right to humanitarian assistance

(A) INTERNATIONAL ARMED CONFLICT

In 1949, the *Geneva Convention relative to the Protection of Civilian Persons in Time of War* was adopted (hereafter the *Fourth Geneva Convention*).[16] This Convention relates to the protection of civilians in international armed conflict. As international law recognises that a State has responsibility for the safety of its own populations and people in its jurisdiction, the *Fourth Geneva Convention* did not provide for the protection of all civilians but only those 'who find themselves

---

13 World Vision commissioned a report to explore the complexities facing multi-mandate agencies in armed conflict: Hugo Slim and Miriam Bradley, *Principled Humanitarian Action and Ethical Tensions in Multi-mandate Organisations in Armed Conflict* (2013). Also see Terry, above n 12; Lin Cotterrell, *Human Rights and Poverty Reduction: Approaches to Human Rights in Humanitarian Crises* (October 2005) The Overseas Development Institute, www.odi.org.uk/sites/odi.org.uk/files/odi-assets/publications-opinion-files/4345.pdf; Hugo Slim and Andrew Bonwick, *Protection: An ALNAP Guide for Humanitarian Agencies* (Overseas Development Institute, 2005); and Edwina Thompson, *Principled Pragmatism: NGO Engagement with Armed Actors* (2008) World Vision International www.eisf.eu/resources/library/ Principledpragmatism.pdf.

14 Human Rights Watch, *Darfur and the ICC: Myths versus Reality* (27 March 2009) HRW www.hrw.org/news/2009/03/27/darfur-and-icc-myths-versus-reality.

15 *Statutes of the International Red Cross and Red Crescent Movement*, preamble.

16 *Convention (IV) Relative to the Protection of Civilian Persons in Time of War*, opened for signature 12 August 1949, 75 UNTS 287 (entered into force 21 October 1950) [*GCIV*].

in case of a conflict or occupation, in the hands of a Party to the conflict or Occupying Power of which they are not Nationals'.[17] Protections are also afforded to those in hospitals and safety zones and localities 'so organised as to protect from the effects of war wounded sick and aged persons, children under fifteen, expectant mothers and mothers of children under seven'.[18]

In addition to the obligation to protect civilians, in international armed conflict where the survival needs of the civilian population are not being met, High Contracting Parties are required to allow the free passage of medical supplies and hospital stores as well as 'consignments of essential foodstuffs, clothing and tonics intended for children under fifteen, expectant mothers and maternity cases'.[19] It should be noted that there are no provisions in the *Fourth Geneva Convention* according obligations to States to either provide for, or allow humanitarian access to, their own populations.[20] In addition to an obligation to provide humanitarian assistance (either directly or through an impartial humanitarian organisation) protected persons may also request assistance from the protecting powers, the International Red Cross Red Crescent Movement, or any other humanitarian organisation.[21]

In international armed conflict, occupying powers have a duty to ensure the food and medical supplies for the population[22] and where their needs are not being met, the occupying power has an obligation to agree to, and facilitate, 'relief schemes'[23] undertaken either by States or by impartial humanitarian organisations.

In 1977, *Additional Protocol I* was adopted and significantly strengthened the rules guiding humanitarian relief in the *Fourth Geneva Convention*.[24] First, all civilians caught up in armed conflict became protected by international law. Second, *Additional Protocol I* required parties to the conflict to undertake humanitarian and impartial relief actions without distinction, and required parties to the conflict and States 'to facilitate rapid and unimpeded passage of all relief consignments equipment and personnel . . . even if such assistance is destined for the civilian population of the adverse Party'.[25] In addition, for the first time, parties to the conflict were required to respect and protect humanitarian personnel.[26]

---

17 Ibid Article 4.
18 Ibid Article 14.
19 Ibid.
20 Ibid.
21 Ibid Article 30(1).
22 Ibid Article 55.
23 Ibid Article 59.
24 *Protocol Additional to the Geneva Conventions of 12 August 1949, and Relating to the Protection of Victims of International Armed Conflicts (Protocol I)*, adopted 8 June 1977 (entered into force 7 December 1978) [*Additional Protocol I*].
25 Ibid Article 70(2).
26 Ibid Article 71(2).

The obligation to ensure that basic needs for the survival of the civilian population are met is reinforced by the prohibition of starvation as a method of warfare and to recognise that attacks on objects indispensable to the survival of the civilian population are prohibited.[27]

(B) NON-INTERNATIONAL ARMED CONFLICT

In the case of non-international armed conflicts, the obligation to provide for humanitarian access can be deduced from Article 3 Common to the four *Geneva Conventions*, particularly in regard to provisions ensuring that those taking no active part in hostilities 'shall in all circumstances be treated humanely'[28] and '[t]he wounded and sick shall be collected and cared for'.[29] When the needs of the civilian population are not being met in situations of armed conflict, whether international or non-international in nature, the refusal of humanitarian assistance has serious and detrimental effects inconsistent with the fundamental obligation for humane treatment.

Common Article 3 also provides for an impartial humanitarian body to offer services to the parties to the conflict in anticipation of a need for humanitarian assistance. This is known as the right of humanitarian initiative.[30] Any such offer of humanitarian assistance may not be considered as providing military assistance or aid to the enemy and should be considered on humanitarian grounds. For offers of assistance to be acceptable they must come from organisations that are 'humanitarian' and 'impartial' and the services offered must also be 'humane' and 'impartial'.[31] Article 3 also encourages parties to the conflict to implement other provisions found in the four *Geneva Conventions* and all the relevant articles pertaining to humanitarian assistance would apply.

The right to humanitarian assistance is also established in Article 18 of *Additional Protocol II*, which reinforces the right of humanitarian initiative and recognises the need of the civilian population suffering undue hardship.[32] Assistance must be provided impartially and is subject to the consent of the High Contracting Party concerned.[33]

---

27   Ibid Article 54.
28   *GCIV* Article 3.
29   Ibid Article 3(2).
30   Jean S Pictet (ed.), *The Geneva Conventions of 12 August 1949: Commentary* (2nd edn) (International Committee of the Red Cross, 1958) 41.
31   Ibid 42.
32   *Protocol Additional to the Geneva Conventions of 12 August 1949, and Relating to the Protection of Victims of Non-International Armed Conflicts (Protocol II)*, adopted 8 June 1977 (entered into force 7 December 1978) [*Additional Protocol II*].
33   Ibid.

(C) HUMAN RIGHTS LAW

The continued applicability of human rights law during armed conflict is well recognised.[34] As stated in the International Court of Justice in its advisory opinion in the *Nuclear Weapons Case* '[t]he protection of the International Covenant on Civil and Political Rights does not cease in times of war, except by operation of Article 4 of the Covenant whereby certain provisions may be derogated from in a time of national emergency'.[35]

Without undertaking an extensive analysis of the application of all human rights protections supporting the provision of humanitarian assistance in armed conflict, States have an obligation to respect and protect the right to life of all individuals within their territory and subject to their jurisdiction. Ruth Abril Stoffels notes that 'this not only implies that States must do all in their power to abstain from directly violating this right, but also . . . that they must take all necessary steps to ensure that this right is not abused'.[36]

Stoffels argues that the obligation to ensure that the right is not abused implies that a State has an obligation to ensure that a population affected by crisis has the supplies necessary for their survival. It is possible to deduce from this that the right to life creates an obligation on States to make adequate preparations for disaster relief. However, if a State is unable to provide the necessary materials and support, then it should allow third parties access to provide the necessary assistance. In this way Stoffels uses human rights law to establish a direct link between the right to life and the right to receive humanitarian assistance in the form of supplies and services essential to the survival of the population.

(D) CUSTOMARY INTERNATIONAL HUMANITARIAN LAW

Customary international law is made up of rules that come from a 'general practice accepted as law'.[37] In 1996, the International Committee of the Red Cross (ICRC) initiated a study into the rules of customary international humanitarian law. This study was conducted for two reasons: first, while there is universal ratification of the *Geneva Conventions*, some States have not ratified other important treaty law; second, the relative weakness of treaty law governing

---

34 Jean-Marie Henckaerts, 'Study on Customary International Humanitarian Law: A Contribution to the Understanding and Respect for the Rule of Law in Armed Conflict' (2005) 87 (857) *International Review of the Red Cross* 175. See also: Jean-Marie Henckaerts and Louise Doswald-Beck, *Customary International Humanitarian Law* (Cambridge University Press, 2005), Chapter 32.

35 *Legality of the Threat or Use of Nuclear Weapons* (Advisory Opinion) [1996] ICJ Reports, 240.

36 Ruth Abril Stoffels, 'Legal Regulation of Humanitarian Assistance in Armed Conflict: Achievements and Gaps' (2004) 86 (855) *International Review of the Red Cross* 515, 517.

37 *Statute of the International Court of Justice* Article 38(1)(b).

non-international armed conflicts had profound implications for the conduct of those conflicts.[38]

In 2005, after 10 years and following a review of current State practice, the ICRC first published its study on customary international humanitarian law.[39] The study identified 161 rules of customary international humanitarian law that constitute the common law binding on all parties to all armed conflicts regardless of the international or non-international status of the conflict.

Several rules of customary international humanitarian law identified in the study contribute to the notion that there is a right to humanitarian assistance. The first is *Rule 31 – Humanitarian relief personnel must be respected and protected.* This is a corollary of *Rule 53 – the prohibition of starvation,* as well as the rule that the wounded and sick must be collected and cared for. The safety and security of humanitarian relief personnel is also essential to ensure access for humanitarian relief to civilians in need (*Rule 55*).

Ultimately, in both international and non-international armed conflict there is a right for civilian populations to ask for and receive humanitarian assistance. Provisions in both the *Fourth Geneva Convention,* the *Additional Protocols,* as well as identified rules of customary international humanitarian law, all contribute to this conclusion and establish obligations on States and non-State Parties to allow for the provision of humanitarian assistance to the civilian population.

However, obligations on parties to the conflict to allow access in the provision of humanitarian relief, and the rights of access for humanitarian actors providing relief, must strike the delicate balance between military necessity and humanity. The obligations on parties to the conflict to ensure the provision of food and medical supplies,[40] as well as 'clothing, bedding, means of shelter [and] other supplies essential to the survival of the civilian population' are not without conditions.[41]

The conditions include the requirement of consent from the High Contracting Party and parties to the conflict. Further conditions include ensuring that there is no serious reason for fearing that consignments may not reach their intended destination; the control of the transportation or distribution of the goods may not be effective; there is no advantage to the 'military efforts or economy of the enemy' through the distribution and substitution of the consignments;[42] and finally, 'only in the case of imperative military necessity may the activities of the relief personnel be limited, or their movements temporarily restricted.'[43]

---

38 International Committee of the Red Cross, *Customary International Humanitarian Law* (2010) ICRC www.icrc.org/eng/war-and-law/treaties-customary-law/customary-law/overview-customary-law.htm.

39 Jean-Marie Henckaerts and Louise Doswald-Beck, *Customary International Humanitarian Law* (Cambridge University Press, 2005).

40 *GCIV* Articles 23 and 55.

41 *Additional Protocol I* Article 69.

42 *GCIV* Article 23.

43 *Additional Protocol I* Article 71(3).

Any party to the conflict or High Contracting Power allowing the free passage of relief consignments has the right to determine the technical arrangements under which access is permitted, make distribution conditional on either local supervision or the supervision of a Protecting Power, and must commit not to divert relief supplies except under urgent necessity and in the interests of the civilian population.[44] Parties to the conflict and High Contracting Powers 'shall encourage and facilitate effective international coordination for the relief actions'.[45]

These conditions and limitations raise interesting questions for humanitarian agencies seeking to provide humanitarian assistance to the civilian population. It is evident that to maintain access a very clear impartiality must be established and maintained. There can be no perception that one side of the conflict is benefiting at the cost of another side. The maintenance of the impartial humanitarian mission, consistent with humanitarian principles, is fundamental to continued access both perceptually, but also legally, and humanitarian agencies perceived to violate any of the above conditions may find their staff being refused continued access. 'The mission of any of the personnel who do not respect the[se] conditions may be terminated'.[46] It is noteworthy that the benefit of this clause is that it is the personnel whose mission may be terminated rather than the entire relief operation.[47] Equally, while these conditions are clearly outlined, the Commentaries suggest that parties to the conflict may not arbitrarily reject relief missions and must use valid reasons for doing so.[48]

The limitations and conditions on relief operations provided for in international humanitarian law allow High Contracting Parties room for negotiation if they are disinclined to allow access for humanitarian actors, relief and supplies. International humanitarian law provides for the requirement to allow humanitarian access to be denied if there are 'serious reasons for fearing' conditions will not be met. However, this measure is highly subjective and open to abuse. On the other hand, in situations of severe insecurity where humanitarian agencies are unable to maintain a permanent presence, some of the conditions, such as security of distribution, may be difficult to guarantee. The question then is, despite the provisions of international humanitarian law requiring access for humanitarian relief and medical supplies, and regardless of these measures having entered into customary international law and therefore considered binding on all parties to a conflict, whether in the worst case scenario humanitarian access is possible.

44 Ibid.
45 Ibid Article 70(5).
46 Ibid Article 71(4).
47 Pictet, above n 30.
48 Ibid 819.

III. Humanitarian assistance and the case of Syria

In the case of Syria the difficulties faced by the UN and humanitarian agencies to access hard-to-reach and besieged areas continues to be a critical issue. Despite the strength of support for humanitarian assistance, and for the protection available to personnel participating in relief actions, aid workers and civilians are increasingly the victims of conflict in Syria and access for humanitarian assistance is often either refused or not facilitated. This part of this chapter will explore the issue of humanitarian access in the case of Syria through a review of UN Security Council Resolution 2139 (2014) and an analysis of its impact as reflected in the reports of the UN Secretary-General on the implementation of this resolution.

The ongoing conflict in Syria poses multiple challenges for the international humanitarian community. More than 10 per cent or 2.5 million people are now refugees in neighbouring countries; 9.5 million people are in need of assistance; and 6.5 million are internally displaced.[49] The United Nations Office for the Coordination of Humanitarian Affairs estimates that $2.3 billion is required for humanitarian assistance inside Syria and that $786 million is needed in the immediate and medium term (March–August 2014) to meet some of the top priority lifesaving needs inside Syria.[50] The situation has been called one of the greatest humanitarian disasters of the twenty-first century,[51] with an estimated 100,000 civilians killed since hostilities began in 2011.[52]

Compounding the humanitarian impact on the civilian population is the use of siege warfare and the instrumentalisation of basic human needs for water, food, shelter and medical supplies as a part of the Government's military strategy.[53] The non-State armed groups have also besieged and encircled areas and cut off electrical and water supplies.[54]

Humanitarian access has been difficult at best, and in some situations access has been denied outright. Madamiyet Elsham has been besieged since late 2012.[55] The UN Security Council has been divided on Syria and effective action

---

49 Office for the Coordination of Humanitarian Affairs, *Humanitarian Bulletin: Syrian Arab Republic* (2014) OCHA http://reliefweb.int/sites/reliefweb.int/files/resources/Syria%20Humanitarian %20Bulletin%2045.pdf.

50 Ibid.

51 William Hague, *Prospect in Conversation with William Hague* (2013) Prospect Magazine www.prospectmagazine.co.uk/blog/william-hague-prospect/.

52 Secretary-General Ban Ki-Moon, 'Remarks at the Second International Humanitarian Pledging Conference on Syria' (Speech delivered at the Second International Humanitarian Pledging Conference on Syria, Kuwait City, 15 January 2014).

53 Human Rights Council, Report of the Independent International Commission of Inquiry on the Syrian Arab Republic, 25th sess, UN Doc A/HRC/25/65 (12 February 2014) [132] [Report on Syria].

54 United Nations Security Council, Report of the Secretary-General on the implementation of Security Council *Resolution 2139* (2014), UN Doc S/2014/525 (23 July 2014).

55 Ibid.

has, therefore, been difficult.[56] However, on 2 October 2013, a UN Security Council Presidential Statement called for all parties to respect the UN guiding principles on humanitarian assistance, condemning violations of human rights and international humanitarian law, and urging all parties to take appropriate steps 'to facilitate safe and unhindered humanitarian access to populations in need of assistance in all areas . . . and across conflict lines'.[57]

In that Presidential Statement the Security Council urged the Syrian authorities to facilitate the expansion of humanitarian activities and lift 'bureaucratic impediments and other obstacles'[58] including: increasing the number of humanitarian agencies approved to work in Syria, improving procedures for implementation including the issuance of visas and travel permits, and the importation of goods and equipment essential to effective humanitarian operations. Parties to the conflict were asked to ensure and facilitate access to populations in need, approve new projects and ensure the safety and security of UN and associated personnel and of all other personnel engaged in humanitarian relief activities. All parties were urged to demilitarise medical facilities, schools and other civilian sites.[59]

By February 2014, the situation in Syria had further deteriorated,[60] and the Security Council responded with Security Council Resolution 2139.[61] This resolution built on and reinforced the requests made in the October Presidential Statement and demanded that the Government and opposition armed groups allow humanitarian access to the civilian population. In a statement to the Security Council, the Secretary-General noted: 'This resolution should not have been necessary. Humanitarian assistance is not something to be negotiated; it is something to be allowed by virtue of international law'.[62] Samantha Power, representative of the United States observed: 'It is remarkable that it has taken three years for the Security Council to recognise basic facts and to call for such basic principles of humanity.'[63]

UN Security Council Resolution 2139 was passed on 22 February 2014, almost two and a half years after the outbreak of hostilities in Syria. 'Appalled'

---

56 United Nations, 'Security Council fails to adopt resolution on Syria', *UN News Centre*, 19 July 2012 www.un.org/apps/news/story.asp?NewsID=42513#.U9sTsv7lpzk.

57 *Statement by the President of the Security Council*, 7039th mtg, UN Doc S/PRST/2013/15 (2 October 2013).

58 Meeting at the Security Council on Safe, Unhindered Passage For Convoys, Demilitarization of Medical Centres, Schools, Water Centres, 7039th mtg, UN Doc SC/11138 (2 October 2013) www.un.org/News/Press/docs/2013/sc11138.doc.htm.

59 Ibid.

60 Meeting at the Security Council on the Protection of Civilians in Armed Conflict, 7109th mtg, UN Doc S/PV/7109 (12 February 2014).

61 *SC Res 2139*, UN Doc S/RES/2139.

62 Meeting at the Security Council on the Situation in the Middle East, 7116th mtg, UN Doc S/PV/7116 (22 February 2014) 2.

63 Ibid 6.

at the unacceptable and escalating level of violence particularly against the civilian population in besieged and hard-to-reach areas, the Security Council passed the resolution with demands relating not only to a cessation of the conduct of hostilities, but, specifically relevant to this chapter, in relation to humanitarian access.

The Resolution demanded that all parties, in particular the Syrian authorities, facilitate the expansion of humanitarian relief operations, in accordance with applicable provisions of international humanitarian law and the UN guiding principles of humanitarian emergency assistance – humanity, impartiality and neutrality. All parties are called upon to lift the sieges of populated areas, allow unhindered evacuation for all civilians wishing to leave and to allow humanitarian pauses facilitating humanitarian access to those besieged areas. All parties should allow and facilitate rapid, safe and unhindered humanitarian access for UN humanitarian agencies, personnel and their implementing partners and personnel. The Resolution went on to demand that all parties respect the principle of medical neutrality and facilitate free passage to all areas for medical personnel, equipment, transport and surgical equipment.[64]

The Resolution notes that it is the responsibility of the Syrian Government to protect its own population and demands all parties to take appropriate steps to do so, including the demilitarisation of medical facilities, schools and other civilian facilities.[65]

Finally, the Resolution encourages all Member States to contribute and increase support to the humanitarian appeals for Syria, and requests the Secretary-General to report on the implementation of the Resolution every 30 days.[66]

The Resolution is a strong call for the parties to the conflict to facilitate and ensure the improvement of the humanitarian situation in Syria. It notes that the 'arbitrary denial of humanitarian access and depriving civilians of objects indispensable to their survival, including wilfully impeding relief supply and access, can constitute a violation of international humanitarian law'.[67]

One month after Security Council Resolution 2139, the Secretary-General made his first report to the Security Council on the implementation of the resolution. In short, there had been no significant progress in the improvement of the humanitarian situation for the Syrian population.[68] In the period to the publication of the first report, fighting continued and a further 500,000 people were displaced from the eastern part of the city of Aleppo between late January and March, and the Secretary-General noted that more people are in fact

---

64   *SC Res 2139*, UN Doc S/RES/2139 [8].

65   Ibid 10.

66   Ibid 17.

67   Ibid 2.

68   United Nations Security Council, *Report of the Secretary-General on the Implementation of Security Council Resolution 2139* (2014), UN Doc S/2014/208 (24 March 2014) [37].

'slipping out of reach of humanitarian organisations with around 3.5 million people now estimated to be in need of assistance in hard-to-reach areas, which is an increase of 1 million since the beginning of 2014'.[69]

As a demonstration of compliance with the Resolution, the Syrian Govern-ment established a working group for the implementation of SC Resolution 2139, and the UN received assurances from the President of the National Coalition of the Syrian Revolutionary and Opposition Forces, pledging the commit-ment of the Coalition and Free Syrian Army that they would comply with the Resolution.[70] However, the Secretary-General reported that significant challenges to the delivery of humanitarian assistance remain and it appears that these commitments have not resulted in behavioural change.[71] The challenges identified by the Secretary-General include the need for multiple requests for approval of convoys, lack of communication of approval to those on the ground causing difficulties and delays at checkpoints, and continued insecurity on the ground where increased fighting has complicated the delivery of assistance. In addition there have been several instances in which aid convoys could not proceed or were prevented from carrying essential items.[72] This is particularly true of medical supplies, which have been removed by government officials from inter-agency convoys to Houla and Adra and Madamiyet Elsham.[73] Since the adoption of Resolution 2139, medical supplies that would have assisted around 201,000 people have been removed from humanitarian convoys and thereby withdrawn from distribution.[74]

On 23 April 2014, the Secretary-General issued his second report on the implementation of Resolution 2139.[75] Significant improvements in the humanitarian situation in Syria remain elusive, even though increasing amounts of assistance were delivered in that month. There are still serious challenges to access those in hard-to-reach locations and areas under siege. The situation of approximately 242,000 people in besieged areas remains gravely concerning and it is estimated that only 10 per cent of them have been reached with limited assistance.[76]

Some of the difficulties can be seen in the situation of Nubul and Zahra where the UN has been negotiating with opposition groups to facilitate access. Originally the opposition groups put forward stringent conditions for the facilitation of assistance including (i) Syrian forces cease shelling in Aleppo; (ii)

---

69 Ibid 19.
70 Ibid 20.
71 Ibid 22.
72 Ibid 32.
73 Ibid 41.
74 Ibid.
75 United Nations Security Council, *Report of the Secretary-General on the Implementation of Security Council Resolution 2139* (2014), UN Doc S/2014/295 (23 April 2014).
76 Ibid 24–25.

the situation in the Aleppo central prison be solved; (iii) humanitarian assistance be delivered to Homs and Rural Damascus; (iv) all women and children be released from detention; and (v) Government forces withdraw from Nubul and Zahra.[77] These negotiating positions were relaxed but there is still no access and Nubul and Zahra have been besieged since April 2013.[78] Humanitarian access should not be used as conditions for military gain or concessions from the adverse party.

Humanitarian access continues to be difficult and dangerous for UN and humanitarian relief personnel. The delivery of medical supplies continues to be restricted by the Government. In April 2014, medical supplies that would have assisted 216,015 people in hard-to-reach and besieged areas were either removed from convoys or not allowed to proceed.[79]

In the conclusion of his report, the Secretary-General notes that '[t]wo months since the adoption of Security Council Resolution 2139 (2014), none of the parties to the conflict have adhered to the demands of the Council. Civilians are not protected and . . . [h]umanitarian access . . . is not improving'.[80] The Secretary-General goes on to note that medical supplies are being denied in an arbitrary and unjustifiable manner, which is a clear violation of international humanitarian law. Almost 3.5 million civilians remain largely without access to humanitarian assistance, and the Secretary-General notes that not to comply with Resolution 2139 constitutes arbitrary denial of access.

The right of the civilian population to receive humanitarian assistance in times of armed conflict is entrenched in international humanitarian law – through the *Geneva Conventions*, the *Additional Protocols* and in customary international law. The nature of this protected humanitarian assistance is clearly defined and includes food, water, shelter, medical supplies and material essential to the survival of the civilian population. The Secretary-General's reports on the implementation of SC Resolution 2139, and the updates provided to the Security Council regarding the situation in Syria, clearly identify breaches of the demands made on the Syrian Government and armed opposition groups to allow and facilitate humanitarian access.

The Secretary-General's suggestion that a failure to implement Resolution 2139 amounts to an 'arbitrary denial of access'[81] lends support to the idea that the parties to the conflict are in breach of their obligations under international humanitarian law, regardless of the permissible conditions and limitations on humanitarian access provided for in international humanitarian law. The independent international commission of the inquiry on the Syrian Arab Republic presented the findings and noted that the denial of humanitarian

---

77   Ibid 24.
78   Ibid 33.
79   Ibid 37.
80   Ibid 52.
81   Ibid 53.

convoys is a violation of armed groups' obligations under international humanitarian law.[82]

IV. Denial of humanitarian assistance as a war crime

If parties to the conflict continue to inhibit, prevent and divert humanitarian assistance in violation of both statutory and customary international humanitarian law, and in contravention of the demands made upon it by the UN Security Council, does that denial of humanitarian assistance amount to a serious violation of international humanitarian law?

The right of civilians to receive humanitarian assistance, the right of access for the delivery of humanitarian assistance, and the obligation on Parties to the Conflict to allow access to humanitarian assistance has been established. The conditions and limitations to access that may be applied by Parties to the Conflict do not allow for the arbitrary denial of access where humanitarian needs of the civilian population are not being addressed. The question is whether the denial of access for humanitarian assistance can be considered a serious violation, or grave breach of international humanitarian law.

Serious violations, or 'grave breaches' of international humanitarian law are war crimes. In most cases war crimes endanger protected persons or objects, or breach important values. The majority of war crimes involve death, injury, destruction or the unlawful taking of property.[83] Many violations of international humanitarian law do not reach the threshold required as 'grave breaches' and therefore may not be considered war crimes. This final section of the chapter will consider whether the denial of humanitarian assistance, in the situation of Syria, may be considered a war crime within existing definition and practice.

Grave breaches of international humanitarian law are defined in the *Geneva Conventions* and *Additional Protocol I* and may amount to war crimes. A war crime may be committed by any person, whether military or civilian,[84] in the context

---

82 HRC, above n 53, [141].

83 International Committee of the Red Cross, What are 'serious violations of international humanitarian law'? Explanatory Note, ICRC, www.icrc.org/eng/assets/files/2012/att-what-are-serious-violations-of-ihl-icrc.pdf.

84 See the provisions on 'grave breaches' of *Convention (I) for the Amelioration of the Condition of the Wounded and Sick in Armed Forces in the Field*, opened for signature 12 August 1949, 75 UNTS 31 (entered into force 21 October 1950) [*GCI*]; *Convention (II) for the Amelioration of the Condition of Wounded, Sick and Shipwrecked Members of Armed Forces at Sea*, opened for signature 12 August 1949, 75 UNTS 85 (entered into force 21 October 1950) [*GCII*]; *Convention (III) Relative to the Treatment of Prisoners of War*, opened for signature 12 August 1949, 75 UNTS 135 (entered into force 21 October 1950) [*GCIII*]; *GCIV*; *Statute of the International Criminal Tribunal for the former Yugoslavia* (as amended on 17 May 2002) opened for signature 25 May 1993, Arts 6 and 7; *Statute of the International Criminal Tribunal for Rwanda* (as last amended on 13 October 2006) opened for signature 8 November 1994, Arts 5 and 6; *Rome Statute of the International Criminal Court*, opened for signature on 17 July 1998, 2187 UNTS 90 (entered into force 1 July 2002), Art 25 [*Rome Statute*].

of an armed conflict. In international armed conflict grave breaches include acts committed against persons or property protected by the *Conventions* and include: 'wilful killing, torture or inhuman treatment, including biological experiments, wilfully causing great suffering or serious injury to body or health, and extensive destruction and appropriation of property, not justified by military necessity'.[85] The *Fourth Geneva Convention* in particular, includes 'unlawful deportation or transfer or unlawful confinement of a protected person, compelling a protected person to serve in the forces of a hostile Power', and refusing access to a fair trial, the taking of hostages.[86] *Additional Protocol I* expanded the definition of grave breaches,[87] but still did not include the denial of humanitarian assistance as one of them.

In non-international armed conflict, Article 3, common to the *Geneva Conventions*, speaks to the prohibition of 'outrages upon personal dignity, in particular humiliating and degrading treatment', and *Additional Protocol II* includes as fundamental guarantees the prohibition of 'violence to the life, health and physical or mental wellbeing of persons'.[88] However these guarantees do not reflect a definition of grave breaches in relation to non-international armed conflict.

Humanitarian supplies and personnel are protected in *Additional Protocol I* and *II*, however, there is no direct mention of the denial of humanitarian assistance as a serious violation of humanitarian law within the *Geneva Conventions* or the *Additional Protocols*. However, it is significant that there is a requirement in Common Article 3 that all protected persons 'shall in all circumstances be treated humanely, without any adverse distinction'. This is a fundamental principle balancing military necessity and humanity – key to the application of international humanitarian law. While 'humane treatment' is not specifically defined it is thought that the detailed rules outlined in international humanitarian and human rights law give meaning to the term.[89] It is likely that the denial of humanitarian assistance leading to unnecessary suffering of the civilian population would not be consistent with the requirement of 'humane treatment'.

The *Rome Statute of the International Criminal Court* has jurisdiction over war crimes in particular when committed as part of a plan or policy or as part of a large-scale commission of such crimes. For the purposes of the *ICC* war crimes include all grave breaches of the *Geneva Conventions* and, in situations of international armed conflict include violations such as:

---

85   *GCI* Article 50.

86   *GCIV* Article 147.

87   *Additional Protocol I* Article 85.

88   *Protocol Additional to the Geneva Conventions of 12 August 1949, and Relating to the Protection of Victims of International Armed Conflicts [Protocol I]*, adopted 8 June 1977 (entered into force 7 December 1978), Art 4(2)(a) [*Additional Protocol II*].

89   Henckaerts and Doswald-Beck, above n 39, Rule 87.

Intentionally using starvation of civilians as a method of warfare by depriving them of objects indispensable to their survival, including wilfully impeding relief supplies as provided for under the *Geneva Conventions*.[90]

Such a provision indicates that the denial of humanitarian assistance, inconsistent with the conditions and limitations outlined in the *Conventions*, and in situations where the consequences result in the starvation of the civilian population, could be considered a war crime.

More pertinent to the Syrian question, as a situation of non-international armed conflict, the *Rome Statute* identifies as a war crime:

Intentionally directing attacks against personnel, installations, material, units or vehicles involved in a humanitarian assistance or peacekeeping mission in accordance with the *Charter of the United Nations*, as long as they are entitled to the protection given to civilians or civilian objects under the international law of armed conflict.[91]

The prohibition of attacks against relief personnel and supplies is a welcome advance in the protection of humanitarian assistance. However, it does not contribute towards the enforcement of the right to humanitarian assistance itself. There is no provision in the *Rome Statute* directly relating to the denial of humanitarian relief, or the prohibition on starvation as a method of warfare, or regarding the 'wilfully impeding relief supplies' in the crimes occurring in non-international armed conflict. This is despite the fact that starvation as a method of warfare is prohibited in non-international armed conflicts in *Additional Protocol II*.[92] One measure of hope may be that in accordance with Article 10 of the *Rome Statute*, the omission of the prohibition of starvation in non-international armed conflicts does not change the customary international law status[93] of the rule.[94]

Therefore, determining whether the denial of humanitarian assistance in non-international armed conflict could be considered a war crime at the *International Criminal Court*, requires a review of the elements of particular offences as defined by the *Rome Statute*.

---

90 *Rome Statute* Article 8(2)(b)(xxv).
91 Ibid Article 8(2)(3(iii).
92 *Additional Protocol II* Article 14.
93 Henckaerts and Doswald-Beck, above n 39, Rule 53.
94 *Rome Statute* Article 10.

A. *Murder, cruel treatment and outrage on personal dignity*

Murder is considered a war crime in both international and non-international armed conflict.[95] While murder is commonly considered to involve the act of homicide, it also includes omissions that may lead to death where that omission is contrary to the law of armed conflict and the perpetrator acts wilfully.[96] That murder can be committed by omission was confirmed by the *International Criminal Tribunal for the former Yugoslavia (ICTY)* and the *International Criminal Tribunal for Rwanda (ICTR).*[97] If civilians therefore die as a result of a decision to refuse humanitarian relief, or to fail to provide, facilitate or expedite humanitarian assistance, it may be possible to argue that such denial of assistance can constitute murder by omission if the denial of permission can be considered arbitrary and in contravention of the conditions for approval specified in the *Conventions.*

Equally the severe physical or mental pain imposed on one or more persons by the knowing denial of humanitarian assistance could constitute the crime of 'cruel treatment' or an 'outrage upon personal dignity'.[98] It is arguable that in the case of Syria, the reports of the Secretary-General indicate widespread suffering consistent with the idea of cruel and inhumane treatment and outrages upon personal dignity.

B. *Collective punishments*

Collective punishments, defined as 'penalties of any kind inflicted on persons or entire groups of persons in defiance of the most elementary principles of humanity, for acts that these persons have not committed'[99] are prohibited in both international and non-international armed conflict,[100] but are not considered grave breaches of the *Conventions.* Despite this, collective punishment qualified as a war crime by the *Statute of the ICTR*, although it does not appear as a crime in the *Statute of the ICC.* However, if humanitarian assistance is denied with the purpose of punishing certain persons, it could be considered as collective punishment and therefore in violation of international humanitarian law. Should the denial of humanitarian assistance as collective punishment reach the situation where those being punished die, then it could be considered to reach a threshold of inhumane treatment and therefore be considered as a war crime.

---

95 *Prosecutor v Zejnil Delalić, Zdravko Mučić aka 'Pavo', Hazim Delić, Esad Landžo aka 'Zenga' (Judgment)* (*ICTY, Trial Chamber*, Case No. IT-96-21-T, 16 November 1998) [423].

96 Pictet, above n 30, 1373.

97 *Prosecutor v Delalić (Judgment)* (*ICTY, Trial Chamber*, Case No. IT-96-21-T, 16 November 1998) [422]; *Prosecutor v Akayesu (Judgment)* (*ICTR, Chamber I,* Case No. ICTR-96-4-T, 2 September 1998) [589].

98 Mark Klamberg (ed.), *Elements of Crime*, International Criminal Law Database and Commentary www.iclklamberg.com/Elements.htm#Article%208(2)(c)(i)-1.

99 Pictet, above n 30, 225.

100 *GCIV* Article 33; *Additional Protocol II* Article 4(2)(b).

V. Conclusion

The situation in Syria indicates that the effects of the lack of access for humanitarian operations, particularly in besieged and hard-to-reach areas, may have reached situations where civilian populations are severely malnourished, if not starving, have died as a result of their deprivation as well as a direct impact of the conflict, have been deprived of access to fundamental medical services, and have been subject to significant and prolonged human suffering. This chapter has shown that the denial of humanitarian assistance can constitute a violation of the rules of international humanitarian law. If that denial reaches certain thresholds (murder, cruel and inhumane treatment, and outrages on the dignity of protected persons) it may also constitute a war crime, judiciable at the *International Criminal Court*.

However, the fact that widespread and often well-documented cases of the denial of humanitarian assistance have not been widely used as a basis for prosecution in prior conflicts, may be indicative of the fact that other grave violations of international humanitarian law are considered more serious, and easier to successfully prosecute.[101] Consequently serious questions arise for the Security Council. When a resolution as strong and condemnatory as SC Resolution 2139 fails to result in a change of behaviour, attitude or impact for the civilian population, it calls into question not only the effectiveness of the Security Council's actions, but also of the international system as a whole. If Security Council demands for humanitarian access are to be taken seriously, in Syria or any other conflict, there must be serious and timely consequences for those arbitrarily denying that humanitarian access. If that is not the case, and given the limited enthusiasm for making the case at the *ICC* for denial of humanitarian access to constitute a war crime, then Security Council resolutions such as 2139 become entirely meaningless. This, in consequence, threatens the humanitarian system established over many years, to provide relief from the suffering and deprivation that are by-products of armed conflict.

---

101 See for example: various Reports by the Special Rapporteur of the Commission on Human Rights for the Former Yugoslavia, in particular: Commission on Human Rights, *Fifth periodic report on the situation of human rights in the territory of the former Yugoslavia submitted by Mr. Tadeusz Mazowiecki, Special Rapporteur of the Commission on Human Rights, pursuant to paragraph 32 of Commission resolution 1993/7 of 23 February 1993*, 50th sess, UN Doc E/CN.4/1994/47 (17 November 1993). Also referenced in Christa Rottenstiener, 'The Denial of Humanitarian Assistance as a Crime Under International Law' (1999) 81(835) *International Review of the Red Cross* 555.

7 The Syrian conflict and the use of cultural property for military purposes

Jadranka Petrovic and Rebecca Hughes[1]

I. Introduction

Cultural property is a tangible form of cultural heritage that includes an array of objects, both movable and immovable, such as artworks, archives, historic churches, monuments and archaeological sites. These objects are inseparable from human lives. Their destruction not only affects the identity and history of the people most immediately concerned, but it also deepens hatred and slows down the process of reconciliation. At the same time, destruction of cultural objects deprives future generations of the rich inheritance of the past and ultimately affects all humanity.[2]

Cultural property has always been an innocent victim of warfare. The ongoing armed conflict in the Syrian Arab Republic (Syria) confirms time and again that this has not changed. In addition to the heavy toll that this conflict has had on Syria's people[3] and infrastructure,[4] cultural property in Syria has

---

1 Dr Jadranka Petrovic (LLB, LLM, SJD, PgradDiplInt'lL, GCAustralLaw (Melb), GCAP (Monash)) teaches and researches in International Law at Monash University. Rebecca Hughes (LLB, BA, DML (Fr), GDLP) is a lawyer with the Northern Land Council, Darwin, Australia. The authors are privileged to be able to contribute to this book to honour Professor Tim McCormack, an outstanding supervisor, mentor and friend.

    The views expressed in this chapter are those of the authors alone and do not represent any institutional position.

2 AAP, 'UN Urges Halt to Attacks on Syria's Cultural Sites', *The Australian* (online), 13 March 2014 www.theaustralian.com.au/in-depth/middle-east-in-turmoil/un-urges-halt-to-atta... (a joint statement by UN Secretary-General, Ban Ki-moon, UNESCO Director-General Irina Bokova and the joint UN-Arab League mediator on Syria, Lakhdar Brahimi).

3 Since March 2011, the Syrian conflict has killed over 190,000 people and driven more than 9 million from their homes, with approximately 3 million refugees and more than 6 million people being internally displaced by the conflict. See, eg, UN General Assembly, Human Rights Council, 27th sess, Agenda item 4: Human rights situation that requires the Council's attention, *Eighth Report of the Independent International Commission of Inquiry on the Syrian Arab Republic*, A/HRC/27/60, 13 August 2014 (published on 27 August 2014, annex III, 'Humanitarian Context', 30 [hereinafter *HRC Eighth Report*]; UN Security Council Resolution 2139 (2014) and UN Security Council *Resolution 2165* (2014); United Nations Association of Australia

also been destroyed at an alarming rate.[5] Since the beginning of the uprising in Syria in 2011, cultural property has suffered incalculable damage. It has been widely reported that cultural property in Syria has been deliberately targeted for ideological reasons, its archaeological sites have been looted on an industrial scale and the concomitant illicit trafficking of cultural objects has reached catastrophic levels.[6] What is particularly disturbing is the use of cultural sites, including those inscribed on the United Nations Educational, Scientific and Cultural Organisation (UNESCO) World Heritage List, for encampment, entrenchment of military vehicles and weapons, and other military purposes, which has resulted in damage to these sites or exposed them to the loss of immunity.[7]

By focusing on the present day Syria, and limiting itself to immovable cultural property, predominantly the World Heritage sites situated in Syria, this chapter explores the issue of the belligerent use of cultural property for military purposes from an International Humanitarian Law and International Criminal Law

Victoria Division, News, '"Stop the Destruction", UN Officials Urge in Plea to Save Syria's Cultural Heritage', 13 March 2014 www.unaavictoria.org.au/news; 'Australian Red Cross' Role in Syria and Iraq', Wednesday, 1 October 2014 www.redcross.org.au/news-syria-iraw-3-oct.aspx.

4 See, eg, UNRWA, 'A War on Development: 2nd Report on Impact of Syria Conflict', 30 October 2013 www.unrwa.org/newsroom/press-release/war-development-2nd-report-impact-... (describing the 'catastrophic impact of the ongoing armed conflict . . . on lives, livelihoods and environments of people in Syria').

5 Assyrian International News Agency, 'Emergency Support for Syria's Cultural Heritage', 17 July 2014 www.penn.museum.

6 See, generally, UNOSAT, *Satellite Imagery Analysis to Assess Cultural Heritage Damage* (UNITAR, Geneva, 22 December 2014) [hereinafter *UNOSAT Report*] (using satellite technology and images to assess and analyse the state of cultural property in 18 cultural heritage areas across Syria) www.unitar.org/unosat-report-damage-cultural-heritage-sites-syria-calls-scaled.... See also, American Association for the Advancement of Science (AAAS) Geospatial Technologies and Human Rights Project, *Ancient History, Modern Destruction: Assessing the Current Status of Syria's World Heritage Sites Using High-Resolution Satellite Imagery* [hereinafter *AAAS Report*] www.aaas.org/page/ancient-history-modern-destruction-assessing-current-status...; Emma Cunliffe, *Damage to the Soul: Syria's Cultural Heritage in Conflict, Report on the Damage to Cultural Property in Syria* (Durham University and Global Heritage Fund, 16 May 2012) [hereinafter *Cunliffe Report*].

7 'UNESCO Director-General Condemns Military Presence and Destruction at World Heritage Sites in Syria', UNESCO, 20 February 2014 http://whc.unesco.org/en/news/1108; *UNOSAT Report*, above n 6; Robert Fisk, 'Syria's Ancient Treasures Pulverised', *The Independent*, Sunday (online), 5 August 2012 www.independent.co.uk/voices/commentators/fisk/robert-fisk-syrias-ancient-tre...; Mark Colvin, 'Fears for Syria's Lost Heritage', PM on ABC News, 3 September 2012 www.abc.net.au/pm/content/2012/s3581988.htm; 'Syria Rebels Battle Army in Landmark Aleppo Mosque', *The Daily Star* (Lebanon) (online), 10 October 2012 www.daily star.com.lb/News/Middle-East/2012/Oct-10/190895-syria-rebels-battle-army-in-landmark-aleppo-mosque.ashx#axzz29Cam5zsu; Anne Barnard, 'Syrian War Takes Heavy Toll at a Crossroad of Cultures', *The New York Times* (online), 16 April 2014 www.nytimes.com/2014/04/17/world/middleast/syrian-war-takes-heavy-toll-at-a-cross....

perspective. In particular, the chapter considers the normative implications of the use of cultural property for military purposes in Syria vis-à-vis the question of whether, when and where those responsible will be brought to justice. The chapter argues that relevant instruments of neither International Humanitarian Law nor International Criminal Law address the question of the use of cultural property for military purposes adequately.

The chapter comprises five parts. Part I briefly introduces the topic. Part II commences with a brief look at Syria's geography and demography and then considers its rich cultural property milieu. This is followed by an overview of the Syrian conflict and the impact of the conflict on cultural property in Syria. Part III canvasses the legal framework emphasising the relevant rules under International Humanitarian Law and International Criminal Law. Part IV evaluates the cultural property situation in Syria. Part V concludes that the current law allows those who expose cultural property of great importance to destruction or damage to walk away with impunity, and sketches ways of how to remedy the problem in the future.

II. The Syrian situation

A. Geography and demography

Syria sits on 186,475 square kilometres of fertile plains, high mountains and deserts on the eastern shore of the Mediterranean Sea in the Middle East. It borders Lebanon and the Mediterranean Sea to the west, Turkey to the north, Iraq to the east, Jordan to the south and Israel to the southwest. The area covered by Syria is steeped in history dating back to and beyond biblical times. Over the centuries, from the Romans and Mongols to the Crusaders and Turks, the area has seen invasions and occupations.[8] Today, the area is populated by roughly 23 million people, including Kurds, Armenians, Assyrians, Christians, Druze, Alawite Shia and Arab Sunnis, the last of who make up a majority of the Muslim population.[9] This ethnic and religious diversity has resulted in one of the most unique and precious cultural environments in the world.

B. Syria's cultural property milieu

1 Syria's cultural property generally

Syria is one of the richest cultural property treasure houses on the planet. An array of cultural property resides in this State, including sites dating back

---

8 BBC News Middle East, 'Syria Profile', 7 October 2014, last updated at 11:30, 1 www.bbc.com/news/world-middle-east-14703856.
9 Ibid.

millennia. Syria has more than 10,000 Mesopotamian tells or archaeological mounds. Many of its archaeological sites date back 6,000 years to the Neolithic Age, while others include clay and bronze artefacts, human skulls and the ruins of habitations from the Roman, Hellenistic, Hittite, Byzantine and Babylonian periods.

The scale of built cultural property in Syria is impressive. Various religious sites, along with other architectural structures, in ancient neighbourhoods of Aleppo and Damascus and elsewhere in Syria, some of which are considered to be the earliest cities in human history, 'if not the earliest',[10] adorn this State's landscape.

In addition, Syria's museums, archives and libraries contain seminal and irreplaceable cultural remains including ceramics, sculptures, ancient cuneiform texts and Islamic manuscripts. For instance, it is claimed that the oldest piece of annotated music known to history comes from Syria and dates back to well over 3,200 years[11] – the Hurrian Hymn to Nikkal from twelfth century BC in the ancient cuneiform script Ugarit found in the early 1950s at a site of Ugarit, present day Ras Sharma.[12] The Ugaritic script is believed to be the oldest alphabet script ever found. It was the basis for the Phoenician alphabet, which in turn was the foundation for the early Greek alphabet.

The volume of Syria's national cultural property is impressive.[13] Equally remarkable is the number of Syria's cultural properties inscribed on the UNESCO World Heritage List and on UNESCO's tentative inscription list.[14]

2. World Heritage sites

Six sites in Syria have been designated as World Cultural Heritage sites by UNESCO.[15] These sites are:

* the Ancient City of Damascus, founded in the third millennium BC, was inscribed on the UNESCO World Heritage List in 1979;[16]
* the Ancient City of Bosra, once the capital of the Roman province of Arabia, was added to the World Heritage List in 1980;[17]

---

10 *Cunliffe Report*, above n 6, 4, 34.
11 Heritage for Peace www.heritageforpeace.org/.
12 Ibid 3.
13 *Cunliffe Report*, above n 6.
14 Ibid.
15 See, UNESCO World Heritage Centre, 'World Heritage List' http://whc.unesco.org/en/list/.
16 UNESCO World Heritage Centre, 'Ancient City of Damascus' http://whc.unesco.org/en/list/20.
17 UNESCO World Heritage Centre, 'Ancient City of Bosra' http://whc.unesco.org/en/list/22.

- the Site of Palmyra, evidencing human settlement since Palaeolithic and Neolithic eras and one of the most important cultural centres of the ancient world, was included in the World Heritage List in 1980;[18]
- the Ancient City of Aleppo, founded in the 2nd millennium BC and demonstrating rare medieval Arab structural styles, was inscribed on the World Heritage List in 1986;[19]
- the Crac des Chevaliers and the Qal'at Salah El-Din (Fortress of Saladin) castles, the most significant examples of fortified architecture in the Near East during the time of the Crusades, were inscribed on the World Heritage List in 2006;[20] and
- the Ancient Villages of Northern Syria, dating back to the 1st–7th Centuries and providing remarkable testimony to rural life in late Antiquity and during the Byzantine period, were added to the World Heritage List in 2011.[21]

Syria has twelve additional sites which are on UNESCO's Tentative Inscription List for future consideration,[22] including Apamea famous for its colonnade and the citadel of Qal'at al-Mudiq, the historic town of Hama, with 'the most splendid norias ever constructed',[23] and Homs, known for its ancient buildings, mosques, churches and the ancient souk.[24]

The forms of cultural property protected by either confirmed or tentative world heritage listing by no means represent the totality of important cultural property in Syria. A national regime for protection established under the *Antiquities Law* also protects a significant collection of important cultural property.[25] Despite being an invaluable part of the cultural heritage of all humankind,[26] Syria's cultural property is extremely vulnerable to damage from the Syrian armed conflict, discussed in the next section.

18 UNESCO World Heritage Centre, 'Site of Palmyra' http://whc.unesco.org/en/list/23.
19 UNESCO World Heritage Centre, 'Ancient City of Aleppo' http://whc.unesco.org/en/list/21.
20 UNESCO World Heritage Centre, 'Crac des Chevaliers and Qal'at Salah El-Din' http://whc.unesco.org/en/list/1229.
21 UNESCO World Heritage Centre, 'Ancient Villages of Northern Syria' http://whc.unesco.org/en/list/1348.
22 See, UNESCO World Heritage Centre, 'World Heritage List' http://whc.unesco.rg/en/list/; Diana Darke, 'How Syria's Ancient Treasures are being Smashed', *BBC News Magazine* (online), 9 July 2014, 2.
23 *Cunliffe Report*, above n 6, 35.
24 Ibid 36.
25 Domestically, cultural property in Syria is protected by the *Antiquities Law* as amended in 1999, administered by the Directorate of Antiquities and Museums.
26 Heritage for Peace 3 http://heritageforpeace.org/.

C. The Syrian armed conflict

Since 1971 Syria has been ruled by the Assad family, coming from the minority Alawite religious group (an offshoot of Shi'ite Islam that comprises an estimated 12 per cent of the total Syrian population). The first in the line was Hafez al-Assad, who was followed by Bashar al-Assad. The Assad government has been known for authoritarian rule in its home State and a strong anti-Western policy abroad. Following the death of Hafez al-Assad in 2000 Syria underwent a brief period of relaxation (due to people's ephemeral belief that the Bashar al-Assad Government was less authoritarian than its predecessor), but the much needed and long-promised economic and political reform never materialised.[27]

It was the failure of the Assad government to deliver these reforms that caused protests in March 2011.[28] The Assad government responded violently to the protests. Reportedly, Syrian security forces used tanks, gunfire and mass arrests to try to crush anti-government street protests. However, the opposition began to organise political and military wings for a long uprising against the Assad government, which led to a full-fledged armed conflict between the Syrian government and the opposition in 2012.[29]

The armed opposition in Syria is fragmented. It consists of various groups that were formed during the course of the conflict, primarily the Free Syrian Army, which was the first to take up arms in 2011, and the Islamic Front formed in 2013. In 2013, Hezbollah, a Lebanon-based Shi'a Islamic militant group, entered the conflict in support of the Syrian army. In the east, Dā'sh (also known as Islamic State of Iraq and the Levant (ISIL), the Islamic State of Iraq and Syria (ISIS), or simply as the self-styled 'Islamic State'), a jihadist militant group originating from Iraq, affiliated with al-Qaeda until 2014 and considered to be the most radical and brutal armed opposition group active in Syria and Iraq, made very rapid military gains in both Syria and Iraq,[30] eventually conflicting with the other rebels. In July 2014, ISIL controlled a third of Syria's territory

---

27 BBC News, 'Syria Profile', above n 8, 1.
28 The first stirrings of insurrections that sparked the war took place in Deraa, in March 2011. See, eg, Martin Chulov, 'Syria's Heritage in Ruins: before-and-after Pictures', *The Guardian* (online), 27 January 2014, 3 www.theguardian.com/world/2014/jan/26/syria-heritage-in-ruins-before-and-aft.... Protests in Syria were inspired by the Arab Spring in Tunisia, Egypt and Libya.
29 BBC News, 'Syria Profile', above n 8, 1.
30 According to Lakhdar Brahimi, UN and League of Arab States Joint Special Representative for Syria, ISIS has carried out 100 operations in Syria and 1,000 operations in Iraq in just three months in 2014. See, Susanne Koelbl, 'Interview with UN Peace Envoy Brahimi: "Syria will Become another Somalia"', *Spiegel Online International*, 7 June 2014, 3 www.spiegel.de/international/world/interview-with-former-un-peace-envoy-to-s....

and most of its oil and gas production, thus establishing itself as the major opposition force.[31]

At the international level, the United Nations (UN) described the conflict as being 'overly sectarian in nature',[32] due to the fighting being between mostly Alawite government forces, militias and other Shia groups against largely Sunni-dominated rebel groups (although this characterisation has been disputed by the opposition).[33]

Syria became an increasingly isolated member of the international community for its support for insurgents in Iraq and over its role in Lebanon (including suspicions that the Syrian Government played a role in the former Lebanese Prime Minister Rafik Hariri's death in 2005). By December 2012 the United States of America (US), Turkey, the Gulf States, France and Great Britain had recognised the main opposition National Coalition of the Syrian Revolution as the 'sole legitimate representative of the Syrian people'.[34] However, the rise of the Al-Nusra front (also known as Jabhat al-Nusra – a branch of al-Qaeda operating in Syria and Lebanon – the hardline Islamist terrorist group fighting the Western-backed Free Syrian Army, as well as other military groups) led to a marked cooling of international and regional support for the opposition in mid-2013. Notwithstanding this, large swathes of Syrian territory remain under rebel control, especially more recently under control of the Islamic State, which has, as noted, made significant gains on the ground in Syria as well as in neighbouring Iraq.[35]

In short, the Syrian conflict is complicated, messy and cruel and neither side has demonstrated much regard for civilian casualties. UN High Commissioner for Human Rights, Navi Pillay, has observed that the number of casualties in Syria is 'truly shocking'.[36] As of April 2014, the death toll stood at more than

31 Patrick Cockburn, 'ISIS Consolidates', LRB (online), 21 August 2014 www.lrb.co.uk/ v36/n16/patrick-cockburn/isis-consolidates. It has been argued that ISIS has not been targeted by the Syrian government 'with quite the same gusto' as other rebel factions. See, Michael Weiss, 'Trust Iran only as far as You Can Throw It', *Foreign Policy* (online), 23 June 2014 www.foreignpolicy.com/2014/06/.../trust-iran-only-as-far-as-you-can-throw-it. Brahimi, too, observes that 'ISIS controls one province and the government never attacks them'. See, Koelbl, above n 30, 3. It has been widely reported that the ISIS military strength is partly due to recruiting and training people including foreign nationals. It is believed that hundreds of German, British, Australian etc nationals have joined ISIS. See, Koelbl, ibid 5.

32 'Nasrallah says Hezbollah will not Bow to Sectarian Threats', *NOW News* (online), 14 June 2013 https://now.mmedia.me/.../ . But see, 'Syria Opposition Contradicts UN. Says Conflict not Sectarian', *Naharnet* (online), 22 December 2012 www.nasharnet.com/.../65685-syria-opposition-contradicts-u-n-says-conflict.

33 Ibid.

34 BBC News, 'Syria Profile, above n 8, 1.

35 Ibid 2.

36 'UN's Syria Death Toll Jumps Dramatically to 60,000-Plus', *CNN* (online), 3 January 2013 www.cnn.com/2013/01/02/world/meast/syria-civil-war.

190,000 people,[37] a high percentage of whom were civilians.[38] The severity of the humanitarian disaster in Syria has been outlined by the UN and many other international organisations. Reportedly, in one instance of a chemical weapons[39] attack in the Damascus suburbs on 21 August 2013 alone, the Syrian government killed 1,429 people, including at least 426 children.[40] The conflict has created about 3 million refugees,[41] turning Syria into the world's second-largest producer of refugees, after Afghanistan.[42] To add to this tragedy, more than 6.5 million Syrians are internally displaced.[43]

The Syrian conflict[44] has had a 'deep cultural dimension'[45] as well. The heavy toll that the conflict has had, and continues to have, on cultural property in Syria has been widely reported. In a joint statement the UN Secretary-General, Ban Ki-moon, UNESCO Director-General, Irina Bokova, and UN and League of Arab States Joint Special Representative for Syria from 2012 until 2014, Lakhdar Brahimi, declared that 'all layers of Syrian culture are now under attack – including pre-Christian, Christian and Muslim'.[46] The conflict has endangered museums and libraries, led to an unprecedented scale of looting and illicit trade in artefacts, and damaged numerous cultural sites including World Heritage sites. Today, in Syria, as the UN Secretary-General observes, '[w]hole urban centres and some of humankind's great architectural and cultural heritage

---

37 Laura Smith, 'More than 191,000 Dead in Syria, UN Rights Chief slams "Global Paralysis"', *CNN* (online), 15 October 2014 www.cnn.com/2014/08/22/world/meast/syria-conflict.

38 PBS Newshour, 'Updated: Your Cheat Sheet to the Syrian Conflict', 2 September 2013 at 5:59 PM EDT, 3 www.pbs.org/newshour/rundown/your-cheat-sheet-to-the-syrian-conflict/ 3.

39 See, eg, Koelbl, above n 30, 4.

40 PBS Newshour, above n 38, 3.

41 Brahimi predicts that in 2015 this number will increase to 4 million. See, Koelbl, above n 30, 2.

42 PBS Newshour, above n 38, 4. According to António Guterres, UN High Commissioner for Refugees, 'Syria has become the great tragedy of this century, a disgraceful humanitarian calamity with suffering and displacement unparalleled in recent history. The only solace is the humanity shown by the neighbouring countries in welcoming and saving the lives of so many refugees.' Ibid 5. See also, UN Security Council Resolution on Syria of 22 February 2014, UNSC Res 2139 (2014).

43 PBS Newshour, above n 38, 5. See also 'Syrian Refugees Biggest Humanitarian Crisis', *Middle East Star* (online), 28 August 2014 www.c1000veld.nl/web/browse.php?u...b=5; *HRC Eighth Report*, above n 3, 30.

44 For a chronology of coverage of the Syrian conflict see, eg, 'Syria', *The New York Times* (online) http://topics.nytimes.com/top/news/international/countriesandterritories/syria/index.html.

45 See, Sandra Roorda, 'Syria's Cultural Heritage in Danger: What Can We Do?' (21 October 2013) Cultural Heritage – Saving Antiquities for Everyone www.savingantiquities.org/tag/cultural-heritage-3/ (quoting Bonnie Burnham, President of the World Monuments Fund).

46 UN Vic, 'Stop the Destruction', above n 3.

lie in ruins'.[47] The result of this tragedy in Syria has been the eradication of Syria's rich cultural diversity – a loss not only for the Syrian people but for all humanity.

D. The impact of the conflict on Syria's cultural property

1. The damage to Syria's cultural property

A number of reports have documented damage to Syria's cultural property.[48] According to the UNITAR's Operational Satellite Applications Programme Report, entitled *Satellite-Based Damage Assessment to Cultural Heritage Sites in Syria* of 23 December 2014 (*UNOSAT Report*), the Syrian conflict has created a cultural catastrophe.[49] Some 93 per cent of Syria's total cultural sites are within areas of conflict and displacement. Graced with thousands of archaeological sites and magnificent historic monuments (including UNESCO World Heritage sites described above) within these areas of conflict, Syria is seeing its cultural property vandalised, looted and destroyed by conflict.[50] The *UNOSAT Report* found that of 290 locations that were examined using commercially available satellite imagery: twenty-four locations were destroyed; 104 severely damaged; eighty-five moderately damaged; and seventy-seven possibly damaged.[51]

---

47 Ban Ki-moon, United Nations Secretary-General, 'Crisis in Syria: Civil War, Global Threat' (25 June 2014) *Huffington Post*, 1 www.huffingtonpost.com/ban-kimoon/crisis-in-syria-civil-war_b_5529973.html.

48 See, generally, *UNOSAT Report*, above n 6 (using satellite technology and images to assess and analyse the state of cultural property in eighteen cultural heritage areas across Syria) www.unitar.org/unosat-report-damage-cultural-heritage-sites-syria-calls-scaled.... See also, *AAAS Report*, above n 6; UNESCO periodic reports, eg, 'Syria' www.unesco.org/new/en/safeguarding-syrian-cultural-heritage/; non-governmental organisations, eg, 'Syrian Heritage' www.asor-syrianheritage.org; cultural property blogs, eg, Illicit Cultural Property http://illicitculturalproperty.com/; and scholarly writing, eg, Al Quntar, 'Syrian Cultural Property in the Crossfire: Reality and Effectiveness of Protection Efforts' (2013) 1(4) *Journal of Eastern Mediterranean Archaeology and Heritage Studies* 348; Emma Cunliffe, 'No Longer Lost in the Wilderness: Cultural Property Crimes in Conflict' (2013) 1(4) *Journal of Eastern Mediterranean Archaeology and Heritage Studies* 343.

49 See, *UNOSAT Report*, above n 6.

50 The Global Heritage Fund's director of Global Projects, Dan Thompson has observed that '[a]ll of the country's world heritage sites have sustained damage, including the UNESCO site cities, and a great many of the other monuments in the country have been damaged, destroyed or have been subject to severe looting.' Chulov, above n 28, 5. Satellite images showed that sites in places like Aleppo have been torn apart by raiders and that thousands of Syrian artefacts are turning up on the black market. In August 2013, UNESCO deemed the situation to be 'catastrophic'. See, Tom Mashberg, 'Obama Asked to Protect Syrian Heritage Sites', *The New York Times* (online), 11 September 2013 www.nytimes.com.

51 *UNOSAT Report*, above n 6.

In 2013, all six of Syria's World Heritage-listed sites were categorised by UNESCO as 'World Heritage in Danger' sites,[52] with some structures already destroyed or seriously damaged by combat or looting.[53] Furthermore, other of Syria's cultural property sites in Syria have also been damaged and are threatened by continued fighting; for instance, the World Monument Fund has decided to list all of the cultural heritage sites within the entire of Syria as part of its 2014 World Monuments Watch List.[54] To give just a few other examples of the risks faced by cultural property in Syria: in Aleppo, the Ummayyad mosque came under artillery fire, destroying its ancient minarets; heavy fighting also damaged the Crusader castle Crac des Chevaliers; museums at Apamea, Aleppo and Raqqa experienced thefts; and the archaeological sites of Mari, Dura Europos, Halbia and Buseria have been damaged by illegal excavations.[55]

The major causes of damage to cultural property in Syria have been shelling, gunfire, looting at various tells, museums and monuments, vandalism, terrorism, uncontrolled/illegal construction and demolition. Cultural property sites have been brought into the battlefield, and Government forces and non-State armed groups (anti-Government armed groups and ISIL) are both responsible.[55] This last-listed cause – the use of cultural property for military purposes – is of the most immediate concern here.

2. The use of Syria's cultural property for military purposes

The use of cultural property for military purposes poses a grave threat to the survival of cultural property. Heavy damage to cultural objects can be caused, *inter alia*, by the mere presence of armed forces at the ancient sites or in their

---

52 'Syria's Six World Heritage Sites Placed on List of World Heritage in Danger' (20 June 2013) UNESCO World Heritage Centre http://whc.unesco.org/en/news/1038.

53 Roorda, above n 45.

54 See, eg, David Sokol, 'World Monuments Fund Releases 2014 Watch List', *Architectural Record*, 9 October 2013 http://archrecord.construction.com/news/2013/10/13/1009-World-Monuments-Fund-R.... Internally (in Syria), a group called Syrian Archaeological Heritage under Threat is monitoring and recording the destruction in an attempt to create a list of heritage sites damaged during the conflict and gain global support for the protection and preservation of Syrian archaeology and architecture. See, eg, Fisk, above n 7.

55 Heritage for Peace, above n 11, 1. Illegal digging is considered a grave danger. UNESCO has warned that illegal excavation at important archaeological sites in Syria is 'extremely dangerous' and 'lethal' to the country's heritage. Syria is witnessing illicit archaeological excavations across the country, including the ancient cities of Ebla, Palmyra, Apamea and Mari. UNESCO Assistant Director-General for Culture, Francesco Bandarin has warned that '[a]ll of them have been subject to this phenomenon, some of them to an extent that is unimaginable ... Apamea is completely destroyed'. See, Sanskrity Sinha, 'Illicit Excavation in Syria Lethal to Ancient Heritage', *IBTimes* (online), 6 February 2014 www.ibtimes.co.uk/illicit-excavation-syria-lethal-ancient-heritage-warns-un-143....

56 See, eg, *UNOSAT Report*, above n 6; *Cunliffe Report*, above n 6; *AAAS Report*, above n 6; Chulov, above n 28, 5.

vicinity (as this focuses the opponents' fire onto such objects), armed forces encampments located within areas of cultural significance, entrenchment of military vehicles and weapons, the movement of tanks over potentially fragile sites, the removal of stones or other materials from cultural sites for construction or other structures, and the use of sites or artefacts for target practice.

The normal elevation of ancient settlement mounds or tells (as a result of numerous episodes of ancient building construction superimposed on each other) makes these landmarks not only culturally important but also militarily attractive. In Syria the tells have been used by all sides to the conflict as gun emplacements and guard houses.[57] Tank positions are often dug into such mounds, as well as mines being placed on and around them to harm opponent parties if the station is captured. Some sites are also bulldozed to get building material for street barricades; others are cut for fire trenches or barrier trenches around cities.[58]

No party in the Syrian conflict has any concern about the protection of cultural property caught up in the conflict irrespective of World Heritage listing. Reportedly, five of six properties in Syria that are on the World Heritage List, as well as numerous other sites, have been used for military purposes. One example is the Crac des Chevaliers – the World Heritage site – which was bombed by the Syrian air forces in March 2014 to dislodge rebel fighters who had based themselves there,[59] leaving the castle in partial ruins.[60] Another World Heritage site caught up in the conflict is the Ancient City of Bosra, where a newly constructed fortified vehicle track through an archaeological area has been observed.[61] It has been suggested that the second century Roman amphitheatre was occupied during the fighting by army snipers and Shabiha militia firing at rebel pockets in this ancient city, its windows piled with sandbags.[62]

The World Heritage site of Palmyra has also been substantially impacted by being used for military purposes.[63] It has been evidenced that at this 2,000-year-old remains of the Roman oasis city the army has dug a road and earth dykes, and installed multiple rocket launchers inside the camp of the emperor Diocletian. Shells have hit the columns of the ancient city's Temple of Bel causing two of them to collapse. The temple is one of the most important religious buildings of its time in the Middle East.[64]

In the Ancient City of Aleppo, too, cultural property came under fire due to being used for military purposes. The 50 metre-tall Seljuk minaret of Aleppo's

---

57 See, *UNOSAT Report*, above n 6; *Cunliffe Report*, above n 6; and *AAAS Report*, above n 6.
58 Damien Huffer, 'Documenting the Damage: An Interview with Dr Simone Mühl' (3 October 2014) Saving Antiquities for Everyone www.savingantiquities.org/tag/cultural-heritage-3/.
59 Darke, above n 22, 1.
60 Chulov, above n 28, 3.
61 See, eg, *AAAS Report*, above n 6, 31; *Cunliffe Report*, above n 6, 8; *UNOSAT Report*, above n 6.
62 *Cunliffe Report*, above n 6, 8.
63 See, eg, Barnard, above n 7; Fisk, above n 7.
64 Darke, above n 22, 1.

Great Mosque, considered a masterpiece of elegance dating from 1095, whose height made it a useful rebel lookout and sniper position, collapsed as a result of shelling in March 2013. One commentator described its destruction as equivalent to the loss of Big Ben from the London skyline.[65] Another example of the use of cultural property for military purposes is when the Free Syrian Army rebels established a headquarters in a bath-house near Aleppo's thirteenth century souk, making it susceptible for attack. In the shelling, an electricity substation caught fire and flames quickly spread, reducing the souk's wooden doors and wares to ash.[66]

In April 2013, the Ebla mound or tell in western Syria, first settled more than 5,000 years ago, featuring ancient tombs and 5,000-year-old cuneiform tablets, had been garrisoned by rebels using them for spotting passing government military planes.[67] The tell Rifa'i, a national heritage site, was also heavily damaged by soldiers using it as a military camp.[68] Other cultural sites have been transformed for use in the battlefield and bombed in pursuit of deserters who take refuge in these places.[69]

These and other instances of the use of cultural property for military purposes and the associated damage and risk of damage have been strongly condemned by the international community,[70] demonstrating not only local but also

65 Ibid 2.
66 Ibid.
67 Derek Fincham, 'Looting at Ebla in Syria' (8 April 2013) Illicit Cultural Property http://illicitculturalproperty.com/author/webmaster/; Derek Fincham, 'Documenting destruction in Syria from afar' (13 December 2012) Illicit Cultural Property http://illicitculturalproperty.com/documenting-destruction-in-syria-from-afar/ ('Emma Cunliffe, an archaeologist, has been tracking the destruction and looting of sites in Syria using Facebook feeds and YouTube videos. She says it is incredible just how much you can find out from these posts. "It's a new world online now," she says. Cunliffe did her PhD research on monitoring Syrian archaeological sites with satellite imagery. When fighting turned fierce in Syria, she began to consult imagery much closer to the ground – videos and photos posted by concerned Syrian citizens. Sites were being damaged and also looted.').
68 See, *Cunliffe Report*, above n 6, 8.
69 Ibid 9.
70 See generally, Statements of the UNESCO Director-General on Syria at the UNESCO World Heritage Centre site http://whc.unesco.org/en/news and in particular, 'UNESCO Director-General Condemns Military Presence and Destruction at World Heritage Sites in Syria' (20 February 2014) UNESCO World Heritage Centre http://whc.unesco.org/en/news/1108. See also, Ban Ki-moon, above n 47; http://huffingpost.com/ban-kimoon/crisis-in-syria-civil-war_b5529973.html; AAP, 'UN Urges Halt to Attacks on Syria's Cultural Sites', above n 2 (a joint statement by the UN Secretary-General, Ban Ki-moon, UNESCO Director-General Irina Bokova and the joint UN-Arab League mediator on Syria, Lakhdar Brahimi, citing 'alarming reports' on attacks on Syria's cultural property and condemning the use of cultural property for military purposes or turning it into battlefields, and calling on all parties to halt immediately all destruction of Syrian heritage and protect the World Heritage sites, in line with UN Security Council Resolution 2139 (2014)); Bonnie Burnham, President of the World Monuments Fund, 'Remarks by Bonnie Burnham, President of World Monuments Fund, at the Press Conference on Heritage and Conflict in Iraq and Syria at the Metropolitan Museum of Art' (22 September, 2014) World Monuments Fund www.wmf.org/journal/remarks-bonnie-burnham-president-world-monuments-fu....

international concern for the protection of cultural property that has outstanding value for the cultural heritage of all humankind. This international concern raises the question of how international law responds to the use of cultural property for military purposes. That question in itself raises many others, including: whether international law distinguishes between the World Cultural Heritage and other cultural property; whether the use of cultural property for military purposes *ipso facto* transforms cultural objects into legitimate military targets; and whether an attack on cultural property made into a legitimate military objective should be carried out without any further consideration.

III. The legal framework

A. An international humanitarian law perspective

1. The applicable law

(A) TREATY LAW

Immovable cultural property is protected in times of conflict by both treaty international law and customary international law. Where treaty law is concerned, a number of international instruments address cultural property. They include (in chronological order): the *Hague Conventions of 1899*[71] and *1907*[72] *with Respect to the Laws and Customs of War on Land*, together with annexed *Regulations* (*1899 Convention II*; *1899 Regulations*; *1907 Convention IV*; *1907 Regulations*); the *Convention of 1907 Concerning Bombardment by Naval Forces in Time of War* (*1907 Convention IX*);[73] the *1954 Hague Convention for the Protection of Cultural Property in the Event of Armed Conflict* (*1954 Convention*);[74] the *1977 Protocol I* and *Protocol II*

---

71 *Convention (II) with respect to the Laws and Customs of War on Land*, opened for signature, The Hague, 29 July 1899, 32 Stat. 1803, TS 403, 26 (entered into force 4 September 1900) [hereinafter *1899 Hague Convention II*]; *Regulations concerning the Laws and Customs of War on Land*, annexed to *Convention (II) with respect to the Laws and Customs of War on Land*, The Hague, 29 July 1899 (entered into force 4 September 1900) [hereinafter *1899 Regulations*].

72 *Convention (IV) respecting the Laws and Customs of War on Land*, The Hague, 18 October 1907, 36 Stat. 2277 (1907), TS 539, 3 (entered into force 26 January 1910) [hereinafter *1907 Hague Convention IV*]; *Regulations concerning the Laws and Customs of War on Land*, The Hague, 18 October 1907 (entered into force 26 January 1910) [hereinafter *1907 Regulations*].

73 *Hague Convention (IX) concerning Bombardment by Naval Forces in Times of War*, The Hague, 18 October 1907, 36 Stat 2351 (entered into force 26 January 1910) [hereinafter *1907 Convention IX*].

74 *Convention for the Protection of Cultural Property in the Event of Armed Conflict*, opened for signature 14 May 1954, 249 UNTS 215 (entered into force 7 August 1956) [hereinafter *1954 Convention*]; *Regulations for the Execution of the Convention for the Protection of Cultural Property in the Event of Armed Conflict*, 14 May 1954 (annexed to the *Convention for the Protection of Cultural Property in the Event of Armed Conflict*, opened for signature 14 May 1954, 249 UNTS 215 (entered into force 7 August 1956)) [hereinafter *1954 Regulations*].

Additional to the Geneva Conventions of 12 August 1949, and relating to the Protection of Victims of International and Non-International Armed Conflict respectively (*Protocol I*; *Protocol II*);[75] and the *1999 Protocol for the Protection of Cultural Property in the Event of Armed Conflict (1999 Protocol).*[76]

The 1972 *Convention concerning the Protection of the World Cultural and Natural Heritage* (*WHC*)[77] predominantly deals with the protection of the world heritage in peacetime, but it also contains provisions that relate to time of armed conflict. Given that a number of properties situated in Syria are on the World Heritage Lists it is important to mention this convention here as well.

(i) 1899 and 1907 Conventions The *1899* and *1907 Conventions* provide protection to a range of objects, including historic monuments and buildings dedicated to religion, art or science, and place the obligation on the besieged to mark these objects by distinctive and visible signs and to give notice to the enemy beforehand.[78] The *1907 Convention IX*, which provides protection for a similar range of objects, specifies this sign.[79] However, these three conventions deal with cultural property rather sporadically. Syria is party to none of them.[80]

(ii) 1954 Convention The *1954 Convention* is the first international multilateral treaty that covers cultural property in armed conflict exclusively. The *Convention* explicitly recognises the dual character of cultural property by instructing that 'damage to cultural property belonging to any people whatsoever means damage to the cultural heritage of all [hu]mankind, since each people makes its contribution to the culture of the world'.[81] In other words, cultural property is not only important at the national level, but is also important universally.[82]

75 *Protocol Additional to the Geneva Conventions of 12 August 1949, and relating to the Protection of Victims of International Armed Conflict*, Geneva, 8 June 1977, 1125 UNTS 3 (entered into force 7 December 1978) [hereinafter *Protocol I*]; *Protocol Additional to the Geneva Conventions of 12 August 1949, and relating to the Protection of Victims of Non-International Armed Conflict*, Geneva, 8 June 1977, 1125 UNTS 609 (entered into force 7 December 1978) [hereinafter *Protocol II*].

76 *Second Protocol to the Hague Convention for the Protection of Cultural Property in the Event of Armed Conflict*, opened for signature 26 March 1999, 38 ILM 769 (entered into force 9 March 2004) [hereinafter *1999 Protocol*].

77 *Convention concerning the Protection of the World Cultural and Natural Heritage*, opened for signature 16 November 1972, 1037 UNTS 151 (entered into force 17 December 1975) [hereinafter *WHC*].

78 See, *1907 Regulations* Articles 27 and 56. Similar prohibition is contained in Article 5(1) of the *1907 Convention IX*.

79 *1907 Convention IX* Article 5(2).

80 Lists of States Parties to the *1899* and *1907 Conventions*, as well as other instruments of international humanitarian law are available at *ICRC* website www.icrc.org/applic/ihl....

81 *1954 Convention*, preamble [2].

82 See, eg, John Merryman, 'Two Ways of Thinking about Cultural Property' (1986) 80 *American Journal of International Law* 831.

This convention provides for two-tier protection: general and special protection. 'General protection' is granted to all movable and immovable property 'of great importance to the cultural heritage of every people' defined as 'cultural' in Article 1 of the *Convention*.[83] In accordance with Articles 2–4 of the *Convention*, all cultural property must be safeguarded in peacetime and respected during time of armed conflict, and may bear a distinctive emblem.[84] 'Special protection', on the other hand, is accorded only to a limited number of refuges intended to shelter movable cultural property in the event of armed conflict, of centres containing monuments and other immovable cultural property 'of very great importance' provided that a set of strict requirements specified in Article 8 of the *Convention* is met.[85] During an armed conflict, cultural property under special protection must be marked by the distinctive emblem of the *Convention*.[86]

The *1954 Convention* applies to both international armed conflict[87] and non-international armed conflict.[88] It obligates High Contracting Parties to refrain from acts of hostility directed against cultural property. Syria is one such Party.[89] All cultural property situated in Syria is protected under a 'general protection' rather than a 'special protection' regime as Syria does not have any property, not even any of its World Heritage sites, entered in the 'International Register of Cultural Property under Special Protection'.[90]

---

83 *1954 Convention* Article 1:
> For the purpose of the present convention, the term 'cultural property' shall cover, irrespective of origin or ownership:
> Movable or immovable property of great importance to the cultural heritage of every people, such as monuments of architecture, art or history, whether religious or secular; archaeological sites; groups of buildings which, as a whole, are of historical or artistic interest; works of art; manuscripts, books and other objects of artistic, historical or archaeological interest; as well as scientific collections and important collections of books or archives or of reproductions of the property defined above;
> Buildings whose main and effective purpose is to preserve or exhibit the movable cultural property defined in sub-paragraph (a) such as museums, large libraries and depositories of archives, and refuges intended to shelter, in the event of armed conflict, the movable cultural property defined in sub-paragraph (a);
> Centres containing a large amount of cultural property as defined in sub-paragraphs (a) and (b), to be known as 'centres containing monuments'.

84 *1954 Convention* Article 6.

85 *1954 Convention* Article 8.

86 *1954 Convention* Article 10.

87 *1954 Convention* Article 18.

88 *1954 Convention* Article 19. See also, Theodor Meron, 'The Protection of Cultural Property in the Event of Armed Conflict within the Caselaw of the International Criminal Tribunal for the Former Yugoslavia' (2005) 57(4) *Museum International* 41, 42–3.

89 Lists of States Parties to legal instruments are available at UNESCO portal at http://portal.unesco.org/en/ev.php.

90 *1954 Convention* Article 8(6). In *Kordić*, the Trial Chamber discussed special protection under Article 8 of the *1954 Convention* and concluded that there was 'little difference between the conditions for the according of general protection and those for the provision of special protection'. *Prosecutor v Kordić and Čerkez (Judgment) (International Criminal Tribunal for the former Yugoslavia, Trial Chamber*, Case No IT-95-14/2-T, 26 February 2001) [361].

(iii) WHC   Although primarily concerned with peacetime, the obligations imposed by the *WHC* do extend to some extent to time of armed conflict as well. This convention protects properties under the rubric of 'cultural heritage'[91] that fall into three categories: monuments, groups of buildings and sites, which are of outstanding historic, artistic or scientific value.[92] Such properties enter the 'World Heritage List'.[93] While noting respect for States Parties sovereignty, Article 6 of the *WHC* highlights the universal character of properties to which protection is granted[94] and requires States Parties not to take any deliberate measures that might damage directly or indirectly the cultural heritage protected by the *Convention*.[95] The *Convention* points to various serious and specific threats to cultural heritage, including the outbreak or the threat of an armed conflict. It also envisages the 'list of World Heritage in Danger' for properties inscribed on the World Heritage List whose conservation requires major operations and for which assistance has been requested.[96]

Syria has been party to the WHC since its accession in 1975. As discussed, six of its properties are inscribed on the World Heritage List, all of which have been included in the World Heritage in Danger List since 2013. A number of properties situated in Syria are also on the World Heritage Tentative List waiting for inscription. Thus Syria is obligated to refrain from taking any deliberate measures that might endanger part of the World Heritage situated within its borders.

(iv) Protocol I and Protocol II   Almost identical provisions of Article 53 of the 1977 *Protocol I* and of Article 16 of *Protocol II* provide protection for historic monuments, works of art or places of worship which constitute the cultural or spiritual heritage of peoples.[97] Article 53 makes it clear that its provisions are without prejudice to the provisions of the *1954 Convention* and other relevant instruments, presumably the *1899* and *1907 Conventions*, and the *1935 Washington* or *Roerich Pact*,[98] as there is a direct reference to these instruments in the preamble to the *1954 Convention*.[99] Syria is party to *Protocol I* applicable to international armed conflict, but it is not party to *Protocol II* applicable to non-international armed conflict.[100] Yet, the Syrian armed conflict is likely to meet

---

91 The *WHC* also covers natural heritage and mixed cultural-natural heritage.
92 See, *WHC* Article 1.
93 *WHC* Article 11(2).
94 *WHC* Article 6(1).
95 *WHC* Article 6(3).
96 *WHC* Article 11(4).
97 *Protocol I* Article 53; *Protocol II* Article 16.
98 *Treaty on the Protection of Artistic and Scientific Institutions and Historic Monuments*, Washington, DC, 15 April 1935, 49 Stat 3267 TS 899, 167 LNTS 289 [hereinafter *Roerich Pact*] www.fletcher.tufts.edu/multi/.roerich.html.
99 See, *1954 Convention*, preamble [4].
100 The list of IHL/ICL treaties to which Syria is party is available at ICRC site at www.icrc. org/applic/ihl/ihl.nsf/vw/TreatiesByCountrySelected.xsp?cp_country....

the requirements of Article 1 of *Protocol II* which defines a non-international armed conflict, namely, an armed conflict which takes place 'in the territory of a High Contracting Party between its armed forces and dissident armed forces or other organised armed groups which, under responsible command, exercise such control over a part of its territory as to enable them to carry out sustained and concerted military operations and to implement this protocol'.[101]

(v) 1999 Protocol   The *1999 Protocol* also applies to both international and non-international armed conflicts. The protocol introduces the third tier of protection for cultural property under the *1954 Convention* regime. This protection is envisaged for cultural property 'of the greatest importance for humanity', the so-called 'enhanced protection'.[102] The 'enhanced protection' is designed to replace the 'special protection' which proved to be ineffective.[103] Syria is not party to this protocol and thus none of the cultural properties situated in this State are under the 'enhanced protection' regime.[104]

The conventions and protocols discussed thus far are essentially legal instruments elaborated and adopted by States. While there are some overlaps and synergies between them, each of the instruments is binding only within its specific scope of application, timeframe and subject matter. Of all the above-

---

101   *Protocol II* Article 1. For discussion about the difference between armed conflict and internal disturbance see, eg, Jean Pictet, *The Geneva Conventions of 12 August 1949, Commentary* (1952) Art 3, at 49–50.

102   *1999 Protocol* Article 10.

103   See, eg, UNESCO World Heritage Committee, 8th sess, Phuket, Thailand, 12–17 December 1994, Information note: International Register of Cultural Property under Special Protection: Coordination of Implementation of Conventions Protecting the Cultural Heritage, WHC-94/CONF.003/INF.12, 16 November 1994; World Heritage Site www.worldheritage site.org/forums/index.php?action=vthread&forum=8&topi.... Due to stringent requirements of Article 8 of the *1954 Convention* there is only a modest number of entries in the International Register of Cultural Property under Special Protection.

104   For further information on 'enhanced protection' see, eg, UNESCO, 'Committee for the Protection of Cultural Property in the Event of Armed Conflict' established by the *1999 Protocol* www.unesco.org/new/en/culture/themes/armed-conflict-and-heritage/the-cimmi...; *Second Protocol to the Hague Convention of 1954 for the Protection of Cultural Property in the Event of Armed Conflict*, Committee for the Protection of Cultural Property in the Event of Armed Conflict, 8th mtg, UNESCO Headquarters, Paris, 18–19 December 2013, Item 11 of the Provisional Agenda: Consideration of requests for the granting of enhanced protection, CLT-13/8.COM/CONF.203/8 Paris, 17 October 2013; Meetings of the Committee for the Protection of Cultural Property in the Event of Armed Conflict (with a link to the List of Cultural Property under Enhanced Protection, total: ten sites, all of them being World Heritage properties: Azerbaijan–2; Belgium–3; Cyprus–3; Italy–1; and Lithuania–1, as at 20 March 2014) www.unesco.org/new/en/culture/themes/armed-conflict-and-heritage/the-commi..., and 9th mtg of the Committee for the Protection of Cultural Property in the Event of Armed Conflict, 18–19 December 2014, CLT-14/9.Com/CONF.203/7, Paris, 15 October 2014 www.unesco.org/new/en/culture/themes/armed-conflict-and-heritage/the-commi....

mentioned international instruments Syria is only party to the *1954 Convention*, the *WHC* and *Protocol I*, and is therefore not bound by the *1899* and *1907 Conventions*, *Protocol II* and the *1999 Protocol* under the rubric of 'treaty international law'. In relation to the *1999 Protocol*, it should be noted that Syria signed this protocol on 17 May 1999. Pursuant to Article 18 of the *Vienna Convention of the Law of Treaties*, signature obligates signatories not to defeat treaty's object and purpose prior to ratification.[105] Thus, Syria is under such obligation vis-à-vis the *1999 Protocol*.

(B) CUSTOMARY LAW

Irrespective of whether they are parties to treaties protecting cultural property in armed conflict, all States have certain obligations to protect cultural property during conflicts by virtue of customary international law. It has been recognised that the provisions of the *1907 Convention IV*,[106] the provisions of the *1954 Convention* concerning 'general protection' of cultural property,[107] and some provisions of *Protocol I* and *Protocol II*, including Articles 53 (of *Protocol I*) and 16 (of *Protocol II*),[108] form part of customary international law.

Based on norms of customary international law, in both international armed conflict and non-international armed conflict, special care must be taken in military operations to avoid damage to buildings dedicated to religion, art, science, education or charitable purposes, and historic monuments unless they are military objectives.[109] Property of great importance to the cultural heritage of every people must not be the object of attack unless imperatively required by

---

105 See, *Convention on the Law of Treaties* 18, 23 May 1969, 1155 UNTS 331, Art 18 [hereinafter *Vienna Convention*]. See also, David S Jonas and Thomas N Saunders, 'The Object and Purpose of a Treaty: Three Interpretative Methods' (2010) 43 *Vanderbilt Journal of Transnational Law* 565, 594–608.

106 See, Report of the Secretary-General Pursuant to Paragraph 2 of Security Council Resolution 808 (1993), paras 41–2, UN Doc S/25704 of 3 May 1993, 32 ILM 1159 [1993 Report of the Secretary-General].

107 See, eg, David Meyer, 'The 1954 Hague Cultural Property Convention and Its Emergence into Customary International Law' (1993) 11 *Boston University International Law Journal* 349; Jean-Marie Henckaerts and Louise Doswald-Beck (eds), *Customary International Humanitarian Law* (2005) vol 1 *Rules*, 129; vol II *Practice*, Chapter 12: Cultural Property, 723 *et seq* [*Customary IHL*]; *Prosecutor v Tadić* (*Decision of the Defence Motion for Interlocutory Appeal on Jurisdiction*) (*International Criminal Tribunal for the former Yugoslavia, Appeals Chamber*, Case No. IT-94-1-AR, 2 October 1995) [127] [*Tadić Jurisdiction Decision*].

108 See, Meyer, above n 107. See also, Christopher Greenwood, 'Customary Law Status of the 1977 Geneva Protocols' in Astrid Delissen and Gerard Tanja (eds), *Essays in Honour of Frits Kalshoven* (Martinus Nijhoff, 1991) 93, 110; *Prosecutor v Strugar* (*Judgment*) (*International Criminal Tribunal for the former Yugoslavia, Trial Chamber II*, Case No. IT-01-42-T, 31 January 2005) [223] [*Strugar Judgment*].

109 Article 52 of *Protocol I*, which prohibits making civilian objects the 'object of attack' has also entered customary international law. See, eg, *Tadić Jurisdiction Decision* [127].

military necessity.[110] States are also under an obligation not to use cultural property of great importance for purposes which are likely to expose it to destruction or damage, unless required by military necessity.[111] The following section considers this last-listed obligation.

2. *The prohibition to use cultural property for military purposes*

(A) CULTURAL PROPERTY GENERALLY

It is a well-established rule of international law that cultural property loses its protection in armed conflict if it is used for military purposes. Article 27 of the *1907 Regulations* stipulates that 'in sieges and bombardments all necessary steps must be taken to spare, as far as possible, buildings dedicated to religion, art, science, or charitable purposes, historic monuments . . . *provided they are not being used at the time for military purposes*'.[112] This rule has been emphasised in the jurisprudence of the international criminal tribunals. For example, in *Kordić* the Trial Chamber of the *International Criminal Tribunal for the former Yugoslavia* (*ICTY*) was of the view that 'protection of whatever type will be lost if cultural property . . . is used for military purpose', which principle the Chamber found to be 'consistent with the custom codified in Article 27' of the *1907 Regulations*.[113]

The same requirement is explicitly referred to in other relevant instruments. Article 53 of *Protocol I* and Article 16 of *Protocol II* prohibit the use of cultural property 'in support of military effort'.[114] The *1954 Convention* goes a step further by prohibiting, in its Article 4(1), the use not only of cultural property but also 'its immediate surroundings or of the appliances in use for its protection for purposes which are likely to expose it to destruction or damage in the event of armed conflict'.[115] This added location requirement is also imposed in Article 8(1)(a) of the *Convention* in relation to cultural property under 'special protection'. This requirement has been rejected in some decisions of the *ICTY*, however. For instance, expressly rejecting this requirement previously announced in *Blaškić*, the *Naletilić* Trial Chamber was of the view that the mere fact that cultural property is in the 'immediate vicinity of the military objective' does not justify

---

110   *1907 Regulations* Articles 23(g) and 27.
111   Ibid Article 27(1) and *1954 Convention* Article 4(1), (2).
112   *1907 Regulations* Article 27(1) (emphasis added).
113   *Prosecutor v Kordić and Čerkez* 361. This requirement was first announced in *Blaškić* and then reiterated in other *ICTY* decisions, including *Naletilić and Martinović* and *Strugar*. See, *Prosecutor v Blaškić* (*Judgment*) (*International Criminal Tribunal for the former Yugoslavia, Trial Chamber*, Case No IT-95-14-T, 3 March 2000) [185]; *Prosecutor v Naletilić and Martinović* (*Judgment*) (*International Criminal Tribunal for the former Yugoslavia, Trial Chamber*, Case No IT-98-34-T, 31 March 2003) [603]; *Strugar Judgment* [310].
114   *Protocol I* Article 53; *Protocol II* Article 16.
115   *1954 Convention* Article 4(1).

its destruction.[116] The *Strugar* Trial Chamber reiterated the conclusion in *Naletilić* noting that 'the preferable view appears to be that it is the use of cultural property and not its location that determines whether and when the cultural property would lose its protection'.[117]

The *1999 Protocol*, too, prohibits the use of cultural property for military purposes. It explicitly requires that cultural property under enhanced protection is not to be used for military purposes or to shield military sites, and that a State Party to the *Protocol* which has control over the cultural property declares that it will not be so used.[118]

Notwithstanding this, unlike the *1907 Regulations* (which point to the use of cultural property 'at the time' concerned), both the *1954 Convention* (with respect to cultural property under 'general protection') and *Protocols I* and *II* are silent on the question of when/for how long an object of cultural property is to be deemed to be used for military purposes.[119]

Furthermore, none of these three instruments defines the concept of the use of cultural property for military purposes under the rubric of 'general protection', either. However, Article 8(3) of the *1954 Convention*, concerned with protection of centres containing monuments under 'special protection', instructs that the centres will be deemed to be used for military purposes whenever they are 'used for the movement of military personnel or material, even in transit' and 'whenever activities directly connected with military operations, the stationing of military personnel, or the production of war material are carried on within the centre'.[120]

---

116 *Naletilić Judgment* [604].

117 *Strugar Judgment* [310]. This view has also been reflected in scholarly writing. See, eg, Jean-Marie Henckaerts, 'New Rules for the Protection of Cultural Property in Armed Conflict' (1999) 835 *International Review of the Red Cross* 593; Roger O'Keefe, *The Protection of Cultural Property in Armed Conflict* (Cambridge University Press, 2006) 254; Jadranka Petrovic, *The Old Bridge of Mostar and Increasing Respect for Cultural Property in Armed Conflict* (Martinus Nijhoff Publishers, 2013), 160.

118 *1999 Protocol* Article 10(1)(c).

119 The *ICRC Commentary* on Article 53 of *Protocol I*: 'if protected objects were used in support of the military effort, this would obviously constitute a violation of Article 53 of the *Protocol*, though it would not necessarily justify attacking them . . . such a right would depend on whether an object is being a military objective, or not, as defined in Article 52, paragraph 2.' Accordingly, 'it is not permitted to destroy a cultural object whose use does not make any contribution to military action, nor a cultural object which has temporarily served as a refuge for combatants, but is no longer used as such.' Yves Sandoz, Christophe Swiranski and Bruno Zimmerman (eds), *Commentary on the Additional Protocols of 8 June 1977 to the Geneva Conventions of 12 August 1949* (ICRC/Martinus Nijhoff, 1987) [2079]. The *1999 Protocol* does provide that cultural property can be used for military purposes on the basis of imperative military necessity 'when and for as long as: (i) that cultural property has, by its function, been made into a military objective'. *1999 Protocol* Art 6(1)(a)(i).

120 *1954 Convention* Article 8(3).

(B) WORLD HERITAGE SITES

The relevant legal instruments governing the use of cultural property for military purposes do not contain provisions dealing specifically with cultural property inscribed on the World Heritage List. In times of armed conflict the cultural properties on this list are governed by the rules envisaged for 'special protection' or 'enhanced protection' provided that such properties are entered in the 'International Register of Cultural Property under Special Protection'[121] and the 'List of Cultural Property under Enhanced Protection'[122] respectively. Otherwise, rules pertinent to cultural property under 'general protection' apply.

In contrast to the rules relating to the 'special' and 'enhanced' protection, which strictly prohibit the use of cultural property for military purposes,[123] the rules applicable to 'general protection' (as discussed below) provide that the prohibition not to use cultural property for military purposes may be waived if military necessity requires such a waiver, even if cultural property is of outstanding universal value and is inscribed on the World Heritage List.

It should be noted that to date, of all 779 cultural properties inscribed on the World Heritage List,[124] only the Vatican City (also known as the Holy See) is included in the 'International Register of Cultural Property under Special Protection'. None of the six World Heritage properties situated in Syria is included in this register.[125] Not any of those six properties is on the 'List of Cultural Property under Enhanced Protection' either. Thus, the rules governing 'general protection' of cultural property, together with the possibility of a waiver on the basis of military necessity, apply to Syria.

3. Military necessity

Paradoxically, the very same law that proscribes the use of cultural property for military purposes permits a holder of cultural property to use cultural property for military purposes on the basis of military necessity even though this may pose

---

121 Ibid Article 8(6).
122 *1999 Protocol* Articles 11(2) and 27(1)(b).
123 See, *1954 Convention* Articles 8(1)(b), 8(5), 9; *1999 Protocol* Article 19(c).
124 As of June 2014, 1,007 sites are listed on the World Heritage List: 779 cultural; 197 natural; and thirty-one mixed properties, in 161 States Parties to the *WHC*. The World Heritage List is available at http://whc.unesco.org/en/statesparties/au.
125 The Committee for the Protection of Cultural Property in the Event of Armed Conflict has been making efforts to develop synergies and complementarity between the *WHC* and the *1999 Protocol*. Potential modifications to the nomination format for the World Heritage List have been explored in order to allow States that are party to both the *WHC* and the *1999 Protocol* to apply simultaneously, at their convenience, for inscription on the World Heritage List and on the List of Cultural Property under Enhanced Protection. It has been considered, however, that an integrated approach to periodic reporting would be more appropriate. See, Committee for the Protection of Cultural Property in the Event of Armed Conflict, 9th mtg 18–19 December 2014, Item 9 of the Provisional Agenda: 'Development of synergies with other relevant UNESCO normative instruments and programmes and strengthening partnership', CLT-14/9.COM/CONF.203/7, Paris, 15 October 2014, [4].

a significant danger to cultural property.[126] Article 4 of the *1954 Convention* first obligates States Parties to refrain 'from any act of hostility directed against [cultural] property' and 'from any use of the property and its immediate surroundings or of the appliances in use for its protection for purposes which are likely to expose it to destruction or damage in the event of armed conflict'.[127] This article then spells out that the obligation to 'refrain from *any use* of the property and its immediate surroundings or of the appliances in use for its protection for purposes which are likely to expose it to destruction or damage in the event of armed conflict',[128] as well as the obligation not to attack cultural property, may be waived in cases where military necessity 'imperatively' requires such a waiver.[129] However, the *Convention* does not define this concept.

Article 6 of the *1999 Protocol* clarifies the notion of 'imperative' military necessity. Pursuant to this article a waiver on the basis of imperative military necessity under Article 4(2) of the *1954 Convention* may only be invoked to direct an act of hostility against cultural property when and for as long as that cultural property has, by its function,[130] been made into a military objective and there is no feasible alternative to obtain a similar military advantage to that offered by directing an act of hostility against that objective.[131] Therefore, both a holder of cultural property and the opponent may invoke military necessity in cases of the use of cultural property for military purposes. This is applicable only to the system of 'general protection'.

In contrast, for cultural property under the 'special protection' the *Convention* does not envisage a waiver of military necessity to use cultural property for military purposes.[132] Pursuant to Article 8 of the *Convention* special protection is granted, *inter alia*, on a condition that cultural property is *not* used for military

---

126 For a discussion on the concept of military necessity see generally, Petrovic, above n 117. See also, Henckaerts, 'New Rules', above n 117; APV Rogers, *Law on the Battlefield* (Manchester University Press, 2004); Jiří Toman, *The Protection of Cultural Property in the Event of Armed Conflict. Commentary on the Convention for the Protection of Cultural Property in the Event of Armed Conflict, signed on 14 May 1954 in The Hague, and on other instruments concerning such protection* (UNESCO Publishing, 1996); William Downey, 'The Law of War and Military Necessity' (1953) 47 *American Journal of International Law* 256; William O'Brien, 'The Meaning of "Military Necessity" in International Law' (1957) 1 *World Polity* 109; Ashlyn Milligan, 'Targeting Cultural Property: The Role of International Law' (2008) 19 *Journal of Public and International Affairs* 91; Elizabeth Varner, 'The Art of Armed Conflicts: An Analysis of the United States' Legal Requirements Towards Cultural Property under the 1954 Hague Convention' (2011) 44 *Creighton Law Review* 1185.

127 *1954 Convention* Article 4(1).

128 *1954 Convention* Article 4(1) (emphasis added).

129 *1954 Convention* Article 4(2).

130 For discussion about the meaning of the phrase 'by its function', see generally, Henckaerts, 'New Rules', above n 117.

131 *1999 Protocol* Article 6(a).

132 See, eg, Milligan, above n 126, 96–7; Thomas Desch, 'The Second Protocol to the 1954 Hague Convention for the Protection of Cultural Property in the Event of Armed Conflict' (1999) 2 *Yearbook of International Humanitarian Law* 63, 75–9; Jiří Toman, *Cultural Property in War: Improvement in Protection. A Commentary on the 1999 Second Protocol to the Hague Convention of 1954 for the Protection of Cultural Property in the Event of Armed Conflict* (UNESCO Publishing, 2009) [*1999 Commentary*].

purposes.[133] This is an absolute prohibition, explicitly stressed in Article 9 of the *1954 Convention* which demands that the High Contracting Parties refrain 'from any use of such property or its surroundings for military purposes'.[134]

Similarly, in accordance with Article 10(c) of the *1999 Protocol*, it is not permissible to use cultural property under the enhanced protection for military purposes or to shield military sites. To this end, the State Party which has control over the cultural property must make a declaration 'confirming that it will not be so used'.[135] Furthermore, Article 12 of the *1999 Protocol* makes it clear that the parties to a conflict must refrain from 'any use of the property or its immediate surroundings in support of military action'.[136] Where cultural property under enhanced protection is being used for military purposes such property may only be the object of attack if 'the attack is the only feasible means of terminating the use of the property [and] all feasible precautions are taken in the choice of means and methods of attack'.[137] If circumstances permit, the attack needs to be ordered at the highest operational level of command, effective advance warning is issued to the opposing forces and reasonable time is given to them to redress the situation.[138] A holder of cultural property included in the List of Cultural Property under Enhanced Protection who intentionally uses such property or its immediate surroundings in support of military action commits an offence and is liable to punishment as a war criminal.[139]

Protocol I and *Protocol II* do not permit the use of 'the historic monuments, works of art or places which constitute the cultural or spiritual heritage of peoples' in support of the military effort on the basis of military necessity.[140] However, Article 53 of *Protocol I* applies 'without prejudice to the provisions of the [*1954*] *Convention*'. In effect, this means that in case of contradiction the *1954 Convention* prevails, and thus imperative military necessity may be invoked, provided that the Parties concerned are bound by the *Convention*.[141]

However, the use of cultural property for military purposes by a holder of cultural property does not *ipso facto* absolve the opponent from its obligation not to attack cultural property,[142] or rather to invoke military necessity to do so. This

---

133 *1954 Convention* Article 8(1)(b).
134 *1954 Convention* Article 9.
135 *1999 Protocol* Article 10(c).
136 *1999 Protocol* Article 12.
137 *1999 Protocol* Articles 13(b) and 13(2)(a)(b).
138 *1999 Protocol* Article 13(2)(c).
139 *1999 Protocol* Article 15(1)(b).
140 *Protocol I* Article 53; *Protocol II* Article 16.
141 See, Sandoz *et al.*, above n 119 [640] ('If one of the Parties is not bound by the Convention Article 53 applies. Moreover, Article 53 applies even if all Parties concerned are bound by another international instrument insofar as it supplements the rules of that instrument'). Ibid.
142 See, eg, Kevin Chamberlain, *War and Cultural Heritage: An Analysis of the 1954 Convention for the Protection of Cultural Property in the Event of Armed Conflict and Its Two Protocols* (Institute of Art and Law, 2004) 37; Varner, above n 126, 1211; Toman, *1996 Commentary*, above n 126, 72.

points to the importance of the question of balance between the exigencies of armed conflict and the desire to preserve for posterity the cultural heritage of humankind,[143] that is, the question of whether the concept of military necessity and humanity generate imperatives and whether these imperatives create norm conflicts. In addressing this question it is useful to look at Nobuo Hayashi's reasoning on the proposition that International Humanitarian Law 'accounts for' military necessity.[144] Hayashi posits that '[i]t is always possible for the belligerent to act in a manner that jointly satisfies military necessity and humanity'.[145] In Hayashi's view, there are numerous instances where performing or forbearing given belligerent conduct is both humane and militarily necessary – or both inhumane and militarily unnecessary – at the same time.[146] From the International Humanitarian Law normative perspective, 'neither military necessity nor military non-necessity really makes the performance or forbearance of any belligerent behaviour mandatory. Rather, it *only permits.*'[147] In other words, normatively, military necessity leaves the belligerent at liberty to pursue material military necessities and to avoid non-necessities: 'even to forbear military necessity conduct and to perform unnecessary conduct . . . normative military necessity does not *per se* prompt the framers of IHL rules to make pursuing material necessities and avoiding material military non-necessities obligatory'.[148] The conduct-kind destroying cultural property in armed conflict as a response to cultural property being used for military purposes is a good example. While there have been numerous instances of the destruction of cultural property on this pretext throughout history, including WWI and WWII,

---

143 See, eg, Milligan, above n 126, 97.
144 See, Nobuo Hayashi, 'Military Necessity as Normative Indifference' (2013) 44 *Georgetown Journal of International Law* 675 [hereinafter 'Military Necessity'] and Nobuo Hayashi, 'Basic Principles', pdf file available at www.militarynecessity.com/.../routledge_loac_handbook_basic_princip... [hereinafter 'Basic Principles'].
145 Hayashi, 'Military Necessity' above n 144, 679. The idea that international humanitarian law has been developed with a view to striking a realistic and meaningful balance between military necessity and humanity finds support in treaty provisions (see, eg, *1907 Convention IV*), as well as scholarly writings (see, eg, Geoffrey Best, 'The Restraints of War in Historical and Philosophical Perspective' in Astrid JM Delissen and Gerard J Tanja (eds), *Humanitarian Law of Armed Conflict Challenges Ahead: Essays in Honour of Frits Kalshoven* (Martinus Nijhoff, 1991) 3, 5; Sandoz *et al.*, above n 119, 389, 392–3; Christopher Greenwood, 'Historical Development and Legal Basis' in Dieter Fleck (ed.), *The Handbook of International Humanitarian Law* (Oxford University Press, 2nd edn, 2008, 1st edn, 1995) 1, 37; Chris af Jochnick and Roger Normand, 'The Legitimation of Violence: A Critical History of the Laws of War' (1994) 35 *Harvard International Law Journal* 49, 53; Michael N Schmitt, 'Military Necessity and Humanity in International Humanitarian Law: Preserving the Delicate Balance' (2010) 50 *Virginia Journal of International Law* 795, 798).
146 Hayashi, 'Military Necessity, above n 144, 679.
147 Ibid 680 (emphasis added).
148 Ibid 684.

and the more recent Balkan conflicts, on a number of occasions cultural property has also been spared even though it has been used for military purposes.[149]

'Material' military necessity (as opposed to 'normative' military necessity) is situation-specific and evaluative in nature.[150] Essentially, it is about calculating the degree of cogency between the means taken or considered, on the one hand, and the ends sought, on the other, under the circumstances prevailing or anticipated at the relevant time.[151]

Military necessity is sometimes equated with military objective.[152] However, this equation is unhelpful,[153] since the former pertains to *conduct* whereas the latter pertains to *objects*.[154] As Hayashi correctly observes, whereas international law permits or tolerates given conduct as militarily necessary or unnecessary, an object which constitutes a military objective or a civilian object, becomes principally liable to or immune from attacks.[155]

At the practical level, humanity's outstanding cultural achievements are 'at the mercy of the relatively parochial interests of certain belligerents',[156] which is dissonant with the main premises of the *1954 Convention*. Put bluntly, as the appropriateness of the 'conduct', or the invocation of military necessity, is essentially in the hands of a military commander, who in some instances may not know anything about the importance of preservation of cultural property, and whose information on the basis of which a decision to harm cultural property is to be made might have ideological connotations.

---

149   During WWII, in Rome in 1943, for example, the US forces spared the enemy's military headquarters (clearly deemed a legitimate military target) as it was situated in the historic city centre, and generally, orders were given that the US planes return with their bombs if the targets were obscured or unidentifiable. See, eg, O'Keefe, *The Protection of Cultural Property in Armed Conflict*, above n 117, 70–73. Another example involves the US commanders' decision not to attack military targets – two MiG fighter aircrafts placed next to the temple of Ur – in Iraq, during the Gulf War in 1991, on the basis of respect for cultural property. See, US Department of Defense, *Final Report to Congress on Conduct in Persian Gulf War* (1992) 612–15.

150   Hayashi, 'Military Necessity' above n 144, 682.

151   Ibid 681.

152   See, eg, *Strugar Judgment* [295]; *Prosecutor v Brđanin* (*Judgment*) (*International Criminal Tribunal for the former Yugoslavia, Appeals Chamber*, Case No IT-99-36-A, 3 April 2007) [337]; *Prosecutor v Strugar* (*Judgment*) (*International Criminal Tribunal for the former Yugoslavia, Appeals Chamber*, Case No IT-01-42-A, 17 July 2008) [*Strugar Appeals Judgment*] [330]; *Prosecutor v Prlić et al.* (*Judgment, Separate and Partially Dissenting Opinion of Presiding Judge, Jean-Claude Antonetti*) (*International Criminal Tribunal for the former Yugoslavia, Trial Chamber III*, Case No IT-04-74-T, 29 May 2013) [*Antonetti Opinion*] vol 6, 316–18. See also, Thomas Desch, 'The Second Protocol to the 1954 Hague Convention for the Protection of Cultural Property in the Event of Armed Conflict' (1999) 2 *Yearbook of International Humanitarian Law* 63, 74 (explaining approaches to Article 6 of the *1999 Protocol* at the 1999 Diplomatic Conference).

153   Hayashi, 'Military Necessity' above n 144.

154   *Protocol I* Article 52(2).

155   Ibid Article 52(1).

156   Merryman, above n 82, 841.

While the *1954 Convention* is silent on the question of who can invoke imperative military necessity to use cultural property for military purposes, or to attack so-used cultural property, the *1999 Protocol* clarifies that for cultural property under 'general protection' the commander must be an officer commanding a force the equivalent of a battalion in size or larger. Notwithstanding this, the *Protocol* also allows a force smaller in size where circumstances do not permit otherwise.[157] What this means is that ultimately the lowest-ranked commander can invoke military necessity and decide the fate of cultural property even if that property is of the most important value to the cultural heritage of all humankind, if 'the circumstances do not permit otherwise'.

Nevertheless, the commander needs to evaluate the information available to her/him at the time of making a decision to harm cultural property, and not the information acquired with the benefit of hindsight or acquired subsequently.[158] However, in practice, during a trial, it may be difficult to prove *ex post facto* whether this was really the case.

In accordance with Article 6 of the *1999 Protocol*, once military necessity is established, this 'necessity' can only last for as long as cultural property is, by its function, made into a military objective.

After military necessity has been established, a military commander needs to determine whether an object of cultural property constitutes a legitimate military objective, and ascertain that there is no feasible alternative available to obtain a similar military advantage to that offered by directing an act of hostility against that object.[159] In the case of invoking military necessity to use cultural property for purposes which are likely to expose it to destruction or damage, the commander must ensure that no choice is possible between such use of the cultural property and another feasible method for obtaining a similar military advantage.[160] While cultural property can be sacrificed on this pretext at the practical level, it should be noted that there are almost always alternatives which allow for cultural property to be spared.

In determining whether an object of cultural property constitutes a legal target, the military objective test within the meaning of Article 52(2) of *Protocol I*[161] needs to be met. This is a two-prong test, both prongs of which need to be meet cumulatively. To this end a military commander first needs to determine whether

---

157 *1999 Protocol* Article 6(c). However, Article 4 of the *1954 Convention* neither defines the concept of imperative military necessity nor specifies who makes a decision and when to invoke it.

158 See, eg, Varner, above n 126, 1204; Sandoz *et al.*, above n 119 [2079]; *Strugar Trial Judgment* [194].

159 See, eg, Varner, above n 126, 1204.

160 *1999 Protocol* Article 6.

161 *Protocol I* Article 52(2) provides that:

Attacks shall be limited strictly to military objectives. Insofar as objects are concerned, military objectives are limited to those objects which by their nature, location, purpose or use make an effective contribution to military action and whose total or partial destruction, capture or neutralisation, in the circumstances ruling at the time, offers a definite military advantage.

the 'nature, location, purpose or use'[162] of given objects 'make an effective contribution' to military action, and then, also establish whether destroying such objects would give a 'definite military advantage' in accordance with the circumstances at the time of the decision.[163]

4. Proportionality and precautions

Where military necessity has been invoked, and where an object of cultural property has been made a military objective, that still does not mean that such object should necessarily be attacked. The proportionality principle also needs to be respected and a range of precautions must be taken.

Proportionality is an element in the law of armed conflict rule that establishes the lawfulness or unlawfulness of an attack directed at a military objective and should not be equated with military necessity.[164] This principle requires that the damage to cultural property does not exceed the 'direct military advantage expected to be gained'.[165] The principle is covered by Articles 51 of *Protocol I*. Under this article the military must assess the anticipated concrete and direct military advantage,[166] based on the information available at the time, against the potential harm (both short and foreseeable long-term effects) to civilians or civilian objects, or a combination thereof.[167] In the recent *Prlić et al Judgment*, the *ICTY* Trial Chamber III discussed the principle of proportionality in relation to the destruction of the Old Bridge of Mostar and held, by a majority, with

---

162 For discussion about the meaning of each component of the first prong see, eg, Henckaerts, 'New Rules', above n 117.

163 *Protocol I* Article 52(2).

164 *Protocol I* Article 51(5)(b); Hayashi, 'Military Necessity', above n 144. But see, David Luban, 'Military Necessity and the Culture of Military Law' (2013) 26 *Leiden Journal of International Law* 315, 343–5.

165 For discussion about the proportionality test, see, eg, Varner, above n 126, 1207–8 and the accompanying footnotes; Rogier Bartels, '*Prlić et al.*: The Destruction of the Old Bridge of Mostar and Proportionality', European Journal of International Law Talk www.ejiltalk.org/wp-content/uploads/2013/07/; Rebecca J. Barber, 'The Proportionality Equation: Balancing Military Objectives with Civilian Lives in the Armed Conflict in Afghanistan' (2010) 15(3) *Journal of Conflict and Security Law* 467.

166 On discussion about the difference between military advantage and military necessity see, Hayashi, 'Basic Principles', above n 144 (noting that 'any difference between military necessity and military advantage or convenience might be seen as one of degrees. The former might involve the act's indispensability, whereas the latter might encompass indispensability as well as mere gain, superiority or expediency. It is doubtful whether the indispensability of belligerent conduct is a viable distinguishing feature here.').

167 See, eg, Tim McCormack and Paramdeep B. Mtharu, 'Expected Civilian Damage and the Proportionality Equation', Asia Pacific Centre for Military Law, University of Melbourne Law School 2006 www.apcml.org/.../un_report_exp_civilian_damage_1106.pdf 10; Barber, above n 165, 481; *Prosecutor v Kupreskić (Judgment) (International Criminal Tribunal for the former Yugoslavia, Trial Chamber*, Case No IT-95-16-T, 14 January 2000) [526].

Judge Antonetti dissenting, that the impact on the civilian population was disproportionate to the concrete and direct military advantage expected by the destruction of this object of cultural property.[168]

The precautions are regulated by Article 57 of *Protocol I* and Article 7 of the *1999 Protocol*. One of the precautions is avoiding the location of military objectives near cultural property.[169] Also, all feasible precautions must be taken in the choice of means and methods of attack with a view to avoiding, and in any event minimising, incidental damage to cultural property, and refraining from or cancelling or suspending an attack which would be excessive in relation to the concrete and direct military advantage anticipated.[170]

5. Summary

International humanitarian law instruments discussed above do not make a distinction between cultural property inscribed on the World Heritage List and other property. Unless World Cultural Heritage properties are included in the International Register of Cultural Property under Special Protection or on the List of Cultural Property under Enhanced Protection, those properties are treated as all other cultural property under 'general protection'. This leaves cultural property situated in Syria, including the six World Heritage-listed properties, only protected under a less stringent system of 'general protection' as none of Syria's cultural property has been included in the mentioned *1954 Convention*'s Register and List.

Despite variations in relevant instruments, and despite the fact that not all instruments are legally binding, a certain amount of consensus has been achieved. In general, under the law of armed conflict, cultural property is shielded against any act of hostility provided that it is not used at the same time for military purposes.[171] Even if cultural property is being used for military purposes cultural property should not be attacked automatically. Before deciding to use cultural property for military purposes, or harming cultural property so used, the military must adhere to the rules of international law regulating military necessity, military objective, the principle of proportionality and precautions in attack, and to the rules concerning the effects of hostilities. A failure to do so may result in

---

168 *Prosecutor v Prlić et al. (Judgment) (International Criminal Tribunal for the former Yugoslavia, Trial Chamber III*, Case No IT-04-74-T, 29 May 2013) vol 3, [1582–7]. But see, *Antonetti Opinion*, vol 6, 301–25 (opining that 'the Old Bridge was a legitimate military objective whose destruction gave the HVO a definite military advantage by cutting off communications and supply of food' and that '[i]f the Old Bridge was a military objective, it quite simply had to be destroyed', and thus 'fail[ing] to see how the principle of proportionality could be applicable in this case'). Ibid 325.

169 *Protocol I* Article 58(b); *1999 Protocol* Article 8(b).

170 *Protocol I* Article 57; *1999 Protocol* Article 7.

171 Heritage for Peace, above n 11, 1.

a commission of a war crime that entails individual criminal responsibility. As discussed, in Syria, all sides to the conflict have used cultural property for military purposes and all sides launched attacks against so used cultural property causing incalculable damage to the cultural heritage of Syria and simultaneously to the cultural heritage of all humankind.[172]

B. An international criminal law perspective

International criminal law allows for the prosecution of individuals for destructive acts or operations against cultural property. Individual criminal responsibility is envisaged for such acts by both treaty international law and customary international law.

1. The applicable legal instruments

(A) 1907 CONVENTION IV

The *1907 Convention IV* and its annexed *Regulations* are part of customary international law.[173]

Article 56(2) of the *1907 Regulations* provides that '[a]ll seizure of, destruction or wilful damage done to institutions of this character, historic monuments, works of art and science, is forbidden and should be made the *subject of legal proceedings*'.[174]

(B) 1954 CONVENTION

The *1954 Convention* deals with the question of individual criminal responsibility in Article 28. This article requires States Parties to 'take, within the framework of their ordinary criminal jurisdiction, all necessary steps to prosecute and impose penal sanctions upon those persons, of whatever nationality, who commit or order to be committed a breach of the . . . Convention'.[175] Article 28 has not been effective as it neither provides a list of possible violations of the *Convention* nor spells out the concrete sanctions that should be imposed.

---

172 See, eg, Human Rights Council, 'Human Right Situations that Require the Council's Attention: Oral Update of the Independent International Commission of Inquiry on the Syrian Arab Republic', 25th sess, Agenda item 4, 18 March 2014, 6–12, esp. [75–80] [*HRC Oral Update*].

173 See, eg, *Judgment of the International Military Tribunal* (1946), 'The Law relating to War Crimes and Crimes against Humanity' www.derchos.org/nizkor/nuremberg/judgment/cap7.html and www.yale.edu/lawweb/avalon/imt/proc/judwarcr.htm; *1993 Report of the Secretary-General*, above n 106.

174 *1907 Regulations* Article 56(2) (emphasis added).

175 *1954 Convention* Article 28.

Protocol I, applicable to international armed conflict, covers grave breaches of its provisions in Article 85. Sub-paragraph (4)(d) of this article concerns a breach of Article 53(a) of *Protocol I* prohibiting acts of hostility directed against the 'clearly-recognised historic monuments, works of art or places of worship which constitute the cultural or spiritual heritage of peoples and to which *special protection* has been given by *special arrangement*, for example, within the framework of a competent international organisation', that is, when these objects are made 'the objects of attack, causing as a result extensive destruction thereof, where there is no evidence of the violation by the adverse Party of Article 53, sub-paragraph (b), and when such [objects] are *not located in the immediate proximity of military objectives*'.[176]

This is a very complex and ambiguous provision. It contains a number of requirements, all of which have to be satisfied. Reference to 'a competent international organisation' could be interpreted to include UNESCO – an international organisation tasked with the protection of cultural property. Properties inscribed on UNESCO's World Heritage List, and properties included in the International Register of Cultural Property under Special Protection or in the List of Cultural Property under Enhanced Protection appear to satisfy the requirement of 'special arrangement'.[177] It is less clear whether properties protected under the 'general protection' under the *1954 Convention* (which is *lex specialis* to the more general provisions of Article 53 of *Protocol I*) are to be considered to be under 'special protection' within the meaning of Article 85(4)(d) of *Protocol I*.[178]

The location requirement in Article 85(4)(d) has been interpreted to mean 'an evidentiary precaution'[179] rather than loss of protection due to a failure to distance cultural property from military objectives. The *ICTY* jurisprudence shows that the mere fact that cultural property is located in the immediate vicinity of military objectives does not justify its destruction.[180]

To qualify as a grave breach of *Protocol I* under Article 85(4)(d) an act must also 'result in extensive destruction' of objects protected by Article 53(a). This deviates from the requirement in Article 53 of *Protocol I* that an act only needs to be 'directed' against cultural property, which, therefore, does not necessarily have to 'result in extensive destruction'.

However, Article 85(4)(d) does not elevate the prohibition in paragraph (b) of Article 53 of *Protocol I* to use objects protected in paragraph (a) of this article

---

176 *Protocol I* Article 85(4)(d) (emphasis added).
177 See, eg, Toman, above n 126, 391–2.
178 See, eg, Roger O'Keefe, 'Protection of Cultural Property under International Criminal Law' (2010) 11 *Melbourne Journal of International Law*, 1, 29.
179 Ibid 31.
180 See, *Naletilić Trial Judgment* [604]; *Strugar Trial Judgment* [310].

in support of the military effort to the level of a grave breach of *Protocol I*. Also, to reiterate, *Protocol I*, with its provision in Article 85(4)(d), applies to international armed conflict. There is no similar provision in *Protocol II* (even though Article 16 of *Protocol II* also prohibits the use of objects in support of military effort).

(D) *1999 PROTOCOL*

The *1999 Protocol* dedicates the whole of Chapter 4 to 'criminal responsibility and jurisdiction'. Article 15 of the protocol specifies offences within the meaning of the *Protocol*. For the first time ever the use of cultural property or its immediate surroundings in support of military action has been criminalised in paragraph (b) of this article.[181] However, this is done only in relation to cultural property under enhanced protection. The use for military purposes of cultural property under general protection is not criminalised at all.

'Using cultural property under enhanced protection or its immediate surroundings in support of military action' (together with 'making cultural property under enhanced protection the object of attack',[182] and 'extensive destruction or appropriation of cultural property protected under the [*1954*] *Convention* and [the *1999*] *Protocol*'[183]) is considered a serious violation of the *Protocol* and has been made subject to universal jurisdiction.[184] This offence is a corollary of the requirements that the enhanced protection is granted on a condition that 'it is not used for military purposes or to shield military sites and a declaration has been made by the Party which has control over the cultural property, confirming that it will not be so used',[185] and that any 'use of the [cultural] property or its immediate surroundings in support of military action' may turn so used cultural property into a military objective.[186]

---

181   *1999 Protocol* Article 15(1)(b).
182   *1999 Protocol* Article 15(1)(a).
183   *1999 Protocol* Article 15(1)(c).
184   See, eg, Micaela Frulli, 'The Criminalization of Offences against Cultural Heritage in Times of Armed Conflict: The Quest for Consistency' (2011) 22(1) *European Journal of International Law* 203, 211 (noting that the *1999 Protocol* 'de facto distinguishes between two classes of offences: those committed against property under enhanced protection entail more serious consequences,' and explaining that '[w]hile all of the offences listed in Article 15 of the *1999 Protocol* are to be considered serious violations, only the first three – among which the first two concern property under enhanced protection – correspond to what are called grave breaches in the *Geneva Conventions* and *Additional Protocols*, and States Parties accordingly also have a duty to try or extradite any person who committed such serious violations, that is to say to exercise universal jurisdiction whenever an alleged offender is present on their territory').
185   *1999 Protocol* Article 10(c).
186   *1999 Protocol* Articles 12 and 13.

The *Rome Statute*[187] of the *International Criminal Court* (*ICC*) criminalises offences against cultural property under the rubrics of war crimes[188] and crimes against humanity – persecution.[189]

In relation to war crimes concerning cultural property, the *ICC* has jurisdiction under Article 8(2)(b)(ix), applicable to international armed conflict, and the identical Article 8(2)(e)(iv), applicable to non-international armed conflict. Cultural property is included in 'other serious violations of the laws and customs', namely, 'intentionally directing attacks against buildings dedicated to religion, education, art, science or charitable purposes, historic monuments, hospitals and places where the sick and wounded are collected, provided they are not military objectives'.[190] These two articles do not require that an attack 'results' in actual damage to cultural property. For an attack to amount to an offence under these two articles it would suffice that an act is intentionally 'directed' against cultural property provided such property is not a military objective.

The *Rome Statute* does not criminalise the conduct of the holder of cultural property, which exposes such property to damage or destruction. The *Statute* only criminalises the conduct of the attacking party. As Frulli notes, 'if acts against cultural property may be justified where the property has become a military objective: the two sides of this coin have to be taken into consideration to enhance the protection of property through criminal sanctions.'[191]

The crime of persecution is covered by Article 7(1)(h) of the *Rome Statute*. Under this article, persecution, which may occur on a variety of grounds, including cultural grounds, needs to be linked to an 'identifiable group or collectivity'.

Syria is not party to the *Rome Statute*. However, Syria signed this treaty on 29 November 2000 and, as with the *1999 Protocol*, in accordance with Article 18 of the *Vienna Convention on the Law of Treaties* (*Vienna Convention*),[192] its signature forbids it from defeating this treaty's object and purpose prior to ratification. The fact that Syria is not party to the *Rome Statute* would not necessarily preclude the *ICC* from exercising its jurisdiction over the Syrian situation if, consistent with Article 13(b) of the *Rome Statute* the UN Security Council acting under Chapter VII of the *Charter of the United Nations* referred the situation to the *ICC* Prosecutor. The Security Council has indeed deemed the Syrian situation as

---

187 See, *Rome Statute of the International Criminal Court*, UN Diplomatic Conference of Plenipotentiaries on the Establishment of an International Criminal Court, opened for signature 17 July 1998, 2187 UNTS 3 (entered into force 1 July 2002) [hereinafter *Rome Statute*].

188 Ibid Articles 8(2)(b)(ix) and 8(2)(e)(iv).

189 Ibid Article 7(1)(h).

190 For discussion about inconsistencies between the *1999 Protocol* and the *Rome Statute*, including the wording of the relevant articles concerning offences against cultural property, see, eg, Frulli, above n 184, 210–12.

191 Ibid 215.

192 *Vienna Convention on the Law of Treaties*, Article 18.

constituting threat to peace and security and, acting under Chapter VII powers, attempted to refer the Syrian situation to the *ICC*. However, this attempt was unsuccessful due to the vetoes of China and the Russian Federation – both permanent members of the Security Council.[193] Notwithstanding this, even if the Syrian situation was referred to the *ICC*, that would not change much in relation to the issue of the use of cultural property for military purposes by a holder of such property, given that the *Rome Statute* does not criminalise such conduct.

2. *Treatment of the World Heritage sites and other cultural property*

At a normative level, International Criminal Law does not explicitly differentiate between cultural property inscribed on the World Heritage List and other cultural property. However, implicitly, the law does assign a higher degree of protection to World Cultural Heritage, by envisaging a grave breach of *Protocol I* only for acts which result in destruction of cultural property for which special arrangements have been made by international organisations within the meaning of Article 85(4)(d) of *Protocol I*. As discussed, the World Heritage sites would satisfy this requirement. Also, by including offences against cultural property under enhanced protection, as envisaged by the *1999 Protocol*, in the list of offences to which universal jurisdiction applies, the protocol assigns more serious consequence for offences involving World Heritage sites. This is evident in relation to offences involving both the use of cultural property under enhanced protection for military purposes, and making such property the object of attack. This proposition is supported by the fact that UNESCO has been making efforts to encourage States to register their properties, which are inscribed on the World Heritage List, also in the List of Cultural Property under Enhanced Protection.[194]

193   See, eg, UN Press Release, Security Council coverage, 'Referral of Syria to International Criminal Court Fails as Negative Votes Prevent Security Council from Adopting Draft Resolution', SC/11407, 22 May 2014 www.un.org/press/en/2014/sc11407.doc.htm; 'Russia, China block Security Council referral of Syria to International Criminal Court' (22 May 2014) United Nations www.un.org/apps/news/story.asp?NewsID=47860; Patrick Maigua, 'UN Envoy: Syrian Crisis a Big Threat to World Peace and Security', United Nations Radio, Geneva www.multimedia.org/radio/english/2013/08/un-envoy-syrian-crisis-a-big-thre....

194   At the time of this writing some World Heritage sites have already been included in the List of Cultural Property under Enhanced Protection. See, eg, Committee for the Protection of Cultural Property in the Event of Armed Conflict, Second Protocol to the Hague Convention of 1954 for the Protection of Cultural Property in the Event of Armed Conflict, Item 11 of the Provisional Agenda: Consideration of requests for the granting of enhanced protection, 8th mtg, UNESCO, 18–19 December 2013, CLT-13/8.COM/CONF.203/8, Paris, 17 October 2013; List of Cultural Property under Enhanced Protection (10 sites, all of them being World Heritage properties) http://unesco.org/.../culture/...protection/.../cultural-property/enhanced-pr....

The differentiation between the World Heritage List properties and other cultural property is particularly illustrated by the weight given to the World Heritage sites at the judicial level. The *ICTY*'s case law provides useful examples. The so-called 'Dubrovnik' cases – *Jokić* and *Strugar* – are cases in point. Although cultural property-related crime pursuant to Article 3(d) of the *ICTY Statute* was only one of the charges in the *Jokić* case and in the *Strugar* case, a great amount of evidence was presented and a substantial amount of time was dedicated in the proceedings, as well as considerable space given in judgments to the damage to the Old City of Dubrovnik – a World Heritage site – by the Yugoslav Army in 1991 during the conflict following the dissolution of the former Yugoslavia.

In *Jokić*, the Trial Chamber explained at length the requirements of 'general protection', as opposed to 'special protection' under the *1954 Convention* and discussed the preamble to the *WHC*, emphasising the universal value of cultural property on the World Heritage List: 'deterioration or disappearance of any of the cultural or natural heritage *constitutes a harmful impoverishment of the heritage of all the nations of the world*'.[195] The Trial Chamber stressed that the entire Old City of Dubrovnik was considered, at the time of the shelling, 'an especially important part of the world cultural property. It was, among other things, an outstanding architectural ensemble illustrating a significant stage in human history . . . The shelling attack on the Old [City] was an attack not only against the history and heritage of the region, but also against the cultural heritage of humankind.'[196] The Chamber underlined that the possibility of restoration does not mitigate the gravity of the crime as it can never bring back the original status of the damaged cultural object.[197]

The *Strugar* case[198] provided closer factual and legal analysis of the attack against the Old City of Dubrovnik than the *Jokić* case as the judgment in the latter was a result of a plea bargain. The *Strugar* Trial Chamber, *inter alia*, analysed in depth the applicable law criminalising the destruction of cultural property.

The *Prlić* case also dedicated a substantial amount of time and space to the destruction of the Old Bridge (*Stari Most*) of Mostar. The Bridge was not inscribed on the World Heritage List at the time of the destruction on 9 November 1993. After it was rebuilt, together with the Old City of Mostar, the Bridge was added to the List in 2005. During the trial, the Bridge was already on the World Heritage List. An analysis of its destruction occupies a significant part of a generally voluminous Trial Judgment. In its Separate and Partially Dissenting Opinion, the Presiding Judge, Jean-Claude Antonetti, noted that 'the destruction of the *Stari Most* is alleged on all conceivable grounds, including Article 2 of the

---

195 *Prosecutor v Jokić (Sentencing Judgment) (International Criminal Tribunal for the former Yugoslavia, Trial Chamber,* Case No IT-01-42/1-S, 18 March 2004 [*Jokić Sentencing Judgment*] [49] (quoting the *WHC*) (emphasis added by the Jokić Trial Chamber).

196 Ibid [51].

197 Ibid [52].

198 See, *Strugar Trial Judgment.*

[*ICTY*] *Statute*, which is without precedent in the case of the destruction of cultural heritage'.[199] Judge Antonetti further noted the 'importance [of the Bridge] at the time of the events and its fame following its inclusion on the UNESCO World Heritage List'[200] and made reference to the *Jokić Decision* underlying that the very teleology of the international system for the protection of cultural heritage was that 'the restoration of the *Stari Most*, made possible by the international community, has no bearing on guilt'.[201] In Judge Antonetti's view '[o]f all the cases before the Tribunal, the destruction of Dubrovnik is – in terms of its symbolic character – the attack directed against cultural heritage that most resembles the destruction of the *Stari Most'.*[202]

A number of other *ICTY* cases included cultural property-related charges but none of them gave cultural property such a prominence as the above-mentioned cases concerning World Heritage sites.[203] At the same time, the case law has been silent on the issue of the use of cultural property for military purposes by the holder of such property. Given the current jurisdiction of the *ICC* where crimes against cultural property are concerned, it is unlikely that this silence will be broken any time soon.

3. Summary

In summary, the relevant international instruments governing protection of cultural property in armed conflict envisage individual criminal responsibility for violations of their provisions. For the first time ever, the use of cultural property for military purposes has been criminalised. However, this has been done only in relation to cultural property under enhanced protection. The use of all other cultural property for military purposes is not criminalised even though such property may also be of outstanding universal value. This leaves such cultural property unprotected simply because it is not included in the List of Cultural Property under Enhanced Protection.

The *ICTY* jurisprudence shows that, at the judicial level, cultural property inscribed on the World Heritage List has been given greater prominence than other cultural property. The *ICC* may well adopt a similar approach. If the Syrian situation is brought before the *ICC* it is likely that cultural property charges generally will not be given an ancillary status to other crimes, largely due to the

---

199 *Antonetti Opinion* (bold in original; here omitted).
200 Ibid 303.
201 Ibid 304.
202 Ibid 313.
203 For a survey of the *ICTY* case law see, eg, Meron, above n 88; *Antonetti Opinion*, above n 152, 301; O'Keefe, 'Protection of Cultural Property under International Criminal Law', above n 178.

World Heritage properties involved. However, the fact remains that those who expose cultural property to the dangers emanating from warfare through encampment, the positioning of snipers, shielding military objectives, the movement of heavy weapons and heavy vehicles, and other military purposes are unlikely to be brought to account.

IV. Evaluation of the Syrian situation

A number of investigations have been made into the evidence of atrocities committed during the Syrian conflict, including the UN Human Rights Council's Commission of Inquiry on Syria.[204] The Commission has documented numerous violations of international humanitarian law, in particular identifying violation of norms providing protection for cultural property. Reportedly, both government forces and pro-government militia, and non-State armed groups have used positioned military objectives in and around protected cultural property sites, used historic churches as bases for military operations and positioned snipers in centuries-old mosque minarets, exposing the buildings to attack by the opponent, to name just a few examples.[205] Such misuse of cultural property has caused immeasurable damage to the Syrian cultural heritage and concomitantly to the cultural heritage of all humankind.[206] This conduct has also clearly breached provisions of the international legal instruments governing the protection of cultural property in armed conflict.

Syria is party to the *1954 Convention* and *Protocol I*. The *Convention* proscribes the use of cultural property for military purposes except in cases of imperative military necessity. *Protocol I* also prohibits the use of the protected objects in support of military effort. However, the *Protocol* does not envisage the exception of military necessity. Because the *Convention* is *lex specialis* to the *Protocol*, the *Convention* takes primacy. However, the question of primacy between these two instruments is irrelevant in the context of the Syrian situation, as the conflict in

---

204 See, eg, *Seventh Report of the UNHRC, Report of the Independent International Commission of Inquiry on the Syrian Arab Republic*, 25th sess, Agenda item 4, A/HRC/25/65 of 12 February 2014 (published 5 March 2014) [hereinafter *HRC 7th Report*]; Human Rights Council, 25th sess, Agenda item 4: 'Human rights situations that require the Council's attention', *Oral Update of the Independent International Commission of Inquiry on the Syrian Arab Republic*, 18 March 2014 [hereinafter *HRC Oral Update*]; *Eighth Report of the UNHRC, Report of the Independent International Commission of Inquiry on the Syrian Arab Republic*, 27th sess, Agenda item 4, A/HRC/27/60 of 13 August 2014 (published on 27 August 2014) [hereinafter *HRC Eighth Report*]; Stephanie Nebehay, 'UN Documents New War Crimes in Syria for Future Prosecution', *Reuters* (online), 25 January 2014 www.reuters.com/article/2014/01/25/us-syria-crisis-warcrimes-idUSBREA0N1SV20140125; 'Briefing: Holding ISIS to Account' (16 October 2014) IRIN www.irinnews.org/report/100720/briefing-holding-isis-to-account.

205 See, eg, *HRC 7th Report*, above n 204 [116–121]; *HRC Oral Update*, above n 204 [75–80].

206 See, eg, *UNOSAT Report*, above n 6.

Syria has been characterised as non-international in nature.[207] In other words, the *Convention* applies to both international and non-international armed conflict, whereas *Protocol I* only applies to international armed conflict. Because of the nature of the conflict in Syria, only the *1954 Convention* applies to the Syrian situation as far as the use of cultural property for military purposes is concerned. As noted, Syria is not party to *Protocol II*, which applies to non-international armed conflicts.

According to the UN Commission of Inquiry on Syria, the Syrian conflict 'once between the Government and a limited number of anti-government armed groups, has morphed into multiple shifting conflicts involving countless actors and frontlines'.[208] Additionally, ISIS has evolved from a loosely organised military group to a self-proclaimed State. Moreover, ISIS has been recruiting and training foreign fighters in Syria.[209] These non-State armed groups are bound by the provisions of the *1954 Convention* by virtue of Article 19 of the *Convention* which provides that in the event of an armed conflict not of an international character 'occurring within the territory of one of the High Contracting Parties, each party to the conflict shall be bound to apply, as a minimum, the provisions of the [*1954*] *Convention* which relate to respect for cultural property'.[210] The obligation to respect cultural property is based on Article 4 of the *Convention*, which, *inter alia*, prohibits the use of cultural property for military purposes and the attacks against cultural property unless such use or attacks are imperatively required by military necessity.[211] Therefore, the *1954 Convention* applies to non-State armed groups in Syria.[212]

Neither Article 4 nor the rest of the *Convention* differs between cultural property inscribed on the World Heritage List and other cultural property. All cultural property situated in Syria is protected under the 'general protection' which allows the holder of cultural property to use such property for military purposes on the basis of imperative military necessity. Had Syria been party to the *1999 Protocol*, and had cultural property in Syria been included in the List of Cultural Property under Enhanced Protection, that would have proscribed more strongly the use of cultural property in support of military action. Such use of cultural property, if done intentionally, would have amounted to a serious violation of

---

207 See, eg, Louise Arimatsu and Mohbuba Choundhury, 'The Legal Classification of the Armed Conflicts in Syria, Yemen and Libya' (March 2014) Chatham House www.chathamhouse. org/.../20140300ClassificationConflicts/ArimatsuCho....

208 *HRC Eighth Report*, above n 204 [136].

209 Reportedly, the international make-up of ISIS forces equals to 11,000 foreign fighters from at least 74 States. See, IRIN, 'Briefing: Holding ISIS to Account', above n 204 www.irinnews.org/report/100720/briefing-holding-isis-to-account.

210 *1954 Convention* Article 19(1).

211 *1954 Convention* Article 4(1), (2).

212 For discussion about the applicability of the *1954 Convention* to non-State actors, see, eg, Zoë Howe, 'Can the 1954 Hague Convention Apply to Non-State Actors? A Study of Iraq and Libya' (2012) 47(2) *Texas International Law Journal* 403.

the *Protocol*, which entails individual criminal responsibility and envisages universal jurisdiction in case of prosecution. Importantly, this protection would have encompassed both international and non-international armed conflicts. However, as Syria is not party to the *1999 Protocol* neither the Syrian Government forces nor the opposition armed groups are bound by its provisions.

This raises the question of whether the holder of cultural property in Syria who exposes such property to damage and destruction by using it for military purposes in the absence of military necessity, can be held accountable under the *1954 Convention*. Article 28 of the *Convention*, concerned with sanctions, does envisage individual criminal responsibility for those individuals who commit or order to be committed a breach of the *Convention*. However, Article 28 does not specify offences. Due to the lack of this specification, Article 28 had been (until the adoption of the *1999 Protocol*) one of the most criticised provisions of the *Convention*.

As noted above, a number of investigations have been made into the evidence of atrocities committed by all sides to the conflict in Syria, including the impact on cultural property.[213] The question is whether, when and where those responsible will be brought to justice. Given the difficulties involved in accessing evidence in the present conflict-torn Syria, it is likely that prosecutions will have to be left for the period after the conflict has finished. This may be an indeterminate postponement. Brahimi, for example, sees the task of achieving peace in Syria to be a mission impossible. In his view, Syria will become another Somalia. 'It will not be divided, as many have predicted. It's going to be a failed State, with warlords all over the place.'[214]

One possibility as to where to prosecute Syrian crimes would be the national level. Article 28 of the *1954 Convention* has been interpreted to mean that any State can prosecute and impose sanctions 'upon those persons, of whatever nationality' who commit or order to be committed a breach of the *Convention* on the basis of universal jurisdiction.[215] Another avenue for the prosecution of crimes against cultural property in the Syrian context would be a mixed national–international level or an entirely international level. An *ad hoc* international criminal tribunal, like *ICTY* or *ICTR*, or mixed (international–national) tribunal, like the Special Court for Sierra Leone or the Extraordinary Chambers in the Courts of Cambodia for Khmer Rouge crimes and the Special Tribunal for Lebanon could also be established, or the Syrian situation could be brought before the *ICC*.

However, Syria is not party to the *Rome Statute* – this of course means that it does not automatically come within the jurisdiction of the *ICC*. Still, Syria may

---

213 For a survey of the international responses to the Syrian conflict in relation to cultural property, see, eg, Silvia Perini and Emma Cunliffe, *Towards a Protection of the Syrian Cultural Heritage: A Summary of the International Responses (March 2011–March 2014)* (Heritage for Peace, April 2014).

214 Koelbl, above n 30, 2, 5.

215 See, eg, Petrovic, above n 117, 200–2 and surrounding footnotes.

voluntarily accept the jurisdiction of the *ICC* in accordance with Article 12(3) of the *Rome Statute*. This scenario is unlikely to be realised under the present Syrian Government, as evidence collected by the UN investigators implicates President Bashar al-Assad and other Syrian high officials.[216] It is to be expected that the possibility envisaged in Article 13(b) of the *Rome Statute* will be pursued, namely, referral to the Prosecutor by the Security Council acting under Chapter VII of the *Charter of the United Nations*. So far the *ICC* has been powerless in relation to the Syrian situation as the Security Council has been unable to adopt a resolution that would have referred the situation to the Court.

Meanwhile, both the Assad Government and the armed opposition groups have been accusing each other of crimes, demanding that those responsible be brought to justice. As it has been observed, '[t]hey both want accountability about what the others do, rather than themselves.'[217]

To reiterate, the *Rome Statute* has jurisdiction over serious violations of the laws and customs concerning acts involving 'intentionally directing attacks against buildings dedicated to religion, education, art, science or charitable purposes, historic monuments, hospitals, and places where the sick and wounded are collected, provided they are not military objectives'.[218] This jurisdiction is applicable in both international and non-international armed conflict. However, this provision only encompasses 'attacks' directed against cultural property provided such property is not a military objective. The provision is silent on the responsibility of those who use cultural property for military purposes. In Syria, the misuse of cultural property by all sides has been well documented. As a consequence, such cultural property has been to a great extent exposed to destruction or damage. It will not be surprising, however, if the prosecution at the *ICC* eventuates, that all sides either blame each other or claim that cultural property against which an attack was directed, was a military objective and that their conduct was based on military necessity – a defence raised in a number of cases involving cultural property-related charges.[219] The concept of military necessity, as discussed above, can be ambiguous or 'elastic'; sometimes more personal convenience than necessity.[220] Equally, 'military advantage' can easily be interpreted by the warring parties to merely mean showcasing military superiority.

If the use of cultural property for military purposes is criminalised under both the 'general protection' and 'enhanced protection' (as there is a corollary

---

216   See, eg, Stephanie Nebehay, above n 204.
217   Ibid (quoting Karen Koning Abu Zayd, an American expert serving on an Independent Commission of Inquiry set up by the UN in 2011).
218   *Rome Statute* Articles 8(2)(b)(ix) and 8(2)(e)(iv).
219   The *Strugar case*, the *Prlić case* and the *Milošević case* are recent examples.
220   See, eg, Hayashi, 'Basic Principles', above n 144 (noting that any difference between military necessity and military advantage or convenience might be seen as one of degrees; the former might involve the act's indispensability, whereas the latter might encompass indispensability as well as mere gain, superiority or expediency).

obligation to respect cultural property under both regimes), then, as Frulli observes,

> no real room is left for military necessity considerations: either it is possible to punish those who attacked the protected property or those who exposed it to the loss of immunity from attack, thus offering stronger protection to cultural property and bearing a much greater potential in terms of deterrence and prevention.[221]

Otherwise the holder of cultural property responsible for exposing cultural property to damage through its use for military purposes will walk away with impunity, as may be the case in Syria given the current state of law on the subject.

V. Conclusion

Across the devastated landscape that is Syria today World Heritage properties and other irreplaceable evidence of past civilisations' achievements lie in ruins. The devastation is partly caused by the use of cultural property for military purposes by all sides involved in the ongoing armed conflict in this state. One of the reasons why this is possible is the absence of legal repercussions for the holder of cultural property.

Of all international legal instruments that govern protection of cultural property in armed conflict only the *1999 Protocol* criminalises the use of cultural property under 'enhanced protection' or its immediate surroundings in support of military action. The use of cultural property under 'general protection' is not criminalised at all. In Syria, neither cultural property inscribed on the World Heritage List, nor the numerous other properties that are exceptionally important to the cultural heritage of humankind are included in the 'List of Cultural Properties under Enhanced Protection' as Syria is not a party to the *1999 Protocol*. The *Rome Statute*, to which Syria is not a party either, but which can become applicable via the referral by the UN Security Council, or if Syria voluntarily seeks out its jurisdiction, is silent on the question of accountability of the holder of cultural property for exposing cultural property to the loss of immunity.

This impunity for the destruction of cultural property in the Syrian context is a major problem for the international community. Immediate steps that could be taken to remedy the current situation include the need to criminalise the use of cultural property for military purposes at a national level; to foster ratification of the *1999 Protocol*; and include as much of cultural property as possible in the List of Cultural Property under Enhanced Protection – the combination of which would enable States to bring to justice those responsible for exposing cultural

---

221 Frulli, above n 184, 216.

property to the loss of immunity in armed conflict on the basis of universal jurisdiction. At the same time, the Syrian situation illustrates the need to consider amending the current international law concerning the protection of cultural property in armed conflict. To this end, criminalisation of the use of cultural property presently envisaged for the system of 'enhanced protection' should also be extended to the system of 'general protection'. Additionally, in order to harmonise the relevant provisions across instruments, it would be necessary to include in the *Rome Statute* offences concerning the use of cultural property under both enhanced protection and general protection in support of military action.

In parallel, it is essential to reinforce the education of military personnel on the significance of the preservation of cultural property for posterity in general, and in particular on the importance of the proper interpretation of provisions of the existing international instruments, all the while making it clear that the use of cultural property in support of military action does not *ipso facto* entitle the opponent to harm cultural property. Since cultural property is precious, not just locally, but also across borders and across generations, its protection must be a matter of the highest priority for the international community.

8 Accountability for violations of the Law of Armed Conflict and the question of the efficacy of International Criminal Law in ameliorating violence in armed conflict

Dale Stephens[1]

I. Introduction

After decades of promise, international criminal law has now found its place as a vibrant and entrenched part of the international legal panoply. The liberal dream of harnessing law's power to universally restrain and criminalise aberrant battlefield violence has finally been realised. There is now a cascade of international courts and tribunals routinely dispensing justice and assigning legal culpability to individuals who have breached the tenets of international criminal law. While there is a developing corpus of respectable legal authority and a growing set of principles of criminal responsibility, it is fair to ask what, if anything, has been missed in this juridification[2] project.

We live in an age where legal normativity, particularly the Law of Armed Conflict (LOAC), has sought to colonise all political and social space on the battlefield. This represents a decisive change from the previously dominant just war tradition that preceded the current positivist framework. Whereas previously individuals were required to undergo a process of ongoing introspective examination regarding their motivation and legal capacities for engaging in such conflict, now the requirement is one of external compliance with positively constructed rules and standards. This conception of LOAC creates a series of binary choices regarding lawful and unlawful behaviour and it acts to remove

---

1 Associate Professor, The University of Adelaide Law School; the author would like to thank Mr Mark Giddings for his valuable research assistance; all errors within this chapter are solely the responsibility of the author.

The views expressed here are those of the author alone and do not necessarily reflect the views of the Adelaide Law School.
2 A term originally and skilfully used and explored by Gerry Simpson, *Law, War & Crime: War Crimes, Trials and the Reinvention of International Law* (Polity Press, 2007) chapter 6.

the role of introspection within decision-making. Such a renunciation is the very point of modern law.[3]

With this seeming triumph of legal positivism in mind, this chapter will examine the influence and role of international criminal law to determine whether we are now living in a more accountable age. It would seem counter-intuitive that the great rise of international criminal law and its application to military operations could result in any diminution of accountability, but there is evidence of this unanticipated outcome. To undertake such a reappraisal is fitting in a volume dedicated to Professor Tim McCormack, since the great skill he has exhibited throughout his professional career has been the patient and forensic questioning of the law and its application. He has that enviable ability to review and skilfully deconstruct assumptions and legal positions tentatively reached, in a manner that is both effective but also very honest. Such ability serves to preserve the integrity of the law and reinforce faith in its method. It is in that spirit that this chapter undertakes its own examination of the role of international criminal law in its application to military operations.

In addition to the general introduction and conclusion, the chapter will comprise three substantive parts. The first substantive part will provide a brief overview of the liberal project of criminalising battlefield conduct and reveal the potential challenges of this endeavour. The second substantive part will examine the resulting case law coming from the *International Criminal Tribunal for the former Yugoslavia (ICTY)*[4] to locate the relevant legal tests for battlefield conduct, and will briefly comment on the framework for the *International Criminal Court*.[5] It is asserted that the growing jurisprudence and resultant frameworks for attributing criminal liability have not served to clarify applicable tests in any kind of consistent or meaningful manner, at least in relation to the mainstream business of targeting under the law of armed conflict (principally Part IV of *Additional Protocol I*).[6] Finally, the third substantive part will examine the nature of legal discourse within contemporary military decision-making contexts. It will be submitted that accountability is better realised at the current time through

---

3 Martii Koskenniemi, 'The Silence of Law/The Voice of Justice' in Laurence Boisson de Chazournes and Philippe Sands (eds), *International Law, The International Court of Justice and Nuclear Weapons* (Cambridge University Press, 1999) 501.

4 *The International Tribunal for the Prosecution of Persons Responsible for Serious Violations of International Humanitarian Law Committed in the Territory of the former Yugoslavia since 1991* [*ICTY*], created pursuant to UNSCR 827 adopted by the Security Council at its 3217th meeting, 25 May 1993 has over the past 20 years developed a considerable body of case law dealing with the law applicable to armed conflict and has, consequently, had a decisive effect in shaping contemporary attitudes to the law applicable in armed conflict.

5 *Rome Statute of the International Criminal Court*, 2187 UNTS 3 (entered into force 1 July 2002) [hereinafter referred to as *ICC Statute*].

6 *Protocol Additional to the Geneva Conventions of 12 August 1949, and relating to the Protection of Victims of International Armed Conflicts*, opened for signature 8 June 1977, 1125 UNTS 3 (entered into force 7 December 1978) [hereinafter *API*].

responding to broader social pressures on such decision-making than any kind of blunt application of international criminal law.

II. International criminal law and liberalism

Liberalism represents one of the dominant schools of modern international relations theory.[7] Through the lens of liberalism, law is seen to possess potential within international statecraft to restrict individual oppression and maximise personal freedom through employment of normative mechanisms.[8] Individuals and private groups acting within domestic and transnational society are seen as fundamental actors in international politics and they are considered rational and risk adverse. The State thus represents a subset of domestic interests and is presupposed to act for the general security of the population.[9] Equal respect for individuality, social dignity and a government of law are all mainstays of classic liberalism. Liberalism also considers that the recognised interdependence between States shapes choices made by such States. This provides a base for an explanatory rationale regarding the celebrated tendency for liberal democratic States not to engage in armed conflict with each other.[10]

Judith Shklar has observed that the rule of law is 'the miracle of liberalism, Government without coercion'.[11] The development of an international legal regime regulating warfare and an allied machinery to enforce normative standards is the realisation of such a liberalist dream. This dream derives from the nineteenth-century movement to ameliorate the excesses of warfare through law, or even achieve its abolition.[12] Such principles saw their triumphant rise through the Wilsonian strain of international liberalism post-World War I, as well as their modified revival after the World War II.

Classic liberalism perceives humanity as possessing an unerring political nature.[13] As David Luban notes, liberalism seeks to manage the 'unsocial sociability' of humanity,[14] and to counterpoise violence to politics [15] The fulfilment of this project is realised through the development of law's capacity

---

7   See generally John Baylis, Steve Smith and Patricia Owens, *The Globalization of World Politics* (Oxford University Press, 2008).

8   Martii Koskenniemi, *Apology To Utopia: The Structure of Legal Argument* (Cambridge University Press, 2006) 71, who notes that liberalism is predicated upon 'an ascending, individualistic argument: social order is ultimately legitimate only insofar as it provides for individual freedom'.

9   Samuel P. Huntington, *The Soldier and the State* (Belknap Press, 1957) 149.

10 Spencer R. Weart, *Never At War: Why Democracies Will Not Fight One Another* (Yale University Press, 2000).

11 Judith Shklar, *Legalism: Law, Morals And Political Trials* (Harvard University Press, 1964) 23.

12 See generally Howard N. Meyer, *The World Court In Action* (Rowman & Littlefield, 2002).

13 David Luban, 'A Theory of Crimes Against Humanity' (2004) 29 *Yale Journal of International Law* 85, 109.

14 Ibid 112 (paraphrasing Kant).

15 Ibid.

to restrict, marginalise and criminalise violence. Firmly within the scope of this ambitious legal regime may be counted those acts of violence over which the *ICC* has subject-matter jurisdiction: crimes against humanity, genocide, the crime against aggression and most relevantly for this discussion, crimes under the law of armed conflict.[16] Indeed, even before the creation of the *ICC* the liberal promise to confine unnecessary violence through law had achieved celebrated victories in the post-war Nuremburg and Tokyo trials. These were followed by the rise of modern international criminal law with the creation of the *ICTY* and the *International Criminal Tribunal for Rwanda (ICTR)*.[17]

The realisation of this vision was not without its historical baggage. Judith Shklar, for example, was very critical of the Nuremburg trials for their reliance on crimes against peace, and even war crimes, given their largely non-criminalised status in pre-war conceptions. By incorporating a universalist underpinning in the assertion of jurisdiction, the Nuremburg Trials were, according to Shklar, characterised by illusions and legal fictions. More scathingly, the Tokyo Trials of post-war defendants were, according to Shklar, a 'complete dud'[18] given the foreign nature of the so-called universal principles being asserted. Such universalism appeared to be based upon conceptions of natural law; as Shklar observes 'what on earth could the Christian-Judaic ethic mean to the Japanese?'[19]

While Shklar was to write in 1964 that 'whatever the future may be, law for the present cannot cope with war',[20] such despair has been overtaken with much energetic devotion to this very promise. The modern age is heavily characterised by liberalism's incessant march to making, refining and invoking law to quell or otherwise mute excessive violence. The profusion of international legal instruments regulating armed conflict shows no hint of subsiding. Notwithstanding the emphatic manner in which the law's optimism has put paid to Shklar's pessimism, there are a number of doubts that may be raised about the contemporary LOAC.

One is whether the current constellation of legal regulation has resulted in the sufficient cabining of violence that liberalism promised. The breathless enthusiasm that presaged the arrival of the *ICC*[21] saw enormous hope placed in

---

16 *ICC Statute*, n 5 Article 5.
17 *Statute of the International Criminal Tribunal for Rwanda*, United Nations Security Council Resolution 955, adopted by the Security Council at its 3453rd mtg, 8 November 1994.
18 Judith Shklar, above n 11, 181.
19 Ibid 183.
20 Ibid 187.
21 For example, Lloyd Axworthy, then Canada's Minister of Foreign Affairs, was one of the most dedicated advocates of the creation of the Court, who declared at the Rome Conference in June 1998: An independent and effective international criminal court will help to deter some of the most serious violations of international humanitarian law. It will help give new meaning and global reach to protecting the vulnerable and innocent. By isolating and stigmatising those who commit war crimes or genocide, and removing them from the community, it will help to end cycles of impunity and retribution. Without justice, there is no reconciliation, and without

the capacity of the Court to guard against aberrant behaviour on the battlefield and to deliver righteous vengeance against those war criminals who overstepped law's boundaries. Certainly the steady completion of trials at the *ICTY* (and now the *ICC*) and the rate of resulting convictions attest to a quantitative measure of modest 'success'. While it is a matter of collective celebration that individuals who recruit child soldiers are held to account[22] or who forcibly transfer civilians contrary to LOAC are convicted of relevant crimes,[23] there is also a broader context at play. The primary business of warfare is based upon legal issues surrounding targeting. Questions of distinction and proportionality are at the core of the main effort of warfare where countless numbers of people are killed and injured and property destroyed under the cover of law. It is here that the various courts and tribunals have not provided any kind of consistent threshold of meaning or durable reference and the question of accountability remains an open one. In this context, Kennedy observes that,

> [h]umanitarians can so enchant an institution like the International Criminal Court as a symbol of humanitarian law that they forgo inquiry into whether the existence and use of the Court – in Yugoslavia or elsewhere, short term and long term – might do more to excuse than condemn the responsible, among the great powers, among Yugoslavian civilians, among international agencies and non-government organizations . . . [t]he institutions of international humanitarian law easily overestimate their neutrality and disengagement and underestimate the distributive and political effects of their initiatives.[24]

Hence, while much attention has been given to sensational violations of specific prohibitions underpinning LOAC, these operate mostly at the periphery and

---

reconciliation, no peace.   (Reproduced in Lana Wylie's, 'We Care What They Think: Prestige and Canadian Foreign Policy'. Paper presented at the 2006 Annual Meeting of the Canadian Political Science Association, York University, Toronto June 3, 2006, 9–10 www.cpsa-acsp.ca/papers-2006/Wylie.pdf). See also comments of the 'NGO Coalition for an International Court' *ICC Update*, Special Edition, 11 April 2002; and Graham Blewitt, 'The International Criminal Tribunals for the Former Yugoslavia and Rwanda' in Mark Lattimer and Philippe Sands (eds), *Justice For Crimes Against Humanity* (Hart Publishing, 2005) 160, ('No longer will political, military or police leaders of countries be able to commit such crimes with impunity. There will be a realistic likelihood that they will be held accountable for their actions in an international criminal court.')

22 *The Prosecutor v Thomas Lubanga Dyilo* (*International Criminal Court, Trial Chamber*, Case No ICC-01/04-01/06 of 14 March 2012) www.icc-cpi.int/en_menus/icc/situations%20and%20cases/Pages/situations%20and%20cases.aspx.

23 *The Prosecutor v Blagojević* (*International Criminal Tribunal for the former Yugoslavia, Trial Chamber*, Case No IT-02-60-T, 17 January 2005) www.icty.org/x/cases/blagojevic_jokic/tjug/en/bla-050117e.pdf.

24 David Kennedy, *Dark Sides of Virtue: Reassessing International Humanitarianism* (Princeton University Press, 2004) 300.

there remains the largely unexamined question as to the routine application of this body of law that justifies or excuses great destruction in the normal course. If the role of international criminal law were to have a decisive effect, it would be here within the mainstream regulation of standard activities of warfare where it should make its presence known. For while much violence is restrained, the law also acts to authorise and permit a large level of institutional violence at the same time.[25] In this context, Kahn poignantly observes in relation to the 1991 Gulf War that '[t]he overwhelming lesson of the conduct of the Gulf War is that there is no direct correlation between complying with international legal rules and minimizing suffering'.[26]

The adequacy with which international criminal law has dealt with the 'big picture' of routine military operations will be examined below in Part III through the jurisprudence of the *ICTY*. It will be established that when it comes to providing consistent guidance as to the boundaries of lawful behaviour in standard targeting contexts, international criminal law has not yet provided a consistent theme. Indeed, as will be revealed in Part IV of this chapter, restraint and accountability for battlefield behaviour derives more faithfully from the application of broad government policy directions as well as the psychological influence and social internalisation of the *Geneva Conventions* and *Additional Protocols* themselves. Moreover, the manner in which modern military decision-making is undertaken is more attuned to social pressures and political measures of accountability than anything emanating from the jurisprudence of international criminal law.

III. War crimes – *ICTY* decision-making and *ICC Statute*

By all outward measures, the LOAC has been one of the great successes of international law. The four *1949 Geneva Conventions*,[27] still rate as the only treaty series to have obtained universal ratification by States. Similarly, the *1977*

---

25 David Kennedy, *Of War and Law* (Princeton University Press, 2006) 106 (observing that 'the international legal standards of self-defense, proportionality and necessity are so broad that they are routinely invoked to refer to the zone of discretion rather than limitation').

26 Paul Kahn, 'Lessons for International Law from the Gulf War' (1992–1993) 45 *Stanford Law Review* 425, 436.

27 *Geneva Convention for the Amelioration of the Condition of the Wounded and Sick in Armed Forces in the Field of August 12, 1949*, opened for signature 12 August 1949, 75 UNTS 31 (entered into force 21 October 1950) [hereinafter *GCI*]; *Geneva Convention for the Amelioration of the Condition of Wounded, Sick and Shipwrecked Members of Armed Forces at Sea of August 12, 1949*, opened for signature 12 August 1949, 75 UNTS 85 (entered into force 21 October 1950) [hereinafter *GCII*]; *Geneva Convention relative to the Treatment of Prisoners of War of August 12, 1949*, opened for signature 12 August 1949, 75 UNTS 135 (entered into force 21 October 1950) [hereinafter *GCIII*]; *Geneva Convention relative to the Protection of Civilian Persons in Time of War of August 12, 1949*, opened for signature 12 August 1949, 75 UNTS 287 (entered into force 21 October 1950) [collectively *Geneva Conventions*] [hereinafter *GCIV*].

Additional Protocols[28] also find large subscription within the international community.[29] Added to these instruments are the impressive array of treaties dealing with, *inter alia*, conventional weapons, protection of cultural property and rules regulating air and naval warfare. Of course the law also deals with more contemporary topics ranging from chemical weapons, biological weapons, anti-personnel landmines and cluster munitions through to laser weapons and, on the close horizon, nanotechnology and autonomous weapons systems. The breadth and depth of legal regulation of armed conflict seems to know no limit. The legal colonisation of land, sea, air and now cyberspace environments, continues unabated and the methodologies and techniques of the interpretative process are now well rehearsed within military and humanitarian groups. Yet at the heart of the legal regime for the regulation of armed conflict, the fundamental concepts of proportionality and distinction remain ambiguous and ill-defined. Upon examination, these principles are far more permissive than most champions of the power of law to regulate war realise. Crucially, the link between these two apparently objective standards and the subjective discretions, which are expressed through the legal framework of the Law of Armed Conflict, remain unclear. However, the law itself does specifically press humanitarian considerations. The celebrated 'Martens clause',[30] which will be addressed more fully below, provides a foundation upon which concepts of 'humanity' and 'public conscience' are asserted and which might provide a link between greater ethical restraint and the positivist framework of LOAC. However, as will be revealed, despite initial efforts by the *ICTY* to give the 'Martens clause' normative force in conditioning the principles of distinction and proportionality, further efforts of development have been curtailed.

A. Martens clause

In an effort to ensure that there are no gaps – no moments where law cannot apply to regulate battlespace violence – treaty law includes the venerable 'Martens clause'. The clause, which found an early expression in the Preamble,

---

28 *API*, above n 6; *Protocol Additional to the Geneva Conventions of 12 August 1949, and relating to the Protection of Victims of Non-International Armed Conflicts*, opened for signature 8 June 1977, 1125 UNTS 609 (entered into force 7 December 1978) [hereinafter *APII*] and *Protocol Additional to the Geneva Conventions of 12 August 1949, and relating to the Adoption of an Additional Distinctive Emblem*, opened for signature 8 December 2005 (entered force 14 January 2007) [hereinafter *APIII*], 8 December 2005; [collectively *Additional Protocols*].

29 As at July 2013, there were 173 States Parties to *Additional Protocol I*; 167 to *Additional Protocol II* as well as 63 to 2005 *Additional Protocol III*.

30 Preamble, *1907 Convention (IV) Respecting the Laws and Customs of War on Land*, as reproduced in A. Roberts and R. Guelff (eds), *Documents on the Laws of War* (Oxford University Press, 3rd edn, 2000) 70.

1907 Convention (IV) Respecting the Laws and Customs of War on Land was subsequently adopted in *Additional Protocols I*[31] and *II*,[32] and provides:

> Until a more complete code of the laws of war is issued, the High Contracting Parties think it right to declare that in cases not included in the Regulations adopted by them, populations and belligerents remain under the protection and empire of the principles of international law, as they result from the usages established between civilized nations, from the laws of humanity and the requirements of the public conscience. [33]

While necessarily ambiguous, it is clear that as a minimum the clause reflects a principle that holds that where there exists uncertainty as to the application of relevant law, operational staff are still to be governed by principles of humanity as well as the dictates of public conscience in their decision-making. As will be canvassed below, the *ICTY* has attempted to give the clause practical application in the context of bracketing the cumulative effects of attacks in accordance with the principles of distinction and proportionality, but even here there has been a lack of subsequent institutional traction.

As previously noted, the principles of distinction and proportionality remain the core legal anchors for lawful targeting in armed conflict. The principle of distinction, as enunciated within *Additional Protocol I* provides:

> In order to ensure respect for and protection of the civilian population and civilian objects, the Parties to the conflict shall at all times distinguish between the civilian population and combatants and between civilian objects and military objectives and accordingly shall direct their operations only against military objectives.[34]

The principle of proportionality as reflected in *Additional Protocol I* provides:

> An attack which may be expected to cause incidental loss of civilian life, injury to civilians, damage to civilian objects, or a combination thereof, which would be excessive in relation to the concrete and direct military advantage anticipated.[35]

Despite their central place there has been considerable debate about the legal thresholds envisaged within these principles. As to distinction, it represents a paradigmatic rule, but like all rules is necessarily over and under inclusive in its

---

31 *API*, above n 6, Art 1(2).
32 *APII*, above n 28, preamble, 4.
33 As reproduced in A. Roberts and R. Guelff, above n 30.
34 *API* above n 6, Art 48.
35 *API* above n 6, Art 51(5)(b) and also represented in Article 57(2)(b).

reach. This has been a central point of contention, especially in the context of determining when a civilian takes a direct part in hostilities thus losing protected status under this principle. Similarly, the principle of proportionality constitutes a standard under the law[36] whose factors concerning assessments of collateral damage to property and incidental injury to civilians need to be balanced and weighed against anticipated 'concrete and direct military advantage'. The principle is one that has not easily been reconciled. Dinstein notes, for example, that there has always been a fundamental disconnect between balancing military considerations against civilian losses, as they are 'dissimilar considerations'.[37] Such a proposition seems experientially sound. It is difficult to comprehend how the loss of life incurred in attacking a bridge or track or even munitions factory can be measured in terms of prospective 'military advantage' outside very clear extremes.

Given the ambiguities associated with these central principles, it might be hoped that the *ICTY* would provide reasoned guidance as to their import. In relation to the 'Martens clause', the *ICTY* in the 2000 *Kupreškić* case[38] did have cause to examine the significance of this provision and sought to apply it in a practical manner to regulate the principles of distinction and proportionality. The *Kupreškić* case itself dealt with accused who were charged with attacking a village in Bosnia on 16 April 1993, where over one hundred inhabitants were killed. The accused raised defences of *tu quoque* and reprisal. The Tribunal dismissed both defences. The Tribunal embarked upon an analysis of customary international law and observed that 'the absolute nature of most obligations imposed by the rules of international humanitarian law reflected the progressive trend towards the so-called "humanisation of international legal obligations"'.[39] The Tribunal expressly invoked 'elementary considerations of humanity'[40] as well as the 'Martens clause'[41] as exemplars of this humanitarian underpinning and also invoked the rise of the separate regime of International Human Rights Law to buttress their decision.[42]

In respect of the 'Martens clause', the Tribunal conducted a lengthy examination of the precautions necessary to be observed when determining

---

36 Useful discussion on the discretionary differentiation between applying a rule and a standard can be found in Pierre Schlag, 'Rules and Standards' (1985–1986) 33 *UCLA Law Review*, 379. See also Duncan Kennedy, 'Form and Substance in Private Law Adjudication' (1976) 89 *Harvard Law Review* 1685, 1687.
37 Yoram Dinstein, *The Conduct of Hostilities Under the Law of International Armed Conflict* (Cambridge University Press, 2004) 122.
38 *Prosecutor v Zoran Kupreškić, Mirjan Kupreškić, Vlatko Kupreškić, Drago Josipović, Dragan Papić, Vladimir Šantić* (*International Criminal Tribunal for the former Yugoslavia, Trial Chamber*, Case No IT-95-16-T, 14 January 2000) www.icty.org/x/cases/kupreskic/tjug/en/kup-tj000114e.pdf.
39 Ibid 518.
40 Ibid 524.
41 Ibid 525.
42 Ibid 529.

whether a target could be attacked as well as the subsequent application of the principle of proportionality. The Tribunal determined that the 'Martens clause' did have customary status, although acknowledged that 'the "principles of humanity" and the "dictates of public conscience" have [not] been elevated to the rank of independent sources of international law'.[43] However the Tribunal did determine that:

> this Clause enjoins, as a minimum, reference to those principles and dictates any time a rule of international humanitarian law is not sufficiently rigorous or precise: in those instances the scope and purport of the rule must be defined with reference to those principles and dictates. In the case under discussion, this would entail that the prescriptions of Articles 57 and 58 (and of the corresponding customary rules) must be interpreted so as to construe as narrowly as possible the discretionary power to attack belligerents and, by the same token, so as to expand the protection accorded to civilians.[44]

In relation to the practical application of the 'Martens clause' in this context the Tribunal determined that:

> As an example of the way in which the Martens clause may be utilised, regard might be had to considerations such as the cumulative effect of attacks on military objectives causing incidental damage to civilians. In other words, it may happen that single attacks on military objectives causing incidental damage to civilians, although they may raise doubts as to their lawfulness, nevertheless do not appear on their face to fall foul *per se* of the loose prescriptions of Articles 57 and 58 (or of the corresponding customary rules). However, in case of repeated attacks, all or most of them falling within the grey area between indisputable legality and unlawfulness, it might be warranted to conclude that the cumulative effect of such acts entails that they may not be in keeping with international law. Indeed, this pattern of military conduct may turn out to jeopardise excessively the lives and assets of civilians, contrary to the demands of humanity.[45]

Hence, the Tribunal sought to fashion a practical rule regarding the manner in which proportionality assessments might be undertaken that expressly involved consideration of cumulative effects of ongoing attacks. To this end, the Tribunal was addressing a latent ambiguity in the conceptual application of Articles 57 and 58 of *Additional Protocol I* and their corresponding representations under the *ICTY Statute* (and also now the *ICC Statute*) in relation to the significance of

43 Ibid 525.
44 Ibid 525.
45 Ibid 526.

cumulative effects. Such a conclusion necessarily spoke to customary law understandings of targeting calculations and would appear contrary to the expressed declarations of a number of States Parties to *Additional Protocol I*.[46]

Given the specificity of this determination regarding both the application of the 'Martens clause' and its impact upon targeting decisions, it is curious that this line of analysis was not repeated in subsequent *ICTY* determinations. The 'Martens clause' was subsequently addressed in the context of the discussion of reprisals in the *Martić*[47] case in a very cursory manner where the views of the Tribunal in *Kupreškić* regarding the operational significance of the clause were essentially ignored. The issue of proportionality was subsequently discussed in the *Galić*[48] case, and again, the reasoning applied by the Tribunal in *Kupreškić* concerning the practical application of the clause in the context of the rules relating to proportionality were overlooked.

In the majority Appeals decision of *Gotovina*,[49] the possibility that inferences might be made as to the cumulative effects of doubtful attacks in relation to aid in either the construction of a substantive rule, or at least as an evidentiary matter going to relevant mental elements, was emphatically rejected. In that instance, the majority decision dismissed evidence relied upon by the Trial decision that a 200 metre impact analysis was determinative of deciding criminal guilt concerning distinction and proportionality assessments relating to an artillery attack on four separate towns. Having rejected the 200-metre standard the Trial Chamber adopted in its analysis, the majority then quickly dismissed the remaining evidence:

> The Trial Chamber's Impact Analysis, which the Appeals Chamber . . . has now found to be erroneous, was at the very core of its finding that the artillery attacks on the Four Towns were indiscriminate, and thus unlawful. The Trial Chamber deemed almost all the additional evidence of unlawful attacks as equivocal when considered independent of the Impact Analysis.

46 See for example, the declaration made by Australia: 'In relation to paragraph 5(b) of Article 51 and to paragraph 2(a)(iii) of Article 57, it is the understanding of Australia that references to the "military advantage" are intended to mean the advantage anticipated from the military attack considered as a whole and not only from isolated or particular parts of that attack' www.icrc.org/applic/ihl/ihl.nsf/Notification.xsp?action=openDocument&documentId=10312 B4E9047086EC1256402003FB253.

47 *Prosecutor v Milan Martić (International Criminal Tribunal for the former Yugoslavia, Trial Chamber*, Case No IT-95-11-T of 12 June 2007), 461 www.icty.org/case/martic/4.

48 *Prosecutor v Stanislav Galić (International Criminal Tribunal for the former Yugoslavia, Trial Chamber*, Case No IT-98-29-T of 5 December 2003), 48–62 which provide a lengthy exposition of the law of targeting without making any reference to the issue of the Martens clause or the *Kupreškić case* in particular www.icty.org/case/galic/4.

49 *Prosecutor v Ante Gotovina, Ivan Čermak, Mladen Markač (Appeals Chamber) (International Criminal Tribunal for the former Yugoslavia, Appeals Chamber*, Case No IT-Case No. IT-06-90-A of 16 November 2012), 61 www.icty.org/x/cases/gotovina/acjug/en/121116_judgement.pdf.

More specifically, the Trial Chamber relied on the Impact Analysis to discount Witness Rajčić's assertion that the 2 August Order called for shelling only lawful military targets. In addition, neither Witness Konings nor Witness Corn suggested that the only interpretation of the 2 August Order was as an instruction to commence indiscriminate attacks on the Four Towns. Given that the relevant portion of the 2 August Order was relatively short, and did not explicitly call for unlawful attacks on the Four Towns, the text of the 2 August Order could not, alone, reasonably be relied upon to support a finding that unlawful artillery attacks took place.[50]

In summary, the *ICTY*'s enunciation of a practical application test for the 'Martens clause' in the *Kupreškić* case registered a tangible manifestation of the provision to contextualise an ambiguous aspect of targeting methodology. It was one that certainly offered greater protection to civilians and civilian objects and thus provided a meaningful threshold in the establishment of a measure of accountability under the law. As indicated above however, this formulation has been ignored by subsequent *ICTY* decisions, let alone by other judicial forums. Indeed, the *Kupreškić* case has been met with hostile academic commentary regarding its methodological approach.[51] It seems clear that this type of contextualised application of the 'Martens clause' to targeting determinations is not one that was capable of being sustained by the Tribunal.

B. The principles of distinction and proportionality

1. Principle of distinction

The International Court of Justice has described distinction as a cardinal principle of LOAC.[52] It is a central concept to the conduct of warfare and is encountered in every targeting decision made in the battlespace, no matter how specifically tactical or grandly strategic. Accordingly, any judicial enunciation of this principle will profoundly impact war fighting generally and make accountable those who cross the threshold requirements. The *ICTY* comprehensively examined the issue of distinction in the 2007 case of *Martić*[53]

---

50   Ibid 77.

51   See for example Michael Schmitt, 'Military Necessity and Humanity in International Humanitarian Law: Preserving the Delicate Balance' (2010) 50(4) *Virginia Journal Of International Law* 795, 820–2.

52   *Legality of the Threat or Use of Nuclear Weapons* (Advisory Opinion), 1996, ICJ 226, 78 [hereinafter *Nuclear Weapons case*] ('The cardinal principles contained in the texts constituting the fabric of humanitarian law are the following. The first is aimed at the protection of the civilian population and civilian objects and establishes the distinction between combatants and non-combatants; States must never make civilians the object of attack . . . ').

53   *Martić*, above n 47.

where the Tribunal dealt with what has become a paradigmatic case of an indiscriminate attack. The essential facts of *Martić* were that M87 Orkan rockets were fired at the city of Zagreb on 2 and 3 May 1995, killing nine and injuring at least 214 people.

The defence in that instance asserted, *inter alia*, that military targets were the focus of the shelling and that the resulting civilian loss was, effectively, proportionate under the law. The Court reviewed the weapon system used, noting that the M87 Orkan rocket was a non-guided cluster munition, with each submunition consisting of 420 pellets of 3 millimetres in size and had a dispersal area of 2 hectares. In that instance the rockets were fired at maximum range of 50 kilometres into a densely populated area where the differentiation between military and non-military objects was very hard to discern. The facts of the case included: that only one bomblet landed anywhere near any target of a possible military nature; the city of Zagreb was densely populated; the statements of the accused indicated that he intended to attack the city; and the weapon was a non-guided high dispersion munition. Having regard to these factors, and given the dubious nature of the military targets in question, coupled with the fact that the M87 in these circumstances was incapable of hitting a specific target and was employed at maximum range, the Trial Chamber held (and the Appeal Chamber upheld) that the M87 Orkan rocket was an indiscriminate weapon in the circumstances ruling at the time. Accordingly, the Trial Chamber determined that its principal effect was to attack civilians in a densely populated area with knowledge that severe casualties would occur that were not susceptible to any balance of military advantage anticipated.[54] The accused, Milan Martić, was duly convicted. This conclusion seems inescapable on the facts presented and is routinely cited as an example of a judicially endorsed standard of indiscriminate attack. Yet, given the facts of the case, such an outcome is hardly surprising. It represents the kind of manifest illegality that all soldiers are required to identify under international law[55] and thus its significance is hardly decisive.

Given this rather obvious breach of the Law of Armed Conflict, it seems unfortunate that it has become something of the threshold standard for violation of the principle of distinction, at least in circumstances where weapon systems of a similar type are used. Hence, the *Final Report to the Prosecutor by the Committee Established to Review the NATO Bombing Campaign Against the Federal Republic of Yugoslavia* that was commissioned to review the use of force employed by NATO during *Operation Allied Force*, relied upon the facts of *Martić* (as outlined at an earlier interlocutory stage) to set a standard for determining the culpability of using such a weapon system vis-á-vis the issue of distinction, and observed:

---

54 Ibid [461–3].
55 *ICC Statute* Article 33 which requires an individual to ascertain whether an order is 'manifestly illegal'. Article 33(2) further provides: 'For the purposes of this article, orders to commit genocide or crimes against humanity are manifestly unlawful'.

It should be noted that the use of cluster bombs was an issue of sorts in the *Martić* Rule 61 Hearing Decision of Trial Chamber I on 8 March 1996. In that decision the Chamber stated there was no formal provision forbidding the use of cluster bombs as such . . . but it regarded the use of the Orkan rocket with a cluster bomb warhead in that particular case as evidence of the intent of the accused to deliberately attack the civilian population because the rocket was inaccurate, it landed in an area with no military objectives nearby, it was used as an antipersonnel weapon launched against the city of Zagreb and the accused indicated he intended to attack the city as such . . . The Chamber concluded that 'the use of the Orkan rocket in this case was not designed to hit military targets but to terrorise the civilians of Zagreb' . . . There is no indication cluster bombs were used in such a fashion by NATO. It is the opinion of the committee, based on information presently available, that the OTP should not commence an investigation into use of cluster bombs as such by NATO.[56]

It is curious that the somewhat unique facts of *Martić* are applied in such a direct fashion in the report. While there are likely many reasons why the NATO bombing effort complied with the rule of distinction under the law, it is unfortunate that the facts of *Martić* were so directly invoked in the report to reference the lawfulness of the NATO attack. The lingering question is the longer-term implications of setting what appears to be such a high standard of criminal responsibility. No professional military force would ever countenance firing cluster munitions into crowded civilian areas where there is doubt as to the proximity of a military objective. It is equally clear that as a test for criminal liability for breaching the principle of distinction the *Martić Decision* sits at an early point of self-evident application. The difficulty arises when progressing down that road of causality and fashioning a test for a particular weapon system that is not so clearly egregious to humanitarian principles. Here the *Martić Decision* and the subsequent committee report offer little practical guidance.

It is notable that, even during *Operation Allied Force*, the relative degrees of constraint that legal and policy factors place upon targeting were exhibited. One incident is of particular relevance, namely the bombing of the airfield in the city of Niš on 7 May 1999 by NATO Forces, which killed fourteen civilians and injured twenty-eight. This incident is instructive because as Human Rights Watch notes '[a]fter the incident in Niš, the White House quietly issued a directive to the Pentagon to restrict cluster bomb use (at least by US forces)'.[57] Such a decision plainly reveals a differentiation between legal and policy

---

56 *The Final Report to the Prosecutor by the Committee Established to Review the NATO Bombing Campaign Against the Federal Republic of Yugoslavia* (The Hague: *ICTY*, released 13 June 2000) 27 www.icty.org/sid/10052.

57 Human Rights Watch Report, *The Crisis in Kosovo* 2000 (see commentary at footnote 84 of the report) www.hrw.org/reports/2000/nato/Natbm200-01.htm.

thresholds of tolerance relating to the acceptability of civilian casualties. Against the background of liberalism's march towards the ever more comprehensive legal regulation of the battlefield, it is sobering to realise that the exercise of political discretion by the US government in this case was a greater check on the conduct of its bombing campaign than the supposedly restrictive constraints of the law.

2. The principle of proportionality

Despite its central significance to assessing the lawfulness of targeting, the issue of proportionality under LOAC has not been comprehensively dealt with by the *ICTY*. In the case of *Galić*[58] when canvassing the concept of proportionality, *inter alia* in respect of Articles 51(5)(b) and 57(2)(a)(iii) of *API*, the Tribunal famously provided that the test of lawfulness was based upon an assessment of 'whether a reasonably well-informed person in the circumstances of the actual perpetrator, making reasonable use of the information available to him or her, could have expected excessive civilian casualties to result from the attack'.[59] This test was re-affirmed on Appeal, where the Tribunal cited with approval a series of factors that the Trial Chamber outlined that would inform such 'reasonableness', which included review of relevant distances at play, identification criteria, relevance of surrounding combat activity and visual issues.[60] Such a finding, in these cases concerning 'reasonableness', is not problematic *per se*, but of course it provides little definitive guidance and conceptually operates to elevate the subjective to the objective, so as to appear a 'natural' outcome with relative ease.[61] The lack of deep analysis as to relevant criteria for bolstering a 'reasonable' determination of anticipated civilian loss under the proportionality test is regrettable.

Within the academic literature, there remains a lingering issue as to whether the term 'excessive' as found in the proportionality formula can be equated with 'extensive'. Professor Dinstein has responded to such a claim as representing a misreading of the *API* text.[62] Such logic is well grounded. It would seem eminently sustainable to understand moments where even extensive damage would still not be excessive. Much rides on the quality of the military advantage thus anticipated, whether it be merely tactical or broadly strategic. Hence, it is unfortunate that when an opportunity arose for clarification on such a key point, as was the case in the *Strugar* prosecution, the Tribunal determined that it was not necessary to determine such questions of the proportionality equation on the facts presented.[63]

---

58 *Galić*, above n 48.
59 Ibid 58.
60 *Prosecutor v Stanislav Galić (International Criminal Tribunal for the former Yugoslavia, Appeals Chamber,* Case No IT-98-29-A of 30 November 2006) 193.
61 Koskenniemi, above n 8, 597.
62 Dinstein, above n 37, 120–1.
63 *Prosecutor v Pavle Struger (International Criminal Tribunal for the former Yugoslavia, Trial Chamber,* Case No IT-01-42-T of 31 January, 2005) 281.

Hence, as will be addressed more fully in Part IV below, in grappling with the issue of proportionality, the imposition of governmental policy dictates in reducing anticipated civilian loss plays a more decisive role in such determinations than anything proffered by the *ICTY*, so far, as a legal test.

3. The ICC framework and the future of LOAC jurisprudence

The *ICTY*'s jurisdictionally limited remit will eventually come to an end – probably in the near future.[64] Focus will be progressively placed on the *ICC* to continue providing judicial guidance in this field. If there were a sense that the *ICC* might provide a more meaningful exposition of legal standards, it would seem that such a hope might be dashed. As some commentators have observed, while States were willing to prescribe reasonably exacting standards for liability for the *ICTY*, this has not been repeated for the *ICC*, where they themselves would be subject to a new regime of criminal liability.[65] In essence, defences are wider and inculpatory provisions narrower under the *ICC Statute* than is the case of the *ICTY*. Concepts like 'manifest illegality' have a wider application as a defence regarding 'superior orders' than what is provided for in the *ICTY Statute*;[66] 'self-defence' is given a much broader application than what is even permitted under most national systems; [67] criminal responsibility for 'ordering' crimes is defined more narrowly;[68] and recklessness as an element for criminal responsibility is downplayed.[69]

Hence, the *ICC* will be subject to a number of structural impediments in its capacity to define liability and requisite standards in a manner that reflects the provisions of the *Geneva Conventions* and *Additional Protocols* themselves, as well as supporting customary international law. To that end, its future impact in defining key elements of lawfulness relating to standard battlefield activity faces a number of significant challenges.

4. Conclusion – international criminal jurisprudence and the conduct of military operations

Modern professional military forces train according to the general provisions of *Geneva Conventions* and the *Additional Protocols*, and apply them in practice. Despite

---

64 The *ICTY* is operating under a general completion strategy policy, which would indicate that its jurisdiction will extend only for a few more years, see List of *ICTY* Completion Strategy Reports at www.icty.org/sid/10016.

65 Robert Cryer, 'The Boundaries of Liability in International Criminal Law, or "Selectivity by Stealth"' in Gerry Simpson (ed.), *War Crimes Law* vol 1 (Dartmouth Publishing Company, 2004) 59, 86.

66 Ibid 67–8, 71–2.

67 Section 10.4 of the *Criminal Code Act 1995* (Cth) at subsection 3(a) expressly provides that self-defence is not available 'if the person uses force that involves the intentional infliction of death or really serious injury . . . to protect property'.

68 Cryer, above n 65, 79.

69 Ibid 80.

the broad thresholds identified in the developing jurisprudence of international criminal law, the substance of LOAC that gets translated into operational 'rules of engagement' is characterised by its highly detailed and nuanced character. It is axiomatic that the thresholds for criminal violation of LOAC as enunciated by bodies such as the *ICTY* provide an obvious minimum standard of compliance expected. In practice and in training, decisions regarding what may be classified as a military objective under the law, what might be tolerated as proportionate civilian loss in any given attack, what precautions are required in any targeting formulation, what levels of confidence are demanded before any decision to use force is made and what opportunities exist for individual decision-makers to refuse to proceed with the prosecution of an attack, are all intricate, complex and highly calibrated.[70] In contrast to the jurisprudence emanating from the *ICTY* and the structural framework for criminal liability represented in the *Rome Statute*, the thresholds and intensive planning required for both deliberate (planned) and/or dynamic (targets of opportunity) targeting decisions by military forces, set necessarily high thresholds that far exceed anything yet enunciated by these forums.

Accordingly, in answer to the unadorned question whether the existing regime of international criminal law provides a level of accountability for decision-making under the law of armed conflict, then the answer is yes. However, as has been discussed above, the nature of the legal tests for establishing criminal liability are set so high that they fail to provide any kind of meaningful standard that actually reflects the internal tolerances usually imposed within the modern operational legal interface. This seems slightly counterintuitive given that violations of the rules and standards applicable to the principles of distinction and proportionality are self-identified as 'grave breaches' of the *Conventions*.[71] Academic commentators have recognised that military forces can impose much higher levels of compliance with such law. Kennedy notes for example that '[p]erhaps contrary to expectations, the military professional cannot be relied upon for an expansive reading of justifications for warfare or a narrow reading of limits'.[72] The broader question then, is how is accountability more realistically met within the military legal context. The final part to this chapter will address

---

70 In seeking to operationalise these obligations, the Australian Defence Force [ADF] has developed a 'six step' targeting process that personifies responsibility and ensures that individual discretion is constantly enlivened and decisions made to comport faithfully with the law at every stage. See generally Air Commodore Paul Cronan AM RAAF, Group Captain Chris Hanna CSC RAAF, Wing Commander Duncan Blake RAAF, Wing Commander Ian Henderson RAAF & Wing Commander Pat Keane RAAF, 'Operations BASTILLE and FALCONER: Legal Support To Commanders' (2011) 184 *Australian Defence Force Journal* 33.

71 *API* above n 6, Art 85(3) provides that 'the following acts shall be regarded as grave breaches of this Protocol . . . (a) making the civilian population or individual civilians the object of attack . . . (b) launching an indiscriminate attack affecting the civilian population or civilian objects in the knowledge that such attack will cause excessive loss of life, injury to civilians or damage to civilian objects, as defined in Article 57, paragraph 2 (a) (iii)'.

72 Kennedy, above n 24, 271.

that issue and demonstrate that while 'black letter' proscriptions have their obvious place, more telling is the role of social and policy influences in relation to questions of legitimacy, that serve to ensure that accountability is maintained more completely for actions taken within the battle space.

IV. Contemporary influences and the question of accountability

Modern warfare takes place within a terrain of dense legal regulation that fuses public with private legal spheres and mobilises legal distinction to legitimise strategic action. Within this realm, it has been observed that 'lines are now harder to draw, both because the world of war has become more mixed up and because ambiguities, gaps and contradictions in the materials we use to draw the lines have become more pronounced'.[73] Persuasion often has greater traction than arguments made under assertions of formal validity. This phenomenon represents a victory for the humanitarian strategy to permanently render law's imprint upon political and military decision-making, but of course this comes at a price. Kennedy asserts '[i]nternational law has become the metric for debating the legitimacy of military action . . . law now shapes the politics of war', and, further:

> In the court of world public opinion, the laws in force are not necessarily the rules that are valid, in some technical sense, but the rules that are persuasive to relevant political constituencies. Whether a norm is or is not legal is a function not of its origin or pedigree, but of its effects. Law has an effect – is law – when it persuades an audience with political clout that something someone else did, or plans to do, is or is not legitimate . . . the fact that the modern law in war is expressed in the keys of both validity and persuasion makes the professional use of its vocabulary both by humanitarian and military professionals a complex challenge'.[74]

As discussed earlier in Part III, the legal tests produced by the *ICTY* for assessing the lawfulness of targeting decisions provide very broad boundaries of discretion. Given the inherent contradictions, vagueness and lack of traction even within like cases, it is hard to currently point to *ICTY* jurisprudence for definitive judgment on applicable legal tests outside very broad, and frankly, self-evident circumstances of violation. While the spectre of criminal prosecution within international or even national courts for violation of LOAC remains a real possibility, LOAC's influence plays out more realistically within a wider audience, through numerous channels of power and through various mediums,

---

73   David Kennedy, 'Lawfare and Warfare' in J Crawford and M Koskenniemi (eds), *The Cambridge Companion To International Law* (Cambridge University Press, 2012) 161.
74   Kennedy, above n 25, 96–7.

including that of perceived legitimacy. Accordingly, within the modern context of LOAC, it has been asserted that understanding restraint in warfare requires greater attention to the work of sociologists or political scientists 'about what functioned as a restraint or a reason [which] became more important than the ruminations of jurists in determining what international law was or was not'.[75]

In this context, the role of legitimacy has a significant impact in the way legal positions are developed, defended and maintained. Legitimacy is a property, a power conferred by the subject upon the powerful.[76] Theoretical frameworks have identified various forms of legitimacy. These include source legitimation, which deals with the norms, rules and institutions of international legal discourse themselves; procedural legitimation which concerns the concept of fairness as perceived locally and necessarily implicates concepts such as accountability and participation and finally, substantive legitimation which is focused upon outcomes and ends.[77] All these forms of legitimacy exert contradictory influences, which makes the struggle irreducibly political. Sitaraman has in fact further condensed the concept into notions of formal (legal) and sociological legitimacy.[78] The former is maintained 'by the authority and procedures established by law' and the latter 'by the beliefs of the population'.[79] It is difficult to anticipate which of these two centrifugal forces will have dominance in any given circumstance.

This phenomenon is manifested most directly in liberal democratic States, but this is not exclusively so. Within the decentralised nature of international legal practice, international norms are accorded relative weight in terms of their persuasiveness to relevant audiences. In this regard, values ranging from constitutionalism, strategic policy preferences, 'ultimate questions' of law and ethics and socio-legal norms all form part of the mix in framing such perspectives. The recognition of this interrelationship has itself been the focus of general theoretical work concerning the relativities of international legal obligation, in terms of notions of 'compliance pull',[80] in theories of transnational politico-legal iteration[81] and 'interactional theories' of international law.[82] Not all law is equal and particular norms have more or less resonance depending on prevailing political cultures.

75 Kennedy, above n 72, 170.
76 Jeni Whalan, *The Power of Legitimacy, Local Cooperation and the Effectiveness of Peace Operations*, (Unpublished PhD dissertation, Oxford University, Chapter II, 67–111 (2010)) (on file with the author).
77 Ibid.
78 Ganesh Sitaraman, *The Counterinsurgent's Constitution* (Oxford University Press, 2013) 197–8.
79 Ibid 197.
80 See generally, Thomas Franck, *The Power Of Legitimacy Among Nations* (Oxford University Press, 1990).
81 Harold Hongju Koh, 'Why Do Nations Obey International Law' (1996–1997) 106 *Yale Law Journal* 2599 and 'Transnational Legal Process' (1996) 75 *Nebraska Law Review* 181.
82 J Brunne and SJ Toope, 'International Law and Constructivism: Elements of an Interactional Theory of International Law' (2000) 39 *Columbia Journal of Transnational Law* 19.

Since at least the Vietnam conflict, it has been evident that modern liberal democracies are decisively impacted by public opinion (both internally and abroad) concerning the perceived legitimacy of participation and conduct within an armed conflict. These lessons have been fully absorbed by military professionals and especially by military lawyers. In modern warfare, the application of force, while always congruent with legal authority, is also always subject to an additional layer of policy oversight, either directly imposed or indirectly anticipated. Such oversight ensures that wide discretions permitted under the law are routinely checked. Watkin records that during the 2003 Iraqi War for example, the US Secretary of Defence was to provide specific approval where an attack was anticipated to result in incidental injury of over fifty civilian casualties.[83] This sends an unmistakable signal to military decision-makers of the sensitivity of actions conducted under the law. The smooth reassurance of an objective legal standard is left behind to enter a new paradigm, 'the domain in which the image of a single dead civilian can make out a persuasive case for violation that trumps the most ponderous technical legal defense'.[84]

Added to the formula of perceived legitimacy is the role of constructivism and social agency. Constructivism is a concept that operates with international relations theory to explain why States behave in the manner they do.[85] It relates to questions of self-identity, where factors such as perceived lawfulness and a 'logic of appropriateness'[86] operate to shape decisions. There seems to be evidence of a similar phenomenon applying in the context of military decision-making. Putting aside all the clever technical legal arguments that can be made to justify battlespace decision-making, there remains nonetheless a dedicated will to act in conformity with the law. As has been observed, the modern military aspires to act not only according to the bare prescriptions of law but also legitimately in its own eyes when dispensing force.[87] This has echoes of an inchoate just war resonance but also the need for an internalisation of legitimate action. To that end, it offers a more meaningful basis for ensuring accountability in the ordinary course of mainstream war fighting than anything yet coming from the *ICTY* (or the *ICC*).

V. Conclusion

The Law of Armed Conflict has become so broad in its range and so dense in its content that it saturates all decision-making relating to the application of force.

---

33 Kenneth Watkin, 'Assessing Proportionality: Moral Complexity and Legal Rules' (2005) 8 *Yearbook Of International Humanitarian Law* 3, 30.

34 Kennedy, above n 25, 97.

35 See generally Jeffrey T Checkel, 'The Constructivist Turn in International Relations Theory' (1998) 50(2) *World Politics* 324.

86 Ryan Goodman and Derek Jinks, 'Toward an Institutional Theory of Sovereignty' (2003) 55 *Stanford Law Review* 1749, 1752.

87 Kennedy, above n 24, 292.

Allied to this legal universe, is the rise of international criminal law and its attendant jurisprudential expressions. The *ICTY*, the *ICTR* and now the *ICC* take their central place as key dispensers of international justice and have a decisive role in defining the boundaries of criminal sanction under their applicable statutes. They provide a welcome and essential role and further the cause of ameliorating excessive violence within the battlespace. The growing jurisprudence being produced by these bodies is steadily defining the thresholds and limits of conduct under applicable criminal law.

It has been a theme of this chapter that the thresholds enunciated for the general conduct of armed conflict by these bodies under the rules relating to targeting are very broad. Such outcomes are perfectly consistent with defining criminal liability, which does necessarily have a specific social focus. In terms of establishing a more general accountability under the law, at least in the context of targeting decisions, such thresholds have limited utility. To this end the rise of international criminal law changes nothing. Modern military forces have always identified a much lower threshold of tolerance for what is acceptable battlespace behaviour. Accountability mechanisms, whether legal, social or political, are more reliably derived from registers of legitimacy than classic recitations on legal validity, especially those applicable under the tenets of international criminal law. Such measures of accountability, particularly within liberal democratic States, have sufficient 'bite' to ensure that the goals of ameliorating battlespace excess are realised. Relevant strategies for framing effective accountability mechanisms should have regard to these inter-disciplinary influences. There is no doubt that the impact of the jurisprudence of international criminal law as developed through bodies such as the *ICTY*, *ICTR* and the *ICC*, as well as national courts under the complementarity principle,[88] will progressively impact the shaping of the thresholds of permitted discretion, but it seems that the early steps in this field are tentative at best. In many ways, however, the mere existence of bodies such as the *ICTY*, *ICTR* and *ICC*, have an impact in operational training and performance by virtue of their symbolism and latent capacities. To that end their very existence serves as a key role in signalling the seriousness in which the international community seeks to re-affirm both accountability and responsibility in decisions made under the Law of Armed Conflict.

---

88 *ICC Statute*, above n 5, Art 17.

9 The fractured relationship between fairness, the rights of the accused, and disclosure at the International Criminal Court

Sophie Rigney[1]

I. Introduction

The permanent *International Criminal Court* (*ICC*), established to prosecute 'the most serious crimes of international concern'[2] and thereby to assist in ending impunity for such crimes,[3] is the pinnacle of efforts to ensure accountability for violations of international humanitarian law. This chapter examines how accountability for violations of international humanitarian and criminal law is affected by the way disclosure is undertaken in *ICC* trials. Disclosure of information relevant to the trial is closely linked to ensuring the procedural rights of an accused, and the fairness of the trial process. Here, I argue that the way disclosure is undertaken at the *ICC* does not give the rights of the accused 'full respect'. While procedural rules should reinforce the rights of an accused and ultimately the principle of a fair trial, in reality the current situation of disclosure at the *ICC* demonstrates the disconnections between procedural rules, rights and trial fairness. This chapter commences by setting out how the rules that govern disclosure at the *ICC* are connected to trial fairness and the rights of an accused. The chapter then moves to an analysis of the disclosure regime at the *ICC*, with

---

1 PhD Candidate and Teaching Fellow, Melbourne Law School; Lecturer, International Criminal Procedure, University of Tasmania (2014); former Legal Assistant and Case Manager (Defence), *International Criminal Tribunal for the former Yugoslavia* (2009–2011). I am delighted to have been asked to contribute a chapter in honour of Tim McCormack, who has guided me from my undergraduate days in Tasmania, to a career in international law in The Hague and an academic vocation in Melbourne. Tim has provided me with significant opportunities and I will always be grateful for his support. He has been a role model for generosity of spirit.
The views expressed in this chapter are those of the author alone and do not necessarily reflect the views of The University of Melbourne.
2 *Rome Statute of the International Criminal Court*, opened for signature 17 July 1998, 2187 UNTS 90 (entered into force 1 July 2002) [*Rome Statute*] Article 1.
3 Ibid Preamble.

particular reference to recent trials at the *ICC*, namely the cases of *The Prosecutor v Lubanga*[4] and *The Prosecutor v Katanga and Ngudjolo Chui*.[5] These cases reveal that disclosure rules are being applied in a way that permits non-disclosure – in particular, of exculpatory material – by both the prosecution and victims' representatives. This non-disclosure may have problematic implications for the rights of an accused, and ultimately the fairness of the trial. As trials are a key mechanism to ensure accountability for violations of international humanitarian and criminal law, the disconnections between rules, rights and fairness are an important area of examination. A fracturing of procedural rules, rights and fairness in these trials may pose difficulties for accountability for such violations.

II. Fairness, rights and disclosure rules: interlinking and mutually enforcing aspects of international criminal trials?

Trial Chambers have a responsibility to ensure trials are 'fair and expeditious and . . . conducted with full respect for the rights of the accused and due regard for the protection of victims and witnesses'.[6] In order to ensure such a trial, procedural rules (including the body of rules that governs how disclosure is effectuated)[7] must be applied in a way consistent with the accused's rights. In this way, trial fairness, the rights of an accused and the procedural rules that govern the conduct of a trial, are interlinked, and in theory, mutually reinforcing. It is worth quoting Salvatore Zappalà at length on this point, as he articulates the link between accountability mechanisms of trial, procedural rules and the rights of an accused:

> Respecting the rules to establish the truth requires full consistency with rights of the accused; these must be seen as an essential component of accurate and truthful fact finding on which punishment is premised. If only one of these rights is violated, in only one aspect, in only one instance, the whole process loses credibility and is likely to fail in its objective of properly establishing the truth and of imposing just punishment.[8]

The rights of an accused are protected at the *ICC* by Article 67 of the *Rome Statute*. These rights are closely modelled on international human rights obligations in

---

4 *Prosecutor v Lubanga* (*International Criminal Court, Trial Chamber I*, Case No. ICC-01/04-01/06).

5 *Prosecutor v Katanga* (*International Criminal Court, Trial Chamber II*, Case No ICC-01/04-01/07-621).

6 *Rome Statute* Article 64(2).

7 *International Criminal Court, Rules of Procedure and Evidence*, Doc No ICC-ASP/1/3 (adopted 9 September 2002) [*ICC Rules*] Rules 76–84; *Rome Statute* Articles 61, 64 and 67. The *ICC Rules* and the *Rome Statute* to be read conjunctively; see Lars Büngener, 'Disclosure of Evidence' in Christoph Safferling (ed.), *International Criminal Proceedings* (Oxford, 2012) 352.

8 Salvatore Zappalà, 'The Rights of Victims v the Rights of the Accused' (2010) 8 *Journal of International Criminal Justice* 137, 145.

the *International Covenant on Civil and Political Rights*,[9] and are also protected in the statutes of other international criminal institutions.[10] The rights of an accused thus have at least three roles: first, they are an integral part of the *ICC*'s governing document; second, they form human rights guarantees; and third, they are also 'part and parcel of the epistemological mechanism for fact finding in criminal proceedings'.[11] Of the several rights the accused enjoys under Article 67 of the *Rome Statute*, there are two rights that are particularly affected by disclosure: the right to know the case alleged by the prosecution,[12] and the right to time and facilities to prepare a defence.[13] These rights are to be enjoyed 'in full equality',[14] and thus, disclosure is also closely connected with the principle of equality of arms. Christoph Safferling refers to a 'kaleidoscope of rights', which includes 'moral principles' such as the equality of arms, as well as particular precise rights which provide the individual with a 'realizable legal claim'.[15] In Safferling's kaleidoscope, these are constitutive of 'fairness'.[16]

The right 'to be informed promptly and in detail of the nature, cause and content of the charge'[17] is closely related to disclosure, because in order to be so informed, the accused must receive disclosure of material that outlines these aspects of the charge. Without receiving such disclosure, the accused cannot know what the prosecution's case is, and therefore what case they must meet. As Lars Büngener correctly points out, the information on the charges generally refers more to the indictment or document containing the charges; disclosure relates to a broader category of information, which includes 'pieces of evidence and factual information which go beyond the contents of an indictment'.[18] There is hence a distinction between the charges themselves and the broader category of disclosable material, which would include witness materials, documents sought to be tendered and potentially exculpatory materials. This information will form the basis for how the prosecution will set out its case, and what evidence might exist to support its attempt to establish guilt beyond a reasonable doubt. Disclosure of this information is therefore closely connected to an accused's

---

9   *International Covenant on Civil and Political Rights*, opened for signature 16 December 1966, 999 UNTS 171 (entered into force 23 March 1976) Art 14.

10   See, eg, SC Res 827, UN SCOR, 48th sess, 3217th mtg, UN Doc S/RES/827 (25 May 1993), as amended by SC Res 1877, UN SCOR, 64th sess, 6155th mtg, UN Doc S/RES/1877 (7 July 2009) Art 20.

11   Zappalà, above n 8, 145.

12   *Rome Statute* Article 67(1)(a).

13   *Rome Statute* Article 67(1)(b).

14   *Rome Statute* Article 67.

15   Christoph J M Safferling, *Towards an International Criminal Procedure* (Oxford University Press, 2001) 30–1.

16   Ibid 31.

17   *Rome Statute* Article 67(1)(a).

18   Büngener, above n 7, 347.

presumption of innocence[19] and the ability of the defence to challenge the prosecutions' case.

The accused's rights to know the case, and rights to time and facilities to prepare a defence, are closely linked.[20] Disclosure affects these rights and how they interact. Without disclosure, a defendant will not know the prosecution case they are expected to address, and thus will not be able to adequately prepare. It is for this reason that Colleen Rohan argues that prosecution disclosure 'is the sole means for affording the accused adequate time and facilities in which to investigate that evidence and prepare to meet it at trial'.[21] International criminal defence lawyer Wayne Jordash also notes the close connection between timely disclosure and the ability to prepare a defence case, particularly in complex cases concerning years of armed conflict and involving allegations of complex modes of liability.[22] He points out that:

> The devil of a Prosecution and Defence case is in the detail provided by this disclosure. The smallest of details may prove important and the more that are available at an early stage the better. This aids the taking of instructions, detailed investigations, the planning of overall strategy, and trial management, including efficient and focused court sessions.[23]

Because the accused enjoys the presumption of innocence and need not run an affirmative defence case (but can simply put the prosecution's case to proof), time and facilities to prepare a defence include an ability to run investigations, and to be able to address the prosecution's evidence and case theory from the commencement of the trial.[24] Time and facilities to prepare a defence should not, therefore, be understood as only relevant to running a defence phase of the trial: rather, the right applies to trial readiness. Disclosure must be provided in a manner that allows it to be integrated into a defence case from the outset; if it is not, the utility of the information could be limited, and there may be a negative impact on the accused's time and facilities to prepare – both in relation to the examination of particular witnesses, and to the overall case.

The accused should be able to enjoy these rights 'in full equality'.[25] The principle of equality of arms includes that neither party is placed at a material

---

19 *Rome Statute* Article 66.
20 See Büngener, above n 7, 347.
21 Colleen Rohan, 'Protecting the Rights of the Accused in International Criminal Proceedings: Lip Service or Affirmative Action?' in William A. Schabas, Yvonne McDermott and Niamh Hayes (eds), *The Ashgate Research Companion to International Criminal Law* (Ashgate, 2013), 289. See also Wayne Jordash, 'Fairness of Karadzic trial in question' (4 October 2010) International Justice Tribune www.rnw.nl/international-justice/article/fairness-karadzic-trial-question.
22 Jordash, above n 21.
23 Ibid.
24 Rohan, above n 21, 290–1.
25 *Rome Statute* Article 67.

disadvantage *viz* the other party, with regards to information.[26] Disclosure regulates the relationship between the parties, through requiring a party with an informational advantage to provide that information to the other party. Such informational parity should ensure that the trial is not an 'ambush'.[27] Disclosure of information between the parties is therefore integral to the right to equality of arms between the parties, and as Masha Fedorova argues, without access to necessary information, 'a meaningful equality of arms cannot be sustained'.[28] While disclosure obligations exist for both the prosecution and the defence,[29] such obligations tend to be more onerous on the prosecution. This is for two main reasons: first, the burden of proof rests on the prosecution, meaning they bear primary responsibility for gathering the evidence (and then disclosing it to the defence); and second, the prosecutor 'enjoys massive advantages in the facilities for the gathering of evidence'.[30] These resources – including investigators, search warrants, the ability to initiate investigations, and certain powers that accompany the status of a prosecutorial office[31] – are usually far in excess of those available to the defence, and grant the prosecution 'superior, and sometimes even sole access to this material'.[32] The ability to obtain material thus necessitates a degree of 'equalising' between the parties,[33] and prosecution disclosure obligations exist, in part, to redress the imbalance between the parties.[34] Disclosure obligations thereby operate to ensure the principle of equality of arms.

The *ICC* has taken further steps to ensure equality of arms, by placing a burden on the prosecutor to investigate incriminating and exonerating circumstances alike, and to disclose all evidence to the defence that appears relevant to both the defence and the prosecution cases.[35] This provision, however, reinforces the need for appropriate disclosure: the prosecutor's duty to investigate exonerating material is only effective if the potentially exculpatory material is disclosed to the defence. As the below analysis will show, the emerging practice

---

26   See Masha Fedorova, *The Principle of Equality of Arms in International Criminal Proceedings* (Intersentia, 2012), 233–302.

27   Ibid.

28   Ibid 233–4.

29   For an examination of defence disclosure obligations, see Kate Gibson and Cainnech Lussiaà-Berdou, 'Disclosure of Evidence' in Karim AA Khan, Caroline Buisman and Christopher Gosnell (eds), *Principles of Evidence in International Criminal Justice* (Oxford University Press, 2010) 306, 338–44.

30   Büngener, above n 7, 350.

31   Ibid; Fedorova, above n 26, 234.

32   *Prosecutor v Kordić and Čerkez (Decision on Appellant's Notice and Supplemental Notice of Prosecution's Non-Compliance with its Disclosure Obligations Under Rule 68 of the Rules) (International Criminal Tribunal for the former Yugoslavia, Trial Chamber III,* Case No IT-95-14/2, 11 February 2004) [17].

33   Fedorova, above n 26, 234.

34   Gibson and Lussiaà-Berdou, above n 29, 306.

35   *Rome Statute* Articles 54(1)(a) and 54(1)(f).

of the *ICC* permits non-disclosure of exculpatory material – which may pose a particular challenge for the full and proper utility of this requirement.

The relationship between disclosure and the rights of an accused is therefore a strong one. As trials are key accountability mechanisms for violations of international humanitarian and criminal law, the relationship between these constituent elements of trial is an important area of enquiry when we examine accountability for such violations. This chapter moves from the theoretical to the practical, with an examination of the relationship between trial fairness, rights and rules in relation to the way disclosure is undertaken at the *ICC*. While there may be other areas of disclosure practices that may be concerning, such as disclosure provided in an untimely manner, this chapter focuses solely on matters of non-disclosure at the *ICC*.

A. Non-disclosure at the ICC: the role of victims and the use of confidentiality agreements by prosecutors

Despite the importance of disclosure outlined above, the *ICC*'s *Rules* – and their implementation by Trial Chambers – permit an environment of non-disclosure. Here, I examine two emerging issues: first, the non-disclosure of exculpatory material in the possession of the prosecution; and second, the lack of clarity around the disclosure responsibilities of Victims' Representatives, and potential non-disclosure of material (including potentially exculpatory material) in the possession of the victims. As a result, the ability of the accused to construct an effective defence is limited, and they may be at an informational disadvantage. The rules permitting non-disclosure also curtail the ability of Trial Chambers to manage the informational disparity and the relationships between the participants of the trial. This environment of non-disclosure at the *ICC* may therefore have a significant effect on the rights of the accused to know the case, the time allowed, and facilities available to prepare a defence, as well as the principle of equality of arms. This demonstrates a fracture between the procedural rules governing disclosure and the rights of the accused. Rather than being mutually reinforcing, the ability of prosecutors and victims to withhold disclosure means that procedural rules permit an environment where the rights of the accused are restricted, rather than such rules being undertaken in a way that ensures the trial is undertaken with 'full respect' for the accused's rights. While trials are a key accountability mechanism for violations of international humanitarian and criminal law, they are presently being conducted in a way that allows these disconnections between procedural rules, rights and trial fairness.

1 Non-disclosure of exculpatory material held by the prosecutor

The first major issue is non-disclosure of potentially exculpatory material in the prosecution's control. Given the importance of disclosure, outlined above, restrictions on disclosure must be strictly limited and non-disclosure must be properly viewed as the exception rather than the rule.[36] However, the *ICC's* disclosure rules include several provisions that allow for non-disclosure of material.[37] There is concern at how these provisions for non-disclosure reconcile with the necessity for prosecution disclosure to the defence of exculpatory materials.

Article 67(2) of the *Rome Statute* places an obligation on the prosecutor to disclose potentially exculpatory material in its possession to the defence as soon as practicable.[38] The fact that this provision is part of the Article in the *Rome Statute* that governs 'Rights of the accused' is demonstrative of the centrality of exculpatory material to the accused's rights. This has been further reinforced by *ICC* Trial Chambers, who have ruled that the right to a fair trial includes an entitlement to disclosure of exculpatory material.[39] Exculpatory material is that which, in the prosecution's view, 'shows or tends to show the innocence of the accused, or to mitigate the guilt of the accused, or which may affect the credibility of prosecution evidence'.[40] In case of any doubt as to the application of this provision, the Court will decide.[41] Yet while the disclosure of potentially exculpatory material is therefore mandated under the disclosure rules, is formulated as constitutive of the rights of the accused, and is understood by Trial Chambers as integral to a fair trial, the *ICC's* governing laws also establish permission for such materials to be withheld. Article 54(3)(e) of the *Rome Statute* (read conjunctively with Rule 82 of the *ICC Rules*) provides for non-disclosure of material that the prosecution has obtained under confidentiality arrangements with sources, and that is to be used solely as 'springboard' information to generate new evidence.[42] This can only be introduced into evidence after the consent of the provider has been given and there has been 'adequate prior

---

36 Bernhard Kuschnik, 'International Criminal Due Process in the Making: New Tendencies in the Proceedings Before the ICC' (2009) 9 *International Criminal Law Review* 157, 166; Büngener, above n 7, 361.

37 Kuschnik, above n 36, 166. Non-disclosure may occur due to the material being an 'internal document'. It may 'prejudice further ongoing investigations' of the OTP. Non-disclosure ensures the confidentiality of the material. It is aimed to 'protect the safety of witnesses and victims and members of their families'. The material may be withheld if it relates to the 'steps that have been taken' by the OTP to either ensure the confidentiality of the information, or the protection of the witnesses, victims and members of their families. See *ICC Rules*, r 81.

38 *Rome Statute* Article 67(2).

39 *Prosecutor v Lubanga (Decision on the Consequences of Non-Disclosure of Exculpatory Materials Covered Article 54(3)(e) Agreements and the Application to Stay the Prosecution of the Accused, Together with Certain other Issues Raised at the Status Conference on 10 June 2008)* (*International Criminal Court, Trial Chamber I,* Case No ICC-01/04-01/06, 13 June 2008) [*Lubanga Decision on the Consequences of Non-Disclosure of Exculpatory Materials*] [34].

40 *Rome Statute* Article 67(2). See also *Lubanga Decision on the Consequences of Non-Disclosure of Exculpatory Materials* (*International Criminal Court, Trial Chamber I,* Case No ICC-01/04-01/06, 13 June 2008) [59].

41 *Rome Statute* Article 67(2).

42 *ICC Rules* r 82 (which regulates non-disclosure pursuant to *Rome Statute* Art 54(3)(e)).

disclosure to the accused'.[43] These provisions – on the one hand, necessitating disclosure of exculpatory material; on the other, permitting its non-disclosure – have been described as constituting a 'collision course' present in the *Rome Statute* itself.[44]

The challenge of necessitating disclosure of exculpatory material, but permitting the non-disclosure of some materials, has been the subject of litigation in both the *Lubanga* and *Katanga* cases. In the *Lubanga* case,[45] the use of information from intermediaries gathered under Article 54(3)(e) and the non-disclosure of exculpatory evidence led to a stay in proceedings: a measure that was closely linked to the rights of the accused and the fairness of the trial.[46] This stay in proceedings has been used as evidence to support an argument that Trial Chambers put 'weight on fairness and impartiality, rather than speediness when conducting the trials'.[47] The stay in proceedings does demonstrate the commitment of that Trial Chamber to ensuring that the defence received the necessary information. This may be seen as a positive indicator, that the Trial Chamber is prepared to do 'anything it takes' to ensure the defence receives the material it requires, that the rights of the accused are upheld, and that the fairness of the proceedings is not compromised. Thus on one interpretation, the stay could be seen as a positive step for the position of the rights of the accused and the fairness of the trial with regards to the procedure governing the conduct of the trial.[48] In the absence of disclosure rules being complied with in a way that reinforces the rights of the accused and trial fairness, the trial cannot be permitted to continue.

However, there is another way of viewing the *Lubanga* stay of proceedings, and an overly optimistic interpretation should be cautioned against. As a

---

43 Ibid.
44 Christian M De Vos, 'Case Note: *Prosecutor v Lubanga*. "Someone Who Comes Between One Person and Another: Lubanga, Local Cooperation and the Right to a Fair Trial"' (2011) 12 *Melbourne Journal of International Law* 217, 231.
45 The details of the Decisions in the *Lubanga case* have been thoroughly addressed by other authors; see, eg, De Vos, above n 44; Sabine Swoboda, 'The ICC Disclosure Regime – A Defence Perspective' (2008) 19 *Criminal Law Forum* 449, 459; Rachel Katzman, 'The Non-Disclosure of Confidential Exculpatory Evidence and the Lubanga Proceedings: How the ICC Defence System Affects the Accused's Right to a Fair Trial' (2009) 8 (1) *Northwestern Journal of International Human Rights* 77; Sara Anoushirvani, 'The Future of the International Criminal Court: The Long Road to Legitimacy Begins with the Trial of Thomas Lubanga Dyilo' (2010) 22 (1) *Pace International Law Review* 213.
46 *Lubanga Decision on the Consequences of Non-Disclosure of Exculpatory Materials* (*International Criminal Court, Trial Chamber I*, Case No ICC-01/04-01/06, 13 June 2008).
47 Kuschnik above n 36, 185. See also Anoushirvani, who argues that the Trial Chamber's 'emphasis on a defendant's right to a fair trial is highlighted in its decision imposing the stay, serving to further legitimise its decision and its role as an impartial international criminal tribunal' (Anoushirvani, above n 45, 224).
48 See, eg, Anoushirvani, who argues that 'By imposing a stay on the proceedings, the ICC is emphasizing the importance of a fair trial' (Anoushirvani, above n 45, 222).

preliminary point, it should be remembered that while ultimately the defence gained the initially undisclosed material, this was 'at the cost of resources, time and extended custody for Mr Lubanga'.[49] In addition, the stay in proceedings demonstrates a significant challenge for the Trial Chamber: that they were unable to regulate the relationship between the parties, uphold procedure and ensure the rights of the Accused and the fairness of the trial, by any less radical means. A stay in proceedings is a significant step for a Trial Chamber to take and will not be entered into lightly. It is *prima facie* incompatible with a Chamber's statutory responsibility to ensure an expeditious trial.[50] It is not satisfactory that, in order for the Trial Chamber to ensure trial safety, they must stop proceedings. Here, the fact that the Trial Chamber had to go to such measures to ensure some acceptable level of informational parity between the parties demonstrates the flaws in the present system.

The proceedings in *Lubanga* are precedent for the fact that a prosecutor cannot use the provision of Article 54(3)(e) to gather materials in a widespread manner and not disclose them. In that case, the prosecutor received over 50 per cent of its documentary evidence on condition of confidentiality.[51] The Trial Chamber deemed this broad use of Article 54(3)(e) in the *Lubanga* case to be incorrect.[52] However, it is still possible for a prosecutor to gather exculpatory material and not disclose it to the defence under this provision. There remains an inherent tension in the *Rome Statute* between the provisions to gather material under confidentiality agreements and to disclose exculpatory material to the defence. While the *Lubanga* stay of proceedings shows that the widespread use of confidentiality agreements is incorrect, and shows how seriously Trial Chambers view the right of the accused to disclosure of exculpatory material, it also demonstrates how difficult this tension in the *Rome Statute* can be for Trial Chambers to resolve. Their role to both properly regulate the relationships of the parties, and to give full respect to the rights of the accused, is limited by this permission of non-disclosure of exculpatory material.

An examination of the *Lubanga* case reveals that non-disclosure of exculpatory materials in the possession of the prosecutor has been a significant issue in the way disclosure is undertaken at the *ICC*. Non-disclosure of material due to confidentiality agreements under Article 54(3)(e) has continued to be problematic in the case of *Katanga*,[53] which shows that the internal inconsistencies in the *Statute*

---

49   Peter Morrissey, 'Applied Rights in International Criminal Law: Defence Counsel and the Right to Disclosure', in Gideon Boas, William A Schabas and Michael P Scharf (eds), *International Criminal Justice: Legitimacy and Coherence* (Edward Elgar, 2012) 68, 90.

50   *Rome Statute* Article 64(2).

51   Swoboda above n 45, 463.

52   *Lubanga Decision on the Consequences of Non-Disclosure of Exculpatory Materials* (International Criminal Court, Trial Chamber I, Case No ICC-01/04-01/06-1401, 13 June 2008).

53   *Prosecutor v Katanga (Decision on Article 54(3)(e) Documents Identified as Potentially Exculpatory or Otherwise Material to the Defence's Preparation for the Confirmation Hearing)* (International Criminal Court, Pre-Trial Chamber I, Case No ICC-01/04-01/07-621, 20 June 2008) [3]–[6].

remain challenging. In spite of the accepted importance of disclosure of exculpatory material, there is nonetheless an environment of non-disclosure, permitted by the rules. Trial Chambers are limited in their ability to manage this, without resorting to the extreme measure of a stay of proceedings. Significant questions are raised around how the rights of an accused can be given full respect in a trial environment that explicitly permits exculpatory materials to be withheld. In turn, the connection between the procedural rules and the accused's rights starts to show a splintering.

2. Non-disclosure by victims

The second major issue emerging from the current disclosure regime at the *ICC* is the non-disclosure of material (both exculpatory and incriminating) held by victims' representatives. Unlike earlier international criminal institutions, where victims could only participate in international criminal trials as witnesses,[54] the *ICC* provides scope for victims to 'participate' in trials. The novel system of increased victim participation brings with it as yet unresolved questions about the management of information and disclosure, as well as the regulation of the disclosure relationship between the trial participants. Mirjan Damaška has noted the tension between this increased role for victims, the fairness of trial and the rights of the accused, when he argued that 'the greatest stress on considerations of fairness toward the defendant comes from the ennobling ambition of [the *ICC*] to place justice for victims at the heart of [its] mission'.[55]

While increased victims participation need not necessarily be prejudicial to the rights of the accused,[56] the broader issue of the appropriate balance between the rights of the accused and the interests of the victims can be examined in the

54 Zappalà, above n 8, 137–8. For a more comprehensive examination of the role of victims participants in ICC proceedings than what is practicable in the current chapter, see: Christine Van den Wyngaert, 'Victims before International Criminal Courts: Some Views and Concerns of an ICC Trial Judge' (2011) 44 *Case Western Reserve Journal of International Law* 475; Claude Jorda and Jérôme de Hemptinne, 'The Status and Role of the Victim', in Antonio Cassese, Paola Gaeta and John RWD Jones (eds), *The Rome Statute of the International Criminal Court: A Commentary*, vol 2 (Oxford University Press, 2002) 1387; Emily Haslam, 'Victim Participation at the International Criminal Court: A Triumph of Hope over Experience?' in Dominic McGoldrick, Peter Rowe and Eric Donnelly (eds), *The Permanent International Criminal Court: Legal and Policy Issues* (Hart, 2004) 315; Håkan Friman, 'The International Criminal Court and Participation of Victims: A Third Party to the Proceedings?' (2009) 22 *Leiden Journal of International Law* 485; Charles P Trumbull IV, 'The Victims of Victim Participation in International Criminal Proceedings' (2008) 29 *Michigan Journal of International Law* 777; and Jo-Anne Wemmers, 'Victims' Rights and the International Criminal Court: Perceptions within the Court regarding the Victims' Right to Participate' (2010) 23 *Leiden Journal of International Law* 629.
55 Mirjan Damaška, 'The Competing Visions of Fairness: The Basic Choice for International Criminal Tribunals' (2001) 36(2) *North Carolina Journal of International Law and Commercial Regulation* 365, 372.
56 Zappalà, above n 8, 139.

framework of the application of particular procedural rules. Here, the rules governing disclosure provide an examination of how victims' participation is conducted and whether the rights of an accused are afforded 'full respect'.

Victims' Representatives are not a party to the trial,[57] and they are fundamentally motivated by different aims than those of the prosecution.[58] However, under Article 68(3), where the 'personal interests' of the victims are affected, the Court shall permit the views and concerns of victims to be presented and considered at an appropriate stage of the proceedings.[59] This will be done in a manner 'not prejudicial to or inconsistent with the rights of the accused and a fair and impartial trial'.[60] In this way, while there is no specific right for victims to present evidence, they may apply to the Trial Chamber to do so.[61] It is likely that victims would have standing on matters of disclosure.[62] Yet while they enjoy these abilities, Victims' Representatives do not hold the same duties or responsibilities of disclosure as do prosecutors.[63] There is no duty of Victims' Representatives to undertake disclosure in the *ICC*'s procedural framework.[64] As the *Lubanga* Trial Chamber reinforced, the disclosure regime only applies to prosecutors: there is 'no positive obligation . . . on the other organs of the Court, the defence or the participants to disclose exculpatory material to the defence under Article 67(2) of the *Statute*, Rule 76 or Rule 77 of the *Rules*'.[65] The *Katanga* Trial Chamber noted the lack of obligation for Victims' Representatives under the *ICC*'s *Statute* and *Rules*, and further noted that, given the lack of a specific right for victims to present evidence, there can be no duty on the victims to disclose evidence.[66] This is true regardless of whether the evidence in their

---

57   See Situation in the Democratic Republic of the Congo (*Decision on the Application for Participation in Proceedings* of VPRS1, VPRS 2-3-4-5-6) (*International Criminal Court, Pre-Trial Chamber I*, Case No ICC-01/04, 17 January 2006) [51], quoting from *Berger v France (Judgment)* (ECHR, App No 48221/99, 3 December 2002) [38] and *Perez v France (Judgment)* (ECHR, App No 47287/99, 12 February 2004) [68].

58   Morrissey argues that 'they are concerned to shield their clients from trauma, to have their story told and accepted, and to secure justice for the victims' (Morrissey, above n 49, 83).

59   *Rome Statute* Article 68 (3).

60   *Rome Statute* Article 68 (3).

61   *Prosecutor v Katanga* ('*Decision on the Modalities of Victim Participation at Trial*') (*International Criminal Court, Trial Chamber II*, Case No ICC-01/04-01/07-1788, 22 January 2010) [*Katanga Decision on Victims Participation*] [105].

62   Morrissey above n 49, 95.

63   *Prosecutor v Katanga* (*Judgment on the Appeal of Mr Katanga against the Decision of the Trial Chamber II of 22 January 2010 entitled 'Decision on the Modalities of Victim Participation at Trial'*) (*International Criminal Court, Appeals Chamber*, Case No ICC-01/04-01/07 OA 11, 16 July 2010) [*Katanga Appeals Decision on Victims Participation*] [85].

64   Büngener notes that 'the procedural framework of the ICC does not foresee [a duty to disclose material], which is also the main reason why the Chambers of the Court have answered this question in the negative' (Büngener, above n 7, 372–3).

65   *Prosecutor v Lubanga* (*Decision on the Defence Application for Disclosure of Victims Applications*) (*International Criminal Court, Trial Chamber I*, Case No ICC-01/04-01/06-1637, 21 January 2009), [10].

66   *Katanga Decision on Victims Participation* (*International Criminal Court, Trial Chamber II*, Case No ICC-01/04-01/07-1788, 22 January 2010) [105].

possession is incriminating or exculpatory.[67] This approach was approved by the Appeals Chamber.[68] Yet in spite of its acceptance by both Trial and Appeals Chambers, such non-disclosure is questionable. As Christine van den Wyngaert, writing extra-judicially, has noted '[t]his might strike some as odd: how can victims have a right to tender incriminating evidence without a corresponding duty to disclose exculpatory material?'[69]

The lack of disclosure obligations means that information which comes under the possession or control of Victims' Representatives may never be provided to the parties – and in particular, to the defence. Victims are not entitled to conduct investigations in order to establish the guilt of the accused, as this would effectively make them second prosecutors and would 'be prejudicial to the rights of the Defence, the principle of equality of arms and the requirements of a fair trial'.[70] However, victims are able to undertake investigations 'in order to collect information with a view to establishing the existence, nature and extent of the harm suffered'.[71] This ability to undertake investigations could result in key material being under their control.[72] Indeed, Victims' Representatives may have even greater access to such materials than prosecution staff, as a result of their role to represent victims. The accused does not then have any access to this material, and given the lack of disclosure obligations on the victims, there is no requirement for them to disclose this material to the defence – regardless of whether the material is incriminating or potentially exculpatory.[73] The problematic nature of this is further reinforced by the fact that, unlike the prosecution, victims are not under an obligation to be objective.[74]

In the *Katanga* case, the Appeals Chamber noted the prosecutor's responsibility to investigate exonerating and incriminating circumstances equally, under Article 54(1)(a) of the *Rome Statute*, and therefore considered that it would be reasonable for the prosecutor's investigation to extend to discovering any exculpatory evidence in the possession of the victims.[75] This information would then have to be disclosed to the accused under Article 67(2) of the *Statute* and Rule 77 of the *ICC Rules*.[76] However, this approach is predicated on an assumption that

---

67 Ibid.
68 *Katanga Appeals Decision on Victims Participation* (*International Criminal Court, Appeals Chamber*, Case No ICC-01/04-01/07 OA 11, 16 July 2010).
69 Van Den Wyngaert, above n 54, 488.
70 *Katanga Decision on Victims Participation* (*International Criminal Court, Trial Chamber II*, ICC-01/04-01/07-1788, 22 January 2010) [102].
71 Ibid [103].
72 Ibid [102–3].
73 *Katanga Appeals Decision on Victims Participation* (*International Criminal Court, Appeals Chamber*, Case No ICC-01/04-01/07 OA 11, 16 July 2010) [83].
74 Büngener, above n 7, 373.
75 *Katanga Appeals Judgment on Victims Participation* (*International Criminal Court, Appeals Chamber*, Case No ICC-01/04-01/07 OA 11, 16 July 2010) [81].
76 Ibid.

the prosecutor will become aware of the existence of this information. There is no guarantee that the prosecutor will discover this information: it may remain solely under the control of, and knowledge of, the victims. There is no legal obligation on the victims to inform the prosecution of such material, or its existence. Indeed, it is difficult to see why Victims' Representatives who have control over exculpatory material would make this known to the prosecution. As aforementioned, the motivations of the Victims' Representatives are different from those of the prosecutor; such motivations may not align with exculpatory material being investigated by the prosecutor. Indeed, it may be in the interests of victims to withhold that information.

As a result, Victims' Representatives may hold exculpatory material which the defence cannot access, and which the victims are under no obligation to provide to the defence (or to notify the prosecutor of, for subsequent investigation and disclosure). The potential impact of this on the accused's right to time and facilities to prepare their case is significant. If the defence cannot access material which suggests their innocence or undermines the credibility of a prosecution witness against them, their ability to mount an effective defence is curtailed. This situation also poses problems for the role of the Trial Chamber to regulate the informational relationship between the prosecution and defence, and to ensure equality of arms between the parties. While the victims are not a party to the trial, they may hold information which affects the prosecution case. For example, the non-disclosure of information which goes to undermine the credibility of a prosecution witness may place the prosecution's evidence at an advantage which the defence could have challenged, had it had access to the exculpatory material. In the absence of an obligation on Victims' Representatives to disclose any exculpatory material in their possession or under their control, the ability of a Trial Chamber to manage this aspect of the disclosure regime and the informational relationship between the parties will be limited.

There is also no clear guidance around the responsibility of Victims' Representatives to provide disclosure of incriminating documents they themselves seek to rely upon in the proceedings. The Ngudjolo Chui defence team in the *Katanga* case argued that allowing victims to lead incriminating evidence would be to effectively make victims a second prosecutor.[77] This argument shows the concern held by some defence teams, regarding equality of arms issues and the ability of victims to lead this evidence. In the *Lubanga* case, the Trial Chamber held that 'victims participating in the proceedings may be permitted to tender and examine evidence if in the view of the Chamber it will assist in the determination of the truth'.[78] This approach has been reiterated by the Appeals

---

77   *Prosecutor v Katanga (Defence for Mathieu Ngudjolo, 'Application to Determine the Modalities of the Participation of Victims at the Trial Stage') (International Criminal Court, Trial Chamber II,* Case No ICC-01/04-01/07, 13 January 2009) [47].

78   *Prosecutor v Lubanga (Decision on Victims' Participation) (International Criminal Court, Trial Chamber I,* Case No ICC-01/04-01/06, 18 January 2008) [108].

Chamber,[79] and by other Trial Chambers.[80] However, the Trial Chamber did not provide guidance as to whether the victims would need to disclose any documents to the defence before seeking to tender them. This issue was appealed, but the Appeals Chamber also failed to provide a Decision on this point. Instead, the Appeals Chamber remitted the issue to the Trial Chamber to decide on a case-by-case basis, noting that the Trial Chamber 'could rule on the modalities for the proper disclosure of such evidence before allowing it to be introduced'.[81]

In the *Katanga* case, the Appeals Chamber found that the Trial Chamber may request the victims to submit evidence that was not previously disclosed to the accused.[82] The Appeals Chamber specifically noted that this was not incompatible with the accused's right to a fair trial.[83] If victims are authorised to present evidence, it is for the Trial Chamber to set the modalities of disclosure 'and to decide on the measures required to safeguard the fairness of the trial, given the need to respect the rights of the accused, but also the interests of the victims'.[84] The *Katanga* Trial Chamber specified a procedure for Victims' Representatives to tender documentary evidence, which would involve making a written application to the Trial Chamber regarding the documents they intend to present, showing their relevance and 'how they may contribute to the determination of the truth'.[85] The application, and the documents, 'must be notified to the parties . . . for their observations'.[86] Such a procedure, however, does not require the disclosure of the actual document to the parties: simply the 'notification' of the document. Non-disclosure of the actual material is therefore still permitted under this procedure. The Chamber will only authorise the presentation of evidence 'provided that it is not prejudicial to the Defence or to the fairness or impartiality of the trial'.[87]

In the *Katanga Decision*, the Appeals Chamber also acknowledged the link between disclosure processes, material held by victims and defence resources. They ruled that, in the case where a Trial Chamber requests the victims to

79 *Prosecutor v Lubanga (Judgment on the Appeals of The Prosecutor and The Defence against Trial Chamber I's Decision on Victims' Participation of 18 January 2008)* (International Criminal Court, Trial Chamber I, Case No ICC-01/04-01/06 OA 9 OA 10, 11 July 2008) [*Lubanga Judgment of Appeal on Victims Participation*].

80 *Katanga Decision on Victims Participation* (International Criminal Court, Trial Chamber II, Case No ICC-01/04-01/07-1788, 22 January 2010) [81].

81 *Lubanga Judgment of Appeal on Victims Participation* (International Criminal Court, Trial Chamber I, Case No ICC-01/04-01/06 OA 9 OA 10, 11 July 2008) [100].

82 *Katanga Appeals Judgment on Victims Participation* (International Criminal Court, Appeals Chamber, Case No ICC-01/04-01/07 OA 11, 16 July 2010) [55].

83 Ibid.

84 *Katanga Decision on Victims Participation* (International Criminal Court, Trial Chamber II, Case No ICC-01/04-01/07-1788, 22 January 2010) [107].

85 Ibid [99].

86 Ibid.

87 Ibid [101].

submit evidence that was not previously disclosed to the accused, the Trial Chamber must order disclosure of this material to the accused 'sufficiently in advance of its presentation at the trial, and take any other measures necessary to ensure the accused's right to a fair trial, in particular the right "to have adequate time and facilities for the preparation of the defence"'.[88] This is the correct approach. Nonetheless, concerns about the effect of victims' participation on defence resources, and thereby the defence's time and facilities to prepare their case, go beyond the question of disclosure of material held by the victims. Another concern is around victim participation on disclosure issues and their potential standing to make submissions in this regard. While victims are not intended to act as a second prosecutor, defence teams face two opponents with the capacity to make submissions on disclosure issues. In the course of responding to such submissions from victims as well as prosecutors, 'defence resources are stretched, time is wasted and disclosure is compromised'.[89] This also poses significant issues for the equality of arms in the proceedings.[90]

There is therefore a multitude of issues regarding the role of victims and non-disclosure of material to the parties (particularly the accused), and these issues may be cumulative. It may be that victims hold exculpatory material which they do not disclose; seek to rely on incriminating documents which they have not previously disclosed; and can intervene in disclosure matters while speaking to the guilt of the accused. The impact of these issues on the rights of the accused to time and facilities to prepare a defence, to know the case, and to equality of arms, has the potential to be significant. The 'splintering' that we have witnessed between rules, rights and fairness, in relation to prosecution non-disclosure of exculpatory material, now deepens. In light of this non-disclosure by victims, we can notice what we might call a 'fracturing' between these trial elements of rules, rights and fairness.

These two issues of non-disclosure of information by victims and prosecution pose challenges for the rights of the accused to time and facilities to prepare their case, to know the case against them and for the principle of equality of arms. If an accused cannot access potentially exculpatory material in the possession of either the Victims' Representatives, or the prosecution, they are at an informational disadvantage in the case; and are at a disadvantage in terms of preparing their defence. These rules contribute to an environment where the rights of an accused are limited rather than given 'full respect'; and the implementation by Trial Chambers of these rules facilitates such an environment. These two issues also demonstrate the difficulties Trial Chambers face in attempting to regulate the relationships between the parties at trial. The rules permitting non-disclosure curtail the ability of Trial Chambers to manage the informational parity between the parties. It has been shown that there is a

---

88 *Katanga Appeals Judgment on Victims Participation* (*International Criminal Court, Appeals Chamber*, Case No ICC-01/04-01/07 OA 11, 16 July 2010) [55].

89 Morrissey, above n 49, 95.

90 See Swoboda, above n 45, 462.

fracture between the way the disclosure is undertaken – namely, that it may be withheld – and the rights of the accused, which are limited by this, rather than reinforced.

III. Fairness, rights and disclosure rules: disconnected and fractured aspects of international criminal trials?

The rules that govern the disclosure regime at the *ICC*, and their application by Trial and Appeals Chambers, provide a particular area of enquiry about the interaction of procedural rules, the rights of the accused and the overall fairness of the trial. In theory, these three elements are mutually dependent: a Trial Chamber has a responsibility to ensure a trial that is fair and conducted with 'full respect' for the rights of an accused; this respect is ensured through processes governed by rules. Specifically, there is a clear connection between disclosure rules and trial fairness, and it has even been said that disclosure is 'arguably the most important mechanism for ensuring that the accused receives a fair trial'.[91]

However, as this chapter shows, there are two emerging issues with how disclosure is undertaken at the *ICC*, which suggests a fracturing between these procedural rules and the rights of an accused. The disclosure rules, and their application by Chambers, permit an environment of non-disclosure to the defence by both prosecutors and victims. There are significant implications for an accused's rights – in particular, to time and facilities to prepare a defence, and to know the case against them – as well as the principle of equality of arms. The ability of Trial Chambers to protect and promote the rights of the accused and to regulate the relationships between the parties, is curtailed in this trial environment. The above may be further evidence of the claim made by Kate Gibson and Cainnech Lussiaà-Berdou, that Chambers 'regularly recall the importance of disclosure as a fundamental component of fair trials', but that nonetheless, 'the effectiveness of the fair trial safeguards contemplated by the disclosure regime in the rules has been reduced'.[92] The question then becomes how this lack of 'full respect' for the rights of an accused ultimately affects the fairness of the trial.

ICC trials are a key mechanism for ensuring accountability for violations of international humanitarian and criminal law. Yet the way that disclosure is being undertaken in these trials – facilitating a fracturing of procedural rules, rights and fairness – may pose difficulties for accountability for such violations. The *ICC*'s mission, to end impunity for 'the most serious crimes of international concern', is not assisted by trials that fail to adhere to their most fundamental requirement: that they are 'fair . . . and conducted with full respect for the rights of the accused'.[93]

91 Gibson and Lussiaà-Berdou, above n 29, 306.
92 Ibid 313.
93 *Rome Statute* Article 64(2).

10 The Australian experience of conducting war crimes trials

Vasko Nastevski[1]

I. Introduction

This chapter will survey the existing war crimes legislation in Australia, which generally reflects international legal developments relating to war crimes, crimes against humanity and genocide since 1945. It will also explore the motivations behind Australia's response to each of these international crimes, exposing the piecemeal nature of the approach taken and resulting in significant shortcomings when dealing with accused war criminals found resident in Australia.

II. *War Crimes Act* (Cth)

The *War Crimes Act 1945* (Cth) (*War Crimes Act*) was introduced to facilitate the trial and punishment of Japanese war criminals by Australian constituted military tribunals. The *War Crimes Act* would ensure that the 'laws of war', in particular *Hague Convention IV of 1907*[2] and the *Geneva Convention of 1929*[3] were given a domestic legislative basis[4] and made 'provision for the trial and punishment of violations of the laws and usages of war'.[5]

The Second Reading Speech encapsulated the prevailing sentiment when it asserted that the establishment of military tribunals 'is necessary in order that

---

1 Dr Vasko Nastevski completed his PhD (2011) under the auspices of the Asia Pacific Centre for Military Law in the Melbourne Law School at the University of Melbourne. This chapter represents a considerably modified version of a specific chapter in his doctoral thesis. The views expressed in this chapter are those of the author alone and do not represent any institutional position.
2 *Hague Convention (IV) Respecting the Laws and Customs of War on Land*, opened for signature 18 October 1907, 1 Bevans 631 (entered into force 26 January 1910).
3 *Geneva Convention of July 27, 1929, for the Amelioration of the Condition of the Wounded and Sick of Armies in the Field*, opened for signature 27 July 1929, 2 Bevans 965 (entered into force 19 June 1931).
4 Michael Carrel, 'Australia's Prosecution of Japanese War Criminals: Stimuli and Constraints' in David A Blumenthal and Timothy LH McCormack (eds), *The Legacy of Nuremberg: Civilising Influence or Institutionalised Vengeance?* (Martinus Nijhoff Publishers, 2008) 242–3.
5 *War Crimes Act 1945* (Cth) Preamble (*War Crimes Act*).

[Japanese] war criminals may be adequately and expeditiously dealt with.'[6] The Opposition appeared even more enthusiastic about prosecuting alleged Japanese war criminals, suggesting that 'the whole community will be relieved to know that this Bill has been introduced, for everybody is anxious that war criminals shall be tried and punished.'[7] In a demonstration of bipartisanship, the Leader of the Opposition commended the Government 'for the strong attitude it has adopted in urging that stern action be taken against war criminals.'[8] The *War Crimes Act* was assented to on 11 October 1945. War crimes were defined as being 'any violation of the laws and usages of war' or 'any war crime committed in any place whatsoever, whether within or beyond Australia, during any war.'[9] The definition included crimes against peace as advocated within the *Charter of the International Military Tribunal for the Far East*[10] and a series of other specific crimes, which reflected antecedent crimes within violations of the laws and usages of war, such as murder, torture, rape, confiscation of property and cannibalism.[11] The *War Crimes Act* 'set up military tribunals . . . to . . . function . . . along the lines of a field general court-martial',[12] which would issue punishments ranging from the death penalty to a fine of any amount.[13]

The first Australian war crimes trial conducted under the auspices of the *War Crimes Act* was held at Morotai during November 1945 and the final trial was held in April 1951 on Manus Island. The majority of trials were held in Papua New Guinea (Rabaul, Manus Island, Wewak), while others were conducted in Indonesia (Morotai), Malaysia (Labuan), Singapore and Hong Kong. Only three trials were conducted on Australian territory, these were located in Darwin.[14] In total 300 trials were conducted of 807 accused. Of these 279 were acquitted, 579 convicted with 137 being sentenced to death.[15] However, the contribution made by Australia in the field of war crimes trials and the significant

6 Commonwealth, *Parliamentary Debates*, House of Representatives, 4 October 1945, 6511 (John Beasley, Minister for Defence).

7 Commonwealth, *Parliamentary Debates*, House of Representatives, 4 October 1945, 6511 (Archie Cameron).

8 Commonwealth, *Parliamentary Debates*, Senate, 4 October 1945, 6464 (George McLeay, Leader of the Opposition).

9 *War Crimes Act* s 3(a)–(b).

10 *Charter of the International Military Tribunal for the Far East*, signed in Tokyo on 19 January 1946, amended 26 April 1946, TIAS 1589, 4 Bevans 20.

11 Philip R Piccigallo, *The Japanese on Trial: Allied War Crimes Operations in the East, 1945–1951* (University of Texas Press, 1979) 124–5.

12 Commonwealth, *Parliamentary Debates*, House of Representatives, 4 October 1945, 6510 (John Beasley, Minister for Defence).

13 Commonwealth, *Parliamentary Debates*, House of Representatives, 4 October 1945, 6511 (John Beasley, Minister for Defence); *War Crimes Act* s 11.

14 David Sissons, 'The Australian War Crimes Trials and Investigations (1942–1951)', (2006) www.ocf.berkeley.edu/~changmin/documents/Sissons%20Final%20War%20Crimes%20Text%2018-3-06.pdf, [17–19].

15 Carrel, above n 4, 246.

participation in the prosecution of Japanese war criminals would come to an abrupt end. As a member of the Commonwealth, Australia was considerably influenced by a British decision during 1948 to scale down and ultimately end war crimes trials. The British Government advice at the time advocated that:

> punishment of war criminals is more a matter of discouraging future generations than meting out retribution to every guilty individual . . . we are convinced that it is now necessary to dispose of the past as soon as possible.[16]

Pressure to close down the trials also came from the United States, which had increasingly hardened in its ideological differences with the Soviet sphere. Essentially, the United States saw a 'strong and prosperous Japan as a counter to the extension of Soviet influence in the Asia-Pacific'.[17] An early end to the Japanese war crimes trials was therefore required.[18]

Australia's lack of enthusiasm in dealing with alleged war criminals was further demonstrated, following a request for extradition by the Soviet Union of accused war criminal and Australian national Ervin Viks. Rejecting the extradition request, Sir Garfield Barwick, in his now familiar speech declared:

> we think the time has come to close the chapter [on pursuing war criminals].[19]

It was only in the 1980s and following a series of public allegations against individuals for being Nazi war criminals that Australia's attention again turned to possible prosecution for war crimes. The *Review of Material Relating to the Entry of Suspected War Criminals into Australia* was submitted to the Special Minister of State on 28 November 1986 with the findings that:

> It is more likely than not that a significant number of persons who committed serious war crimes in World War II have entered Australia and some of these are now resident in Australia; certainly the likelihood of this is such that some action needs to be now taken.[20]

---

16   Telegram dated 13 July 1948 by the British Commonwealth Relations Office sent to the seven Dominions, extract found in Honourable Jules Deschênes, Commissioner, *Commission of Inquiry on War Criminals Report*, Part 1: Public, Ottawa, Canada, 30 December 1986, 27.

17   Carrel, above n 4, 255.

18   Ibid.

19   Commonwealth, *Parliamentary Debates*, House of Representatives, 22 March 1961, 449 (Sir Garfield Barwick, Acting Minister for External Affairs and Attorney General), 451–2.

20   Department of the Special Minister of State, *Review of Material Relating to the Entry of Suspected War Criminals into Australia* (Australian Government Publishing Service, 1987) 177.

The Report's most notable recommendation included that:

> The Government make a clear and positive statement to the effect that, as regards serious war crimes, it does not regard the Chapter as closed . . . and that it will take appropriate action under the law to bring to justice persons who have committed serious war crimes found in Australia . . . [21]

The Report made a further reference to 'amending the *War Crimes Act* so as to permit a civil court to deal with a war crime'.[22]

III. *War Crimes Amendment Act* (Cth)

The *War Crimes Amendment Act 1988* (Cth) *(War Crimes Amendment Act)* came into effect on 25 January 1989, having made extensive changes to the *War Crimes Act*. Important differences included enabling prosecution of alleged war criminals by domestic Australian criminal courts and extending application to crimes committed by citizens of the Axis countries against their own populations.[23] Section 9 of the *War Crimes Amendment Act* outlined that a person who:

(a)   on or after 1 September 1939 and on or before 8 May 1945; and
(b)   whether as an individual or as a member of an organisation;

committed a war crime, is guilty of an indictable offence against this Act.[24]

This immediately limited its jurisdiction to a specific time period. The narrowness of the legislation is further prescribed through Section 7, whereby a *serious crime* will constitute a *war crime* only if it was committed:

(a)   in the course of hostilities in a *war*;
(b)   in the course of an *occupation*;
(c)   in pursuing a policy associated with the conduct of a *war* or with an *occupation*; or
(d)   on behalf of, or in the interests of, a power conducting a *war* or engaged in an *occupation*.[25]

21   Ibid 180.
22   Ibid 182. [Italics not in original]
23   Gillian Triggs, 'Australia's War Crimes Trials: All Pity Choked' in Tim McCormack and Gerry Simpson (eds), *The Law of War Crimes: National and International Approaches* (Kluwer Law International, 1997) 123, 125.
24   *War Crimes Amendment Act* 1988 (Cth) s 9 *(War Crimes Amendment Act)*.
25   Ibid s 7(1) (emphasis added).

The terms *war* and *occupation* play an instructive role in interpreting the provisions. First, 'war' is given the following meaning:

(a)   a war, whether declared or not;
(b)   any other armed conflict between countries; or
(c)   a civil war or similar armed conflict;
(whether or not involving Australia or a country allied or associated with Australia) *in so far as it occurred in Europe in the period beginning on 1 September 1939 and ending on 8 May 1945.*[26]

The time period is re-emphasised but includes a geographical particularity concerning only *Europe*. When the War Crimes Amendment Bill 1987 (Cth) (War Crimes Amendment Bill) was first read in Parliament, the definition of *war* was much broader, extending its reach to 'Europe, the Atlantic, Northern Africa, the Middle East, Asia or the Pacific (including New Guinea and Northern Australia)'.[27] The effect of such a list was to include theatres of war that were more likely to involve Australians and would have technically exposed Australian service personnel to the possibility of prosecution.

The Opposition argued at the time that Australian servicemen were already subject to Australian jurisdiction and to Australian military law, therefore it was unnecessary for them to be included under these circumstances.[28] Undoubtedly, any exposure of Australian service personnel to this legislation had the potential to generate electoral discontent for the Government. The early amendment to the initial War Crimes Amendment Bill ensured that the exposure of Australians would be so limited that it effectively ruled out possible prosecution of Australian service personnel.

The Explanatory Memorandum, based on the initial War Crimes Amendment Bill, elucidates that 'the date 1 September 1939 is the commencing day for the purposes of the Nuremberg Tribunal's jurisdiction to try war crimes'.[29] The date 8 May 1945 reflects the application of the *War Crimes Amendment Act* to the European theatre of War as it is the date on which Germany surrendered in Europe.[30]

The term 'occupation' is given the following meaning:

(a)   an occupation of territory arising out of a war; or
(b)   without limiting the generality of paragraph (a), an occupation of territory in Latvia, Lithuania or Estonia as a direct or indirect result of:

---

26   Ibid s 5 (emphasis added).
27   War Crimes Amendment Bill 1987 (Cth) (as read a first time) 28 October 1987, s 5.
28   Commonwealth, *Parliamentary Debates*, Senate, 15 December 1988, 4250 (Robert Hill).
29   Explanatory Memorandum, War Crimes Amendment Bill 1987 (Cth) 5.
30   Commonwealth, *Parliamentary Debates*, Senate, 20 December 1988, 4572 (Michael Tate).

(i)   the agreement of 23 August 1939 between Germany and the Union of Soviet Socialist Republics; or

(ii) any protocol to that agreement.[31]

An occupation for the purposes of the *War Crimes Amendment Act* could have occurred only in Europe (between 1 September 1939 and 8 May 1945) and with a separate emphasis to the three Baltic States, reflecting the many requests from within the Australian community to recognise the occupation of territory in Latvia, Lithuania and Estonia, either by Germany or the Union of Soviet Socialist Republics, and without distinguishing the 'horrific crimes that were committed during that period of occupation'.[32] A 'war crime' is further defined under Section 7(3) of the *War Crimes Amendment Act* so that an act constituted a war crime if it was:

(a) committed:
   (i)   in the course of political, racial or religious persecution; or
   (ii) with intent to destroy in whole or in part a national, ethnic, racial or religious group, as such; and
(b) committed in the territory of a country when the country was involved in a war or when territory of the country was subject to an occupation.[33]

The formulation of this provision derived partly from Article 6(c) of the *Charter of the International Military Tribunal (IMT)*,[34] which defined *crimes against humanity*.[35] Unsurprisingly, it has been accused of creating 'a mishmash of language' by invoking the alternative international crimes of crimes against humanity and genocide to define war crimes.[36] Section 6 provides a list of acts that are considered a *serious crime* if they were done in a part of Australia and were under the law then in force, an offence such as:

(a) murder
(b) manslaughter

---

31   *War Crimes Amendment Act* s 5. The initial Bill only included sub-paragraph (a), but was expanded following further pressure from the Opposition.

32   Commonwealth, *Parliamentary Debates*, Senate, 15 December 1988, 4250 (Robert Hill).

33   *War Crimes Amendment Act* s 7(3).

34   Explanatory Memorandum, War Crimes Amendment Bill 1987 (Cth) 7.

35   Charter of the International Military Tribunal, annexed to Agreement for the Prosecution and Punishment of the Major War Criminals of the European Axis, signed in London 8 August 1945, 82 UNTS 279,
definition included: persecutions on political, racial or religious grounds in execution of or in connection with any crime within the jurisdiction of the Tribunal, whether or not in violation of the domestic law of the country where perpetrated.

36   Gideon Boas, 'War Crimes Prosecutions in Australia and Other Common Law Countries: Some Observations' (2010) 21 *Criminal Law Forum* 313, 318.

(c)   causing grievous bodily harm

(d)   wounding

(e)   rape

(f)   indecent assault

(g)   abduction, or procuring, for immoral purposes.[37]

Section 6(4) extends the definition of a *serious crime* to 'the deportation of a person to, or the internment of a person in, a death camp, a slave labour camp, or a place where persons are subjected to treatment similar to that undergone in a death camp or slave labour camp'.[38] Where these offences are committed in the manner set out under Section 7, they will constitute *war crimes*. The intention appears to be to 'characterise in terms already found in Australian law the acts which constitute war crimes under international law'.[39]

Section 11 provides that a person shall not be charged with an offence 'unless he or she is an Australian citizen; or a resident of Australia or of an external Territory'.[40] However, it was not necessary for the individual to be an Australian citizen or resident at the time of the commission of the offences.

Section 16 provides that superior orders are not a defence to an offence listed under the *War Crimes Amendment Act*, but if a person is convicted for an offence under the *War Crimes Amendment Act*, superior orders will be 'taken into account in determining the proper sentence'.[41] Nevertheless, arguably any claim of superior orders may also play a part in proof of tests such as *mens rea*. Conceivably, where a person did not know a particular order was illegal, nor had a reason to think that it was illegal, this may allow for some form of implicit mitigation in establishing actual criminality.[42] This clause is also to be read in conjunction with Section 6(2), which requires that 'regard shall be had to any defence under that law that could have been established in a proceeding for the offence'.[43] Accordingly, a court is able to consider any defence available in a State or territory for offences characteristic of one of the serious crimes listed under Section 6(1).[44] This is further supplemented by Section 13(2)(f) to the extent that:

> all defences under the law in force in that State or Territory when the person is charged with the offence had been defences under the law in force in that State or Territory *at the time of the act*.[45]

---

37   *War Crimes Amendment Act* s 6(1).

38   Ibid s 6(4).

39   Explanatory Memorandum, War Crimes Amendment Bill 1987 (Cth) 5.

40   *War Crimes Amendment Act* s 11.

41   Ibid s 16.

42   Irene Nemes, 'Punishing Nazi War Criminals in Australia: Issues of Law and Morality' (1992) 4(2) *Current Issues in Criminal Justice* 141, 151 n 56.

43   *War Crimes Amendment Act* s 6(2).

44   Explanatory Memorandum, War Crimes Amendment Bill 1987 (Cth) 6.

45   *War Crimes Amendment Act* s 13(2)(f) (emphasis added).

Perhaps somewhat counter-intuitively, Section 17(2) introduced principles of international law as a further avenue of defence, where it provided that:

> it is a defence if the doing by the defendant of the act alleged to be the offence:
>
> (a) was permitted by the laws, customs and usages of war; and
> (b) was not under international law a crime against humanity.[46]

Section 17(3) further stated that:

> To avoid doubt, the doing of the act by the defendant was permitted by the laws, customs and usages of war if it was reasonably justified by the exigencies and necessities of the conduct of war.[47]

These provisions effectively provided a further defence in situations where an act was committed that was 'regarded under international law as acceptable when performed in the course of war'.[48] Although they seem to be qualified to some extent by Section 17(4) and (5), in that 'evidence of the existence of the facts constituting the defence' is required in order for a defendant to be entitled to rely on a defence under Subsection (2).[49] In cases where such evidence does exist, 'the onus of establishing beyond a reasonable doubt, that those facts either do not exist or do not constitute the defence lies on the prosecution'.[50]

An incongruity that is highlighted by these provisions is that a trial judge may be forced to consider principles and definitions under international law, despite the *War Crimes Amendment Act* seeking to avoid such considerations in the earlier provisions when defining a *war crime* based on recognised Australian terminology.[51] Deferring to known crimes and principles under Australian criminal law in order to now define a *war crime* for the purposes of the *War Crimes Amendment Act* resulted from concerns about the possibility of legal challenges to the jurisdiction of Australian courts and/or to the retrospectivity of the legislation. As Senator Hill outlined during debates at the second reading of the War Crimes Amendment Bill:

> it seeks to create in Australia an offence for an event which occurred out of Australia. The offence would have been committed against somebody, not an Australian, by somebody, probably not an Australian . . . worse still, it is creating a new offence – that of a war crime and retrospectively applying it to events which occurred almost 50 years ago.[52]

---

46 Ibid s 17(2).
47 Ibid s 17(3).
48 Explanatory Memorandum, War Crimes Amendment Bill 1987 (Cth) 9.
49 *War Crimes Amendment Act* s 17(4).
50 Ibid s 17(5).
51 Gillian Triggs, 'Australia's War Crimes Act: Justice Delayed or Denied?' [1990] (March) *Law Institute Journal* 153, 154.
52 Commonwealth, *Parliamentary Debates*, Senate, 15 December 1988, 4246 (Robert Hill).

Despite initial bipartisanship on the issue of pursuing alleged war criminals residing in Australia, some quite bitter and often rancorous debate preceded the commencement of the legislation. There are also significant limitations to be found in the *War Crimes Amendment Act* in that it only applies to a 'narrow slice of time'[53] and limits the possible location of the offences to Europe.

A. *Prosecutions under the* War Crimes Amendment Act 1988 *(Cth)*

There were three prosecutions initiated under the *War Crimes Amendment Act*, all of which were beset by issues around the age of the defendants and the adequacy of evidence given the lapse of time between the commission of the acts and the trial.

1 Ivan Polyukhovich

The first case was that of Ivan Polyukhovich, who was ultimately charged with the murder of eight men, nine women and eight children, and being knowingly concerned in the murder of approximately 850 persons.[54] Committal proceedings against Mr Polyukhovich commenced on 28 October 1991 in the Adelaide Magistrates Court and on 5 June 1992 the Magistrate committed Mr Polyukhovich to the Supreme Court of South Australia on two of the eight counts made against him.[55] Notably the Director of Public Prosecutions (DPP) did subsequently relay three additional charges.[56] Some of the witnesses that the prosecution was to rely on died after the commencement of the proceedings, while others were simply too ill to travel.[57] On 18 May 1993 the Supreme Court acquitted Mr Polyukhovich of all charges for lack of evidence as well as not being satisfied as to the credibility of the evidence that was presented.[58] The case against Mr Polyukhovich would inevitably set the tone for Australia's disappointing experience in bringing to justice war criminals.

2 Mikolay Berezowsky

The second person indicted under the *War Crimes Amendment Act* was Mikolay Berezowsky. He was charged with being 'directly knowingly concerned in or

---

53 Gillian Triggs, above n 23, 129.

54 Attorney-General's Department, *Special Investigations Unit – Annual Report 1989* (1990) 2–4.

55 Attorney-General's Department, *Report of the Investigations of War Criminals in Australia* (1993) 57.

56 Triggs, above n 23, 130.

57 Michael Kirby, 'War Crimes Prosecutions – An Australian Update' (1993) 10 *Australian Bar Review* 109, 111.

58 Triggs, above n 23, 132. See also David Bevan, *A Case to Answer: The Story of Australia's First European War Crimes Prosecution* (Wakefield Press, 1994) xii.

party to the murder of 102 Jewish people'.[59] Committal proceedings were commenced on 22 June 1992 and concluded one month later. The case against Mr Berezowsky floundered due to identification difficulties[60] and as with the Polyukhovich proceedings, the case was inhibited due to important overseas witnesses not being able to travel to Australia because of ill health, while others had died.[61] The case against Mr Berezowsky was dismissed on 29 July 1992 due to insufficient evidence.[62]

3. Heinrich Wagner

The third case involved Heinrich Wagner, who on 5 September 1991 was charged for being 'directly knowingly concerned in or party to the murders of about 104 Jewish people'.[63] Committal proceedings began on 1 June 1992, were adjourned and recommenced on 10 August 1992. The Magistrate concluded on 20 November 1992 that Mr Wagner had a case to answer on all of the three counts made against him.[64] However, Mr Wagner soon after suffered a heart attack[65] and the case was dropped as the DPP decided that he was too ill to continue.[66]

There was considerable public criticism of the ineffective trials, coupled with concerns over the significant expenditure of public money, which by June 1992 had cost $15.4 million.[67] Agitation from different ethnic groups who had raised concerns about adverse imputations being made against their communities and finally doubts about the possibilities of successfully securing convictions given the experience with the first three attempts, all prevailed upon the Government at the time to close down the investigation of alleged war criminals as of June 1992.[68]

IV. *Genocide Convention Act 1949* (Cth)

The *Convention on the Prevention and Punishment of the Crime of Genocide (Genocide Convention)* was introduced in 1948 and came into force on 12 July 1951.[69] Article

---

59 Attorney-General's Department, *Report of the Investigations of War Criminals in Australia* (1993) 57.
60 Triggs, above n 23, 123.
61 Attorney-General's Department, above n 59, 59.
62 Bevan, above n 58, xii.
63 Attorney-General's Department, above n 59, 60.
64 Ibid 61.
65 Triggs, above n 23, 134.
66 Bevan, above n 58, xii.
67 Attorney-General's Department, *Report on the Operations of the War Crimes Act 1945 to June 1992* (1992) 6.
68 Triggs, above n 23, 134.
69 *Convention on the Prevention and Punishment of the Crime of Genocide*, opened for signature 9 December 1948, 78 UNTS 277 (entered into force 12 January 1951).

2 of the *Genocide Convention* provides a list of acts that will constitute genocide if 'committed with intent to destroy, in whole or in part, a national, ethnical, racial or religious group, as such'.[70] The list of acts includes:

(a) Killing members of the group;
(b) Causing serious bodily or mental harm to members of the group;
(c) Deliberately inflicting on the group conditions of life calculated to bring about its physical destruction in whole or in part;
(d) Imposing measures intended to prevent births within the group;
(e) Forcibly transferring children of the group to another group.[71]

Article 3 makes punishable any acts of genocide, any conspiracy, direct and public incitement or attempt to commit genocide and complicity in genocide.[72] Article 5 obliges States Party 'to enact . . . the necessary legislation to give effect to [its] provisions . . . and, in particular, to provide effective penalties for persons guilty of genocide'.[73]

The Australian Parliament seemed comfortable enough responding rhetorically at least to the calls for action against the crime of genocide, as it 'has long shocked the conscience of mankind'.[74] The Genocide Convention Bill 1949 (Cth) (Genocide Bill) was introduced with the purpose of seeking 'approval of the Parliament for Australian ratification' of the *Genocide Convention*.[75] Australian parliamentarians at the time viewed ratification as part of an obvious exercise that would see Australia taking 'its place with other nations in condemning' genocide.[76] However, belying the acceptance of these moral obligations to ratify the *Genocide Convention* was an underlying sense of cynicism as to the effectiveness of international conventions. This is perhaps best captured in a statement made by Sir Robert Menzies as Leader of the Opposition at the time:

> I have no faith in conventions. However, the last thing I should dream of doing would be to speak or vote in such a way as to cast any doubt on the proposition that in Australia we abominate the crime of genocide . . . if it needs our subscription to a convention to advertise our feeling to the world, then let us subscribe to it.[77]

---

70 Ibid Article 2.
71 Ibid.
72 Ibid Article 3.
73 Ibid Article 5.
74 Commonwealth, *Parliamentary Debates*, House of Representatives, 19 May 1949, 92 (Joseph Chifley, Prime Minister).
75 Ibid.
76 Commonwealth, *Parliamentary Debates*, House of Representatives, 30 June 1949, 1865 (Herbert Evatt, Attorney-General and Minister for External Affairs).
77 Commonwealth, *Parliamentary Debates*, House of Representatives, 30 June 1949, 1865 (Robert Menzies, Leader of Opposition).

Australia ratified the *Genocide Convention* on 8 July 1949 through the enactment of the *Genocide Convention Act 1949* (Cth) (*Genocide Act*), thereby acknowledging genocide as a crime under international law. However, genocide was not incorporated as a crime in Australia's domestic criminal law nor has 'the [*Genocide*] *Convention* . . . formed part of Australian domestic law.'[78] Indeed this was acknowledged from the outset, in that the Genocide Bill was merely seen to be ratifying the *Genocide Convention* and that 'subsequently, no doubt, legislation will be put [forward] to make genocide a crime inside Australia, *if that becomes necessary*'.[79]

One of the principal reasons that was consistently given as to why the crime of genocide had not been made a crime domestically is that it was thought that such a crime could simply not occur in Australia. For example, statements were made that 'persecution of that kind has never been tolerated in Australia';[80] 'in this country we are extremely unlikely to commit any of those crimes';[81] 'it has no effect or relevance inside our own country';[82] indeed 'it deals with a crime of which no Anglo-Saxon nation could be guilty'.[83] Some of the more extreme speeches denounced the Genocide Bill as 'nothing more nor less than a piece of pious humbug',[84] 'a piece of eyewash . . . [not] worth the paper on which it is printed'[85] and that:

> No one in his right senses believes that the Commonwealth of Australia will be called before the bar of public opinion, if there is such a thing, and asked to answer for any of the things which are enumerated in this convention.[86]

Some of the reasons for not making *genocide* a crime through specific domestic legislation at the time included constitutional uncertainty over the capacity of the Commonwealth to legislate to implement treaties and a perceived lack of precision in the *Genocide Convention* definition of genocide. It was said to be all

---

78   *Kruger v Commonwealth* (1997) 190 CLR 1, 70 (Dawson J).
79   Commonwealth, *Parliamentary Debates*, House of Representatives, 30 June 1949, 1864 (Robert Menzies, Leader of Opposition).
80   Ibid 1865.
81   Commonwealth, *Parliamentary Debates*, House of Representatives, 30 June 1949, 1865 (Henry Gullett).
82   Commonwealth, *Parliamentary Debates*, House of Representatives, 30 June 1949, 1872 (Robert Menzies, Leader of Opposition).
83   Commonwealth, *Parliamentary Debates*, House of Representatives, 30 June 1949, 1874 (Adair Blain).
84   Commonwealth, *Parliamentary Debates*, House of Representatives, 30 June 1949, 1865 (Henry Gullett).
85   Commonwealth, *Parliamentary Debates*, House of Representatives, 30 June 1949, 1867 (Joseph Abbott).
86   Commonwealth, *Parliamentary Debates*, House of Representatives, 30 June 1949, 1871 (Archie Cameron).

too hard.[87] Successive Governments then provided a standard position for not criminalising genocide, which was conveniently summarised by Crispin J:

> the legislature took the view that its obligation to provide effective penalties for persons guilty of acts falling within the definition of genocide could be adequately fulfilled by reliance upon the existing provisions of the criminal law.[88]

The response by Australia in relation to the *Genocide Convention* has been described as being typical of its 'general approach' to 'human rights obligations.'[89] In addition to the view that it was irrelevant to Australia, the Australian Government took the view that existing laws, as they relate to murder, manslaughter, assault, conspiracy and incitement, and others were 'sufficient to enable Australia to comply with its obligations under the *Genocide Convention*'.[90] However, advice from the Attorney-General's Department at the time indicated that 'the criminal laws of the Commonwealth did not provide penalties for all of the acts described in the *Genocide Convention*'.[91] For example, the physical elements of 'causing serious bodily or mental harm' and 'deliberately inflicting on the group conditions of life calculated to bring about its physical destruction in whole or in part' were deemed inadequately covered under Commonwealth law.[92]

The common law is similarly deficient in providing for the crime of genocide. On one view, the prohibition against genocide is a customary norm of international law giving rise to non-derogable enforcement obligations by each State to the entire international community. As such, the crime of genocide, as recognised in customary international law, should be a source of the common law and be incorporated in the absence of conflicting domestic law. Indeed, it has been contended that it is 'morally repugnant to suggest that genocide is not a crime in Australia'.[93] However, Wilcox J concluded differently:

---

87 Shirley Scott, 'Why Wasn't Genocide A Crime in Australia?: Accounting For the Half-century Delay in Australia Implementing the Genocide Convention' (2004) 10(2) *Australian Journal of Human Rights* 22.

88 In the matter of an application for a writ of mandamus directed to Phillip R Thompson Ex parte Wadjularbinna Nulyarimma, Isobel Coe, Billy Craigie and Robbie Thorpe (Applicants), Tom Trevorrow, Irene Watson, Kevin Buzzacott and Michael J Anderson (Intervenors) [1998] ACTSC 136 [71] (18 December 1998) (Crispin J).

89 Andrew Mitchell, 'Genocide, Human Rights Implementation and the Relationship between International and Domestic Law: *Nulyarimma v Thompson*' (2000) 24 *Melbourne University Law Review* 15, 22.

90 Ibid. See also Commonwealth, *Parliamentary Debates*, Senate, 15 August 1974, 965 (Donald Willesee, Minister for Foreign Affairs). (Italics omitted in original).

91 Ibid. Mitchell refers to a Memorandum from the Acting Secretary of the Attorney-General's Department, GA Watson, to the Secretary of the Department of External Affairs, 6 April 1949, Ref 47/740. (Italics omitted in original).

92 Ibid.

93 Douglas Guilfoyle, '*Nulyarimma v Thompson*: Is Genocide a Crime at Common Law in Australia?' (2001) 29 *Federal Law Review* 1, 36.

Ratification of a convention does not directly affect Australian domestic law unless and until implementing legislation is enacted. This seems to be the position even where the ratification has received Parliamentary approval, as in the case of the *Genocide Convention*.[94]

The position adopted by Australian courts seems to reflect an 'entrenched resistance to the use of international law in domestic courts',[95] which has ultimately imposed 'a chilling effect on the pursuit of international legal rights through the Australian courts'.[96] There have been governmental and parliamentary reviews that have similarly concluded that the position of Australian law in relation to the *Genocide Convention* is clearly 'unsatisfactory'[97] or that 'Australia's common law and criminal code . . . only partially address the acts listed in the [*Genocide*] *Convention*'.[98]

While it is possible that some of the acts listed as constituting genocide can be prosecuted as offences under existing domestic criminal laws, notably, to prosecute an act of genocide, in addition to proving the physical elements of these acts, it is a requirement to prove that genocide is committed against a specific category or *group*. Generally, existing domestic laws provide for offences committed against individuals.[99] As a result, domestic laws are unlikely to address the 'very precise and high threshold mental element' of the crime of *genocide*, in that it would have to be proved beyond a reasonable doubt that the accused committed the acts 'with intent to destroy, in whole or in part' one of the specified groups.[100]

Nor would they satisfy jurisdictional requirements without specific provisions giving extraterritorial effect, especially for genocidal acts committed outside Australia.[101] Where the accused perpetrators and victims were not Australian citizens at the time of the commission of offences and when perpetrated outside Australia, universal jurisdiction provides the most suitable opportunity to make out such a nexus. However, this would need to be present in the criminal law being invoked. Courts do not assume criminal jurisdiction for offences committed extraterritorially except where it has been specifically provided for by statute.[102]

---

94 *Nulyarimma v Thompson* (1999) 96 FCR 153, 162 (Wilcox J).
95 Guilfoyle, above n 93, 33.
96 Gillian Triggs, 'Implementation of the Rome Statute for the International Criminal Court: A Quiet Revolution in Australian Law' (2003) 25 *Sydney Law Review* 507, 521.
97 Attorney-General's Department, *Review of Commonwealth Criminal Law: Final Report* (1991) 86–7.
98 Legal and Constitutional References Committee, Senate, Humanity Diminished: The Crime of Genocide – Inquiry into the Anti-Genocide Bill 1999 (2000) 19.
99 Mitchell, above n 89, 22.
100 Katherine L Doherty and Timothy LH McCormack, 'Complementarity as a Catalyst for Comprehensive Domestic Penal Legislation' (1999) 5 *University of California Davis Journal of International Law and Policy* 147, 165.
101 Ibid.
102 Ivan Shearer, 'Jurisdiction' in Sam Blay, Ryszard Piotrowicz and Martin Tsamenyi (eds), *Public International Law: An Australian Perspective* (Oxford University Press, first published 1997, 2nd edn, 2005) 161.

In Australian criminal law, jurisdiction for the domestic crime of *murder* or *rape* is generally based on territoriality, so that a clear nexus exists between the State and the offence.[103] The position held by successive Australian Governments that domestic criminal laws relating to murder or manslaughter would be sufficient to enable Australia to satisfy its obligations with respect to the *Genocide Convention*,[104] would therefore appear to be misguided.

Moreover, given that the *Genocide Act* did not provide for the trial and punishment of the crime of genocide by Australian courts, this has potentially left Australia in breach of its international obligations under the *Genocide Convention*. Article 5 of the *Genocide Convention* provides that contracting parties 'undertake to enact . . . the necessary legislation . . . and, in particular, to provide effective penalties for persons guilty of genocide or any of the other acts enumerated in article III'.[105] The *Genocide Act* has clearly failed to proscribe the crime of genocide and Australia's domestic laws and indeed the common law do not meet the necessary requirements.[106] The only way to fulfil Australia's obligation under the *Genocide Convention* is to enact comprehensive legislation that declares genocide a crime under domestic Australian law.

The consequence of the approach taken in respect of the *Genocide Act* is that alleged war criminals found in Australia, cannot be charged with the crime of genocide pursuant to the *Genocide Convention*. Unfortunately, this proposition leaves Australia's criminal justice system exposed, given the deficiency in the laws to cover the crime of genocide.[107] As Saul pronounces, 'Australia remains a grim black hole in the aspirational universe of protection – and a depressing safe haven for perpetrators of genocide'.[108]

V. *Geneva Conventions Act 1957* (Cth)

At a diplomatic conference held in Geneva in 1949, four international conventions (*Geneva Conventions*) were developed dealing with the protection of war victims. All four *Geneva Conventions* provide for measures to be taken to prevent *grave breaches*, designed to protect specific categories of people. The *grave breaches* include:

> wilful killing, torture or inhuman treatment, including biological experiments, wilfully causing great suffering or serious injury to body or health,

---

103   Ibid.
104   Triggs, above n 96, 520.
105   *Convention on the Prevention and Punishment of the Crime of Genocide*, above n 69, Art 5.
106   Mitchell, above n 89, 45.
107   Genocide has subsequently been made an explicit crime in Australia by the amendments to the *Criminal Code Act 1995* (Cth) (*Criminal Code*) as a result of implementing the requirements under the International Criminal Court.
108   Ben Saul, 'The International Crime of Genocide in Australian Law' (2000) 22 *Sydney Law Review* 527, 529. This is true at least for the period until ratification of the ICC.

and extensive destruction and appropriation of property, not justified by military necessity and carried out unlawfully and wantonly.[109]

The *Geneva Conventions* not only provided a legal definition of the most serious crimes committed against other human beings, but they also present States Parties with the obligation to enact legislation to bring to justice those individuals perpetrating these crimes.[110] The *Geneva Conventions* impose three fundamental obligations on contracting parties. First they provide that States 'undertake to enact any legislation necessary to provide effective penal sanctions for persons committing, or ordering to be committed, any of the grave breaches'; second to 'search for persons alleged to have committed' any of the grave breaches; and third to try such persons or to hand them over for trial to another State concerned.[111] In recognition of its obligation under the *Geneva Conventions*, Australia enacted the *Geneva Conventions Act 1957* (Cth) *(Geneva Conventions Act)*, albeit some 8 years after the *Geneva Conventions* were introduced. In doing so, it was asserted that '[it] is the true moral obligation which we owe to all humanity, through the United Nations, and through this aspect of public international law'.[112]

Importantly, by Section 7 the *Geneva Conventions Act* provided for the domestic prosecution of persons accused of grave breaches.[113] Section 10 subsequently vested jurisdiction in the Supreme Court of each State and territory to conduct trials of offences against the *Geneva Conventions Act*.[114] Amendments were made in 1991 that added the possibility of prosecution against breaches of *Additional Protocol I*.[115] The scope of its potential application did not go unnoticed at the time of its emergence, it was described as representing:

> quite a milestone in the history of our own internal law . . . that an offender can be punished under Australian law, whether the offence for which he is being punished or tried was committed in Australia or elsewhere.[116]

---

109   *First Geneva Convention* Article 50; *Second Geneva Convention* Article 51; *Third Geneva Convention* Article 130; *Fourth Geneva Convention* Article 147.

110   GIAD Draper, *The Red Cross Conventions* (Stevens and Sons Limited, 1958) 24–5.

111   *First Geneva Convention*, above n 109, Art 49; *Second Geneva Convention* Article 50; *Third Geneva Convention* Article 129; *Fourth Geneva Convention* Article 146.

112   Commonwealth, *Parliamentary Debates*, House of Representatives, 12 November 1957, 2769 (Harold Holt).

113   *Geneva Conventions Act 1957* (Cth) s 7(1) [*Geneva Conventions Act*]. The provision stated that 'a person who, in Australia or elsewhere, commits . . . a grave breach of any of the Conventions is guilty of an indictable offence'.

114   Ibid s 10.

115   Australia ratified *Additional Protocol I* (dealing with international armed conflicts) and *Additional Protocol II* (dealing with internal armed conflicts) in 1991. The *Geneva Conventions Amendment Act 1991* (Cth) included grave breaches of *Protocol I* as indictable offences in the *Geneva Conventions Act*.

116   Commonwealth, *Parliamentary Debates*, House of Representatives, 12 November 1957, 2749 (Gough Whitlam).

Section 7(3) further added that the provisions apply 'to persons regardless of their nationality or citizenship',[117] thereby providing an 'unlimited ambit' in its application to international crimes and distinguishing its jurisdictional reach from the more limited *War Crimes Act* and other domestic criminal law.[118] Essentially, there is no requirement that the alleged war criminals or victims are Australian citizens or even that Australia is a participant in the armed conflict.

The principal legislation was commended as 'historic and unprecedented' in that it advanced the 'creation of legal rights in defence of justice' by establishing 'justiciable rights' in relation to war crimes.[119] It would make the prosecution of war crimes 'amenable to our courts'.[120] However, any interest that may have existed in realising the effectiveness of the *Geneva Conventions Act* was almost immediately tempered. Statements made during debate over the principal legislation about the terminology that is employed by the scheduled *Geneva Conventions* reads ominously. For example, it was stated that:

> One hopes that this will never have to be interpreted by our courts . . . the language of these conventions has that blissful, airy, vague quality which attaches to treaties and declarations of human rights. It is quite unlike our statutory language.[121]

It was asserted that if 'legislators prescribe a vague and indefinite rule, correspondingly loose is the protection which the court of interpretation is able to give'.[122] The attitude given expression here is symptomatic of Australia's historical approach to international law. While there seems to be acceptance of Australia's role participating in an articulation of some international conscience through international treaties and conventions, at the same time, Australia's attitude is derisory of international laws' utility for domestic implementation.[123]

The *Geneva Conventions Act* is also limited to war crimes committed in the context of an international armed conflict. Common Article 2 of each of the *Geneva Conventions* provides that they 'shall apply to all cases of declared war or of any other armed conflict which may arise between two or more of the High Contracting Parties' or in cases of 'occupation of the territory of a High Contracting Party'.[124] Common Article 3 does outline the minimum standards that need to

---

117 *Geneva Conventions Act* s 7(3).
118 Doherty and McCormack, above n 100, 171.
119 Commonwealth, *Parliamentary Debates*, Senate, 5 December 1957, 1754–5 (Reginald Wright).
120 Ibid.
121 Commonwealth, *Parliamentary Debates*, House of Representatives, 12 November 1957, 2749 (Gough Whitlam).
122 Commonwealth, *Parliamentary Debates*, Senate, 5 December 1957, 1756 (Reginald Wright).
123 The enactment of the *War Crimes Amendment Act* and the amendments made to the *Criminal Code* to give effect to the provisions of the *International Criminal Court* were a deliberate effort to overcome this attitude.
124 Article 2 of all four *Geneva Conventions*, above n 109.

be adhered to by parties in conflicts not of an international character. However that provision does not contain any grave breaches mandating criminal punishment. Indeed the *Geneva Conventions* deliberately avoid according criminal liability and enforcement provisions to internal armed conflicts.[125]

Australia did ratify *Additional Protocol II*, which was developed to strengthen the rules applicable for internal conflicts. However, the *Geneva Conventions Act* does not directly address serious violations of this protocol.[126] Perhaps not surprisingly, a great majority of armed conflicts since World War II have been of a non-international character, therefore immediately limiting the number of war crimes that can be prosecutable in Australian domestic criminal courts through the *Geneva Conventions Act* by automatically excluding the vast majority of armed conflicts.

Finally, the *Geneva Conventions Act* excludes the possibility of prosecuting crimes committed prior to 1957, which is when the legislation was made effective, therefore excluding all persons who may now be living in Australia and who have committed serious war crimes prior to this time. So, although there exists a legislative basis and a legal obligation in Australia to prosecute for war crimes committed after the ratification of the *Geneva Conventions*, there is 'no such obligation in relation to acts occurring before that time'.[127] Significantly, whether through deference to the early dismissive attitude towards the *Geneva Conventions* or otherwise, no person has ever been charged under the *Geneva Conventions Act*.[128] This omission comes despite clear accusations of war criminality, such as the case of the 'Balibo Five'. For example, in 2007 the New South Wales Coroner concluded that the killing of the journalists at Balibo might amount to a war crime[129] that is prosecutable under the *Geneva Conventions Act*.[130]

VI. *Crimes (Torture) Act 1988* (Cth)

Australia enacted the *Crimes (Torture) Act 1988* (Cth) (*Torture Act*) to give effect to certain provisions of the *Convention Against Torture and Other Cruel, Inhuman or Degrading Treatment or Punishment* (*Torture Convention*). The Attorney-General at that time commented during the Second Reading of the Crimes (Torture) Bill

---

125 Steven Ratner, 'The Schizophrenias of International Criminal Law' (1998) 33(2) *Texas International Law Review* 237, 240.
126 Doherty and McCormack, above n 100, 172. It has been suggested that ratification of *Additional Protocol II* 'does not require legislative action'. Commonwealth, *Parliamentary Debates*, House of Representatives, 12 February 1991, 380 (Gavan Duffy).
127 Gillian Triggs, 'Australia's War Crimes Trials: A Moral Necessity or Legal Minefield?' (1987) 16 *Melbourne University Law Review* 382, 397.
128 Doherty and McCormack, above n 100, 171.
129 *Inquest into the Death of Brian Raymond Peters* (Unreported, Coroner's Court of New South Wales, Magistrate Pinch, 16 November 2007), [121–3].
130 Ben Saul, 'Prosecuting War Criminals at Balibo Under Australian Law: The Killing of Five Journalists in East Timor by Indonesia' (2009) 31 *Sydney Law Review* 83, 107–9.

1988 (Cth) (Torture Bill) that the 'main purpose [of the Torture Bill] is to deny a safe haven in Australia to any person who, while acting officially, or at the instigation or behest of a person so acting, is involved in the torture of a person in another country'.[131] Torture is one of the acts which can constitute a crime against humanity and was given the same definition as that found in the *Torture Convention*.[132] The rhetoric that accompanied all the commendations for the legislation also included the usual moral posturing, such as:

> we are fortunate to live in a society in which we not only express moral repugnance about torture but also carry it through in practice by condemning and punishing any instances of brutality or wrong treatment of those in custody or under official protection.[133]

However, despite this language, there have been no prosecutions under the *Torture Act*.[134] The Attorney-General's later remarks in the Second Reading Speech are perhaps instructive in this respect where he states:

> The passage of this Bill will be a significant step in the international effort to combat torture. Whether or not the occasion ever arises for the legislation to be invoked, its existence will be a clear indication to the international community that Australia will never become a safe haven for those who breach fundamental human rights.[135]

131   Commonwealth, *Parliamentary Debates*, House of Representatives, 23 March 1988, 1227 (Lionel Bowen, Attorney-General).

132   *Crimes (Torture) Act 1988* (Cth) s 3(1) [*Torture Act*] provides that an act of torture means 'any act by which severe pain or suffering, whether physical or mental, is intentionally inflicted on a person' and
(a) for such purposes as:
(i) obtaining from the person or from a third person information or a confession;
(ii) punishing the person for an act which that person or a third person has committed or is suspected of having committed; or
(iii) intimidating or coercing the person or a third person; or
(b) for any reason based on discrimination of any kind.
See also *Convention against Torture and Other Cruel, Inhuman or Degrading Treatment or Punishment*, opened for signature 10 December 1984, 1465 UNTS 85 (entry into force 26 June 1987) Art 1.

133   Commonwealth, *Parliamentary Debates*, House of Representatives, 20 April 1988, 1831 (Duncan Kerr).

134   Human Rights and Equal Opportunity Commission, 'Australia's Compliance with the Convention Against Torture and Other Cruel, Inhuman and Degrading Treatment or Punishment' (Sydney, April 2008) 6.

135   Commonwealth, *Parliamentary Debates*, House of Representatives, 23 March 1988, 1227 (Lionel Bowen, Attorney-General).

There are two revealing elements in this statement. First there is an acknowledgment that the legislation may never lead to a prosecution of any person suspected of committing torture. The result being that the legislation merely appears as a 'motherhood statement' of this country's 'distaste, even hatred, of torture'.[136] The second aspect of the statement provides an insight into the motivations behind the ratification of the *Torture Convention*. Indeed, members of Parliament were candid in their justifications, suggesting that it 'recognises our place in the international community' and the legislation introduces into the domestic law of Australia 'a recognition that we live in a world which is now ordered by international perceptions of legal responsibilities'.[137] The bipartisan support for the Torture Bill extended to the reasons for enacting it, such that even the Opposition at the time understood that 'it is worth having mostly because of our international obligations, but nobody should delude himself that this legislation will be effective.'[138]

The *Torture Act* also has inherent policy and technical limitations that defy its effectiveness to bring about a prosecution and conviction for torture under the legislation. First, the *Torture Act* makes *torture* an offence in Australia from 1989, thereby only providing Australian courts jurisdiction to try individuals accused of performing an act of *torture* from this moment in time. Moreover, the *Torture Act* seems to make a distinction between *torture* and *cruel, inhuman or degrading treatment*. In other words, it does not criminalise *cruel, inhuman or degrading treatment*. As Fairhall highlights, 'there is a potential gap here: if the conduct is held to amount to cruel and degrading punishment, it would seem to fall outside the [*Torture Act*]'.[139] Significantly, Fairhall goes on to explain that:

> This matter is not merely of academic interest. In the leaked confidential briefing from the US Justice Department to the Counsel to the President, the distinction between torture, on the one hand, and cruel and inhuman treatment, on the other, was one basis for arguing that certain interrogation methods falling short of extreme torture might be lawful under US domestic law designed to implement the *Convention Against Torture*. A similar argument might well be raised under the *Commonwealth Crimes (Torture) Act*.[140]

---

136 Commonwealth, *Parliamentary Debates*, House of Representatives, 20 April 1988, 1853 (Peter McGauran).

137 Commonwealth, *Parliamentary Debates*, House of Representatives, 20 April 1988, 1831 (Duncan Kerr).

138 Commonwealth, *Parliamentary Debates*, House of Representatives, 20 April 1988, 1853 (Peter McGauran).

139 Paul Ames Fairhall, 'Reflections on Necessity as a Justification for Torture' (2004) 11 *James Cook University Law Review* 21, 32.

140 Ibid.

A prosecution under the *Torture Act* can only be brought against a person if they are currently present in Australia or are an Australian citizen.[141] Moreover, the legislation only applies to a person who 'does outside Australia an act that is an act of torture',[142] effectively limiting the application of the legislation to acts committed outside of Australia. The rationale for this decision was that the laws of the States and territories are already adequate to fulfil such an obligation should such an act occur within Australia.[143] However, as the Human Rights and Equal Opportunity Commission (HREOC) made clear, some Australian States and territories do not have specific offences of torture.[144]

The Australian Government took a noticeably narrow approach at the time of introducing the *Torture Act*. However, more recently it seems to have provided a broader scope for the prosecution of acts of torture. In May 2009, the United Nations Committee Against Torture made concluding observations on Australia's obligations under the *Torture Convention* that Australia 'does not have an offence of torture at the Federal level and that there are gaps in the criminalization of torture in certain States and Territories'.[145] Accordingly it recommended that Australia 'ensure that torture is adequately defined and specifically criminalized' at both levels.[146] In response, the Australian Government inserted a new Division 274 into the *Criminal Code Act 1995* (Cth) (*Criminal Code*) to 'criminalise acts of torture committed both within and outside Australia'[147] and 'to operate concurrently with [any] existing State and Territory offences'.[148]

The new provisions outlining the offence of torture essentially replicate those found in the *Torture Act* and they provide 'the offence extraterritorial application', which is also a 'key aim of the [*Torture Convention*]'.[149] As a result the new provisions addressing the crime of torture would have a broader application than that found in the *Torture Act*. But again, 'a fairly conservative drafting approach

---

141   *Torture Act* s 7.
142   Ibid s 6(1).
143   Commonwealth, *Parliamentary Debates*, House of Representatives, 23 March 1988, 1227 (Lionel Bowen, Attorney-General).
144   Human Rights and Equal Opportunity Commission, above n 134, 6. The HREOC does also suggest that acts of torture may be criminalised under the provisions of other criminal offences, for example assault.
145   United Nations Committee Against Torture, *Concluding Observations of the Committee against Torture, Australia*, 40th sess, UN Doc CAT/C/AUS/CO/3 (22 May 2008) 2 [8].
146   Ibid.
147   Explanatory Memorandum, Crimes Legislation Amendment (Torture Prohibition and Death Penalty Abolition) Bill 2009 (Cth) 1.
148   Ibid 2.
149   Commonwealth, *Parliamentary Debates*, House of Representatives, 19 November 2009, 12197 (Robert McClelland, Attorney-General). *Crimes Legislation Amendment (Torture Prohibition and Death Penalty Abolition) Act 2010* (Cth) Schedule 1 (*Torture Amendment Act*) provides that the *Criminal Code* s 15.4 (extended geographical jurisdiction – category D) applies to an offence of torture as outlined in this legislation.

is adopted in extending the range of *Criminal Code* torture offences'.[150] For example, the purposes for which a torture offence can be committed are restrictive and do not adequately reflect the potentially broad listing of torture purposes in the *Torture Convention*.[151] Neither do the new provisions criminalise acts involving cruel, inhuman or degrading treatment or punishment. This seems a crucial omission, especially when considering the obligations reflected under the *Torture Convention* itself. For example, the obligation to prevent torture is described by the United Nations Committee Against Torture as being 'wide-ranging' and that it is 'interdependent, indivisible and interrelated' with the obligation to prevent cruel, inhuman or degrading treatment or punishment.[152] Moreover, this obligation 'overlaps with and is largely congruent with the obligation to prevent torture'.[153] In any event, the new provisions only operate prospectively from 14 April 2010.[154]

VII. *International Criminal Court Act 2002* (Cth) and *International Criminal Court (Consequential Amendments) Act 2002* (Cth)

The most recent enactments in Australia relating to war crimes are the *International Criminal Court Act 2002* (Cth) (*ICC Act*) and the *International Criminal Court (Consequential Amendments) Act 2002* (Cth) (*Consequential Amendments Act*). The legislation was introduced in order to comply with the requirements of the *Rome Statute of the International Criminal Court* (*ICC*) and also made important amendments to the Australian Criminal Code. The *ICC Act* provides the legislative framework regulating Australia's relationship with the *ICC* itself,[155] while the *Consequential Amendments Act* criminalises the offences within the subject jurisdiction of the *ICC* under Australian law.[156] In this respect, the legislative approach adopted by Australia was to include provisions outlining the precise elements of each of the offences, being war crimes, crimes against humanity,

---

150 Greg Carne, 'Is Near Enough Good Enough? – Implementing Australia's International Human Rights Torture Criminalisation and Prohibition Obligations in the *Criminal Code* (Cth)' (2012) 33 *Adelaide Law Review* 229, 249.

151 Ibid 259–60.

152 General Comment 2 on Implementation of Article 2 by States Parties of the Convention Against Torture and Other Cruel, Inhuman Or Degrading Treatment Or Punishment (UN Doc CAT/C/GC/@/CRP.1/Rev.4) (23 November 2007), 3.

153 Ibid.

154 *Torture Amendment Act* s 2 provides that the legislation commences on the day after it receives the Royal Assent, which was 13 April 2010. As a result of this enactment, the *Torture Act* itself has been repealed in its entirety: at clause 4.

155 Timothy LH McCormack, 'Australia's Legislation for the Implementation of the Rome Statute' in Matthias Neuner (ed.), *National Legislation Incorporating International Crimes* (BWV, 2003) 66.

156 Ibid 67.

genocide and crimes against the administration of justice of the *ICC*, comparable to the Elements of Crime for the *ICC*.[157]

The amendments to the *Criminal Code* made the crime of *genocide* a prosecutable offence under Australian law for the first time by outlining five offences that can constitute genocide,[158] each of which requires that they are committed against a 'person or persons [who] belong to a particular national, ethnical, racial or religious group' and that the 'perpetrator intends to destroy, in whole or in part, that national, ethnical, racial or religious group, as such'.[159]

The amendments also made certain the status of the category of crimes against humanity, which previously only had 'a limited place in Australian law as a defence' under the *War Crimes Amendment Act*.[160] Moreover, the *War Crimes Amendment Act* did not define *crimes against humanity* nor did it make it a separate category of offence under domestic Australian criminal law.[161] Under the new legislation, a crime against humanity occurs where the acts have been committed as part of a widespread or systematic attack directed against a civilian population, the crimes are a result of either a State or organisation's policy to commit that attack and the perpetrator's conduct is committed intentionally or knowingly.[162]

The *Consequential Amendments Act* also replicated the categories of *war crimes* as defined in the *Elements of Crimes of the ICC*. The four categories include grave breaches of the *Geneva Conventions* and of *Additional Protocol I*,[163] other serious war crimes that are committed in the course of an international armed conflict,[164] serious violations of Common Article 3 which are committed in the course of a non-international armed conflict,[165] and other serious violations of the laws and customs applicable in a non-international armed conflict.[166] In addition to these categories, Australia also separately included war crimes that are grave breaches of *Additional Protocol I*, even though these did not form part of the *ICC*. However, because these were previously crimes pursuant to the *Geneva Conventions Act*, they were incorporated as part of the amendments.[167] The comprehensive nature of the amendments confirms that *war crimes* are able to be committed in both international and non-international armed conflict.

---

157 Ibid.
158 *Criminal Code* ss 268.3–268.7.
159 Ibid ss 268.3(b)–(c), 268.4(b)–(c), 268.5(b)–(c), 268.6(b)–(c), 268.7(b)–(c).
160 Triggs, above n 96, 523. Section 17(2)(b) of the *War Crimes Amendment Act* provides a defence where the alleged act was not under international law a *crime against humanity*.
161 McCormack, above n 155, 72.
162 Explanatory Memorandum, *International Criminal Court (Consequential Amendments) Bill 2002* (Cth) 1.
163 *Criminal Code* Subdivision D.
164 Ibid Subdivision E.
165 Ibid Subdivision F.
166 Ibid Subdivision G.
167 *International Criminal Court (Consequential Amendments) Act 2002* (Cth) Division 268, Subdivision H (*Consequential Amendment Act*); Explanatory Memorandum, *International Criminal Court (Consequential Amendments) Bill 2002* (Cth).

The *Consequential Amendments Act* also introduces a defence of superior orders for *war crimes* only. Section 268.116 explicitly rejects such a defence where a *crime against humanity* and *genocide* has been committed, stating that it 'does not relieve the person of criminal responsibility'.[168] For the purposes of a war crime, the defence of superior orders will be allowed where the accused was under a legal obligation to obey the order, the accused did not know that the order was unlawful and the order was not manifestly unlawful.[169] This is also contrary to the *War Crimes Amendment Act*, which is categorical that there is no defence of superior orders, although it may act to mitigate the sentence.[170] The difference in approach reflects the context of the 'unique circumstances' of World War II and the magnitude of the crimes committed, which were all deemed to be manifestly illegal.[171] Accordingly, the *IMT* prohibited the defence of superior orders.[172] The *War Crimes Amendment Act*, which was concerned specifically with war crimes committed during World War II, imitated the *IMT* and 'excluded any defence based on superior orders, consistent with proceedings at Nuremberg'.[173] Outside the *IMT* however, the defence of superior orders has been regularly invoked, especially where 'the realities of justice may mean that a strict prohibition of the defence of superior orders is in fact legally and ethically untenable'.[174] Therefore, including the defence of superior orders as part of the *ICC* implementing legislation recognises both the exceptionality of the facts that led to the drafting of the *IMT*, but also the development of international criminal law since Nuremberg.[175]

The difference in approach also keeps the implementing *ICC* legislation consistent with the defences that would be available under the *ICC* itself should it assert its jurisdiction.[176] While the defence of superior orders has not yet been invoked in criminal proceedings in Australia, as no war crimes trials have taken place under this legislation, the defence of superior orders has been considered in proceedings determining refugee claims for protection.[177] In doing so, Australian courts have provided 'thoroughly researched judgements' and 'canvassed developments in conventional and customary international humanitarian law and international criminal law', including in relation to the defence of superior orders, that will have resonance for Australia's various war crimes

---

168   Ibid Division 268, s 268.116(1).
169   Ibid s 268.116(3).
170   *War Crimes Amendment Act* s 16.
171   Lachlan Harris, 'The International Criminal Court and the Superior Orders Defence' (2004) 22(2) *University of Tasmania Law Review* 200, 207.
172   Charter of the International Military Tribunal, above n 35, Art 8.
173   Explanatory Memorandum, War Crimes Amendment Bill 1987 (Cth), General Outline.
174   Harris, above n 171, 211.
175   Ibid see generally.
176   Triggs, above n 96, 530. See *Rome Statute of the International Criminal Court*, opened for signature 17 July 1998, 2187 UNTS 90 (entered into force 1 July 2002) Art 33.
177   See *SRYYY v Minister for Immigration & Multicultural & Indigenous Affairs* (2005) 147 FCR 1.

legislation.[178] Furthermore, as a matter of statutory interpretation, there is a presumption that existing defences will apply unless there is clear evidence to the contrary. To this effect, no such clear evidence exists, meaning that the normal defences applicable in Australian criminal law will equally apply to criminal charges stemming from the new *ICC* provisions.[179]

At the time of the implementing legislation, some concern was raised as to the definitions of the crimes in the *ICC*. More particularly, they were said to be vague, open to wide interpretation and thus potentially to abuse.[180] However, the crimes under the *Statute of the ICC* were not new and the definitions draw upon long-established principles of law, both customary and treaty.[181] Moreover, the definitions are to be read in conjunction with the *Elements of Crimes*. To this effect, the provisions in the *Consequential Amendments Act* have been formulated 'consistent with Commonwealth criminal law policy, with a focus on detailing the precise conduct which is prohibited in express terms, and the mental elements that are required.[182] By legislating separately for each individual offence and including the precise elements that will constitute the individual offences, parliament reflected the style and form of the provisions in the *Criminal Code*.[183]

The approach is also a profound departure from the general attitude that has historically characterised Australia's response to international treaty implementation for war crimes. Therefore, it arguably provides for greater certainty to all parties involved in the criminal trial process.[184] Furthermore, drafting the implementing *ICC* legislation in a manner that is considered consistent with Australia's existing legal traditions also seems to signal a desire to consolidate Australia's competence to prosecute war criminals without the matters proceeding to the *ICC* itself.[185] The Explanatory Memorandum makes it clear from its very first sentence that:

> Australia retains the right and power to prosecute any person accused of a crime under the Statute in Australia *rather than surrender that person for trial in the International Criminal Court.*[186]

---

178   Peter Johnston and Claire Harris, 'Case Notes: SRYYY v Minister for Immigration and Multicultural and Indigenous Affairs: War Crimes and the *Refugee Convention*' (2007) 8(1) *Melbourne Journal of International Law* 108.

179   McCormack, above n 155, 79.

180   Joint Standing Committee on Treaties, Parliament of the Commonwealth of Australia, *Report 45: The Statute of the International Criminal Court* (2002) 42–4.

181   Ibid 81.

182   Explanatory Memorandum, *International Criminal Court (Consequential Amendments) Bill 2002* (Cth).

183   McCormack, above n 155, 69.

184   Ibid 70.

185   Joint Standing Committee on Treaties, above n 180, 70.

186   Explanatory Memorandum, *International Criminal Court (Consequential Amendments) Bill 2002* (Cth) (emphasis added).

The Explanatory Memorandum goes on to state that:

> By creating crimes in Australian law that mirror the crimes in the Statute, Australia will always be able to prosecute a person accused of a crime under the Statute in Australia rather than surrender that person for trial in the ICC.[187]

Effectively, the amendments enable Australian criminal courts to assert primary jurisdiction over international crimes. The concept of complementarity provides Australian courts with competence to prosecute war criminals by giving Australia first rights to institute criminal proceedings against accused war criminals found in Australia.[188] Indeed, the report by the Joint Standing Committee on Treaties (JSCOT) on the *ICC* made a point of emphasising the relevant parts of the preamble to the *ICC* when it stated that:

> it is the duty of every State to exercise its criminal jurisdiction over those responsible for international crimes and the International Criminal Court . . . shall be complementary to national criminal jurisdictions.[189]

This approach also reflected the declaration Australia attached to its instrument of ratification. The declaration essentially provided that it is Australia's right to exercise its jurisdictional primacy with respect to the crimes within the jurisdiction of the *ICC*; that nobody would be surrendered to the *ICC* without the consent of the Attorney-General; and that the offences will be interpreted and applied in a way that accords with the way they are implemented in Australian domestic law.[190] However, Australia's declaration has been accused of being a 'hindrance to the smooth cooperation with the *ICC*'; that it 'changes the *Rome Statute's* legal effect, resulting in vagueness'; and that 'it is an unnecessary obstacle, inconsistent with the object and purpose of the Statute', all of which lends itself to being construed as a reservation, which is incongruously prohibited by Article 20 of the *Statute of the ICC*.[191] The declaration and the nature of the amendments in the *ICC* implementing legislation was a response to various submissions made at the time that consideration was being given to ratifying the *ICC*. These submissions suggested that ratification would diminish the control that Australia could exercise over its affairs by ceding jurisdictional

---

187   Ibid.

188   *Rome Statute of the International Criminal Court*, above n 176, Art 17: the 'Court . . . shall be complementary to national criminal jurisdictions.'

189   Joint Standing Committee on Treaties, above n 180, 77.

190   Australian Declaration attached to instrument of ratification for the *Rome Statute of the International Criminal Court* (Rome, 17 July 1998), 1 July 2002.

191   Pauline Collins, 'What is Good for the Goose should be Good for the Gander: The Operation of the *Rome Statute* in the Australian Context' (2009) 32(1) *UNSW Law Journal* 106, 131.

authority to an international (foreign) court.[192] In other words, there was concern over Australia's sovereignty.

However, national war crimes trials play an equally important role in ensuring there is accountability for such crimes. Indeed, it is the development of national laws such as the *ICC* implementing legislation 'that may represent the most important criteria by which the effectiveness of the system of *international* criminal justice should be measured'.[193] Ironically, the lack of coverage in Australian law for war crimes committed between the end of World War II and the beginning of the *ICC* implementing legislation highlights that the prosecution and punishment of war crimes was already completely dependent on national jurisdictions. Therefore, any imperative to introduce war crimes legislation and conduct national trials should be viewed from the perspective that it is providing for the accountability for the commission of war crimes rather than overcoming competing jurisdictional sovereignties.

Given the 'piecemeal and restricted' nature of previous war crimes legislation enacted in Australia, the comprehensiveness of the *ICC* legislation and its clear deference to national jurisdictions, seems to represent a 'unique commitment' to prosecuting international crimes in Australian domestic courts.[194] Indeed, while the *ICC* may intervene and assume jurisdiction when a State is 'unwilling or unable genuinely to carry out the investigation or prosecution',[195] the Explanatory Memorandum to the *Consequential Amendments Act* assures that Australia 'will always be in a position to investigate and, if appropriate, prosecute a person who is accused of a crime under the Statute', indeed '*we will never be "unable" to*'.[196] However, Australia's motivation for enacting such comprehensive war crimes legislation has also been accused of being an 'ignoble one' because it is premised on an 'avoidance strategy'. In other words, by having such comprehensive war crimes legislation, Australia can never be accused of being 'genuinely unable' to try a person for want of effective domestic legislation.[197] Nevertheless, assuming that an Australian Government was actually willing and

---

192   Joint Standing Committee on Treaties, above n 180, 716. This was thoroughly repudiated in the Report of JSCOT, where it stated that ratification would not give away the judicial responsibility that Australian courts have always exercised [71–2]; that ratification would not create a universal court capable of overturning decisions made by domestic Australian courts [72–3]; and ratification would not automatically expose Australian nationals to the jurisdiction of the ICC [73].

193   Steven Freeland, 'The Effectiveness of International Criminal Justice' (2008) *ALTA Law Research Series* 16.

194   Triggs, above n 96, 534.

195   *Rome Statute of the International Criminal Court*, above n 176, Art 17.

196   Explanatory Memorandum, *International Criminal Court (Consequential Amendments) Bill 2002* (Cth).

197   Tim McCormack, 'The Contribution of the International Criminal Court to Increasing Respect for International Humanitarian Law' (2009) 27(1) *The University of Tasmania Law Review* 22, 45.

able to investigate and to prosecute based on the legislation giving effect to the provisions of the *ICC*, the provisions only operate prospectively. The *ICC* itself came into force on 1 July 2002.[198] This leaves the potential to excuse many war criminals from prosecution in Australia's criminal justice system. Notably, there have been no prosecutions in Australia for war crimes since the adoption of the *ICC* and the amendments made to the Australian *Criminal Code*. It seems that the enactment of such comprehensive war crimes legislation in Australia is yet 'to be fully appreciated', instead it perpetuates Australia's less than committed attitude to the prosecution of war criminals located in its territory.[199]

VIII. Conclusion

The Australian experience of undertaking war crimes trials since the end of World War II has been largely unsatisfactory. Australian Governments have enlisted the use of appropriate moral rhetoric when participating in the various international efforts to introduce accountability for international crimes, yet this apparent concern has not manifested itself into enforceable domestic laws or appropriate levels of interest to undertake war crimes trials. Indeed, the consistent lack of political will by successive Australian governments to prosecute war crimes has been described as 'widely deficient'.[200] The motivations behind Australia's response to the various international legal developments since World War II in relation to international crimes seems to be more about political convenience than any entrenched desire to prosecute alleged war criminals resident in Australia. It seems that the sentiment expressed by Sir Garfield Barwick in 1961 to 'close the chapter' on war crimes prosecutions 'still reverberates in Australia's contemporary attitude to war criminals'.[201] As a result, the Australian landscape in relation to war crimes legislation is piecemeal and mostly ineffective for dealing with accused war criminals.

Yet there is no doubt that there are individuals now living in Australia, most of whom are probably Australian citizens, who are responsible for some of the most abhorrent crimes committed in various parts of the world.[202]

---

198 *Rome Statute of the International Criminal Court*, above n 176, entered into force on 1 July 2002, sixty days after sixty States became parties to the *Statute* through ratification or accession.

199 Boas, above n 36, 321–2.

200 David MacGregor, 'Bringing War Criminals To Justice in Australia: Upholding International Criminal Law and the Principle of Non-Refoulement' (2007) 32(3) *Alternative Law Journal* 154, 154.

201 Boas, above n 36, 316.

202 See for example ABC Radio National, 'War Criminals in Australia', *Background Briefing*, 18 October 2009 www.abc.net.au/rn/backgroundbriefing/stories/2009/2715237.htm; Fergus Hansen, 'Confronting Reality: Responding to War Criminals Living in Australia' (Policy Brief, Lowy Institute for International Policy, February 2009); and Mark Aarons, *War Criminals Welcome: Australia, A Sanctuary for Fugitive War Criminals Since 1945* (Black Inc, 2001).

The importance of ensuring accountability for violations of international humanitarian law is perhaps cogently encapsulated by Vera Ranki:

> It is imperative to prosecute because the alternative is not to prosecute. And not to prosecute means that there is nothing to prosecute for: the action was not a crime.[203]

203 Vera Ranki, 'Holocaust History and the Law: 1985–1995' (1997) 3 *Law Text Culture* 53, 69.

11 The *ICJ*'s role in determining accountability for violations of International Humanitarian Law

Andrew Coleman[1]

> I decided to come before this Tribunal and admit that a crime happened in Srebrenica in which I myself participated and for which I expect adequate punishment. I sincerely wish before this Chamber and before the public, especially the Bosniak public, to express my deep and sincere remorse and regret because of the crime that occurred and to apologise to the victims, their families, and the Bosniak people for my participation in this crime.
>
> —*Momir Nikolić, Bosnian Serb Army*[2]

I. Introduction

Momir Nikolić served in the Bosnian Serb Army in Srebrenica, in July 1995. He was an Assistant Commander for Security and Intelligence and as such was fully informed of the plans to deport Muslim women and children and to kill their men. He did nothing to stop the murder of thousands of human beings. Instead, he personally supervised the exhumation and re-burial of victims' bodies in an attempt to prevent their discovery. Nikolić was found guilty of crimes against humanity and sentenced to 20 years' imprisonment by the *International Criminal Tribunal for the former Yugoslavia (ICTY)*.[3]

The Nikolić case is one of sixty-one completed cases brought before the *ICTY*. This tribunal, together with other *ad hoc* tribunals, such as the *International*

---

1 Dr Andrew Coleman, Monash University, BLT (BA, LLB, LLM, PhD). It is a great pleasure to contribute to this monograph in honour of a wonderful man, Professor Timothy McCormack. Parts of this chapter are based on my two previous works: *Resolving Claims to Self-Determination* (Routledge, 2013) and 'The International Court of Justice and Highly Political Matters' 4(1) *Melbourne Journal of International Law* (2003) 29–75.

    This chapter was written in the author's personal capacity and does not necessarily represent the views of Monash University.

2 *Statements of Guilt*, Momir Nikolić www.icty.org/sid/218.

3 Ibid. See also the case information sheet: www.icty.org/x/cses/nikolic/cis/en/cis_nikolic_momir_1.pdf.

Criminal Tribunal for Rwanda (*ICTR*),[4] and the permanent *International Criminal Court* (*ICC*), has been responsible for handling matters of international humanitarian law and determining individual accountability for international crimes. The *International Court of Justice* (*ICJ*),[5] on the other hand, has been primarily concerned with States' behaviour. But does this court also play a role in protecting international humanitarian values? International humanitarian law clearly falls within the Court's competence.[6] In fact, the *ICJ*'s jurisdiction is broader than the jurisdiction of all other international tribunals, including the *ICTY* or the *ICC*.[7] And yet, compared to the *ICTY*, there is a relative paucity of matters involving principles of international humanitarian law that have been brought before the *ICJ*.[8]

There are two simple reasons for this. First, the *Genocide Convention* was drafted in the aftermath of the Nuremberg Trials, and the mantra espoused at Nuremberg was: 'Crimes against international law are committed by men not abstract entities.'[9] As such the drafters of the *Genocide Convention* envisaged individuals would be prosecuted before a specialised international criminal court.[10] Second, the intended role of the *ICJ* is to resolve disputes between States

---

4 See, eg, the International Committee of the Red Cross's (ICRC) website: www.icrc.org/eng/war-and-law/intertnational-criminal-jurisdiction/ad-hoc-tribuanls/index.jsp.

5 *International Court of Justice* [*ICJ* or 'the Court'] is often referred to as 'the World Court'.

6 The *ICJ* has both a contentious and advisory jurisdiction. When exercising its contentious jurisdiction the Court is able to hear *all* matters that the litigants bring before the Court, as well as 'all matters specifically provided for in the Charter of the United Nations.' See, *Statute of the International Court of Justice*: Articles 35(1) and 36(1) [*ICJ Statute*]. In relation to its advisory jurisdiction Article 65(1) of the *Statute of the ICJ* states that the Court is able to give an advisory opinion on *any* legal question at the request of an authorised body.

7 Fabian O Raimondo, 'The International Court of Justice as Guardian of the Unity of Humanitarian Law' (2007) 20 (3) *Leiden Journal of International Law* 593, at 593.

8 Prior to 1993 the *ICJ* had adjudicated over sixty disputes in its contentious jurisdiction and supplied seventeen Advisory Opinions, but it had only considered matters involving international humanitarian law in two contentious cases, and in one Request for an Advisory Opinion. By 2007, this total had risen to three contentious matters, and two Advisory Opinions from a total of 22 Opinions. By comparison the *ICTY* alone has indicted approximately 161 individuals for breaching international humanitarian law. This result is perhaps not surprising given the more specialised nature of the *ICTY*'s jurisdiction.

9 The so-called 'Nuremberg Legacy': *Trial of the Major War Criminals Before the International Military Tribunal: Nuremberg, 14 November 1945–1 October 1946*, vol 1, 223 (1947); Dermot Groome, 'Adjudicating Genocide: Is the International Court of Justice Capable of Judging State Criminal Responsibility?' (2007) 31(4) *Fordham International Law Journal* 911, 921. See also the Library of Congress website, Military Legal Resources www.loc.gove/rr/frd/Military_Law/pdf/NT-Vol-1.pdf.

10 See Article VI of the *Genocide Convention*; *Convention on the Prevention and Punishment of the Crime of Genocide*, opened for signature 9 December 1948, 78 UNTS 277 (entered into force 12 January 1951) https://trewaties.un.org/doc/Publication/UNTS/Volume%2078/volume-78-I-1021-English; Paola Gaeta, 'On What Conditions Can a State be Held Responsible for Genocide?' (2007) 18(4) *European Journal of International Law* 631, 634.

(the Court's contentious jurisdiction), or to provide guidance to authorised organs of the UN (the Court's advisory jurisdiction).[11] It is, in a manner of speaking, a 'civil' court, and not 'designed' to prosecute individuals as is the case with the *ICTY* and other international war crimes tribunals.

Then in 2007 the *ICJ* decided in the *Bosnian Genocide Case* that States could be held accountable for genocide,[12] thus clarifying that the *ICJ could* play a role in the protection of international humanitarian values. However, the *Bosnian Genocide Case* received strident criticism from commentators, not because of this finding, but because of the Court's failure to find Serbia accountable for acts of genocide.[13] The criticism extended to the norms developed and applied by the Court and even went as far as describing the decision as a political compromise, an attempt to appease Serbia in view of the impending question of Kosovo's claim to independence.[14]

This last criticism is interesting since, not long after the Court handed down its decision in the *Bosnian Genocide Case*, the General Assembly requested the *ICJ* to provide an Advisory Opinion on the legality of Kosovo's Unilateral Declaration of Independence (UDI).[15] The Court's Opinion, essentially that the UDI was not illegal, also received strident criticism along similar lines as the *Bosnian Genocide Case*, that the Court was too conservative and was shaped by political considerations. These criticisms highlight the question of whether the *ICJ* should play a major role in determining accountability for breaches of international humanitarian law.

In considering this question, this chapter first examines the role of the *ICJ*, and looks at the ways in which this court can contribute to determining accountability through advancing the development of norms of international law. This part sets the scene for the second part of the chapter, namely examining the *Bosnian Genocide Case* and the *Kosovo Opinion*, and the implications they have on the Court's role as outlined in Part I. Finally, the chapter examines whether the Court can be *trusted*, that is, whether it is sufficiently free of political influence. The chapter argues that the Court exercises its judicial functions free of political influence and that indeed it has made a significant contribution to the area of accountability for war crimes.

---

11 *UN Charter* Article 92. Only States have standing to appear before the Court's contentious jurisdiction, *ICJ Statute* Article 34(1).

12 *Application of the Convention on the Prevention and Punishment of the Crime of Genocide (Bosnia and Herzegovina v Serbia and Montenegro) (Judgment)* ICJ Rep [2007] 43, 222 [431] *(Bosnian Genocide Case).*

13 Ibid 237, at [471]. SáCouto describes this as ironic: Susana SáCouto, 'Reflections on the Judgment of the International Court of Justice in Bosnia's Genocide Case Against Serbia and Montenegro', 15 *Human Rights Brief* 2, 5.

14 Martin Shaw, 'The International Court of Justice, Serbia, Bosnia, and Genocide', *Open Democracy* (28 February 2007) www.opendemocracy.net/node/4392/.

15 *Accordance with International Law of the Unilateral Declaration of Independence in Respect of Kosovo* (Advisory Opinion), [2010] ICJ Rep 403 *(Kosovo Opinion).*

II. Role of the *ICJ*

The *ICJ* is the principal judicial organ of the UN.[16] As such the Court's role is to assist the UN to achieve its prime objective: the maintenance of peace and security.[17] The *ICJ* is empowered by its *Statute* to do this in two ways: first, by resolving disputes between States in its contentious jurisdiction, and second, through the provision of an Advisory Opinion, which aims to answer a legal question that would assist the UN political organs in their duties.[18] Raimondo, writing in 2007, argues that there is a third way in which the Court assists the international community: shaping the norms to govern international humanitarian law.[19] Many commentators would agree that the Court makes a significant contribution to the maintenance of peace and security through the refinement, clarification and development of norms of international law, but they refer to areas other than international humanitarian law.[20] Raimondo argues that clarification and development of norms of international laws are as important as determining accountability for offences.[21]

A. Developing of norms of international humanitarian law

Raimondo noted that prior to the *Bosnian Genocide Case* the Court had considered international humanitarian law in three contentious matters: *Corfu Channel Case*,[22] *Nicaragua Case*,[23] and the *Armed Activities in the Congo*;[24] and in two Advisory Opinions: *the Nuclear Weapons Opinion*,[25] and the *Wall in Palestine Opinion*.[26] He argues very persuasively that the Court's contribution to the refinement of the norms of international humanitarian law in these matters more than compensates for their relative small numbers.

---

16   *UN Charter* Article 92. The Court is an integral part of the UN.
17   Ibid.
18   *UN Charter* Article 96; *Reservations to the Convention on the Prevention and Punishment of the Crime of Genocide* (Advisory Opinion) [1951] ICJ Rep 19 [Reservations Opinion]. See generally, Mahasen M Aljaghoub, *The Advisory Jurisdiction of the International Court of Justice (1946–2005)*, (2006).
19   Raimondo, above n 7, 595–6.
20   Vincent Chetail, 'The Contribution of the International Court of Justice to International Humanitarian Law' (June 2003) 850(85) *International Review of the Red Cross* 235, 237; Raimondo, above n 7, 610; Andrew Coleman, 'The International Court of Justice and Highly Political Matters' (2003) 4(1) *Melbourne Journal of International Law* 29–75.
21   Raimondo, above n 7, 595–6.
22   *Corfu Channel* Case (*UK v Albania*) (Merits) [1949] ICJ Rep 35 [*Corfu Channel Case*].
23   *Military and Paramilitary Activities in and against Nicaragua (Nicaragua v United States of America)* (Merits) [1986] ICJ Rep 14 [*Nicaragua Case*].
24   *Case Concerning Armed Activities on the Territory of the Congo (Democratic Republic of the Congo v Uganda) (Unreported Judgment)* see www.icj-cij.org/docket/index?p1=3&p2=3&code=crw&case=126.
25   *Legality of the Threat or Use of Nuclear Weapons* (Advisory Opinion) [1996] ICJ Rep 226.
26   *Legal Consequences of the Construction of a Wall in the Occupied Palestinian Territory* (Advisory Opinion) (2004) ICJ Rep 136.

For example, in the *Corfu Channel Case* the Court held that 'elementary considerations of humanity' applied in wartime as well as peacetime.[27] The significance of this conclusion is, as Raimondo points out, that it completely avoids difficult questions of what is/is not an armed conflict, thus removing a dubious and technical potential means of avoiding liability. The finding also removed any doubts raised by commentators regarding the normative value of 'considerations of humanity' which then formed the foundations for later decisions such as the *Nicaragua Case*.[28]

The *Nicaragua Case* concerned an application brought by Nicaragua against the US for losses and damage caused by the US mining in Nicaraguan territorial waters, as well as through support given by the US to the *contras*. The Court held that the US actions breached its duties under customary international law as well as its obligations in its *Treaty of Friendship, Commerce and Navigation* with Nicaragua, and that accordingly it should pay reparations.[29] However, the Court held that in order to prove US responsibility for breaches by the *contras*, Nicaragua had to prove that the *contras* had 'complete dependence' on the US.[30] Nicaragua also had to prove that the US was in 'effective control' of the *contras*.[31] Nicaragua failed to do this, and so the US was not responsible for harm caused by the *contras*.[32]

Raimondo argues that this conclusion may have been controversial, but the *Nicaragua Case* did much to advance the cause of international humanitarian law.[33] For example, the Court's conclusion that considerations of humanity were norms of customary law, and thus, common Article 1 of the 1949 *Geneva Conventions*, namely the obligation to ensure respect for the *Geneva Conventions*, applied to internal as well as external or international conflicts.[34]

---

27 In this case the Court faced a claim made by the UK against Albania. Two British destroyers struck mines in Albanian waters in the Corfu Strait and suffered damage, and many sailors lost their lives or were severely wounded. *Corfu Channel Case* [1949] ICJ Rep 35.

28 Raimondo, above n 7, 596–8.

29 *Nicaragua Case* [1986] ICJ Rep 14, 147–9 [292].

30 Ibid 62 [109].

31 Ibid 64–5 [115]. 'For this conduct to give rise to legal responsibility of the United States, it would have in principle have to be proved that that State had effective control of the military or paramilitary operations in the course of which the alleged violations were committed.' These two 'tests' are often conflated in one test known as the 'effective control test', but they are technically separate: Kalle Kirss, 'Role of the International Court of Justice: Example of the Genocide Case' (2007–2008) 3 *Acta Societatis Martensis* 143, 151–5.

32 The Court concluded the evidence indicated that the *contras* were not totally dependent upon the US, since their attacks continued after the withdrawal of US support and finance and that even the US action of training financing, selecting and installing the leaders of the *contras* was insufficient proof of the required level of dependency. *Nicaragua Case* [1986] ICJ Rep 14, 62 [110], [112], [115].

33 Raimondo, above n 7, 599.

34 Ibid. *Convention (I) for the Amelioration of the Condition of the Wounded and Sick in Armed Forces in the Field*; *Convention (II) for the Amelioration of the Condition of Wounded, Sick and Shipwrecked Members of Armed Forces at Sea*; *Convention (III) Relative to the Treatment of Prisoners of War*; *Convention (IV) Relative to the Protection of Civilian Persons in Time of War*. Geneva, opened for signature 12 August 1949, 75 UNTS 287 (entered into force 21 October 1950) [*Geneva Conventions*]; *Nicaragua Case* [1986] ICJ Rep 14, 114 [218], [220].

B. Clarifying international law

How does clarification of international humanitarian law assist with account-ability? Obviously norms create a structure for States' interaction. States themselves recognise that it is in the self-interest of all States that a structure imposed by the rule of law, as opposed to the rule of power, provides a greater opportunity for States to prosper and grow,[35] even in a community where there is no 'policeman'.[36] Such a system would also assist with the prevention of potential breaches of international humanitarian law by outlawing specific actions, like genocide.

Despite the inherent weaknesses in the international legal system norms influence States' behaviour. As noted by Hurrell: 'It is impossible to think seriously about international relations today without reference to norms prohibiting the aggressive use of force or proscribing genocide, or up-holding self-determination and human rights'.[37] However, in Roth's view, what is more important is that the *right type of behaviour becomes accepted as customary*.[38] Development of international law by the *ICJ* has an important advantage over norms created by States: impartiality.

International law contains a paradox of sorts. One source of international law is the customary practices of States (through the treaties they sign and through their involvement in the political organs of the UN).[39] But can States be trusted to create custom that does not reflect their vested interests?[40] For example,

---

35   Sir Arthur Watts, 'The Importance of International Law' in Michael Byers (ed.), *The Role of International Law in International Politics: Essays in International Relations and International Law* (Oxford University Press, 2000) 5, 7.

36   Philippe Sands, *Lawless World, America and the Making and Breaking of Global Rules* (Penguin, 2005) 237; Watts, above n 35, 7; Bamidele Ojo, *Human Rights and the New World Order: Universality, Acceptability and Human Diversity* (Nova Science Publishers Inc, 1997) 53; Jonathan Charney, 'Disputes Implicating the Institutional Credibility of the Court: Problems of Non-Appearance, Non-Participation, and Non-Performance' in Lori Damrosch (ed.), *The International Court of Justice at a Crossroads* (1987) 288, 303–4.

37   Andrew Hurrell, 'Conclusion, International Law and the Changing Constitution of International Society' in Michael Byers (ed.), *The Role of Law in International Politics* (Oxford University Press, 2000) 327, 335; Watts, above n 35, 7. See *Legal Consequences for States of the Continued Presence of South Africa in Namibia (South West Africa) Notwithstanding Security Council Resolution 276* [1971] ICJ Rep 16; *Western Sahara Opinion* [1975] ICJ Rep 12; *Wall in Palestine Opinion* [2004] ICJ Rep 136 [156]; David Miller, 'Secession and the Principle of Nationality' in Margaret Moore (ed.), *National Self-Determination and Secession* (Oxford University Press, 1998) 62, 65.

38   Brad R Roth, *Governmental Illegitimacy in International Law* (Clarendon Press, 1999), 125.

39   Gillian D Triggs, *International Law, Contemporary Principles and Practices* (LexisNexis, 2006) 43.

40   Luncheon Address by Pieter Hendrik Kooijmans, 'Human Rights: the Actors and the Play' in Wybo Heere (ed.), *Contemporary International Law Issues: New Forms New Applications* (Proceedings of the Fourth Hague Joint Conference held in the Hague, The Netherlands, 2–5 July 1997) (1997) 110, 112; Anna Meijknecht, *Towards International Personality: The Position of Minorities and Indigenous Peoples in International Law* (Intersentia-Hart, 2001) 20.

Meijknecht asks whether 'a sovereign State, who itself poses the greatest danger to minorities and indigenous peoples [can] be entrusted with their protection'.[41]

The answer can be found in arguments presented by States in matters before the Court. For example, the US in the *Nicaragua Case* argued that the customary rules of international law relating to self-defence had been 'subsumed' and replaced by Article 51 of the *UN Charter*.[42] In relation to treaties, even multilateral treaties can reflect the desires of States to protect and maintain their position and influence. One important example is the much criticised veto power of the permanent members of the Security Council.[43] Thus, while States might agree that genocide is a grave offence of international law they will interpret custom to conveniently ensure *their* actions are not considered to be genocidal.

In comparison the *ICJ* has no interests to protect other than the maintenance of international peace and security, and so it develops norms in a manner consistent with the common interest of the entire international community, rather than a single member. Impartiality is as important as the norms being applied.[44] This ensures greater acceptance and potential compliance with the norm by all States.[45] However, in two matters, the *Bosnian Genocide Case* and the *Kosovo Opinion* the Court's impartiality and competence was questioned.

C. The Bosnian Genocide Case *and the* Kosovo Opinion

The *Bosnian Genocide Case* was the first, and the *Kosovo Opinion* the most recent, of a series of extremely difficult and controversial legal matters created by the bloody dissolution of the Socialist Federal Republic of Yugoslavia (SFRY).[46] Each matter before the Court was extremely difficult and loaded with political dynamite.[47] They highlight the challenges facing the Court, as well as underlining

---

41 Ibid 9, 20–1.

42 This argument was rejected by the Court. *Nicaragua Case* [1986] ICJ Rep 14, 94–5.

43 In essence the veto power is used to protect the positions of the permanent members. Paul Kennedy, *The Parliament of Man, the United Nations and the Quest for World Government* (Allen Lane, 2006) 51–9.

44 JG Merrills, *International Dispute Settlement* (5th edn) (Cambridge University Press, 2011) 292.

45 Lung-Chu Chen, *An Introduction to Contemporary International Law: A Policy-Orientated Approach* (Yale University Press, 1989) 3.

46 Other cases include the matters brought by Serbia and Montenegro against the NATO States, which involved Serbia seeking provisional measures, and the NATO States objecting to the *ICJ* exercising jurisdiction: eg, *Case Concerning the Legality of the Use of Force (Serbia and Montenegro v Belgium) (Provisional Measures)* [1999] ICJ Rep 124 140 [51] and *Case Concerning the Legality of the Use of Force (Serbia and Montenegro v Belgium)* ICJ Rep [2004] 279. Currently there is another matter arising from this bloody event before the *ICJ*. The oral proceedings recently finished in April 2014. See *Application of the Convention on the Prevention and Punishment of the Crime of Genocide (Croatia v Serbia)*. Refer to the list of pending cases on the *ICJ*'s website: www.icj-cij.org/docket/index.php?p1=3&p2=1&ode=cry&case=118&k=73.

47 Nikolas Rajković, 'On "Bad Law" and "Good Politics": The Politics of the ICJ Genocide Case and Its Interpretation' (2008) 21 *Leiden Journal of International Law* 885, 893.

the significance of the Court's contribution to protecting international humanitarian values.

1. Bosnian Genocide Case

The *Bosnian Genocide Case* involved the claim by Bosnia-Herzegovina that Serbia had violated Article IX of the *Genocide Convention*.[48] The claim referred to a whole range of events and activities throughout Bosnia-Herzegovina, but the most heinous and tragic of these came to include the deaths of 7,000–8,000 military-aged Bosnian Muslim males in and around Srebrenica, during 1995.[49] In a landmark decision the Court ruled that States could be held accountable for acts of genocide, even in the absence of individuals being found guilty.[50] The Court rejected Serbia's arguments and interpretations of the *Genocide Convention*,[51] and in doing so it also corrected the 'Nuremberg Legacy' as a misperception of the findings of the Nuremberg tribunals.[52]

The Court went on to state:

> Thus, if an organ of the State, or a person or group whose acts are legally attributable to the State, commits any of the acts proscribed by Article III of the Convention, the international responsibility of that State is incurred.[53]

After examining the evidence the *ICJ* concluded that while there were widespread acts throughout Bosnia that amounted to crimes against humanity, genocide had only occurred outside Srebrenica. This finding was due to the Court's decision that it was unable to determine the existence of the specific intent (*dolus specialis*) to destroy a group for the events in Srebrenica, but not for the pattern of attacks throughout the remainder of Bosnia-Herzegovina.[54] The Court noted however, that these actions probably constituted crimes against humanity, but was unable to ultimately determine accountability because their jurisdiction was confined to breaches of the *Genocide Convention*.[55] Furthermore, while the Court was satisfied sufficient intent and the elements of genocide were proven for the massacre in Srebrenica, there was neither sufficient evidence to prove that the Belgrade government was responsible for the commission of genocide[56] nor that it was complicit.[57] The *ICJ* then went on to hold that Serbia

48 *Bosnian Genocide Case* [2007] ICJ Rep 43, 155 [278].
49 The application was lodged on 20 March 1993. Judgment was not handed down until 14 years later (in 2007).
50 *Bosnian Genocide Case* [2007] ICJ Rep 43, 119–20 [181]–[182].
51 Ibid 108 [156].
52 Ibid 115 [172].
53 Ibid 118–19 [179].
54 Ibid 155 [277], 194 [370].
55 Ibid.
56 Ibid 237 [471(2)].
57 Ibid 238 [471(2)].

had failed to prevent the massacre[58] and also had failed to punish those who were responsible for the massacre.[59]

The *Bosnian Genocide Case* was significant for a few major reasons. First, this was the first time that a party to the *Genocide Convention* had brought an action alleging a breach of the Convention against another party before the Court.[60] The application to initiate proceedings was also made at a time when international 'criminal law' was in its infancy.[61] The Third Court's decision attracted a vast volume of criticism.[62] Many commentators welcomed the decision to hold States accountable as a landmark contribution,[63] but they felt that the Court's decision, that Serbia was not responsible for the actions of the Bosnian Serb forces, cheated the Bosnian people of rightful justice.[64]

Critics argued that the Court's reasoning was flawed because, first, it was on a narrow conservative approach to the definition of genocide,[65] and second, because the Court erred by insisting on a level of proof that equated to reasonable doubt when this was a 'civil' matter. Third, the Court also erred by upholding the 'effective control' test developed in the *Nicaragua Case*, as the appropriate test

---

58 The Court held that the State in question must exercise a form of 'due diligence'. Ibid 221 [430]–[431].

59 The Court's finding was not unanimous and was decided by thirteen votes to two. Ibid [471(5)].

60 Groome, above n 9, 912.

61 It should be remembered that not only had no individuals been found guilty of genocide, but also the *ICTY* was not formed until May 1993, months before proceedings were initiated; SáCouto, above n 13, 2. Radislav Krstić was the first person convicted of genocide by the *ICTY* in 2001, although on appeal it was reduced to aiding and abetting. Please refer to the *ICTY* website: www.icty.org/sid/7964. *Prosecutor v Radislav Krstić (Judgment) (International Criminal Tribunal for the former Yugoslavia, Appeals Chamber*, Case No IT-98-33-A 19 April 2004) 12 [36].

62 Here is a sample of the commentary regarding the Court's decision: Ademola Abass, 'Proving State Responsibility for Genocide: the ICJ in *Bosnia v Serbia* and the International Commission of Inquiry for Darfur' [2008] 31 *Fordham International Law Journal* 871; CF Amerasinghe, 'Hague International Tribunals, the *Bosnia Genocide* Case' (2008) 21 *Leiden Journal of International Law* 411, 412; SáCouto, above n 13; Vojin Dimitrijević and Marko Milanović, 'The Strange Story of the Bosnian Genocide Case' (2007) 20 *Leiden Journal of International Law* 65; Gaeta, above n 10; Groome, above n 9; Marko Attila Hoare, 'A Case Study in Underachievement: the International Courts and Genocide in Bosnia-Herzegovina' (2011) 6(1) *Genocide Studies and Prevention* 81; Rajković, above n 47, 885; David Scheffer, 'The World Court's Fractured Ruling on Genocide' (2007) 2(2) *Genocide Studies and Prevention* 123; Douglas Singleterry, '"Ethnic Cleansing" and Genocidal Intent: A Failure of Judicial Interpretation?' (2010) 5(1) *Genocide Studies and Prevention* 39.

63 See, Singleterry, above n 62, 40; SáCouto, above n 13, 3; Amerasinghe, above n 62, 420; Hoare, above n 62, 95; Scheffer, above n 62, 124. But note Gaeta's preference for individual accountability: Gaeta, above n 10, 635.

64 See for example the list of protests by commentators in the media at the date the judgment was finalised in Rajković, above n 47, 866, at the author's note 4; Hoare, above n 62, 93.

65 For example, some commentators suggest that a pattern of evidence as used by the *ICTY* could infer the intent to destroy a group, the key element of genocide. See the list of cases in Groome at his note 129. Groome, above n 9, 943.

for State accountability, rather than the 'overall control' test developed by the *ICTY* in the *Tadić Case*.[66] Finally, some commentators were baffled by the Court's fact-finding process, in particular its choice not to pursue the Supreme Defence Council (SDC) reports and relevant information from the Milošević trial. While some commentators argued that this choice rendered the decision as an 'underachievement',[67] others felt that the *ICJ*'s decision was a 'political compromise' and proof that the *ICJ* had in fact 'subrogated itself to Serbia'.[68]

I disagree with some of these criticisms. The Court's conservative approach, its strict definition of genocide and its use of beyond reasonable doubt – a standard used in criminal jurisdictions throughout many domestic jurisdictions – to determine genocide, is consistent with the nature of genocide being an international 'crime'. And there is little doubt that States consider genocide to be a crime.[69] This status is evident in Article II of the *Genocide Convention*, which defines genocide as follows:

> In the present Convention, genocide means any of the following acts committed with intent to destroy, in whole or in part, a national, ethnical, racial or religious group as such:
> (a) Killing members of the group;
> (b) Causing serious bodily or mental harm to members of the group;
> (c) Deliberately inflicting on the group conditions of life calculated to bring about its physical destruction in whole or in part;
> (d) Imposing measures intended to prevent births within the group;
> (e) Forcibly transferring children of the group to another group.[70]

Clearly Article II refers to the two components of a crime: the 'guilty actions' as listed in paragraphs (a)–(e) – the *actus reus*, and the intention of wrongdoing, the 'guilty mind' – the *mens rea*, or in international law the *dolus specialis*. However, genocide is not a minor offence. It is described as the 'crime of crimes'[71], the 'supreme international crime',[72] *the* crime at the apex of tragic offences in

---

66 Groome, above n 9, 94; SáCouto, above n 13, 4; *Prosecutor v Tadić* (*Appeals Chamber*) Case No IT-94-1-AR72 (2 October 1995) [24] [Tadić].

67 Hoare, above n 62, 91–2.

68 Abass, above n 62, 908–9.

69 As evidenced again by the specific use of the term 'crime' to describe genocide, eg: 'The Crime of Genocide' GA Res 96(I), (C.6, 55th plen mtg,), UN Doc A/PV.65, (11 December 1946) where genocide was comparable to murder of individuals. Refer also to the full title of the *Genocide Convention* (see below, n 70).

70 *Convention on the Prevention and Punishment of the Crime of Genocide* adopted by Resolution 260 (III) A of the United Nations General Assembly 9 December 1948 [*Genocide Convention*].

71 Groome, above n 9, 917; Singleterry, above n 62, 43; Gaeta, above n 10, 643; Abass, above n 62, 899.

72 M Shaw, 'The International Court of Justice: Serbia, Bosnia, and Genocide', *Open Democracy*, 28 February 2007 www.opendemocracy.net/node/4392.jsp.

international humanitarian law, as recognised by States,[73] individual judges of the *ICJ*,[74] and even the *ICTY Appeals Chamber* in the *Krstić Case*:[75]

> Among the grievous crimes this Tribunal has the duty to punish, the crime of genocide is singled out for special condemnation and opprobrium. The crime is horrific in its scope; its perpetrators identify entire human groups for extinction.[76]

Thus the Court's insistence on desiring clearly established evidence, rather than to infer the intent to destroy from a pattern of attacks is perfectly reasonable given the nature of the crime, as so eloquently described above.[77] As the Court stated, its insistence was neither a civil or criminal standard of proof. Rather 'the Court requires proof at a high level of certainty appropriate to the seriousness of the allegation'.[78] The argument that a level of proof should reflect the 'civil' nature of the Court is simply inconsistent with the genocide being the crime of crimes. Second, the *ICJ* is not intended to act as a civil court in the same manner as a domestic court with clearly defined and separated jurisdictions.[79] It is the 'World Court' intended to have a 'universal jurisdiction' encompassing any and all legal matters that States choose to bring before it.[80] Finally, given the implications of holding a State accountable, it is quite appropriate to demand clear and conclusive proof.[81] The Court's perception of the serious nature of the crime of genocide also explains its preference for the use of the 'effective control' test developed in the *Nicaragua Case* rather than the 'overall control' test

---

73 As evidenced again by the specific use of the term 'crime' to describe genocide, eg: 'The Crime of Genocide' GA Res 96(I), (C.6, 55th plen mtg,), UN Doc A/PV.65, (11 December 1946) where genocide was described as 'a denial of the right of existence of entire human groups, as homicide is the denial of the right to live of individual human beings; such denial of the right of existence shocks the conscience of mankind'.

74 The Court uses the expression 'exceptional gravity'. *Bosnian Genocide Case* 129 [209]. Her Excellency Judge Higgins described genocide in these terms in the Press Statement after the judgment was released to the public: 'Given the exceptional gravity of the crime of genocide . . . ' See *Statement to the Press by HE Judge Rosalyn Higgins, President of the International Court of Justice*, 26 February 2007 at the Court's website: www.icj-cij.org/docket/index.php?pr=1897&code=bhy&p1=3&p2=3&p3=6&case=91&k=f4.

75 *Prosecutor v Radislav Krstić (Judgment) (International Criminal Tribunal for the former Yugoslavia, Appeals Chamber*, Case No IT-98-33-A 19 April 2004) 12 [36].

76 Ibid.

77 Gaeta above n 10, 643; Singleterry, above n 62, 43–4.

78 *Bosnian Genocide Case* [2007] ICJ Rep 43, 130 [210].

79 The applicant Bosnia and Herzegovina presented this argument. *Bosnian Genocide Case*, 129 [208].

80 The Court has a 'universal and general function'. Raimondo, above n 7, 593.

81 See the discussion regarding politics in Part C below.

developed in the *Tadić Case*.[82] Essentially the Court felt that to adopt the overall control test would lower the standard of proof.[83]

While the Court's decision to adopt the effective control test is in keeping with the theme or nature of genocide as the 'crime of crimes' it does have serious practical implications.[84] It is conceivable that State governments could easily avoid accountability through destroying any evidence of plan or intent to destroy a particular group.[85] Cassese also argues that the effective control test would be easily circumvented if State governments act through terrorist cells whose links with the State government are difficult if not impossible to discover.[86] However, would the overall control test also be satisfied? Evidence of instructions can be destroyed regardless of which test is used, and as evidenced by the chaos in Syria, insurgent groups often do not have a centralised organised hierarchical structure.[87]

The Court's reluctance to examine relevant evidence relating to the trial of Slobodan Milošević by the *ICTY*,[88] and also to demand that Serbia provide the full detail of redacted reports of the SDC,[89] is more problematic and puzzling since it appeared the Court approved of Bosnia's extensive use of documents and evidence that it received from the *ICTY*. In fact, the Court relied upon such evidence itself, in particular where it had been subject to cross-examination.[90] Although some commentators have inferred that this decision was motivated by political pressure[91] the simplest explanation is that the Court was conscious that directing the Serbian government to produce the full version of the SDC files may have simply been ignored by Serbia.[92] At the time proceedings were initiated in 1993, violence was ongoing, and two orders for provisional measures

---

82 Effective control requires clear proof of directives, orders, instructions being given to the individual body for each breach, whereas overall control does not require instructions for each event, but is satisfied by the existence of an organised hierarchical structure. See *Tadić Case* [131]–[137] and the *Nicaragua Case* 64 [115], above n 29 where the Court stated that evidence of 'planning the whole of its operation' was still insufficient to prove control. For a detailed comparison see Antonio Cassesse, 'The Nicaragua and Tadić Tests Revisited in Light of the ICJ Judgment on Genocide in Bosnia' (2007) 18 (4) *European Journal of International Law* 649, 654–63.

83 *Bosnian Genocide Case*, [2007] ICJ Rep 43, 201 [401].

84 Rajković argues that the Court's choice was also motivated by policy concerns, namely the desire to prevent a norm from being abused. Rajković, above n 47, 901.

85 Cassesse, above n 82, 653–4.

86 Ibid 653–4 and 665–6.

87 They not only have different agendas, but often fight each other. Although intent can be inferred, as the Court held in the *Genocide Case* it is questionable whether an inference is sufficient for the 'crime of crimes'.

88 Groome, n 9, 914, 925–93.

89 *Bosnian Genocide Case* [2007] ICJ Rep 43, 128 [205].

90 Ibid 129 [206] and 131 [214].

91 SáCouto, above n 13, 5.

92 A request for evidence would be made pursuant to Article 44 of the *ICJ Statute*.

made by the Court were ignored by Serbia and the violence continued, ultimately including the tragic events that occurred in Srebrenica.[93] Furthermore, there was already an abundance of evidence available to the applicant (Bosnia and Herzegovina) and to the Court.[94] What this issue reveals is rather than the Court buckling to political pressure, the Court simply lacked the relevant resources to adequately determine the 'best evidence'.[95]

2. Kosovo Opinion

Kosovo was a province of Serbia that also sought independence from Serbia. Serbian attempts to prevent Kosovo's claim to statehood escalated into a humanitarian situation which became more horrific with each passing day.[96] Faced with a serious humanitarian tragedy the UN Security Council, acting in accordance with Chapter VII of the *UN Charter*, adopted Resolution 1244 in June of 1999.[97] The purpose of Resolution 1244 was to first put an end to the conflict, and second, to authorise the UN Secretary-General to establish an interim administration/government pending a final political solution.[98] Subsequently, the United Nations Interim Administration Kosovo, headed by a Special Representative of the Secretary-General,[99] created the interim Provisional Institutions of Self-Government (PISG).[100]

In November 2005 the UN Secretary-General appointed Martti Ahtisaari as his Special Envoy to determine the future status for Kosovo. After a series of unsuccessful negotiations between representatives of Serbia and Kosovo, the Special Envoy prepared the Comprehensive Proposal for the Kosovo Status Settlement that concluded that the only viable alternative for Kosovo was independent statehood.[101]

---

93 See Rajković, above n 47, 890.
94 This point is made clear by the diverse range of sources used by the Court and is implied by Groome, who was critical of the Court's fact-finding process. Groome, above n 9, 930–1. See also Her Excellency Judge Higgins' Press Statement in relation to the *Bosnian Genocide Case*, where she mentioned that fact-finding absorbed almost one-third of the judgment. The Press Statement was delivered immediately after the decision was made on 26 February 2007. See the Court's website www.icj-cij.org/docket/index.php?pr=1897&code=bhy&p1=3&p2=3&p3=6&case=91&k=f4.
95 In essence it lacks the *ICTY*'s Prosecutor's office: Groome, above n 9.
96 See for example Marc Weller, *Contested Statehood, Kosovo's Struggle for Independence* (Oxford University Press, 2009).
97 *Kosovo Opinion* [2010] ICJ Rep 403, 426 [58]; 'The Situation in Kosovo' UN Doc S/Res/1244 (10 June 1999) adopted at its 4011th mtg, 2 [3]–[5] and [10]; annex 2 to the resolution [5].
98 *Kosovo Opinion* [2010] ICJ Rep 403, 426–7 [58].
99 Ibid 427–31 [59]–[63]
100 Ibid.
101 'The Comprehensive Proposal for Kosovo Status Settlement, Report of the Special Envoy of the Secretary-General on Kosovo's Future Status' (hereinafter 'The Ahtisaari Report') available at the United Nations office of the Special Envoy for Kosovo website: www.unosek.org/unosek/en/statusproposal.html; Ibid 24–6 [69].

Although the UN Secretary-General as well as the European Union and the US fully supported the Comprehensive Proposal and the idea of statehood for Kosovo, not surprisingly Serbia's ally, Russia, did not. Russia opposed the adoption of the Comprehensive Proposal for the Kosovo Status Settlement by the Security Council and proposed that the Security Council appoint its own 'mission' to report on the future of Kosovo.[102] This proposal also floundered, so representatives of the European Union, the Russian Federation and the US formed the 'Troika' to conduct negotiations between the protagonists; all the Troika achieved was recognition that a deadlock existed.[103]

This deadlock resulted in the Kosovo Assembly, part of the PISG, holding an extraordinary meeting on 17 February 2008 and adopting, by 109 out of the 120 members (including the Prime Minister of Kosovo and the President of Kosovo who was not a member of the Assembly) a Unilateral Declaration of Independence, which *inter alia* stated:[104]

> We, the democratically-elected leaders of our people, hereby declare Kosovo to be an independent and sovereign state. This declaration reflects the will of our people and it is in full accordance with the recommendations of UN Special Envoy Martti Ahtisaari and his Comprehensive Proposal for the Kosovo Status Settlement.[105]

In response to the UDI, Serbia drafted a Request for the *ICJ*'s Advisory Opinion,[106] which the General Assembly adopted on 8 October 2008.[107] The

---

102   Report of the Security Council Mission on the Kosovo Issue, UNSCOR 62nd sess, 5672nd mtg, UN Doc S/PV.5672 (2 May 2007); Report of the Security Council Mission on the Kosovo Issue, UNSCOR 62nd sess, 5673rd mtg, UN Doc S/PV.5673 (10 May 2007). For information regarding the Comprehensive Proposal for the Kosovo Status Settlement, and the Security Council's discussions refer to the website for the United Nations Office of the Special Envoy for Kosovo: www.unosek.org/. The findings of the Security Council mission can be found in: Report of the Security Council Mission on the Kosovo Issue UN Doc S/2007/256, 4 May 2007.

103   Report of the European Union/United States/Russian Federation Troika on Kosovo, 4 December 2007, annexed to S/2007/723; *Kosovo Opinion* [2010] ICJ Rep 403, 433 [72].

104   Ten members of the Assembly representing the Kosovo Serb community and one member representing the Kosovo Gorani community did not attend the meeting. *Kosovo Opinion* [2010] ICJ Rep 403, 434 [75].

105   *Kosovo Opinion* [2010] ICJ Rep 403, 435 [76].

106   The draft question to the Court was introduced in the General Assembly by the then Serbian Foreign Minister Vuk Jeremić: 'Request for an Advisory Opinion of the International Court of Justice on Whether the Unilateral Declaration of Independence of Kosovo Is in Accordance with International Law', UN Doc. A/63/L.2 63rd sess, Agenda item 71 (2008) (23 September 2008); 'Backing Request by Serbia, General Assembly Decides to seek International Court of Justice Ruling on Legality of Kosovo's Independence' UN Doc GA/10764, 63rd plen sess, 22nd mtg (8 October 2008).

107   Request for an Advisory Opinion of the International Court of Justice on Whether the Unilateral Declaration of Independence of Kosovo is in Accordance with International Law, 63rd sess, 22nd plen mtg, UN Doc A/Res 63/3 (8 October 2008).

Request contained a very simple question: 'Is the unilateral declaration of independence by the Provisional Institutions of Self-Government in accordance with international law?'[108]

The Court unanimously concluded that it had jurisdiction.[109] By a vote of 10 to 4 the Court found that the UDI did not breach general international law;[110]nor the *lex specialis* created by Resolution 1244; nor the Constitutional Framework.[111] However, this was not a unanimous decision, a total of nine judges provided Declarations, Dissenting or Separate Opinions.[112]

In coming to the conclusion that there was no general prohibition in international law, the Court responded to a number of arguments presented during the Written and Oral proceedings: (1) that the Security Council had in the past condemned UDI, for example in relation to Rhodesia, Northern Cyprus and *Republika Srpska*; and (2) that the principle of territorial integrity prohibited UDI.

In relation to the first argument the Court stated:[113]

> The Court notes, however, that in all of those instances the Security Council was making a determination as regards the concrete situation existing at the time that those declarations of independence were made; the illegality attached to the declarations of independence thus stemmed not from the unilateral character of these declarations as such, but from the fact that they were, or would have been, connected with the unlawful use of force or other egregious violations of norms of general international law, in particular those of a peremptory character *(jus cogens)*. In the context of Kosovo, the Security Council has never taken this position.[114]

In response to the issue regarding territorial integrity the Court made a bold and controversial conclusion: 'the scope of the principle of territorial integrity is confined to the sphere of relations between States'.[115]

---

108   *Kosovo Opinion* [2010] ICJ Rep 403, 407, [1].
109   However, it was only by nine votes to five that the Court decided to accept the Request. Their Excellencies Judges Keith and Tomka felt that the General Assembly was not seized of the matter, and only the Security Council could legitimately make a request. His Excellency Judge Bennouna felt that the Request was 'frivolous' and that the Court was exposing itself to an attempt to exploit its Opinion. Separate Opinion of Judge Keith, ibid 2, at [6]; Declaration of His Excellency Vice-President Tomka, *Kosovo Opinion* 2 [9]; Dissenting Opinion of His Excellency Judge Bennouna, ibid 1 [3].
110   *Kosovo Opinion* [2010] ICJ Rep 403, 436–8 [79–84]. The four dissenting judges were: His Excellency Vice-President Tomka, Judges Koroma, Bennouna and Skotnikov.
111   *Kosovo Opinion* [2010] ICJ Rep 403, 447–8 [119]–[122].
112   Not quite a record but indicative of the divisions within the bench.
113   Ibid 437 [80]–[81].
114   Ibid [81].
115   Ibid.

The Court recognised Resolution 1244 as a *lex specialis* that could prohibit a UDI. So after much analysis the Court held that the purpose of Resolution 1244 was to create an interim civil administration, a legal regime, to govern Kosovo,[116] *not to* settle Kosovo's final status, and accordingly did not prohibit a UDI.[117] Crucial to this finding was the Court's opinion that the authors of the UDI were not acting within their capacity as members of the PISG, although they were still acting as representatives of the Kosovar people.[118] If the authors were not official representatives, or not acting within their capacity as members of the PSIG, but merely as a group of individuals, then Security Council Resolution 1244 *could not* prohibit them from making a UDI.[119] Consequently, they also could not violate the Constitutional Framework.[120]

Unsurprisingly, the Court's Opinion generated a great deal of commentary and criticism.[121] The three major criticisms raised by commentators were: (1) that the Court by adopting a narrow approach to the interpretation of the question in the Request lost an opportunity to resolve many questions about self-determination; (2) that the Court erred in finding that the UDI did not breach Security Council Resolution 1244; and (3) that the outcome was influenced by political considerations.[122] Other commentators questioned the wisdom in the conclusion that territorial integrity only applied to States, arguing it jeopardised the future ability of the UN to resolve conflicts because the Court's conclusion effectively nullified and rendered meaningless any future Security Council 'guarantees' regarding territorial integrity.[123] Perhaps the harshest criticism came from Acharya:

> It is unfortunate for international law, international justice, international lawyers and the system of international governance as a whole if the International Court of Justice, the supreme judiciary of the international

---

116 *Kosovo Opinion* [2010] ICJ Rep 403, 444 [100].

117 Ibid 449 [114].

118 Ibid 445 [105]; Jure Vidmar, 'Remedial Secession in International Law: Theory and (Lack of) Practice' (2010) 6 (1) *St Anthony's International Review* 37, 114. This is based on the argument presented by Professor James Crawford, which was influential in the Court's ultimate decision.

119 *Kosovo Opinion* [2010] ICJ Rep 403, 449–52 [114]–[119].

120 Ibid 452 [120]–[121].

121 See the themed articles in the following journals: (2010) 11 *German Law Journal*, the 'Agora' in (2011) 105(1) *American Journal of International Law*; and the Symposium in (2011) 24 *Leiden Journal of International Law*.

122 For example, Theodore Christakis, 'The ICJ Advisory Opinion on Kosovo: Has International Law Something to Say about Secession?' (2011) 24 (1) *Leiden Journal of International Law* 73, 74; Hurst Hannum, 'The Advisory Opinion on Kosovo: An Opportunity Lost, or a Poisoned Chalice Refused?' (2011) 24(1) *Leiden Journal of International Law* 157; Marcelo G Kohen and Katherine del Mar, 'The Kosovo Advisory Opinion and UNSCR 1244 (1999): A Declaration of "Independence from International Law"?' (2011) 24 (1) *Leiden Journal of International Law* 109–14. Criticism also came from members of the Bench: see Separate Opinion of His Excellency Judge Yusuf, *Kosovo Opinion* [2010] ICJ Rep 403 [2]; Declaration of His Excellency Vice-President Tomka, *Kosovo Opinion* [2010] ICJ Rep 403, 454 [1].

123 Kohen and del Mar, above n 122.

governing system, acts as a rubber stamp for the dominant power of the Security Council and the judges' national political affiliations by adopting an economy of judicial reasoning in its decisions. The ICJ's recent advisory opinion on Kosovo's unilateral declaration of independence from Serbia seems to fall within this unsatisfactory category.[124]

The Court's conclusion, although somewhat controversial, *is* significant. The status of territorial integrity within international law and its importance to the maintenance of the security and stability of the international community are both unquestionable and well recognised in treaties,[125] as well as by States.[126] The desire to protect territorial integrity is one of the most powerful counter-arguments to an application for self-determination, simply because a successful claim to independence results in a physical alteration of the territory of the parent State.

The Court's decision ensures that States cannot use the norm of territorial integrity to justify breaches of international humanitarian law:

> The famous principle of territorial integrity is morally progressive in so far as it forbids aggressive interstate wars; but it cannot be treated as legitimating *any* possible action of a government within its internationally secured frontiers.[127]

Accordingly, the Court has resolved one of the seemingly intractable issues at the heart of self-determination, namely its consistency with the norm of territorial integrity, and puts to rest the conundrum that has consistently plagued claims to self-determination. As noted by Shelton:

> From the breakup of the Austro-Hungarian and Ottoman Empires after World War I to the struggle of colonial territories for independence following World War II and the later dissolution of the former Yugoslavia, there has been an unavoidable conflict between the efforts of peoples to achieve independence and the demands of exiting states to preserve their territorial integrity.[128]

As Sharmazanov (spokesperson for the ruling Republican Party of Armenia) recognised, for the first time peoples' right to self-determination was more

---

124 Upendra D. Acharya, 'ICJ's Kosovo Decision: Economical Reasoning of Law and Question of Legitimacy of the Court' (2012) 12 Chi-Kent J. Int'l & Comp Law 1, 1 (discussing Falk's paper: Richard Falk, 'The Kosovo Advisory Opinion' (2011) 105 (1) *American Journal of International Law* 50, 50).

125 See, eg, *Covenant of the League of Nations* Article 10; *UN Charter* Articles 2(4) and 2(7).

126 John Dugard, *Recognition and the United Nations* (Grotius Publications Limited, 1987) 35–8.

127 Wayne Norman, 'The Ethics of Secession as the Regulation of Secessionist Politics' in Margaret Moore (ed.), *National Self-Determination and Secession* (Oxford University Press, 1998) 34, 43.

128 Dinah Shelton, 'Self-Determination in Regional Human Rights Law: from Kosovo to Cameroon' (2011) 105 (1) *American Journal of International Law* 60, 60 citing Antonio Cassese, *Self-Determination of Peoples: a Legal Reappraisal* (Cambridge University Press, 1995).

important than a State's right to the territorial integrity.[129] Thus putting human rights, specifically peoples' rights before the rights of States, which has far-reaching consequences and implications for the international legal system that has been overwhelmingly dominated by States for so long.

3. Summary

Sadly commentators appear to overlook the development of legal norms in the above-discussed cases. Commentators such as Groome rightly question the Court's competency by pointing out that the *ICJ* is simply not well equipped for the exhausting and painstaking process of fact-finding in criminal matters. This conclusion is supported by comments made by Her Excellency Judge Higgins in the Press Statement that one-third of the decision in the *Bosnian Genocide Case* was devoted to fact-finding, and still the Court did not access the best evidence possible, and arguably with its current structure and facilities it will not be able to, and instead will be dependent upon other tribunals such as the *ICTY*.[130] In other words, the Court is incapable of acting as a criminal tribunal, and yet its decision that States could be held accountable meant that it may be called upon in the future to act as a criminal tribunal.[131] This problem is not insurmountable. It can be fixed if the Court was provided with a fact-finding body as suggested by SáCouto.[132]

Commentators examining both the *Bosnian Genocide Case* and the *Kosovo Opinion* felt the Court had missed an important opportunity to cure some of mankind's evils.[133] Furthermore, some commentators suggested that the Court's failure to resist external or political influences explains some of the Court's more baffling pronouncements.[134]

---

129 Author unknown, 'Armenia Hails Court Ruling on Kosovo Independence', *Radio Free Europe* www.rferl.org/content/Armenia_Hails_Court_Ruling_On_Kosovo_Independence/ 2109757 26 July 1010.

130 Groome, above n 9, 988–9.

131 In fact there is another 'criminal' matter now before the Court, *Application of the Convention on the Prevention and Punishment of the Crime of Genocide (Croatia v Serbia)* www.icj-cij.org/docket/index.php?p1=3&p2=1&ode=cry&case=118&k=73.

132 SáCouto, above n 13, 5; Groome, above n 9, 980; Singleterry, above n 62,47; Mark Angehr, 'The International Court of Justice's Advisory Jurisdiction and the Review of Security Council and General Assembly Resolutions' (2009) 103(2) *Northwestern University Law Review* 1007, 1031–6.

133 Cassese, above n 82, 667. In the *Nuclear Weapons Opinion* similar comments were made by members of the Bench: see, eg, Judge Weeramantry who criticised his brethren for failing to seize the day and denounce the use of nuclear weapons as always being illegal. See generally *Nuclear Weapons Opinion* [1996] ICJ Rep 226, 433 (Dissenting Opinion of Judge Weeramantry).

134 In relation to the *Bosnian Genocide Case* see, eg, Abass, above n 62, 909 and SáCouto, above n 13, 5. In relation to the *Kosovo Opinion* see Richard Falk, 'The *Kosovo* Advisory Opinion: Conflict Resolution and Precedent' (2011) 105 (1) *American Journal of International Law* 50.

To summarise these criticisms, the Court is unable to play a role protecting international humanitarian values because it is: (1) not *competent*; (2) not *trusted*; and (3) too *conservative*. The last two criticisms are sufficiently strong criticisms to warrant further examination before concluding.

D. Should the ICJ play a role in protecting international humanitarian values?

Aspects of the Court's approach and findings are baffling to an extent, but to suggest political interference is excessive. In order to better understand the Court's conservative approach and thus, be able to address these criticisms it is perhaps wise to be reminded of the context in which the *ICJ* operates, and in which these decisions were made.[135]

1. Political context

First, the international community is dominated by a particular form of international legal person (State) that considers themselves to be independent sovereigns and free from the authority of a higher political entity.[136] And this is proven by the legal system that States have designed to govern themselves, one based on consensual jurisdiction, and one that, despite Article 94(2) of the *UN Charter*,[137] lacks any real enforcement power.[138] These features *must* influence how the Court approaches controversial legal matters, such as genocide or crimes against humanity or self-determination.[139] As unpalatable as it may be the

---

135 Rajković argues the *ICJ*'s decisions should not be viewed in isolation from their surrounding political context, and even implies that any criticism is questionable if it fails to do so: Rajković, above n 47, 894.

136 Edward McWhinney, *Judicial Settlement of International Disputes: Jurisdiction, Justiciability and Judicial Law-Making on the Contemporary International Court* (1991) 39.

137 Article 94(2) *UN Charter* empowers a State to request action from the Security Council to enforce any legal obligation created by a judgment of the *ICJ*.

138 Renata Szafraz, *The Compulsory Jurisdiction of the International Court of Justice* (1993) 3; P Couvreur, 'The Effectiveness of the International Court of Justice in the Peaceful Settlement of International Disputes' in AS Muller, D Raič and JM Thuránszky (eds), *The International Court of Justice: Its Future Role after Fifty Years* (Kluwer Law International, Martinus-Nijhoff Publishers, 1997) 83, 111; Ojo, above n 36, 53; Charney, above n 36, 303–4; RP Anand, 'Role of International Adjudication' in Leo Goss (ed.), *The Future of the International Court of Justice* (Oceana Publications, 1976) vol 1, 1, 1.

139 The difficulty of achieving anything against States' wishes is perhaps evidenced by the failure to impose a 'true' compulsory jurisdiction. Originally the Committee of Jurists that was tasked with designing the new world court intended to make the jurisdiction of the *ICJ* completely compulsory. However, the opposition to compulsory jurisdiction was so intense that it was felt that if compulsory jurisdiction were pursued, it would jeopardise the very existence not just of the *ICJ*, but also of the UN. Helmut Steinberger, 'The International Court of Justice', in *Judicial Settlement of International Disputes* (1974), 196; Stanmir Alexandrov, *Reservations in Unilateral Declarations Accepting the Compulsory Jurisdiction of the International Court of Justice* (1995) 8.

Court has to consider that its decision, if challenged or ignored, jeopardises its whole credibility, and consequently, its ability to maintain international peace and security. Consequently, the Court must take measured steps in changing norms, rather than embark upon a crusade of judicial activism or 'entrepreneurship'.

Second, each case took place in the context of one of the most politically and emotionally charged backgrounds in the Court's history.[140] Dimitrijević and Milanović describe the *Bosnian Genocide Case* as follows:

> There is no other ICJ case which meant so much to so many people, no other case in which internal politics so manifestly prevented an applicant from arguing its best legal position, and no other ICJ judgment which has been so badly misinterpreted, again due to politics.[141]

Burri summarised the surrounding context of the *Kosovo Opinion* in this way:

> It . . . involved war. International forces had intervened to stop ethnic cleansing. It . . . polarized the entire international community . . . [the] legal assessment was *challenging* . . . the stakes were *high*. Nothing less than the foundation of the international order was at issue.[142]

Such highly charged political matters take place in a 'jungle' of competing 'national interests' of States, and unsurprisingly this has significant effects.[143] First, litigation, and the Court itself, can easily be used as a weapon in the strategy of States. Indeed, Rajković writes that:

> Genocide litigation at the level of state responsibility is more than an exercise of legal imperatives it is also a profoundly political act in terms of both intent and effect.[144]

He argues Bosnia's act of lodging an application for proceedings was motivated by the desire to win international support in an ongoing conflict. The Bosnian government sought to force the *ICJ*, and by extension the international community, to choose 'sides'.[145] His argument makes a lot of sense since at that time Bosnian forces were heavily outmatched by Serbian forces and were in

---

140 Dimitrijević and Milanović, above n 62, 85–6.
141 Ibid 92. Singleterry described the *Bosnian Genocide Case* as a 'problem from hell'. Singleterry, above n 62, 41.
142 Thomas Burri, 'The Kosovo Opinion and Secession: the Sounds of Silence and Missing Links' (2010) 11 *German Law Journal* 881.
143 Anand, above n 138, 1.
144 Rajković, above n 47, 889.
145 Ibid 891–3; Dimitrijević and Milanović, above n 62, 69.

desperate need of assistance, which had been denied by the arms embargo created by Security Council Resolution 713.[146] Arguing they were the victims of genocide could prompt assistance since commentators also have argued that genocide would justify humanitarian intervention by other States.[147] Certainly the Bosnian government sought to use claims of genocide as a means to persuade the *ICJ* to declare Security Council Resolution 713 and the arms embargo as illegal in its application for provisional measures.[148] Third, the *ICTY* had found in three cases that Bosnian forces were also guilty of crimes against humanity.[149] A claim of genocide would deflect attention from these actions and 'remind' international actors of who were the 'true perpetrators' and who were the 'true' victims.

Similar comments have been made about the background to the *Kosovo Opinion*. The General Assembly may have made the Request, but Serbia drafted the question. In fact, Serbia was the sole sponsor of the question and thus arguably was totally 'responsible' for the format of the question.[150] No doubt Serbia chose a specific and narrow question for strategic reasons, namely believing that a narrow question would result in the UDI being considered illegal. Receiving such a declaration could have enabled Serbia to take action before the UN General Assembly to reassert its authority over Kosovo. With Serbia's ally Russia retaining a veto power in the Security Council this is not far-fetched.[151] Thus, Serbia sought to gain a political advantage from the Opinion by persuading States to not grant recognition.[152] Peters goes one step further:

---

146 Letter dated 19 September 1991, from the Permanent Representative of Austria to the United Nations Addressed to the President of the Security Council, SC Res 713, UNSCOR (3009th mtg) UN Doc S/Res/713 (1991) [6].

147 Tania Voon, 'Closing the Gap Between Legitimacy and Legality of Humanitarian Intervention: Lessons from East Timor and Kosovo' (2002–2003) 7 *UCLA Journal of International Law and Foreign Affairs* 31, 58–64; Andrew Field, 'The Legality of Humanitarian Intervention and the Use of Force in the Absence of United Nations Authority' (2000) 26 *Monash University Law Review* 339, 339.

148 *Application of the Convention on the Prevention and Punishment of the Crime of Genocide (Bosnia and Herzegovina v Serbia and Montenegro)* (Provisional Measures, Order of 8 April 1993), ICJ Rep [1993] 3, 6 [2(o)]. As noted by Dimitrijević and Milanović, this was another misuse of alleged genocide that justified the *ICJ* choosing a narrow definition of genocide: Dimitrijević and Milanović, above n 62, 69.

149 *Prosecutor v Delalić et al.*, Case No IT-96-21; *Prosecutor v Hadžihasanović and Kubura*, Case No IT-01-47; *Prosecutor v Rasim Delić*, Case No IT-04-83; See Rajković, n 47, 894.

150 Hannum, above n 122, 159; Marc Weller, 'Modesty can be a Virtue: Judicial Economy in the *Kosovo Opinion*?' (2011) 24 *Leiden Journal of International Law* 130.

151 Weller, above n 150, 131.

152 The expression enlightenment was part of a quote used by Serbia in its Written Submission from the *Peace Treaties* Advisory Opinion. See Serbia's Written Statement filed by Serbia 17 April 2009, 46, [91] www.icj-cji.org/docket/index.php?pl=3&p2=4&k21&case=141&code=kos&p3=1.

'a negative answer might have inspired Serbian actors to propagate a *reconquista* of Kosovo with military means.'[153]

The second significant effect of highly political matters taking place in the international 'jungle' is that regardless of what the Court's decision will be it is going to receive criticism: either for being too conservative or for exceeding its mandate.[154] In a manner of speaking 'damned' if it was too conservative and 'damned' if it was too radical.[155] Again looking at the *Bosnian Genocide Case* its background must have placed immense pressure on the Court to adopt a populist definition of genocide, one that includes other crimes heinous in nature, *but which are different offences*. The Court, and even its then President, Her Excellency Judge Higgins, made this point adamantly clear. It is obvious that the Court was *frustrated* by the restriction in the pleadings to confine themselves to the *Genocide Convention* and not consider other crimes, such as crimes against humanity.

In the *Kosovo Opinion* the failure of the Court to examine remedial self-determination received criticism. As Hannum quite rightly suggests, the Court's refusal is consistent with States' desires. Very few States, but in particular States like Russia or the PRC, for example, *would have wanted* to draft a broader question. One that could have enticed the Court to set guidelines, or pre-conditions that *permitted* or at least legitimised a self-determination claim.[156] A fear clearly held by those States that argued that Kosovo was 'unique':[157] an obvious attempt to minimise the precedent value of the Opinion.[158]

Despite the intense pressure and the political hype faced by the Court in both matters the Court did not buckle. For example, it applied what it believed to be *a legal definition* of Genocide, and the Court's findings in the *Bosnian Genocide Case* in no way dismissed the events that happened in Srebrenica. In fact the Court emphasised that crimes against humanity had indeed occurred. In the *Kosovo Opinion* despite not considering remedial self-determination, commentators like Falk who were highly critical of the Court's approach, believed that it was the *correct and 'right' decision*:

> From the standpoint of human rights, as well as political realism, the Kosovo claim is highly reasonable. It would be irresponsible and extremely destabilizing to insist on a legal reversal of the de facto independence that

---

153   Anne Peters, 'Does Kosovo Lie in the *Lotus-Land* of Freedom?' (2011) 24(1) *Leiden Journal of International Law* 95, 108.

154   Weller, above n 150, 130.

155   Thomas Burri, 'The Kosovo Opinion and Secession: The Sounds of Silence and Missing Links' (2010) 11 *German Law Journal* 881; Weller, above n 150, 129–31.

156   Hannum above n 122, 158–9; Falk, above n 134, 58; Christakis, above n 122, 80.

157   See for example the 'Written Comments Kosovo Opinion', filed by the UK of 15 July 2009 [11]–[14]; www.icj-cji.org/docket/index.php?pl=3&p2=4&k21&case=141&code=kos&p3=1 and the commentary by Hannum, above n 122, 159.

158   See, the statement by the then President of Serbia, Tadić, in UNSC, 63rd year, 5839th mtg, 18 February 2008, UN Doc. S/PV.5839 (2008) 5.

Kosovo has enjoyed, with UN backing and administration, and regional and geopolitical reinforcement . . . for more than a decade.[159]

And finally, Tams concluded:

> The problem with the Court's answer is not that it is wrong, but that it is right. In giving the correct answer to the General Assembly's curiously formulated question, the Court has drawn attention to a serious gap in the international legal system: international law's failure to provide meaningful rules that give normative guidance on how the international community should deal with claims to statehood.[160]

In other words, even though the decision may have disappointed commentators it *still* made a contribution in the advancement of international humanitarian law by drawing the international community's attention to what *must be* changed. Arguably the Court did a similar thing in the *Bosnian Genocide Case* by drawing attention to the gulf between genocide and crimes against humanity.

By not 'buckling' the Court sends a clear message to potential protagonists: the *ICJ* is not to be used to advance extra-legal agendas.[161] And so in answer to the question can *the Court be trusted?* The answer is 'yes'. [162] As Merrills so rightly stated in his monograph, *International Dispute Settlement*, trust is crucial in any legal system, but even more so in the international system since the decision of the Court may vindicate a party's behaviour in the eyes of the international community.[163] Consequently, in the *Bosnian Genocide Case*, a finding by the Court that no genocide took place could have been perceived by the Serbian authorities as a validation of their actions, and even of the lawful existence of the *Republika Srpska*, and Bosnian Muslims would consider anything other than a guilty verdict as ignoring the illegality of Serbian aggression.[164] This perception is often

---

159 Falk, above n 134, 58.
160 Christian J Tams, 'The Kosovo Opinion', *EJIL Talk!* www.ejiltalk.org/the-kosovo-opinion/.
161 Rajković, above n 47, 900.
162 Hoare raised the issue of impartiality in the *Bosnian Genocide Case*. Academics have attempted to measure the impartiality of the *ICJ* by examining the voting patterns of individual judges. The conclusion that commentators have drawn from such quantitative research is that it is more likely that judges are influenced by cultural values and other subtle influences that their legal training and experience have given them, rather than actually being guilty of voting in the national interest. Hoare, above n 62, 93; Thomas Hensley, 'National Bias and the International Court of Justice' (1968) 12 *Midwest Journal of Political Science* 568, 568–9; Il Ro Suh, 'Voting Behaviour of National Judges in International Courts' (1969) 63 *American Journal of International Law* 224, 226; EB Weiss, 'Judicial Independence and Impartiality' in Lori Damrosch (ed.), *The International Court of Justice at a Crossroads* (1987) 123.
163 Merrills, above n 44, 292–3, 296. Trust is particularly important in the international sphere due to the consensual nature of the Court's jurisdiction. No State would consent (or would withdraw their consent) to a matter being adjudicated by the *ICJ* if it could not be trusted to be impartial.
164 Dimitrijević and Milanović, above n 62, 88.

caused by or worsened by ethnic affiliations. As wisely noted by Merrills, any complex case will give rise to different interpretations and different conclusions.[165] Furthermore:

> there will always be bad losers, and consequently the rejection of a decision by a state may be no more than a sign the Court has done what it is supposed to do and has applied the law without fear or favour.[166]

III. Conclusion

In terms of accountability for violations of norms of IHL there is some truth in the criticisms raised by commentators about the *ICJ*'s ability or rather inability, to determine facts – the best evidence possible – and that it does lack the structural advantages and resources of the Prosecutor's office of the *ICTY* or other international criminal tribunal. There is also some truth in the difficulty in holding a State accountable due to the standard of proof and the definition of genocide used by the Court. However, sadly, like so many of the *ICJ*'s decisions the Court's contribution to advancing international humanitarian values in both the *Bosnian Genocide Case* and the *Kosovo Opinion* was lost in all the political hype surrounding the decisions, and also in commentators' well-intentioned desires to end *all* crimes against humanity.

Once the smoke finally clears then these two landmark decisions will finally be recognised as such, and not as an opportunity missed.[167] Why? Because not only can States be held accountable, they will be held accountable for failing to prevent genocide, which translates into States now having a *positive* duty to take action. And this obligation is arguably far easier to prove than proving responsibility for committing an act of genocide and avoids the issue of which test of control should be adopted. Furthermore, these two decisions, the *Kosovo Opinion* particularly, reinforce the continuing and rightful evolution of peoples' rights, and arguably their superiority over State sovereignty, which has kept international relations, international law and peoples in its tight stranglehold for far too long.

It is tragic that the Bosnian people feel cheated of justice, but it is even more tragic that lives were lost in the first place. Accountability is important for many reasons. Holding perpetrators accountable is a means of trying to promote closure for the victims, but accountability takes place after the dead are well and truly buried. As Momir Nikolić in his statement of guilt noted: 'I am aware that I cannot bring back the dead, that I cannot mitigate the pain of the families by my confession . . . '.[168] The Court's decisions in the *Bosnian Genocide Case* and the *Kosovo Opinion* have promoted the idea of prevention by establishing a code of conduct that promotes peoples' rights, of international humanitarian values over antiquated notions of sovereignty and States' rights.

165 Merrills, above n 44, 304.
166 Ibid.
167 This will take time: SáCouto, above n 13, 5.
168 *Statements of Guilt*, above n 2.

12 Moving from the mechanics of accountability to a culture of accountability

What more can be done in addition to prosecuting war crimes?

Helen Durham and Eve Massingham[1]

I. Introduction

The practice of holding individuals criminally responsible for certain categories of international crimes is a well-accepted element of international humanitarian law (IHL). In the last 20 years there has been a raft of procedural and practical developments in the area of international criminal law. However, the creation of a number of international enforcement mechanisms, and the publicity given to the prosecution of 'war criminals', has sometimes overshadowed the wider and deeper obligations found in IHL. As this chapter will discuss, the *Geneva Conventions*[2] and other components of the IHL regime, do require the State Parties

---

1 Dr Helen Durham is the Director of International Humanitarian Law, Strategy, Planning and Research at the Australian Red Cross. Eve Massingham is an International Humanitarian Law Officer at the Australian Red Cross. In dedication to a man who taught and inspired many of us – with thanks.
   This chapter was written in the authors' personal capacity and does not necessarily represent the views of the Red Cross.

2 *Geneva Convention for the Amelioration of the Condition of the Wounded and Sick in Armed Forces in the Field*, 12 August 1949, 75 UNTS 31 (entered into force 21 October 1950) [hereinafter *GCI*]; *Geneva Convention for the Amelioration of the Condition of Wounded, Sick and Shipwrecked Members of Armed Forces at Sea*, 12 August 1949, 75 UNTS 85 (entered into force 21 October 1950) [hereinafter *GCII*]; *Geneva Convention relative to the Treatment of Prisoners of War*, 12 August 1949, 75 UNTS 135 (entered into force 21 October 1950) [hereinafter *GCIII*]; *Geneva Convention relative to the Protection of Civilian Persons in Time of War*, 12 August 1949, 75 UNTS 287 (entered into force 21 October 1950) [hereinafter *GCIV*]; *Protocol Additional to the Geneva Conventions of 12 August 1949, and relating to the Protection of Victims of International Armed Conflicts*, 8 June 1977, 1125 UNTS 3 (entered into force 7 December 1979) [hereinafter *API*]; *Protocol Additional to the Geneva Conventions of 12 August 1949, and relating to the Protection of Victims of Non-International Armed Conflicts*, 8 June 1977, 1125 UNTS 609 (entered into force 7 December 1979) [hereinafter *APII*]; *Protocol Additional to the Geneva Conventions of 12 August 1949, and relating to the Adoption of an Additional Distinctive Emblem*, 8 December 2005, 2404 UNTS 261 (entered into force 14 January 2007) [hereinafter *APIII*].

to develop legal processes for prosecution. However, the normative value of this area of international law is more comprehensive and requires a range of positive actions (such as identification of cultural property, the creation of safety zones and dissemination of IHL) which encourage compliance with IHL.[3] Indeed, for IHL to adequately ensure protection for those not, or no longer, engaged in hostilities, the implementation of obligations before, during and after armed conflict, which reach above and beyond prosecution, is necessary.

Other chapters in this book touch on issues involved with the creation of the *ad hoc*, hybrid and special tribunals and the development of the *International Criminal Court*. These initiatives all came about some time after Gustave Moynier, one of the founders of the International Red Cross and Red Crescent Movement, had proposed such a concept in 1870.[4] This demonstrates that the recent focus on the capacity for international prosecution is new in implementation, not new as an idea. Initially Moynier was not in favour of an international court, instead thinking that reliance on public pressure would be sufficient. However, following the Franco–Prussian War, it became clear to Moynier that public opinion was not enough and he began work on a proposal for the establishment by treaty of an international tribunal. The proposal was presented at a meeting of the International Committee of the Red Cross (ICRC) in 1872 and published in the predecessor to the *International Review of the Red Cross*. He used for his model the arbitral tribunal established under the *Treaty of Washington* to adjudicate claims by the United States against Great Britain for damage to American shipping by a Confederate raider.[5] Several key ideas put forward in the proposal, which consisted of ten short articles, show the incredible foresight Moynier had over a century ago. Importantly, he argued that the court should be a permanent institution, which would be automatically activated when war broke out (Article 1). His proposal also articulated that judicial remedies should not be left to belligerents (Article 2) and that the terms of the *Geneva Convention* were inadequate to impose criminal responsibility and thus violations and penalties should be defined under a separate treaty (Article 5). Moynier's proposal also included suggestions not just related to judgments and penalties but also to victim compensation (Article 7).

Many eminent jurists at the time, including Francis Lieber and de Holtzendorff responded to his suggestion. Among the various criticisms were Lieber's argument that the absence of a police force to implement the tribunal's decisions was crucial and de Holtzendorff's concern that other means such as the importance of teaching the rules of the *Geneva Conventions* were just as important. It is impossible to assess the impact of Moynier's idea of a permanent

---

3 ICRC, *State Parties to the Following International Humanitarian Law and Other Related Treaties* (29 January 2014) ICRC www.law.unimelb.edu.au/files/dmfile/FinalOnlinePDF-2012Reprint. pdf.

4 Christopher Hall, 'The First Proposal for an International Criminal Court' (1998) 322 *International Review of the Red Cross* www.icrc.org/eng/resources/documents/misc/57jp4m.htm.

5 Ibid.

international criminal court on today's international criminal law landscape, however the idea seems to have been forgotten for quite some time given the fairly lukewarm response it received at the time.[6]

Looking to the future there is no doubt that international and hybrid courts and tribunals will of course continue to play a significant role in improving compliance with IHL. Debates about the actual role war crimes prosecution plays in relation to the prevention of the commission of atrocities are important[7] and within many of the institutions themselves this connection is implied. For example, within the preamble of the *International Criminal Court* is the commitment: '[d]etermined to put an end to impunity for the perpetrators of these crimes and thus to contribute to the prevention of such crimes'.[8]

Commentators such as Boas have also noted the complexity about what role international criminal law plays in the search for wider international criminal justice.

> International Criminal Justice is about more than responses. How do we learn from history, or sometimes fail to do so? Can we use our understanding of human psychology to respond better to mass atrocity, or to prevent or address it sooner? What of the sociological elements that are infused in our response to heinous international crimes; how do these affect our understanding and practice of international criminal justice?[9]

The ability to prosecute individuals for the most heinous of international crimes is a 'powerful tool in the armoury of international criminal justice'.[10] However, there is a range of responses to deal with such atrocities. Over thirty Truth and Reconciliation Commissions, community-based approaches that reflect culturally specific responses to these crimes and the emerging use of other disciplines beyond just the law, provide a broader look at the patchwork approaches to dealing with international crimes committed during times of war.[11]

There are however a number of other factors that contribute to IHL compliance, much of which involves the core business of the International Red Cross and Red Crescent Movement – the dissemination of IHL.[12] This chapter

---

6 Ibid.
7 See for example Payuam Akhavan, 'Beyond Impunity: Can International Criminal Justice Prevent Future Atrocities?' (2001) 95(1) *The American Journal of International Law* 7–31.
8 *Rome Statute of the International Criminal Court*, opened for signature 17 July 1998, 2187 UNTS 90 (entered into force 1 July 2002).
9 Gideon Boas *et al.* (eds), *International Criminal Justice: Legitimacy and Coherence* (Edward Elgar Publishing, 2012) 1.
10 Ibid 2.
11 Ibid 3.
12 *Statutes of the International Red Cross and Red Crescent Movement*, adopted by the 25th International Conference of the Red Cross at Geneva in 1986 and amended in 1995 and 2006, particularly Articles 3(2), 5(2)(g) and 5(4)(a).

outlines the nature of the various obligations on States to prevent IHL violations before looking at broader cultural, social and political factors that encourage compliance with IHL.

II. Accountability mechanisms in the *Geneva Conventions*

One of the most dramatic elements of the updating of the *Geneva Conventions* in 1945 were the obligations these multilateral treaties contained in relation to the domestic prosecution of those accused of war crimes. The *Geneva Conventions* include provisions for the 'repression of abuses and infractions', which require the States Party to the *Geneva Conventions* to 'provide effective penal sanctions for a person committing, or ordering to be committed' grave breaches of the *Geneva Conventions*.[13] States Parties are also required to search for individuals suspected of war crimes and bring them to justice.[14] These provisions and, as mentioned above, the proliferation of international courts and tribunals in recent history have placed a strong focus on international criminal law. However, in addition to these prosecutorial accountability mechanisms there are a number of other mechanisms littered throughout the *Geneva Conventions* that act to limit the suffering of war.

A. The obligation to disseminate the text of the Geneva Conventions

Disseminating the texts of the *Geneva Conventions* is one of these mechanisms. That is, as widely as possible, including to military personnel and medical personnel, States Parties to the *Geneva Conventions* must disseminate the texts 'so that the principles thereof may become known to the entire population'.[15] This places a key positive obligation on governments to ensure that education about the rules of war is a part of a variety of education programmes. Clearly education is a key pillar of any legal system. How can you obey the law if you do not know what it says? Governments must ensure that no soldier, sailor or air force personnel can legitimately say they had never heard of the *Geneva Conventions* or did not know that a particular act was a grave breach. This is an obligation also placed on components of the International Red Cross and Red Crescent Movement through the *Statutes of the Movement*,[16] and one which governments work closely with components of the Movement to ensure is fulfilled.

---

13   *GCI* Articles 49, 50; *GCII* Articles 50, 51; *GCIII* Articles 129, 130; *GCIV* Articles 146, 147. See also, *API* Article 85.
14   Ibid.
15   *GCI* Article 47; *GCII* Article 48; *GCIII* Article 127; *GCIV* Article 144; *API* Article 83; *APII* Article 19.
16   *Statutes of the International Red Cross and Red Crescent Movement*, above n 12.

B. The obligation to seek legal advice

An extension of this is the specific obligation on States to 'ensure that legal advisors are available, when necessary, to advise military commanders at the appropriate level on the application of the *Conventions* and this *Protocol*'.[17] The inclusion of this provision in the post-Vietnam era is reflective of the fact that with an increasing complexity in the law of armed conflict, commanders cannot be expected to master the complexity of the law. Rather, this mastery can be left to legal advisers and commanders can be left to 'master the art of exercising command over their troops'.[18] It is recognised that pre-Vietnam the role of lawyers was not one on the battlefield but, should they actually have anything to do with rules of war, it would be in the pre- and post-deployment capacity – perhaps policy, or (to a limited degree) prosecution. However, the operational military lawyer is very much a part of modern-day conflict. The involvement of military lawyers in reviewing aspects of the battle such as rules of engagement and targeting decisions is seen as very beneficial to ensuring IHL compliance. Indeed Brigadier General Charles Dunlap is quoted as saying 'savvy American commanders seldom go to war without their attorneys'.[19]

This is very important for ensuring compliance with IHL. As the ICRC *Roots of Behaviour in War* study notes, 'most men subjected to an authority that they perceive as legitimate will obey orders even when doing so creates a painful conflict with their conscience or moral standards'.[20] The study concludes that violations are 'mostly the result of deliberate policies which either encourage or tolerate such behaviour . . . those who perpetrate these acts are often obeying those who instigate them'.[21] Consequently 'supervision of weapons-bearers, strict orders relating to proper conduct and effective penalties for failure to obey those orders are essential'.[22]

C. The obligation to take precautions against the effects of attacks

One aspect of the *Geneva Conventions* that rarely attracts the same attention – both in terms of discourse and in terms of prosecution – as the various prohibitions on attack, is Article 58 of *Additional Protocol I (API)* – Precautions against the effects of attacks. Article 58 provides:

---

17 *API* Article 82.
18 Y Sandoz *et al.* (eds), *Commentary on the Additional Protocols of 8 June 1977 to the Geneva Conventions of 12 August 1949* (Martinus Nijhoff, 1987) 948.
19 MF Lohr and S Gallotta, 'Legal Support in War: The Role of Military Lawyers' (2003) 4 *Chicago Journal of International Law* 465, 467.
20 Jean-Jacques Frésard, *Roots of Behaviour in War; A Survey of the Literature* (ICRC, 2004) www.icrc.org/eng/resources/documents/misc/5zbggl.htm 105.
21 Ibid 108.
22 Ibid 110.

The Parties to the conflict shall, to the maximum extent feasible:

(a) . . . endeavour to remove the civilian population, individual civilians and civilian objects under their control from the vicinity of military objectives;

(b) avoid locating military objectives within or near densely populated areas;

(c) take the other necessary precautions to protect the civilian population, individual civilians and civilian objects under their control against the dangers resulting from military operations.

That is, the obligation is not only on the party to the conflict launching an attack to take appropriate measures to limit civilian losses, but rather that all parties to a conflict have responsibilities in this regard. As the *Commentary to API* points out, through Article 58,

States have subscribed here to a triple duty to act, which must imperatively be translated into instructions to be given, and first of all into measures to be taken already in peacetime, even though, strictly speaking, the article is only addressed to Parties to a conflict. Some of these measures have a preventive or precautionary character since they are concerned with preventing the construction of certain buildings in particular places, or removing objectives from an area where such buildings are located, or otherwise separating the population and their homes from dangerous places. For that matter, as stated above, it is in their own interest that States should take such measures.[23]

Article 56 *API* further requires that the Parties to the conflict shall endeavour to avoid locating any military objectives in the vicinity of dangerous works or installations. Such provisions are crucial to ensuring the principle of distinction works to protect civilian lives and property. By clearly providing that both parties have obligations with regards to separating the fight from the civilian population the likelihood of 'collateral damage' can be decreased.

The lack of attention to the provisions in Articles 56 and 58 of *API* are quite evident in peacetime society. These accountability mechanisms appear all but unknown to town planners in most peacetime countries. The location of significant military installations in urban areas is very common in many countries. Clearly military personnel need access to services including schools and places of employment for their spouses and other family members, and urban sprawl often puts traditionally more remote military facilities in urban areas. However, one wonders what contingency plans these countries have in place for separating the military and civilian population should conflict reach the borders of these nations.

---

23 Sandoz *et al.* (eds), above n 18, 692.

D. The obligation to review new means and methods of warfare

Another accountability mechanism is the process provided for in Article 36 of *API* to consider the compatibility of new weapons technologies with the fundamental principles of IHL. Over the years the ICRC has taken a number of measures in an attempt to encourage States to adopt formal systems for compliance with Article 36. The 27th International Conference of the Red Cross and Red Crescent in 1999 and the 28th Conference in 2003 both 'called on states to establish mechanisms and procedures to determine the conformity of weapons with international law'.[24] However, to date only a handful of States have such mechanisms in place.[25] The Article 36 obligation implies that a State would have a mandatory procedure to check a weapon's compliance with the principles of IHL, an obligation which is activated when a new weapon is developed or acquired.[26] Compliance with this kind of accountability mechanism is vital to the parts of the *Geneva Conventions* which are concerned with distinction, proportionality and unnecessary suffering.

As Durham has noted elsewhere, implementing the *Geneva Conventions* requires significant expertise, resources and commitment from the implementing State, and may include assistance from the international community.[27] Further, it is a process that requires involvement from a range of areas within government and society including town planners, educational institutions, hospitals, the press, civil society, weapons manufacturers, civil defence, shipping and aircraft authorities and environmental advisers.[28] In addition to the provisions mentioned in more detail above, implementation also requires:

- Ensuring that medical and religious personnel have adequate identification (such as a distinctive emblem and identity card);
- Ensuring that civilian hospitals are able to be marked with the emblem and are not located near military sites;
- Identifying potential hospital and safety zones;
- Identifying which aircraft would potentially function as medical transportation;
- Ensuring that there is the capacity and process to create a national information bureau for prisoners of war and civilians detained.[29]

---

24 Kathleen Lawland, 'Reviewing the Legality of New Weapons, Means and Methods of Warfare' (2006) 88 (864) *International Review of the Red Cross* 925, 926.
25 ICRC, *A Guide to the Legal Review of New Weapons, Means and Methods of Warfare* (January 2006) ICRC www.icrc.org/eng/assets/files/other/icrc_002_0902.pdf 5.
26 Kathleen Lawland, above n 24, 927.
27 Helen Durham, 'From Paper to Practice: The Role of Treaty Ratification Post Conflict' in B Bowden *et al.* (eds), *The Role of International Law in Rebuilding Societies after Conflict* (CUP, 2009) 180.
28 Ibid 182.
29 *GCIII* Article 122; *GCIV* Article 137.

E. Common Article 1 obligations

Finally, it is worth noting that Article 1, common to all four *Geneva Conventions* and Article 1(1) of *Additional Protocols I and III to the Geneva Conventions* (hereinafter Common Article 1), provides that '[t]he High Contracting Parties undertake to respect and to ensure respect for the [. . .] *Convention* [and *Protocol*] in all circumstances'. Many of the measures which States must take, by way of compliance with the obligation to respect the *Geneva Conventions*, are specifically discussed above. Other aspects of 'respect' include the legislative work required for treaty compliance. For IHL this includes the introduction of legislation to protect the red cross, red crescent and red crystal emblems,[30] the requirement to enact legislation to provide effective penal sanction for breaches provisions[31] and the incorporation of other IHL treaties a State is a party to in domestic laws. It is also clear that there is an obligation on States to ensure that their armed forces comply with IHL when abroad.[32] Of course some of these 'respect' obligations are applicable in times of peace as well as in times of war.

So while 'respect' is a reference to the obligation on States to ensure that those actors within their territory or jurisdiction comply with the provisions of the *Geneva Conventions*, there is clearly some ambiguity about the meaning of 'undertake to . . . ensure respect' for the *Geneva Conventions*. Some advocate the idea that 'ensure respect' is little different in meaning to 'respect', while others assert that it refers to the rights or duties of third party States to take measures to ensure respect for the *Geneva Conventions* by those violating, or in danger of violating them.[33] This later approach has been articulated by many (and taken as assumed by many). Sassoli asserts that the Common Article 1 obligation 'is today unanimously understood as referring to violations by other States'.[34] Gasser notes that 'States not involved in a conflict have not only a right – even a duty – to take seriously their role as guardians of the humanitarian *Geneva Conventions*, but also have an interest in doing so'.[35] And even those who dispute the legal basis for this, such as Kalshoven, see it as a moral obligation: 'when it comes to reading into Article 1 any effect beyond the sphere of the State's internal

---

30 *GCI* Article 53; see also *APIII*.

31 *GCI* Article 49; *GCII* Article 50; *GCIII* Article 129; *GCIV* Article 146; *API* Article 88.

32 *Prosecutor v Tadić (Judgment) (International Criminal Tribunal for the former Yugoslavia, Appeals Chamber,* Case No IT-94-1-A, 15 July 1999).

33 See Carlo Focarelli, 'Common Article 1 of the 1949 Geneva Conventions: A Soap Bubble?' (2010) 21(1) *The European Journal of International Law* 125, 137. See also Laurence Boisson de Chazournes and Luigi Condorelli, 'Common Article 1 of the Geneva Conventions Revisited: Protecting Collective Interests' (2000) 837 *International Review of the Red Cross* 67, 69.

34 Marco Sassoli, 'State Responsibility for Violations of International Humanitarian Law' (2002) 846 *International Review of the Red Cross* 401, 421.

35 Hans-Peter Gasser, 'Ensuring respect for the Geneva Conventions and Protocols: The Role of Third States and the United Nations' in Michael Meyer (ed.), *Effecting Compliance: Armed Conflict and the New Law* vol 2 (British Institute of International and Comparative Law, 1993) 48.

affairs, it lies in adding to the State's *right* as a Party to the *Conventions* to make other States respect their terms, a *moral incentive* or "obligation" to do so'.[36]

As such, there is arguably an aspect of accountability for IHL that third States have also accepted responsibility for in their signature and ratification of the *Geneva Conventions.* A number of authors have given consideration to measures a State can take to ensure that a third State respects IHL – both in times of peace and in times of conflict. Palwankar, for example, notes that in peacetime State actions could include the provision of legal advisers to assist in developing or adapting national legislation and penal codes for effective implementation of IHL, training legal advisers within the armed forces, teaching IHL as part of military cooperation, holding regional and international seminars with the participation of States to debate the issues and helping set up regional databanks on various aspects related to national measures and their implementation.[37] Gasser makes an important point that 'influencing the way humanitarian obligations are carried out by a belligerent party must necessarily be clearly explained, convincingly justified and properly carried out if such action is not to be misunderstood as improper interference in the internal affairs of a sovereign State'.[38] As such, while potentially a difficult landscape to manoeuvre, this is clearly another aspect of accountability for IHL violations that deserves greater attention.

III. Cultural and social influences on IHL accountability

As noted previously in this chapter, while prosecution is an essential part of ensuring accountability for IHL, there is also a need to review other options to restrict and reduce suffering during times of armed conflict. A review of the role cultural and social influences play in urging compliance with IHL is a complex theme to examine and requires more detail than can be provided in this section of the chapter. However, it is necessary to touch on some of the major discussion involved in attempts to move from the mechanics of accountability to a culture of accountability.

There are dangers in invoking 'cultural norms' as a reason to follow and adhere to IHL or any other area of international law. To start with, culture itself has evaded a universally agreed definition.[39] Furthermore, culture and law (in

---

36 Frits Kalshoven, 'The Undertaking to Respect and Ensure Respect in All Circumstances: From Tiny Seed to Ripening Fruit' (1999) 2 *Yearbook of International Humanitarian Law* 3, 60.

37 Umesh Palwankar, 'Measures Available to States for Fulfilling their Obligation to Ensure Respect for International Humanitarian Law' (1994) 298 *International Review of the Red Cross* 9, 11.

38 Gasser, above n 35, 27.

39 Helen Durham, 'The Laws of War and Traditional Cultures' (2008) 34(4) *Commonwealth Law Bulletin* 836.

particular international law that often claims 'universality' and a global reach) have a fraught relationship. There can be perils involved in placing so-called 'universal' and secular norms of IHL into local and often contrary contexts. Such situations often result in tension being created between the law wanting to have strong connections to local communities while concurrently wanting to transform traditional practices that do not adhere to the aims of the legal framework. As Sally Engle Merry has stated '[r]ights need to be presented in local cultural terms in order to be persuasive, but they must challenge existing relations of power in order to be effective'.[40]

Taking into account such complexities, work has been done to find connections between the principles found in IHL and traditional cultural practices of warfare in a number of different locations. *Under the Protection of the Palm: Wars of Dignity in the Pacific*[41] is a study which demonstrates that traditional warfare in the Pacific did contain limitations – in many instances in areas that echo the legal principles found in IHL. For example, the saying from the Papua New Guinea Highlands that 'if more than three or four people are killed in a single fight, there may be an outcry that the enemy is "shooting like wild pigs"'[42] reflects elements of the principle of proportionality under IHL (as articulated by *API* Articles 51 and 57) and also an accountability element. The 'outcry' that such action creates is a form of accountability through social pressure and shame. Accountability through social pressure is also very evident in the fact that in the Highlands those breaking the rules of combat were not punished in an individual sense but rather their society as a whole was exposed to the same sort of act they had imposed upon their opponents.[43] In holding warring parties to account and trying to limit some of the suffering during the conflict it was noted that '[i]n general, matters of pride and honour were strong sources of social control and limitations placed on warfare and served humanitarian purposes as well as broader social functions'.[44] Many of the most fundamental tenants of IHL were reflected in various traditional practices across a diverse range of Pacific cultures. For example, restrictions on children fighting in conflict were noted in several countries including Vanuatu and the Solomon Islands and humane treatment of captured enemies was noted in communities in Fiji, Samoa and the Solomon Islands.[45] Rules relating to the protection of cultural property and of warriors being easily distinguished were also very relevant to certain Pacific cultures.[46]

---

40   Sally Merry, *Human Rights and Gender Violence: Translating International Law into Local Justice* (University of Chicago Press, 2006) 5.
41   ICRC, *Under the Protection of the Palm: Wars of Dignity in the Pacific* (ICRC, 2009).
42   Ibid 43.
43   Ibid 39.
44   Durham, 'The Laws of War and Traditional Cultures', above n 39, 838.
45   Ibid 839.
46   Ibid 840.

Other documents such as *Spared by the Spear*,[47] *African Customary Humanitarian Law*[48] and *Arabian Epics*[49] raise similar examples of traditional practices and customs that have broad philosophical connections to the aims of modern IHL through examples of oral history and other cultural practices. Finding these linkages between traditional and cultural practices and attempts to hold warring parties to account is an interesting and unexplored area of research. It must be factored into the wider debates of accountability but needs to be done with caution and care.

One author who has done significant work in reflecting upon the best methods to ensure accountability for the norms found within IHL outside the process of prosecution is Hugo Slim. In his book *Killing Civilians*[50] he argues that there is a need to challenge an 'anti-civilian' thinking and encourage pro-civilian ideologues to develop. Anti-civilian thinking involves ideologies which regard people as purely enemies and can sometimes reject the notion that civilians (especially on the 'other side') are even people. He notes that there is ample evidence of how people find reasons to kill and hurt civilians during conflict and how sufficient people can be recruited and enabled to carry out these tasks. He writes:

> Any practical effect to encourage the contrary ideology of limited warfare and its central concern for civilian protection will need to go head-to-head with these various anti-civilian ideologies and challenge the social and psychological conditioning that makes people agree to and enact them.[51]

Slim's call to action involves making an impact on the wide public arena in a process of long-term political change. He advocates using governments, community and religious leaders, professionals, young people and others as 'connectors' to convince people that deliberately harming and killing civilians during war is wrong. It is a call that is similar to the 'dissemination' of IHL but works at a broader, ethical level and challenges deep-rooted traditions of cultures of violence within societies.

In some senses, recent debates relating to policies such as Responsibility to Protect (R2P)[52] are political attempts to challenge global cultures of impunity

---

47 ICRC, *Spared by the Spear: Traditional Somali Behaviour in Warfare* (ICRC, 1997).
48 Emmanuel Bello, 'Shared Legal Concepts' in *African Customary Humanitarian Law* (University of California, 1980).
49 ICRC, *Arabian Epics* (ICRC Cairo, 1997).
50 Hugo Slim, *Killing Civilians: Methods, Madness and Morality in War* (Hurst & Company, 2007).
51 Ibid 250.
52 UNGA (60th session) 2005 World Summit Outcome (15 September 2005) UNDoc A/Res/60/1 http://daccessdds.un.org/doc/UNDOC/GEN/N05/487/60/PDF/N0548760.pdf?OpenElement; UNGA (63rd session) Implementing the Responsibility to Protect (12 January 2009) UNDoc A/63/677 http://daccessdds.un.org/doc/UNDOC/GEN/N05/487/60/PDF/N0548760.pdf?OpenElement.

and lack of genuine accountability. R2P could be seen as a discourse regarding the appropriate response of the international community, not only to the most heinous of international crimes, but to taking responsibility to prevent such crimes occurring in the first place. The three pillars approach to the Responsibility to Protect doctrine (that a State has primary responsibility to protect those under its jurisdiction from the crimes of genocide, war crimes, ethnic cleansing and crimes against humanity; that all members of the international community have a responsibility to assist States to fulfil this responsibility; that if a State is 'manifestly failing to protect' then the international community is 'prepared to take collective action in a timely and decision manner'[53]) includes a focus on State responsibility and international support and capacity-building towards prevention.

There are many ways to attempt to locate an appreciation of responsibility for war crimes and an urging for limitations to be followed during conflict. It can be done through a review of traditional practices; challenges to cultures of violence or via the development of agreements on new approaches, including at the international level. More nebulous to capture than an enforcement mechanism, such elements play an important role in the ongoing debates.

IV. The role of quasi-judicial and non-judicial bodies in the interpretation and application of IHL

Quasi-judicial bodies, such as truth and reconciliation commissions, and mechanisms such as commissions of enquiry also contribute in varying ways to accountability for violations of IHL. Such measures are used for a variety of reasons, including the rationale that those methods may assist with a peace process and/or moving towards a better future for the population as well as practical considerations such as the sheer numbers of people who may need to be dealt with by the system.[54] Such measures are not without controversy as notions such as accountability, truth and justice 'are always socially constructed and culturally constituted'.[55] Whether truth and reconciliation, for example, is effective as an accountability measure has attracted much attention. Gibson notes

---

53 UNGA (63rd session) above n 52, [139].
54 The existence of some accountability mechanisms clearly comes from the impracticality of prosecution in some circumstances. The Gacaca Court System established in Rwanda in the aftermath of the 1994 genocide in that country is one such example. Anne Aghion's documentary films about the post-genocide reconciliation work in Rwanda note that by 2000, there were over 130,000 genocide prisoners and thousands yet to be tried, and the government had to find a way to expedite both the justice and healing processes leading to the release of many to local tribunals, with the ultimate goal of having the truth revealed rather than punishing the criminals http://bostonfilms.wordpress.com/2009/08/19/truth-and-reconciliation-in-rwanda/.
55 Kevin Avruch and Beatriz Vejarano, 'Truth and Reconciliation Commissions: A Review Essay and Annotated Bibliography' (2002) 4(2) *The Online Journal of Peace and Conflict Resolution* 37, 43.

that the South African truth and reconciliation experience was based on the idea that 'national unity and reconciliation could be achieved only, it was argued, if the truth about past violations became publicly known and acknowledged', but his findings indicate that the reality is not so simple.[56] Further, culture and context play a significant role. Avruch and Vejarano encapsulate this conclusion well when they note:

> for whatever the value of these commissions may be, they will certainly face new sets of challenges if and when they seek to work to ascertain truth(s), or to effect reconciliation, in cultural settings different from the ones attempted thus far – and, perhaps even more so, if and when they seek to do their work across significant cultural borders.[57]

A recent commission of inquiry – commissioned by the UN Human Rights Council – called for independent international fact-finding into Israel's military campaign in Gaza between December 2008 and January 2009. The resulting Goldstone findings reported evidence indicating actions amounting to war crimes and possibly crimes against humanity that were committed by both sides and recommended that both parties, Hamas and Israel, investigate transparently and in good faith, the incidents referred to in the report. A subsequent report by McGowen Davis has found that Israel has 'dedicated significant resources to investigate over 400 allegations of operational misconduct in Gaza reported by the [International Independent Fact-Finding Mission] and others',[58] although issues such as transparency, the participation of victims and witnesses in investigations, the promptness of some investigations and the duration of the ongoing investigations into the allegations remain of concern.[59] The finding is that the de facto Gaza authorities have not conducted any investigations into the launching of rocket and mortar attacks against Israel.[60] This would suggest this approach has struggled to influence accountability.

The Commission of Inquiry approach is also being used currently by the UN Human Rights Council in Syria. The Independent International Commission of Inquiry on the Syrian Arab Republic was established on 22 August 2011. It has a mandate to investigate all alleged violations of international human rights law since March 2011 in the Syrian Arab Republic. The Commission has also been tasked to:

---

56 James Gibson, 'Does Truth Lead to Reconciliation? Testing the Causal Assumptions of the South African Truth and Reconciliation Process' (2004) 48(2) *American Journal of Political Science* 201, 202.

57 Kevin Avruch and Beatriz Vejarano, above n 55, 43.

58 Human Rights Council, *Report of the Committee of Independent Experts in International Humanitarian and Human Rights Law Established Pursuant to Council Resolution 13/9* A/HRC/16/24 (18 March 2011) 21.

59 Ibid 22.

60 Ibid 23.

establish the facts and circumstances that may amount to such violations and of the crimes perpetrated and, where possible, to identify those responsible with a view to ensuring that perpetrators of violations, including those that may constitute crimes against humanity, are held accountable.[61]

An interesting model of accountability is the payment of reparation for violations of international humanitarian law. For example, between 2000 and 2009, the Eritrea-Ethiopia Claims Commission decided through binding arbitration all claims between the two governments and between private entities for loss, damage or injury related to the conflict and resulting from violations of international humanitarian law or other violations of international law.[62]

Another model, the United Nations Compensation Commission, established by the Security Council in 1991, interestingly compensates losses arising as a direct result of Iraq's invasion and occupation of Kuwait, regardless of whether or not they were caused by a violation of IHL.[63] Gillard also notes the *1995 General Framework Agreement for Peace in Bosnia and Herzegovina*, concluded between Croatia, Bosnia-Herzegovina and the former Yugoslavia, which expressly addressed the plight of civilians who, as a result of hostilities and wartime legislation, suffered widespread loss of property rights. The agreement established an innovative mechanism for the return of real property by setting up a Commission for Real Property Claims of Displaced Persons and Refugees which had the authority to make final and legally binding decisions on claims for real property and occupancy rights which must be respected by both entities in Bosnia and Herzegovina.[64]

V. Conclusion

The role of international criminal law has been usefully highlighted in the last decade. Eminent academics such as McCormack have led the way in raising the critical need for international prosecutions and the specific benefits that result in due process and fair trials.[65] Today there is a comfort level by the public and

---

61 United Nations Human Rights Council, *Independent International Commission of Inquiry on the Syrian Arab Republic*, 2012 www.ohchr.org/EN/HRBodies/HRC/IICISyria/Pages/AboutCo I.aspx.

62 Emanuela-Chiara Gillard, 'Reparations for Violations of International Humanitarian Law' (2003) 851 *International Review of the Red Cross* 529, 534.

63 SC Res 692, 2987th mtg, UN Doc Un S/RES/692 (20 May 1991) www.uncc.ch/resolutio/ res0692.pdf; Ibid 541.

64 Gillard, above n 62, 544.

65 Tim McCormack, 'Contributions of the Nuremberg Trial to the Subsequent Development of International Law' in David Blumenthal and Tim McCormack (eds), *The Legacy of Nuremberg: Civilising Influence or Institutionalised Vengeance?* (Martinus Nijhoff, 2008) 101–29; Tim McCormack, 'The Contribution of the International Criminal Court to Increasing Respect for International Humanitarian Law' (2008) 27(1) *University of Tasmania Law Review* 22.

even an understanding by global leaders of the need to ensure that impunity is not an automatic right of those in power and that international courts and tribunals play a legitimate role in the discourse of accountability. However as has been discussed in this chapter, accountability involves more than prosecutions and a wider examination, not just of normative legal obligations, but ways to find connections to ideas of a culture of accountability is increasingly important. If we are to continue to strive for Gustav Moynier's vision of each State being 'ultimately the best guardian of the limits it has itself imposed' we need to be multi-focused and multi-disciplined – prosecuting, educating, connecting, implementing and finding new ways to inspire accountability.

Bibliography

Cases

IMT

United States v Wilhelm von Leeb et al. (*Judgment*), Case No 12 in *Trials of War Criminals before the Nuernberg Military Tribunals under Control Council No 10, Nuernberg, October 1946–April 1949* (US Government Printing Office, 1950) vol XI, 462

United States v Wilhelm List et al. (*Judgment*), Case No 7 in *Trials of War Criminals before the Nuernberg Military Tribunals under Control Council No 10, Nuernberg, October 1946–April 1949* (US Government Printing Office, 1950) vol XI, 1230

United States of America v List (*Hostages Trial*), in H. Lauterpacht (ed.), *Annual Digest and Reports of Public International Law Cases: Being a Selection from the Decisions of International Courts and Tribunals and Military Courts given during the year 1948* (Butterworth, 1953) 632

Trial of Karl Buck and Ten Others (British Military Court, Wuppertal, Germany, 6–10 May 1946), Case No 29 in United Nations War Crimes Commission, *Law Reports of Trials of War Criminals* (His Majesty's Stationery Office, 1948) vol 5, 39

United States et al. v Göring et al., 1 TMWC 171 (1946) 223

ICTY

Prosecutor v Prlić et al. (*Judgment*) (International Criminal Tribunal for the Former Yugoslavia, Trial Chamber III, Case No IT-04–74-T, 29 May 2013)

Prosecutor v Prlić et al. (*Judgment, Separate and Partially Dissenting Opinion of Presiding Judge, Jean-Claude Antonetti*) (International Criminal Tribunal for the Former Yugoslavia, Trial Chamber III, Case No IT-04–74-T, 29 May 2013) vol 6

Prosecutor v Gotovina et al. (*Judgment*) (International Criminal Tribunal for the Former Yugoslavia, Appeals Chamber, Case No. IT-06–90-A, 16 November 2012)

Prosecutor v Đorđević (*Judgment*) (International Criminal Tribunal for the Former Yugoslavia, Trial Chamber II, Case No IT-05–87/1, 23 February 2011)

Prosecutor v Boškoski and Tarčulovski (*Judgment*) (International Criminal Tribunal for the Former Yugoslavia, Appeals Chamber, Case No IT-04–82, 19 May 2010)

Prosecutor v Milutinović et al. (*Judgment*) (International Criminal Tribunal for the Former Yugoslavia, Trial Chamber III, Case No IT-05–87, 26 February 2009)

Prosecutor v Delić (*Judgment*) (International Criminal Tribunal for the Former Yugoslavia, Trial Chamber I, Case No IT-04–83, 15 September 2008)

Prosecutor v Strugar (Judgment) (International Criminal Tribunal for the Former Yugoslavia, Appeals Chamber, Case No IT-01–42-A, 17 July 2008)

Prosecutor v Martić (International Criminal Tribunal for the Former Yugoslavia, Trial Chamber, Case No IT-95–11-T, 12 June 2007)

Prosecutor v Brđanin (Judgment) (International Criminal Tribunal for the Former Yugoslavia, Appeals Chamber, Case No IT-99–36-A, 3 April 2007)

Prosecutor v Galić (International Criminal Tribunal for the Former Yugoslavia, Appeals Chamber, Case No IT-98–29-A, 30 November 2006)

Prosecutor v Hadžihasanović and Kubura (International Criminal Tribunal for the Former Yugoslavia, Case No IT-01–47, 15 March 2006)

Prosecutor v Strugar (Judgment) (International Criminal Tribunal for the Former Yugoslavia, Trial Chamber II, Case No IT-01–42-T, 31 January 2005)

Prosecutor v Blagojević (International Criminal Tribunal for the Former Yugoslavia, Trial Chamber, Case No IT-02–60-T, 17 January 2005)

Prosecutor v Kordić and Čerkez (Judgment) (International Criminal Tribunal for the Former Yugoslavia, Appeals Chamber, Case No IT-95–14/2, 17 December 2004)

Prosecutor v Brđanin (Judgment) (International Criminal Tribunal for the Former Yugoslavia, Trial Chamber II, Case No IT-99–36, 1 September 2004)

Prosecutor v Blaškić (Judgment) (International Criminal Tribunal for the Former Yugoslavia, Appeals Chamber, Case No IT-95–14, 29 July 2004)

Prosecutor v Milošević (Decision on Motion for Judgment of Acquittal) (International Criminal Tribunal for the Former Yugoslavia, Trial Chamber III, Case No IT-02–54-T, 16 June 2004)

Prosecutor v Jokić (Sentencing Judgment) (International Criminal Tribunal for the Former Yugoslavia, Trial Chamber, Case No IT-01–42/1-S, 18 March 2004)

Prosecutor v Kordić and Čerkez (Decision on Appellant's Notice and Supplemental Notice of Prosecution's Non-Compliance with its Disclosure Obligations Under Rule 68 of the Rules) (International Criminal Tribunal for the Former Yugoslavia, Trial Chamber III, Case No IT-95–14/2, 11 February 2004)

Prosecutor v Galić (International Criminal Tribunal for the Former Yugoslavia, Trial Chamber, Case No IT-98–29-T, 5 December 2003)

Prosecutor v Naletilić and Martinović (Judgment) (International Criminal Tribunal for the Former Yugoslavia, Trial Chamber I, Case No IT-98–34, 31 March 2003)

Prosecutor v Kordić and Čerkez (Judgment) (International Criminal Tribunal for the Former Yugoslavia, Trial Chamber III, Case No IT-95–14/2, 26 February 2001)

Prosecutor v Delalić et al. (Judgment) (International Criminal Tribunal for the Former Yugoslavia, Appeals Chamber, Case No IT-96–21-A, 20 February 2001)

Prosecutor v Blaškić (Judgment) (International Criminal Tribunal for the Former Yugoslavia, Trial Chamber, Case No IT-95–14-T, 3 March 2000)

Prosecutor v Kupreškić et al. (Judgment) (International Criminal Tribunal for the Former Yugoslavia, Trial Chamber, Case No IT–95–16-T, 14 January 2000)

Prosecutor v Delalić et al. (Judgment) (International Criminal Tribunal for the Former Yugoslavia, Trial Chamber II, Case No IT-96–21, 16 November 1998)

Prosecutor v Erdemović (Sentencing Judgment) (International Criminal Tribunal for the Former Yugoslavia, Trial Chamber, Case No IT-96–22-Tbis, 5 March 1998)

Prosecutor v Tadić (Decision of the Defence Motion for Interlocutory Appeal on Jurisdiction) (International Criminal Tribunal for the Former Yugoslavia, Appeals Chamber, Case No IT-94–1-AR, 2 October 1995)

ICTR

Prosecutor v Ndindiliyimana et al. (*Judgment*) (International Criminal Tribunal for Rwanda, Appeals Chamber, Case No ICTR-00–56-A, 27 February 2014)

Prosecutor v Karera (*Judgment*) (International Criminal Tribunal for Rwanda, Appeals Chamber, Case No ICTR-01–74, 2 February 2009)

Prosecutor v Nahimana et al. (*Judgment*) (International Criminal Tribunal for Rwanda, Appeals Chamber, Case No ICTR-99–52, 28 November 2007)

Prosecutor v Muvunyi (*Judgment*) (International Criminal Tribunal for Rwanda, Trial Chamber II, Case No ICTR-00–55, 12 September 2006)

Prosecutor v Kamuhanda (*Judgment*) (International Criminal Tribunal for Rwanda, Appeals Chamber, Case No ICTR-99–54A, 19 September 2005)

Prosecutor v Semanza (*Judgment*) (International Criminal Tribunal for Rwanda, Appeals Chamber, Case No ICTR-97–20, 20 May 2005)

Prosecutor v Gacumbitsi (*Judgment*) (International Criminal Tribunal for Rwanda, Trial Chamber III, Case No ICTR-01–64, 17 June 2004)

Prosecutor v Kamuhanda (*Judgment*) (International Criminal Tribunal for Rwanda, Trial Chamber II, Case No ICTR-99–54, 22 January 2004)

Prosecutor v Semanza (*Judgment*) (International Criminal Tribunal for Rwanda, Trial Chamber III, Case No ICTR-97–20, 15 May 2003)

Prosecutor v Akayesu (*Judgment*) (International Criminal Tribunal for Rwanda, Trial Chamber I, Case No ICTR-96–4, 2 September 1998)

ICJ

Application of the Convention on the Prevention and Punishment of the Crime of Genocide (*Croatia v Serbia*) (The list of pending cases is available on the ICJ's website: www.icj-cij.org)

Case Concerning Armed Activities on the Territory of the Congo (*Democratic Republic of the Congo v Uganda*) (*Unreported Judgment*)

Armed Activities in the Territory of the Democratic Republic of Congo (*DRC v Uganda*) (2005) ICJ Rep 7

Legal Consequences of the Construction of a Wall in the Occupied Palestinian Territory (Advisory Opinion) (2004) ICJ Rep 136

Legality of Use of Force (*Yugoslavia v United Kingdom*) (Provisional Measures) (1999) ICJ Rep 826

Legality of the Threat or Use of Nuclear Weapons (Advisory Opinion) (1996) ICJ Rep 226

Application of the Convention on the Prevention and Punishment of the Crime of Genocide (*Bosnia-Herzegovina v Yugoslavia*) (Provisional Measures) (1993) ICJ Rep 325

Military and Paramilitary Activities in and Against Nicaragua (*Nicaragua v United States of America*) (Merits) (1986) ICJ Rep 14

Case of Military and Paramilitary Activities in and against Nicaragua (*Nicaragua v the United States of America*) (Jurisdiction and Admissibility) (1984) ICJ Rep 551

Military and Paramilitary Activities in and against Nicaragua (*Nicaragua v United States of America*) (Provisional Measures) (1984) ICJ Rep 392

Reservations to the Convention on the Prevention and Punishment of the Crime of Genocide (1950–1951) (Advisory Opinion) (1951) ICJ Rep 15

Competence of the General Assembly for the Admission of a State to the United Nations (1949–1950) (Advisory Opinion) (1950) ICJ Rep 57

Corfu Channel Case (*United Kingdom v Albania*) (Merits) (1949) ICJ Rep 35

Conditions of Admission of a State to Membership in the United Nations (Article 4 of Charter) (Advisory Opinion) (1947–1948) ICJ Rep 57

Corfu Channel Case (*United Kingdom v Albania*) (Preliminary Objections) (1947–1948) ICJ Rep 15

Case Concerning the Application of the Convention on the Prevention and Punishment of the Crime of Genocide (*Bosnia Herzegovina v Yugoslavia*) (Provisional Measures) (1933) ICJ Rep 3

ICC

Prosecutor v Bosco Ntaganda (Decision Pursuant to Article 61(7)(a) and (b) of the Rome Statute on the Charges of the Prosecutor against Bosco Ntaganda) (International Criminal Court, Pre-Trial Chamber II, Case No ICC-01/04-02/06) (*Ntaganda Confirmation* Decision)

Prosecutor v Laurent Gbagbo and Charles Blé Goudé (Decision on Prosecution Requests to Join the Cases and Related Matters) (International Criminal Court, Trial Chamber I, Case Nos ICC-02/11-01/11 and ICC-02/11-02/11, 11 March 2015)

Prosecutor v Bosco Ntaganda (Updated Document Containing the Charges) (International Criminal Court, Pre-Trial Chamber II, Case No ICC-01/04-02/06, 16 February 2015) [1], [5]–[6] (*Ntaganda DCC*)

Prosecutor v Gharles Blé Goudé (Decision on the Confirmation of Charges against Charles Blé Goudé) (International Criminal Court, Pre-Trial Chamber I, Case No ICC-02/11-02/11, 11 December 2014)

Prosecutor v Thomas Lubanga Dyilo (Judgment on the Appeal of Mr Thomas Lubanga Dyilo against His Conviction) (International Criminal Court, Appeals Chamber, Case No ICC/01/04-01/06 A 5, 1 December 2014)

Prosecutor v Laurent Gbagbo (Decision on the Confirmation of Charges against Laurent Gbagbo) (International Criminal Court, Pre-Trial Chamber I, Case No ICC-02/11-01/11, 12 June 2014)

Prosecutor v Ntaganda (Transcript of Confirmation Hearing) (International Criminal Court, Pre-Trial Chamber I, Case No ICC-01/04–02/06, 12 February 2014)

Prosecutor v Ntaganda (Document Containing the Charges) (International Criminal Court, Pre-Trial Chamber I, Case No ICC-01/04–02/06, 10 January 2014)

Prosecutor v William Samoei Ruto and Joshua Arap Sang (Prosecution's Updated Pre-Trial Brief) (International Criminal Court, Trial Chamber V(A), Case No ICC-01/09–01/11, 9 September 2013)

Prosecutor v Ngudjolo (Judgment pursuant to Article 74 of the Statute: Concurring Opinion of Judge Van den Wyngaert) (International Criminal Court, Trial Chamber II, Case No ICC-01/04–02/12, 18 December 2012)

Prosecutor v William Samoei Ruto and Joshua Arap Sang (Prosecution Filing in Compliance with the Chamber's 'Order Regarding Applications for Notice of Possibility of Variation of Legal Characterisation') (International Criminal Court, Trial Chamber V(A), Case No ICC-01/09–01/11, 17 September 2012) Annex A

Prosecutor v Mudacumura (Decision on the Prosecutor's Application under Article 58) (International Criminal Court, Pre-Trial Chamber II, Case No ICC-01/04–01/12, 13 July 2012)

Prosecutor v Mudacumura (Second Prosecution's Application under Article 58) (International Criminal Court, Pre-Trial Chamber II, Case No ICC-01/04, 4 July 2012)

Prosecutor v William Samoei Ruto and Joshua Arap Sang (*Prosecution's Submissions on the Law of Indirect Co-perpetration under Article 25(3)(a) of the Statute and Application for Notice to Be Given under Regulation 55(2) with respect to William Samoei Ruto's Individual Criminal Responsibility*) (International Criminal Court, Trial Chamber V, Case No ICC-01/09–01/11, 3 July 2012)

Prosecutor v Lubanga (*Judgment: Separate Opinion of Judge Fulford*) (International Criminal Court, Trial Chamber I, Case No ICC-01/04–01/06, 14 March 2012)

Prosecutor v Katanga (*Judgment on the Appeal of Mr Katanga against the Decision of the Trial Chamber II of 22 January 2010 entitled 'Decision on the Modalities of Victim Participation at Trial'*) (International Criminal Court, Appeals Chamber, Case No ICC-01/04–01/07 OA 11, 16 July 2010)

Prosecutor v Katanga (*Decision on the Modalities of Victim Participation at Trial*) (International Criminal Court, Trial Chamber II, Case No ICC-01/04–01/07–1788, 22 January 2010) (*Katanga Decision on Victims Participation*)

Prosecutor v Lubanga (*Decision on the Defence Application for Disclosure of Victims Applications*) (International Criminal Court, Trial Chamber I, Case No ICC-01/04- 01/06–1637, 21 January 2009)

Prosecutor v Katanga (*Defence for Mathieu Ngudjolo, 'Application to Determine the Modalities of the Participation of Victims at the Trial Stage'*) (International Criminal Court, Trial Chamber II, Case No ICC-01/04–01/07, 13 January 2009)

Prosecutor v Katanga and Mathieu Ngudjolo Chui (*Decision on the Confirmation of Charges*) (International Criminal Court, Pre-Trial Chamber I, Case No ICC-01/04–01/07, 30 September 2008)

Prosecutor v Lubanga (*Judgment on the appeals of The Prosecutor and The Defence against Trial Chamber I's Decision on Victims' Participation of 18 January 2008*) (International Criminal Court, Trial Chamber I, Case No ICC-01/04–01/06 OA 9 OA 10, 11 July 2008)

Prosecutor v Katanga (*Decision on Article 54(3)(e) Documents Identified as Potentially Exculpatory or Otherwise Material to the Defence's Preparation for the Confirmation Hearing*) (International Criminal Court, Pre-Trial Chamber I, Case No ICC-01/04–01/07–621, 20 June 2008)

Prosecutor v Lubanga (*Decision on the Consequences of Non-Disclosure of Exculpatory Materials Covered by Article 54(3)(e) Agreements and the Application to Stay the Prosecution of the Accused, Together with Certain other Issues Raised at the Status Conference on 10 June 2008*) (International Criminal Court, Trial Chamber I, Case No ICC-01/04–01/06, 13 June 2008)

Prosecutor v Lubanga (*Decision on Victims' Participation*) (International Criminal Court, Trial Chamber I, Case No ICC-01/04–01/06, 18 January 2008)

Prosecutor v Lubanga (*Decision on Confirmation of Charges*) (International Criminal Court, Pre-Trial Chamber I, Case No ICC/01/04–01/06, 29 January 2007)

Situation in Uganda (*Warrant of Arrest for Dominic Ongwen*) (International Criminal Court, Pre-Trial Chamber II, Case No ICC/02/04, 8 July 2005)

Other

R v Gul (Appellant) [2013] UKSC 64

Al-Skeini v UK (ECtHR, Grand Chamber, Application No 55721/07, 7 July 2011)

Tabet v Attorney-General (2011) HCJ 474/02

Al-Marri v Pucciarelli 534 F 3d 213 (4th Cir, 2008)

Yoav Hess v Judge Advocate General (2008) HCJ 8794/03

Case of the Ituango Massacres (*Judgment*) (IACtHR, Ser C, No 148, 1 July 2006).

Public Committee against Torture in Israel v Government of Israel [2006] HCJ 769/02

Case of the 'Mapiripan Massacre' (Judgment) (IACtHR, Ser C, No 134, 15 September 2005)
Isayeva v Russia (2005) 41 EHRR 38
SRYYY v Minister for Immigration and Multicultural and Indigenous Affairs (2005) 147 FCR 1
Ergi v Turkey (2001) 32 EHRR 18, [85]
McKerr v UK (2001) 34 EHRR 553, 559
Coard et al. v US (1999) IACiHR
Nulyarimma v Thompson (1999) 96 FCR 153
In the matter of an application for a writ of mandamus directed to Phillip R Thompson
    Ex parte Wadjularbinna Nulyarimma, Isobel Coe, Billy Craigie and Robbie Thorpe
    (Applicants), Tom Trevorrow, Irene Watson, Kevin Buzzacott and Michael J Anderson
    (Intervenors) [1998] ACTSC 136 (18 December 1998)
Kruger v Commonwealth (1997) 190 CLR 1
McCann v UK (1996) 21 EHRR 97
United States v McMonagle 38 MJ 53 (CMA 1993)
Dietrich v The Queen (1992) 177 CLR 292
People v Adams (1972) 9 Ill App 3d 61
Public Prosecutor v Oie Hee Koi and others (Malaysia) [1967] UKPC 21
R v Page [1954] 1 QB 170
Chow Hung Ching and Another v The King (1949) 77 CLR 449
Henwood v People (1913) 54 Colo 188

Instruments

National legislation

Crimes Legislation Amendment (Torture Prohibition and Death Penalty Abolition) Act
    2010 (Cth)
Explanatory Memorandum, Crimes Legislation Amendment (Torture Prohibition and
    Death Penalty Abolition) Bill 2009 (Cth)
International Criminal Court (Consequential Amendments) Act 2002 (Cth)
International Criminal Court Act 2002 (Cth)
Explanatory Memorandum, International Criminal Court (Consequential Amendments)
    Bill 2002 (Cth)
Criminal Code Act 1995 (Cth)
Geneva Conventions Amendment Act 1991 (Cth)
Crimes (Torture) Act 1988 (Cth)
War Crimes Amendment Act 1988 (Cth)
War Crimes Amendment Bill 1987 (Cth)
Defence Force Discipline Act 1982 (Cth)
Crimes Act 1961 (NZ)
Geneva Conventions Act 1957 (Cth)
Genocide Convention Act 1949 (Cth)
Genocide Convention Bill 1949 (Cth)
War Crimes Act 1945 (Cth)

Treaties

Charter of the International Military Tribunal, annexed to Agreement for the Prosecution
    and Punishment of the Major War Criminals of the European Axis, signed in London
    8 August 1945, 82 UNTS 279

Charter of the International Military Tribunal for the Far East, signed in Tokyo on 19 January 1946, amended 26 April 1946, TIAS 1589, 4 Bevans 20

Convention (II) with respect to the Laws and Customs of War on Land, opened for signature, The Hague, 29 July 1899, 32 Stat. 1803, TS 403, 26 (entered into force 4 September 1900)

Convention for the Pacific Settlement of International Disputes (Hague Convention I), opened for signature 18 October 1907, UKTS 6 (entered into force 26 January 1910)

Convention relative to the Opening of Hostilities (Hague Convention III), opened for signature 18 October 1907, 205 CTS 264 (entered into force 26 January 1910)

Convention (IV) respecting the Laws and Customs of War on Land, The Hague, 18 October 1907, 36 Stat. 2277 (1907), TS 539, 3 (entered into force 26 January 1910)

Convention (IX) concerning Bombardment by Naval Forces in Times of War, The Hague, 18 October 1907, 36 Stat 2351 (entered into force 26 January 1910)

Convention on the Prevention and Punishment of the Crime of Genocide (*Genocide Convention*), opened for signature 9 December 1948, 78 UNTS 277 (entered into force 12 January 1951)

Convention (I) for the Amelioration of the Condition of the Wounded and Sick in Armed Forces in the Field, opened for signature 12 August 1949, 75 UNTS 31 (entered into force 21 October 1950)

Convention (II) for the Amelioration of the Condition of Wounded, Sick and Shipwrecked Members of Armed Forces at Sea, opened for signature 12 August 1949, 75 UNTS 85 (entered into force 21 October 1950)

Convention (III) Relative to the Treatment of Prisoners of War, opened for signature 12 August 1949, 75 UNTS 135 (entered into force 21 October 1950)

Convention (IV) Relative to the Protection of Civilian Persons in Time of War, opened for signature 12 August 1949, 75 UNTS 287 (entered into force 21 October 1950)

Convention for the Protection of Cultural Property in the Event of Armed Conflict, opened for signature 14 May 1954, 249 UNTS 215 (entered into force 7 August 1956)

Convention on the Law of Treaties, opened for signature 23 May 1969, 1155 UNTS 331 (entered into force 27 January 1980)

Convention concerning the Protection of the World Cultural and Natural Heritage, opened for signature 16 November 1972, 1037 UNTS 151 (entered into force 17 December 1975)

Convention against Torture and Other Cruel, Inhuman or Degrading Treatment or Punishment, opened for signature 10 December 1984, 1465 UNTS 85 (entered into force 26 June 1987)

Geneva Convention of July 27, 1929, for the Amelioration of the Condition of the Wounded and Sick of Armies in the Field, opened for signature 27 July 1929, 2 Bevans 965 (entered into force 19 June 1931)

International Covenant on Civil and Political Rights, opened for signature 16 December 1966, 999 UNTS 171 (entered into force 23 March 1976)

Protocol Additional to the Geneva Conventions of 12 August 1949, and Relating to the Adoption of an Additional Distinctive Emblem, opened for signature 8 December 2005, 75 UNTS 31 (entered into force 14 January 2007)

Protocol Additional to the Geneva Conventions of 12 August 1949, and Relating to the Protection of Victims of International Armed Conflicts (Protocol I), adopted 8 June 1977, 1125 UNTS 3 (entered into force 7 December 1978)

Protocol Additional to the Geneva Conventions of 12 August 1949, and Relating to the Protection of Victims of Non-International Armed Conflicts (Protocol II), adopted 8 June 1977, 1125 UNTS 609 (entered into force 7 December 1978)

Rome Statute of the International Criminal Court, opened for signature 17 July 1998, 2187 UNTS 3 (entered into force 1 July 2002)

Second Protocol to the Hague Convention for the Protection of Cultural Property in the Event of Armed Conflict, opened for signature 26 March 1999, 38 ILM 769 (entered into force 9 March 2004)

Special Proclamation by the Supreme Commander for the Allied Powers at Tokyo (Tokyo Charter), adopted 19 January 1946

Statute of the International Court of Justice, 33 UNTS 993

Treaty of Peace between the Allied and Associated Powers and Germany (Peace Treaty of Versailles), signed 28 June 1919, UKTS 4 (entered into force 20 January 1920)

Treaty of Peace between the Allied Powers and Turkey (Peace Treaty of Sevres), signed 10 August 1920

Treaty on the Protection of Artistic and Scientific Institutions and Historic Monuments, signed 15 April 1935 at Washington, D.C., 49 Stat 3267 TS 899, 167 LNTS 289 (entered into force 26 August 1935)

UN Documents

2005 World Summit Outcome, GA Res 60/1, 60th sess, UN Doc A/Res/60/1 (24 October 2005)

Basic Principles on the Use of Force and Firearms by Law Enforcement Officials, adopted by the Eighth United Nations Congress on the Prevention of Crime and the Treatment of Offenders, Havana, Cuba, 27 August to 7 September 1990 www2.ohchr.org/english/law/firearms.htm

Civil and Political Rights, including the Question of Disappearances and Summary Executions: Extrajudicial, Summary or Arbitrary Executions: Report of the Special Rapporteur, Philip Alston: Addendum, UN ESCOR, UN Doc E/CN.4/2006/53/Add.1 (26 March 2006)

Commission on Human Rights, *Fifth Periodic Report on the Situation of Human Rights in the Territory of the Former Yugoslavia Submitted by Mr. Tadeusz Mazowiecki, Special Rapporteur of the Commission on Human Rights, Pursuant to Paragraph 32 of Commission Resolution 1993/7 of 23 February* 1993, 50th sess, UN Doc E/CN.4/1994/47 (17 November 1993)

Committee for the Protection of Cultural Property in the Event of Armed Conflict, Second Protocol to the Hague Convention of 1954 for the Protection of Cultural Property in the Event of Armed Conflict, Item 11 of the Provisional Agenda: *Consideration of Requests for the Granting of Enhanced Protection*, 8th mtg, UNESCO, 18–19 December 2013, CLT-13/8.COM/CONF.203/8, Paris, 17 October 2013; List of Cultural Property under Enhanced Protection (10 sites, all of them being World Heritage properties) http://unesco.org/.../culture/...protection/.../cultural-property/enhanced-pr...

Control Council Law No 10: Punishment of Persons Guilty of War Crimes, Crimes against Peace and against Humanity, signed 20 December 1945, 3 *Official Gazette of the Control Council for Germany* 50–55 (31 January 1946)

Decisions Taken by the Preparatory Committee at its Session Held from 11–21 February 1997, UN Doc A/AC.249/1997/L.5 (12 March 1997) annex II (*Report of the Working Group on General Principles of Criminal Law and Penalties*)

Emmerson, Ben, *Promotion and Protection of Human Rights and Fundamental Freedoms while Countering Terrorism* (Interim Report), 68th Sess, UN Doc A/68/389 (18 September 2013)

Final Report Submitted by Barbara Frey, Special Rapporteur, in accordance with Sub-Commission Resolution 2002/25 – Prevention of Human Rights Violations Committed with Small Arms and Light Weapons, UN Doc A/HRC/Sub.1/58/27 (2006)

General Comment 2 on Implementation of Article 2 by States Parties of the Convention Against Torture and Other Cruel, Inhuman Or Degrading Treatment Or Punishment (UN Doc CAT/C/GC/@/CRP.1/Rev.4) (23 November 2007)

Heyns, Christof, *Report of the Special Rapporteur on Extrajudicial, Summary or Arbitrary Executions*, 68th Sess, UN Doc A/68/382 (13 September 2013)

Human Rights Committee, *General Comment No 29: States of Emergency (Article 4)*, UN Doc CCPR/C/21/Rev.1/Add.11 (31 August 2001)

Human Rights Committee, *General Comment No.31: The Nature of the General Legal Obligation Imposed on States Parties to the Covenant*, UN Doc CCPR/C/21/Rev.1/Add.13 (26 May 2004)

Human Rights Committee, *Views: Communication No R.11/45*, 37th sess, UN Doc A/37/40 (5 February 1979) 137 (*de Guerrero v Colombia*)

Human Rights Committee, *Views: Communication No. 563/1993* (27 October 1995) (*Bautista de Arellana v Columbia*)

Human Rights Council, *Report of the Committee of Independent Experts in International Humanitarian and Human Rights Law to Monitor and Assess any Domestic, Legal or other Proceedings Undertaken by both the Government of Israel and the Palestinian side, in Light of General Assembly Resolution 64/245, Including the Independence, Effectiveness, Genuineness of these Investigations and their Conformity with International Standards*, UN Doc A/HRC/15/50 (23 September 2010)

Human Rights Council, *Report of the Independent International Commission of Inquiry on the Syrian Arab Republic*, 25th sess, UN Doc A/HRC/25/65 (12 February 2014)

Human Rights in Palestine and Other Occupied Arab Territories: Report of the United Nations Fact Finding Mission on the Gaza Conflict, UN Doc A/HRC/12/48 (23 September 2009)

Human Rights Council, 25th sess, Agenda item 4: Human Rights Situations that Require the Council's Attention, *Oral Update of the Independent International Commission of Inquiry on the Syrian Arab Republic* (18 March 2014)

International Criminal Court, *Rules of Procedure and Evidence*, Doc No ICC-ASP/1/3 (adopted 9 September 2002)

Meeting at the Security Council on Safe, Unhindered Passage for Convoys, Demilitarization of Medical Centres, Schools, Water Centres, 7039th mtg, UN Doc SC/11138 (2 October 2013) www.un.org/News/Press/docs/2013/sc11138.doc.htm

Meeting at the Security Council on the Protection of Civilians in Armed Conflict, 7109th mtg, UN Doc S/PV/7109 (12 February 2014)

Meeting at the Security Council on the Situation in the Middle East, 7116th mtg, UN Doc S/PV/7116 (22 February 2014)

Principles on the Effective Investigation and Documentation of Torture and Other Cruel, Inhuman or Degrading Treatment or Punishment, GA Res 55/89, UN GAOR, UN Doc A/RES/55/89 (22 February 2001)

Principles on the Effective Prevention and Investigation of Extra-Legal, Arbitrary and Summary Executions, ESC Res 1989/65, UN ESCOR, 15th plen mtg, UN Doc E/RES/1989/65 (24 May 1989)

Report of the Preparatory Committee on the Establishment of an International Criminal Court, UN Doc A/Conf.183/2/Add.1 (14 April 1998) Add (*Part One: Draft Statute for the International Criminal Court*)

Report of the Secretary-General Pursuant to Paragraph 2 of Security Council Resolution 808 (1993) UN Doc S/25704 of 3 May 1993, 32 ILM 1159

Second Protocol to the Hague Convention of 1954 for the Protection of Cultural Property in the Event of Armed Conflict, Committee for the Protection of Cultural Property in the Event of Armed Conflict, 8th mtg, UNESCO Headquarters, Paris, 18–19 December 2013, Item 11 of the Provisional Agenda: Consideration of Requests for the Granting of Enhanced Protection, CLT-13/8.COM/CONF.203/8 (17 October 2013)

Second Protocol to the Hague Convention of 1954 for the Protection of Cultural Property in the Event of Armed Conflict, Committee for the Protection of Cultural Property in the Event of Armed Conflict, 9th mtg, UNESCO Headquarters, Paris, 18–19 December 2014, Item 3 of the Provisional Agenda, CLT-14/9.Com/CONF.203/7 (22 October 2014)

Statement by the President of the Security Council, 7039th mtg, UN Doc S/PRST/2013/15 (2 October 2013)

Statute of the International Criminal Tribunal for Rwanda (as last amended on 13 October 2006), adopted 8 November 1994, annexed to SC Res 955 (1994), UN Doc S/RES/955

Statute of the International Criminal Tribunal for the Former Yugoslavia (as amended on 17 May 2002), adopted 25 May 1993, annexed to SC Res 827 (1993), UN Doc S/RES/827

Strengthening of the coordination of humanitarian emergency assistance of the United Nations, GA Res 46, 78th plen mtg, UN Doc A/RES/46/182 (19 December 1991)

The Basic Principles and Guidelines on the Right to Remedy and Reparations for Victims of Violations of International Human Rights and Serious Violations of International Humanitarian Law, 16 December 2005, UN Doc. A/RES/60/147 (2006)

United Nations Committee Against Torture, *Concluding Observations of the Committee against Torture, Australia,* 40th sess, UN Doc CAT/C/AUS/CO/3 (22 May 2008)

UNESCO World Heritage Committee, 8th sess, Phuket, Thailand, 12–17 December 1994, Information note: *International Register of Cultural Property under Special Protection: Coordination of Implementation of Conventions Protecting the Cultural Heritage,* WHC-94/CONF.003/INF.12 (16 November 1994)

UNGA (63rd sess) *Implementing the Responsibility to Protect* (12 January 2009) UNDoc A/63/677 http://daccessdds.un.org/doc/UNDOC/GEN/N05/487/60/PDF/N0548760.pdf?OpenElement

UNGA (60th sess) *2005 World Summit Outcome* (15 September 2005) UNDoc A/Res/60/1 http://daccessdds.un.org/doc/UNDOC/GEN/N05/487/60/PDF/N0548760.pdf?OpenElement

UN General Assembly, Human Rights Council, 27th sess, Agenda Item 4: Human Rights Situation that Requires the Council's Attention, *Eighth Report of the Independent International Commission of Inquiry on the Syrian Arab Republic,* A/HRC/27/60, 13 August 2014 (published on 27 August 2014)

UN General Assembly, Human Rights Council, 25th sess, Agenda Item 4: Human Rights Situation that Requires the Council's Attention, *Seventh Report of the Independent International Commission of Enquiry on the Syrian Arab Republic,* A/HRC/25/65, 12 February 2014 (published 5 March 2014)

United Nations Security Council, *Report of the Secretary-General on the implementation of Security Council Resolution 2139 (2014),* UN Doc S/2014/525 (23 July 2014)

United Nations Security Council, *Report of the Secretary-General on the implementation of Security Council Resolution 2139 (2014),* UN Doc S/2014/208 (24 March 2014)

United Nations Security Council Resolution, SC Res 2165, 7216th mtg, UN Doc S/RES/2165 (14 July 2014)

United Nations Security Council Resolution, SC Res 2139, 7116th mtg, UN Doc S/RES/2139 (22 February 2014) para 4 (*SC Resolution 2139, UN Doc S/RES/2139*)
United Nations Security Council Resolution, SC Res 692, 2987th mtg, UN Doc S/RES/692 (20 May 1991)

Other

Declaration of St. James's Palace (*St James Declaration (1941)*)
Declaration on Security (*The Moscow Declaration (1943)*)
Statutes of the International Red Cross and Red Crescent Movement, adopted by the 25th International Conference of the Red Cross at Geneva in 1986 and amended in 1995 and 2006

Books

Aarons, Mark, *War Criminals Welcome: Australia, A Sanctuary for Fugitive War Criminals Since 1945* (Black Inc, 2001)
Akkerman, Robert J, Peter Van Krieken and Charles Pannenborg (eds), *Declarations on Principles: A Quest for Universal Peace* (Sijthoff, 1979)
Alexandrov, Stanimir A, *Reservations in Unilateral Declarations Accepting the Compulsory Jurisdiction of the International Court of Justice* (Martinus Nijhoff Publishers, 1995)
Aljaghoub, Mahasen M, *The Advisory Jurisdiction of the International Court of Justice (1946–2005)* (Springer, Berlin, 2006)
American Law Institute, *Restatement of the Law, Foreign Relations Law of the United States* (Office of the Legal Adviser, Department of State, 1986)
American Law Institute, *Model Penal Code and Commentaries* (The Institute, 1980)
Baker, Ray Stannard, *Woodrow Wilson and World Settlement* (Doubleday, Page & Co, 1922)
Ball, Howard, *Prosecuting War Crimes and Genocide: The Twentieth Century Experience* (University Press of Kansas, 1999)
Bantekas, Ilias, *Principles of Direct and Superior Responsibility in International Humanitarian Law* (Manchester University Press, 2002)
Bassiouni, M Cherif, *Crimes against Humanity in International Criminal Law* (Brill, Martinus Nijhoff, 2nd revised edn, 1999)
Bassiouni, M Cherif, *International Crimes: Digest/Index of International Instruments 1815–1985* (Oceana Publications, 1986)
Baylis, John, Steve Smith and Patricia Owens, *The Globalization of World Politics* (Oxford University Press, 2008)
Bello, Emmanuel, 'Shared Legal Concepts' in *African Customary Humanitarian Law* (University of California, 1980)
Ben-Naftali, Orna (ed.), *International Humanitarian Law and International Human Rights Law: Pas de Deux* (Oxford University Press, 2011)
Bevan, David, *A Case to Answer: The Story of Australia's First European War Crimes Prosecution* (Wakefield Press, 1994)
Blewitt, Graham, 'The International Criminal Tribunals for the Former Yugoslavia and Rwanda' in Mark Lattimer and Philippe Sands (eds), *Justice for Crimes against Humanity* (Hart Publishing, 2005)
Blumenthal, DA and TLH McCormack (eds), *The Legacy of Nuremberg: Civilising Influence or Institutionalised Vengeance?* (Martinus Nijhoff Publishers, 2008)

Boas, Gideon, James Bischoff and Natalie Reid, *International Criminal Law Practitioner Library Volume 1: Forms of Responsibility in International Criminal Law* (Cambridge University Press, 2007)

Bothe, Michael, Karl Josef Partsch and Waldemar Solf, *New Rules for Victims of Armed Conflicts: Commentary on the Two 1977 Protocols Additional to the Geneva Conventions of 1949* (Brill, Martinus Nijhoff, 1982)

British Manual of Military Law, No 443 (London, 1914)

Büngener, Lars, 'Disclosure of Evidence' in Christoph Safferling (ed.), *International Criminal Proceedings* (Oxford University Press, 2012)

Byers, Michael (ed.), *The Role of International Law in International Politics: Essays in International Relations and International Law* (Oxford University Press, 2000)

Carrel, Michael, 'Australia's Prosecution of Japanese War Criminals: Stimuli and Constraints' in David A Blumenthal and Timothy LH McCormack (eds), *The Legacy of Nuremberg: Civilising Influence or Institutionalised Vengeance?* (Martinus Nijhoff Publishers, 2008)

Chamberlain, Kevin, *War and Cultural Heritage: An Analysis of the 1954 Convention for the Protection of Cultural Property in the Event of Armed Conflict and Its Two Protocols* (Institute of Art and Law, 2004)

Chen, Lung-Chu, *An Introduction to Contemporary International Law: A Policy-Orientated Approach* (Yale University Press, 1989)

Crawford, Emily, *The Treatment of Combatants and Insurgents under the Law of Armed Conflict* (Oxford University Press, 2010)

Cryer, Robert, 'The Boundaries of Liability in International Criminal Law, or "Selectivity by Stealth"' in Gerry Simpson (ed.), *War Crimes Law* vol 1 (Dartmouth Publishing Company, 2004)

Damrosch, Lori (ed.), *The International Court of Justice at a Crossroads* (Transnational Publishers, Inc, 1987)

Delissen, Astrid JM and Gerard J Tanja (eds), *Humanitarian Law of Armed Conflict Challenges Ahead: Essays in Honour of Frits Kalshoven* (Brill, Martinus Nijhoff, 1991)

Department of the Special Minister of State, *Review of Material Relating to the Entry of Suspected War Criminals into Australia* (Australian Government Publishing Service, 1987)

Deschênes, Jules, *Commission of Inquiry on War Criminals Report* (Alti Rodal for the Deschênes Commission, 1986)

Detter, Ingrid, *The Law of War* (Cambridge University Press, 2nd edn, 2000)

Dinstein, Yoram, *The Conduct of Hostilities under the Law of International Armed Conflict* (Cambridge University Press, 2nd edn, 2010)

Draper, GIAD, *The Red Cross Conventions* (Stevens and Sons Limited, 1958)

Dugard, John, *Recognition and the United Nations* (Grotius Publications Limited, 1987)

Durham, Helen, 'From Paper to Practice: The Role of Treaty Ratification Post Conflict' in B Bowden, H Charlesworth and J Farrall (eds), *The Role of International Law in Rebuilding Societies after Conflict* (Cambridge University Press, 2009)

Durham, H and TLH McCormack (eds), *The Changing Face of Conflict and the Efficacy of International Humanitarian Law* (Kluwer Law International, 1999)

Fedorova, Masha, *The Principle of Equality of Arms in International Criminal Proceedings* (Intersentia, 2012)

Ferencz, Benjamin B, *An International Criminal Court, a Step Toward World Peace: A Documentary History and Analysis* (Oceana Publications, 1980)

Finnin, Sarah, *Elements of Accessorial Modes of Liability: Article 25(3)(b) and (c) of the Rome Statute of the International Criminal Court* (Martinus Nijhoff, 2012)

Fite, Katherine B, *The Nuernberg Judgment, A Summary* (US Government Printing Office, 1947)

Fleck, Dieter (ed.), *The Handbook of Humanitarian Law in Armed Conflict* (Oxford University Press, 2nd edn, 2008)

Franck, Thomas, *The Power Of Legitimacy Among Nations* (Oxford University Press, 1990)

Gasser, HP, 'Ensuring Respect for the Geneva Conventions and Protocols: The Role of Third States and the United Nations' in M Meyer (ed.), *Effecting Compliance: Armed Conflict and the New Law* vol 2 (British Institute of International and Comparative Law, 1993)

Gibson, Kate and Cainnech Lussiaà-Berdou, 'Disclosure of Evidence' in Karim AA Khan, Caroline Buisman and Christopher Gosnell (eds), *Principles of Evidence in International Criminal Justice* (Oxford University Press, 2010)

Green, Leslie C, *The Contemporary Law of Armed Conflict* (Melland Schill Studies in International Law, 3rd edn, 2008)

Greenwood, Christopher, 'Historical Development and Legal Basis' in Dieter Fleck (ed.), *The Handbook of International Humanitarian Law* (Oxford University Press, 2nd edn, 2008, 1st edn, 1995)

Greenwood, Christopher, 'Customary Law Status of the 1977 Geneva Protocols' in Astrid Delissen and Gerard Tanja (eds), *Essays in Honour of Frits Kalshoven* (Brill, Martinus Nijhoff, 1991) 93

Gutman, Roy and David Reiff (eds), *Crimes of War: What the Public Should Know* (Norton and Co, 1999)

Haslam, Emily, 'Victim Participation at the International Criminal Court: A Triumph of Hope over Experience?' in Dominic McGoldrick, Peter Rowe and Eric Donnelly (eds), *The Permanent International Criminal Court: Legal and Policy Issues* (Hart, 2004) 315

Heere, Wybo (ed.), *Contemporary International Law Issues: New Forms New Applications* (Proceedings of the Fourth Hague Joint Conference held in the Hague, The Netherlands, 2–5 July 1997) (TMC Asser Institute, 1997)

Heller, Kevin, 'The Rome Statute of the International Criminal Court' in Kevin Heller and Markus Dubber (eds), *The Handbook of Comparative Criminal Law* (Stanford University Press, 2010) 593

Henckaerts, Jean-Marie and Louise Doswald-Beck (eds), *Customary International Humanitarian Law* (Cambridge University Press, 2005)

Henderson, Ian, *The Contemporary Law of Targeting: Military Objectives, Proportionality and Precautions in Attack under Additional Protocol I* (Martinus Nijhoff, 2009)

Higgins, Rosalyn, *Problems and Process, International Law and How We Use It* (Clarendon Press, 1994)

Horne, Charles F, *The Great Events of the War* (National Alumni, 1923)

Howard, J and TLH McCormack, 'Australia' in B Brandon and M du Plessis (eds), *The Prosecution of International Crimes: A Practical Guide to the Prosecution of ICC Crimes in Commonwealth States* (Commonwealth Secretariat, 2005) 127

Howard, Michael, *Franco-Prussian War: The German Invasion of France 1870–1871* (Macmillan & Co, 1962)

Huntington, Samuel P, *The Soldier And The State* (Belknap Press, 1957)

International and Operational Law Department, Judge Advocate General's Legal Centre and School US Army, *Operational Law Handbook* (Law Department, the Judge Advocate General's Legal Centre and School, 2013)

International Institute of Humanitarian Law, *Rules of Engagement Handbook* (International Institute of Humanitarian Law, 2009)

Jorda, Claude and Jerôme de Hemptinne, 'The Status and Role of the Victim', in Antonio Cassese, Paola Gaeta and John RWD Jones (eds), *The Rome Statute of the International Criminal Court: A Commentary* vol 2 (Oxford University Press, 2002) 1387

Kelly, MJ and TLH McCormack, 'Contributions of the Nuremberg Trial to the Subsequent Development of International Law' in DA Blumenthal and TLH McCormack (eds), *The Legacy of Nuremberg: Civilising Influence or Institutionalised Vengeance?* (Martinus Nijhoff, 2008) 101

Kennedy, David, 'Lawfare and Warfare' in J Crawford and M Koskenniemi (eds), *The Cambridge Companion to International Law* (Cambridge University Press, 2012)

Kennedy, David, *Of War and Law* (Princeton University Press, 2006)

Kennedy, David, *Dark Sides of Virtue: Reassessing International Humanitarianism* (Princeton University Press, 2004)

Kennedy, Paul, *The Parliament of Man, The United Nations and the Quest for World Government* (Allen Lane, 2006)

Kennedy, Paul, *The Rise and Fall of the Great Powers, Economic Change and Military Conflict from 1500–2000* (Fontana Press, 1989)

Koskenniemi, Martii, *Apology to Utopia: The Structure of Legal Argument* (Cambridge University Press, 2006)

Koskenniemi, Martii, 'The Silence of Law/The Voice of Justice' in Laurence Boisson de Chazournes and Philippe Sands (eds), *International Law, The International Court Of Justice and Nuclear Weapons* (Cambridge University Press, 1999)

Lauterpacht, Hersch (ed.), *Oppenheim's International Law: Disputes, War and Neutrality* (Longman, 7th edn, 1952)

Leverick, Fiona, *Killing in Self-Defence* (Oxford University Press, 2006)

Lubell, Noam, *Extraterritorial Use of Force Against Non-State Actors* (Oxford University Press, 2010)

Maogoto, Jackson N, 'Reading the Shadows of History – The Bridges between Turkish and Ethiopian "Internationalised" Domestic Crime Trials' in Gerry J Simpson and Kevin J Heller (eds), *Untold Stories: Hidden Histories of War Crimes Trials* (Oxford University Press, 2013)

Maogoto, Jackson N, *International Criminal Law and State Sovereignty: Versailles to Rome* (Transnational Publishers, 2003)

McCormack, TLH, 'War Crimes' in Valerie Tomaselli and Ingrid Wenzler (eds), *World at Risk: A Global Issues Sourcebook* (CQ Press, 2nd edn, 2010) 568

McCormack, Tim, 'Contributions of the Nuremberg Trial to the Subsequent Development of International Law' in D Blumenthal and T McCormack (eds), *The Legacy of Nuremberg: Civilising Influence or Institutionalised Vengeance?* (Brill, Martinus Nijhoff, 2008) 101

McCormack, TLH, 'An Australian Perspective on the ICRC Customary Law Study' in Anthony M Helm (ed.), *The Law of War in the 21st Century: Weaponry and the Use of Force* (Naval War College, 2006) 81

McCormack, TLH 'Use of Force' in S Blay, R Piotrowicz and B Martin Tsamenyi (eds), *Public International Law: An Australian Perspective* (Oxford University Press, 2nd edn, 2005) 223

McCormack, TLH, 'The Importance of Effective Enforcement of International Humanitarian Law' in Liesbeth Ljinzaad, Johanna van Sambeek and Bahia Tahzib-Lie (eds), *Making the Voice of Humanity Heard: Essays on Humanitarian Assistance and International Humanitarian Law in Honour of HRH Princess Margriet of The Netherlands* (Martinus Nijhoff Publishers, 2004) 319

McCormack, TLH, 'Crimes Against Humanity' in Dominic McGoldrick, Peter Rowe and Eric Donnelly (eds), *The Permanent International Criminal Court: Legal and Policy Issues* (Hart Publishing, 2004) 179

McCormack, TLH, 'Their Atrocities and Our Misdemeanours: The Reticence of States to Try Their Own Nationals for International Crimes' in Mark Lattimer and Philippe Sands (eds), *Justice for Crimes Against Humanity* (Hart Publishing, 2003)

McCormack, TLH, 'Australia's Legislation for the Implementation of the Rome Statute' in Matthias Neuner (ed.), *National Legislation Incorporating International Crimes: Approaches of Civil and Common Law Countries* (Berliner Wissenschafts-Verlag, 2003) 65

McCormack, TLH, 'War Crimes' in Valerie Tomaselli and Sonja Matanovic (eds), *World at Risk: A Global Issues Sourcebook* (CQ Press, 2002) 585

McCormack, TLH, 'From Sun Tzu to the Sixth Committee: The Evolution of an International Criminal Law Regime' in T McCormack and G Simpson (eds), *The Law of War Crimes: National and International Approaches* (Kluwer Law International, 1997) 31

McCormack, TLH, 'The Use of Force' in H Reicher (ed.), *Australian International Law: Cases and Materials* (Law Book Co, 1995) 1028

McCormack, TLH and P Mtharu, 'Cluster Munitions, Proportionality and the Foreseeability of Civilian Damage' in O Engdahl and P Wrange (eds), *Law at War: The Law as it Was and the Law as it Should Be: Liber Amicorum Ove Bring* (Martinus Nijhoff, 2008) 19

McCormack, T and BM Oswald, 'The Maintenance of Law and Order in Military Operations' in Terry D Gill and Dieter Fleck (eds), *The Handbook of the International Law of Military Operations* (Oxford University Press, 2010) 445

McCormack, TLH, M Tilbury and GT Triggs (eds), *A Century of War and Peace: Asia-Pacific Perspectives on the Centenary of the 1899 Hague Peace Conference* (Kluwer Law International, 2001)

McCormack, TLH and GJ Simpson (eds), *The Law of War Crimes: National and International Approaches* (Kluwer Law International, 1997)

McCormack TLH and GJ Simpson, 'Achieving the Promise of Nuremberg: A New International Criminal Law Regime?' in T McCormack and G Simpson (eds), *The Law of War Crimes: National and International Approaches* (Kluwer Law International, 1997) 229

McWhinney, Edward, *Judicial Settlement of International Disputes: Jurisdiction, Justiciability and Judicial Law-Making on the Contemporary International Court* (Brill, Martinus Nijhoff, 1991)

Meijknecht, Anna, *Towards International Personality: The Position of Minorities and Indigenous Peoples in International Law* (Intersentia-Hart, 2001)

Melzer, Nils, *Interpretive Guidance on the Notion of Direct Participation in Hostilities Under International Humanitarian Law* (International Committee of the Red Cross, 2009)

Melzer, Nils, *Targeted Killing in International Law* (Oxford University Press, 2008)

Merrills, JG, *International Dispute Settlement* (Cambridge University Press, 5th edn, 2011)

Merry, Sally, *Human Rights & Gender Violence: Translating International Law into Local Justice* (University of Chicago Press, 2006)

Meyer, Howard N, *The World Court in Action* (Rowman & Littlefield, 2002)

Milanović, Marko, *Extraterritorial Application of Human Rights Treaties: Law, Principles and Policy* (Oxford University Press, 2011)

Moore, Margaret (ed.), *National Self-Determination and Secession* (Oxford University Press, 1998)

Moore, Michael, *Causation and Responsibility: An Essay in Law, Morals, and Metaphysics* (Oxford University Press, 2010)

Morrissey, Peter, 'Applied Rights in International Criminal Law: Defence Counsel and the Right to Disclosure' in Gideon Boas, William A Schabas and Michael P Scharf (eds), *International Criminal Justice: Legitimacy and Coherence* (Edward Elgar, 2012) 68

Muller, AS, D Raič and JM Thuránszky (eds), *The International Court of Justice: Its Future Role after Fifty Years* (Kluwer Law International, Martinus-Nijhoff Publishers, 1997)

Nowak, Manfred, *UN Covenant on Civil and Political Rights: CCPR Commentary* (Engel Publishers, 2nd revised edn, 2005)

Odgers, Stephen, *Principles of Federal Criminal Law* (Thomson Reuters, 2nd edn, 2010)

Ojo, Bamidele, *Human Rights and the New World Order: Universality, Acceptability and Human Diversity* (Nova Science Publishers Inc, 1997)

O'Keefe, Roger, *The Protection of Cultural Property in Armed Conflict* (Cambridge University Press, 2006)

Oppenheim, Lassa, *International Law: A Treatise (War)* (Longmans, Green and Co, 1st edn, 1906)

Petrovic, Jadranka, *The Old Bridge of Mostar and Increasing Respect for Cultural Property in Armed Conflict* (Martinus Nijhoff, 2013)

Petrovic, Jadranka, 'A Monument, Identity and Nationhood: The Case of the Old Bridge of Mostar' in Duncan French (ed.), *Statehood and Self-Determination: Reconciling Tradition and Modernity in International Law* (Cambridge University Press, 2013) 429

Piccigallo, Philip R, *The Japanese on Trial; Allied War Crimes Operations in the East, 1945–1951* (University of Texas Press, 1979)

Pictet, Jean S (ed.), *The Geneva Conventions of 12 August 1949: Commentary* (International Committee of the Red Cross, 1958)

Pictet, Jean (ed.), *The Geneva Conventions of 12 August 1949: Commentary* (International Committee of the Red Cross, 1956)

Roberts, A and R Guelff (eds), *Documents on the Laws of War* (Oxford University Press, 3rd edn, 2000)

Rogers, APV, *Law on the Battlefield* (Melland Schill Studies in International Law, 3rd edn, 2012)

Rogers, APV *Law on the Battlefield* (Manchester University Press, 2004)

Rohan, Colleen, 'Protecting the Rights of the Accused in International Criminal Proceedings: Lip Service or Affirmative Action?' in William A Schabas, Yvonne McDermott and Niamh Hayes (eds), *The Ashgate Research Companion to International Criminal Law* (Ashgate, 2013) 289

Roling, BVA, *The Tokyo Trial and Beyond: Reflections of a Peacemonger* (Polity Press, 1993)

Roth, Brad R, *Governmental Illegitimacy in International Law* (Clarendon Press, 1999)

Safferling, Christoph JM, *Towards an International Criminal Procedure* (Oxford University Press, 2001)

Sandoz, Yves, Christophe Swinarski and Bruno Zimmerman (eds), *Commentary on the Additional Protocols of 8 June 1977 to the Geneva Conventions of 12 August 1949* (Martinus Nijhoff, 1987)

Sands, Philippe, *Lawless World, America and the Making and Breaking of Global Rules* (Penguin, 2005)

Schmitt, Michael, 'The Status of Opposition Fighters in a Non-International Armed Conflict' in Kenneth Watkin and Andrew Norris (eds), *Non-International Armed Conflict in the Twenty-first Century* (International Law Studies, 2012) vol 88, 119

Schmitt, Michael, Charles Garraway and Yoram Dinstein (drafting committee), *The Manual on the Law of Non-International Armed Conflict: With Commentary* (International Institute of Humanitarian Law, 2006)

Scott, James Brown (ed.), *Texts of the Peace Conferences at The Hague, 1899 and 1907* (Boston, 1908)

Shearer, Ivan, 'Jurisdiction' in Sam Blay, Ryszard Piotrowicz and Martin Tsamenyi (eds), *Public International Law: An Australian Perspective* (Oxford University Press, 1st published 1997, 2nd edn, 2005)

Shklar, Judith, *Legalism: Law, Morals and Political Trials* (Harvard University Press, 1964)

Simpson, Gerry, *Law, War & Crime: War Crimes, Trials and the Reinvention of International Law* (Polity, 2007)

Sitaraman, Ganesh, *The Counterinsurgent's Constitution* (Oxford University Press, 2013)

Slim, Hugo, *Killing Civilians: Methods, Madness and Morality in War* (Hurst & Company, 2007)

Slim, Hugo and Miriam Bradley, *Principled Humanitarian Action and Ethical Tensions in Multi-mandate Organisations in Armed Conflict* (World Vision, 2013)

Slim, Hugo and Andrew Bonwick, *Protection: An ALNAP Guide for Humanitarian Agencies* (Overseas Development Institute, 2005)

Steinberger, Helmut, 'The International Court of Justice', in H Steinberger (ed.), *Judicial Settlement of International Disputes* (Springer, 1974)

Straubing, Harold Elk (ed.), *The Last Magnificent War and Eyewitness Accounts of World War I* (Paragon House, 1989)

Szafraz, Renata, *The Compulsory Jurisdiction of the International Court of Justice* (Kluwer Law International incorporating Martinus Nijhoff Publishers, 1993)

Tanaka, Y, T McCormack and G Simpson (eds), *Beyond Victors' Justice: The Tokyo Trial Revisited* (Martinus Nijhoff, 2011)

Taylor, JP, *The Struggle for Mastery in Europe 1848–1918* (Oxford University Press, 1954)

Toman, Jiří, *Cultural Property in War: Improvement in Protection*, A Commentary on the 1999 Second Protocol to the Hague Convention of 1954 for the Protection of Cultural Property in the Event of Armed Conflict (UNESCO Publishing, 2009)

Toman, Jiří, *The Protection of Cultural Property in the Event of Armed Conflict*, Commentary on the Convention for the Protection of Cultural Property in the Event of Armed Conflict, signed on 14 May 1954 in The Hague, and on other instruments concerning such protection (UNESCO Publishing, 1996)

Triffterer, Otto, 'Article 33: Superior Orders and Prescription of Law' in Otto Triffterer (ed.), *Commentary on the Rome Statute of the International Criminal Court: Observers' Notes, Article by Article* (Hart, 2nd edn, 2008)

Triffterer, Otto, 'The New International Criminal Law: Its General Principles Establishing Individual Criminal Responsibility' in Kalliopi Koufa (ed.), *The New International Criminal Law* (Sakkoulas Publications, 2003) 639

Triggs, Gillian, *International Law, Contemporary Principles and Practices* (LexisNexis, 2006)

Triggs, Gillian, 'Australia's War Crimes Trials: All Pity Choked' in Tim McCormack and Gerry Simpson (eds), *The Law of War Crimes; National and International Approaches* (Kluwer Law International, 1997)

UK Ministry of Defence, *The Manual of the Law of Armed Conflict* (Oxford University Press, 2004)

United Nations War Crimes Commission, *History of The United Nations War Crimes Commission and the Development of The Laws of War* (UNWCC by His Majesty's Stationery Office in London, 1948)

Walworth, Arthur, *Wilson and His Peacemakers: American Diplomacy at the Paris Peace Conference 1919* (Norton and Co, 1986)

Walworth, Arthur, *America's Moment: 1918* (Norton and Co, 1918)

Watts, Sean, 'Present and Future Conceptions of the Status of Government Forces in Non-International Armed Conflict' in Kenneth Watkin and Andrew Norris (eds), *Non-International Armed Conflict in the Twenty-first Century* (International Law Studies, 2012) vol 88, 145

Weart, Spencer R, *Never At War: Why Democracies Will Not Fight One Another* (Yale University Press, 2000)

Weller, Marc, *Contested Statehood, Kosovo's Struggle for Independence* (Oxford University Press, 2009)

Werle, Gerhard, *Principles of International Criminal Law* (TMC Asser Press, 2nd edn, 2009)

Journal articles

Abass, Ademola, 'Proving State Responsibility for Genocide: The ICJ in *Bosnia v Serbia* and the International Commission of Inquiry for Darfur' (2008) 31 *Fordham International Law Journal* 871

Akhavan, Payam, 'Beyond Impunity: Can International Criminal Justice Prevent Future Atrocities?' (2001) 95(1) *The American Journal of International Law* 7

Alston, Philip, 'The CIA and Targeted Killings Beyond Borders' (2011) 2 *Harvard National Security Journal* 283

Amerasinghe, CF, 'Hague International Tribunals: The *Bosnia Genocide* Case' (2008) 21 *Leiden Journal of International Law* 411

Angehr, Mark, 'The International Court of Justice's Advisory Jurisdiction and the Review of Security Council and General Assembly Resolutions' (2009) 103(2) *Northwestern University Law Review* 1007

Anoushirvani, Sara, 'The Future of the International Criminal Court: The Long Road to Legitimacy Begins with the Trial of Thomas Lubanga Dyilo' (2010) 22(1) *Pace International Law Review* 213

Arnison, Nancy D, 'International Law and Non-Intervention: When Do Humanitarian Concerns Supersede Sovereignty?' (1993) 17 *Fletcher Forum of World Affairs* 199

Avruch, Kevin and Beatriz Vejarano, 'Truth and Reconciliation Commissions: A Review Essay and Annotated Bibliography' (2002) 4(2) *The Online Journal of Peace and Conflict Resolution* 37

Barber, Rebecca J, 'The Proportionality Equation: Balancing Military Objectives with Civilian Lives in the Armed Conflict in Afghanistan' (2010) 15(3) *Journal of Conflict and Security Law* 467

Ben-Naftali, Orna and Keren Michaeli, ' "We Must Not Make a Scarecrow of the Law": A Legal Analysis of the Israeli Policy of Targeted Killing' (2003) 36 *Cornell International Law Journal* 233

Blum, Gabriella and Philip Heymann, 'Law and Policy of Targeted Killing' (2010) 1 *Harvard National Security Journal* 145

Boas, Gideon, 'War Crimes Prosecutions in Australia and Other Common Law Countries: Some Observations' (2010) 21 *Criminal Law Forum* 313

Boisson de Chazournes, Laurence and Luigi Condorelli, 'Common Article 1 of the Geneva Conventions Revisited: Protecting Collective Interests' (2000) 837 *International Review of the Red Cross* 67

Brunne, J and SJ Toope, 'International Law and Constructivism: Elements of an Interactional Theory of International Law' (2000) 39 *Columbia Journal of Transnational Law* 19

Burri, Thomas, 'The Kosovo Opinion and Secession: The Sounds of Silence and Missing Links' (2010) 11 *German Law Journal* 881

Carne, Greg, 'Is Near Enough Good Enough? – Implementing Australia's International Human Rights Torture Criminalisation and Prohibition Obligations in the *Criminal Code* (Cth)' (2012) 33 *Adelaide Law Review* 229

Cassesse, Antonio, 'The Nicaragua and Tadic Tests Revisited in Light of the ICJ Judgment on Genocide in Bosnia' (2007) 18(4) *European Journal of International Law* 649

Checkel, Jeffrey T, 'The Constructivist Turn in International Relations Theory' (1998) 50(2) *World Politics* 324

Chetail, Vincent, 'The Contribution of the International Court of Justice to International Humanitarian Law' (June 2003) 85(850) *International Review of the Red Cross* 235

Christakis, Theodore, 'The ICJ Advisory Opinion on Kosovo: Has International Law Something to Say about Secession?' (2011) 24(1) *Leiden Journal of International Law* 73

Clark, Roger, 'Drafting a General Part to a Penal Code: Some Thoughts Inspired by the Negotiations on the Rome Statute of the International Criminal Court and by the Court's First Substantive Law Discussion in the *Lubanga Dyilo* Confirmation Proceedings' (2008) 19 *Criminal Law Forum* 519

Clark, Roger, 'The Mental Element in International Criminal Law: The Rome Statute of the International Criminal Court and the Elements of Offences' (2001) 12 *Criminal Law Forum* 291

Cohen, Amichai and Yuval Shany, 'Beyond the Grave Breaches Regime: The Duty to Investigate Alleged Violations of International Law Governing Armed Conflict' (2011) 14 *Yearbook of International Humanitarian Law* 37

Cohen, Amichai and Yuval Shany, 'A Development of Modest Proportions: The Application of the Principle of Proportionality in the *Targeted Killings* Case' (2007) 5 *Journal of International Criminal Justice* 310

Coleman, Andrew, 'The International Court of Justice and Highly Political Matters' (2003) 4(1) *Melbourne Journal of International Law* 29

Collins, Pauline, 'What is Good for the Goose should be Good for the Gander: The Operation of the *Rome Statute* in the Australian Context' (2009) 32(1) *UNSW Law Journal* 106

Corten, Oliver, 'Territorial Integrity Narrowly Interpreted: Reasserting the Classical Inter-State Paradigm of International Law' (2011) 24 (1) *Leiden Journal of International Law* 90

Cronan, Paul, Chris Hanna, Duncan Blake, Ian Henderson and Pat Keane, 'Operations BASTILLE and FALCONER: Legal Support To Commanders' (2011) 184 *Australian Defence Force Journal* 33

Cunliffe, Emma, 'No Longer Lost in the Wilderness: Cultural Property Crimes in Conflict' (2013) 1(4) *Journal of Eastern Mediterranean Archaeology and Heritage Studies* 343

Damaška, Mirjan, 'The Competing Visions of Fairness: The Basic Choice for International Criminal Tribunals' (2001) 36(2) *North Carolina Journal of International Law and Commercial Regulation* 365

Desch, Thomas, 'The Second Protocol to the 1954 Hague Convention for the Protection of Cultural Property in the Event of Armed Conflict' (1999) 2 *Yearbook of International Humanitarian Law* 63

De Vos, Christian M, Case Note: *Prosecutor v Lubanga.* ' "Someone Who Comes Between One Person and Another": *Lubanga*, Local Cooperation and the Right to a Fair Trial' (2011) 12 *Melbourne Journal of International Law* 217

Dimitrijević, Vojin and Marko Milanović, 'The Strange Story of the Bosnian Genocide Case' (2008) 21 *Leiden Journal of International Law* 65

Doherty, Katherine L and Timothy LH McCormack, 'Complementarity as a Catalyst for Comprehensive Domestic Penal Legislation' (1999) 5 *University of California Davis Journal of International Law and Policy* 147

Downey, William, 'The Law of War and Military Necessity' (1953) 47 *American Journal of International Law* 256

Dressler, Joshua, 'Reforming Complicity Law: Trivial Assistance as a Lesser Offense?' (2008) 5 *Ohio State Journal of Criminal Law* 427

Dressler, Joshua, 'Reassessing the Theoretical Underpinnings of Accomplice Liability: New Solutions to an Old Problem' (1985) 37 *Hastings Law Journal* 91

Droege, Cordula, 'Elective Affinities? Human Rights and Humanitarian Law' (2008) 90 *International Review of the Red Cross* 501

Durham, Helen, 'The Laws of War and Traditional Cultures' (2008) 34(4) *Commonwealth Law Bulletin* 836

Fairhall, Paul Ames, 'Reflections on Necessity as a Justification for Torture' (2004) 11 *James Cook University Law Review* 21

Falk, Richard, 'The *Kosovo* Advisory Opinion: Conflict Resolution and Precedent' (2011) 105(1) *American Journal of International Law* 50

Field, Andrew, 'The Legality of Humanitarian Intervention and the Use of Force in the Absence of United Nations Authority' (2000) 26 *Monash University Law Review* 339

Finnin, Sarah, 'Mental Elements under Article 30 of the Rome Statute of the International Criminal Court: A Comparative Analysis' (2012) 61 *International and Comparative Law Quarterly* 325

Focarelli, Carlo, 'Common Article 1 of the 1949 Geneva Conventions: A Soap Bubble?' (2010) 21 *European Journal of International Law* 125

Freeland, Steven, 'The Effectiveness of International Criminal Justice' (2008) *ALTA Law Research Series* 16

Friman, Håkan, 'The International Criminal Court and Participation of Victims: A Third Party to the Proceedings?' (2009) 22 *Leiden Journal of International Law* 485

Frulli, Micaela, 'The Criminalization of Offences Against Cultural Heritage in Times of Armed Conflict: The Quest for Consistency' (2011) 22(1) *European Journal of International Law* 203

Gardam, Judith, 'Proportionality and Force in International Law' (1993) 87 *American Journal of International Law* 391

Gibson, James, 'Does Truth Lead to Reconciliation? Testing the Causal Assumptions of the South African Truth and Reconciliation Process' (2004) 48(2) *American Journal of Political Science* 202

Goodman, Ryan and Derek Jinks, 'Toward an Institutional Theory of Sovereignty' (2003) 55 *Stanford Law Review* 1749

Groome, Dermot, 'Adjudicating Genocide: Is the International Court of Justice Capable of Judging State Criminal Responsibility?' (2007) 31(4) *Fordham International Law Journal* 911

Guilfoyle, Douglas, 'Nulyarimma v Thompson: Is Genocide a Crime at Common Law in Australia?' (2001) 29 *Federal Law Review* 1

Hall, Christopher, 'The First Proposal for an International Criminal Court' (1998) 322 *International Review of the Red Cross* 59

Hannum, Hurst, 'The Advisory Opinion on Kosovo: An Opportunity Lost, or a Poisoned Chalice Refused?' (2011) 24(1) *Leiden Journal of International Law* 15

Harris, Lachlan, 'The International Criminal Court and the Superior Orders Defence' (2004) 22(2) *University of Tasmania Law Review* 200

Hayashi, Nobuo, 'Military Necessity as Normative Indifference' (2013) 44 *Georgetown Journal of International Law* 675

Hays Parks, W, 'Part IX of the ICRC "Direct Participation in Hostilities" Study: No Mandate, No Expertise and Legally Incorrect' (2010) 42 *International Law and Politics* 769

Henckaerts, Jean-Marie, 'Study on Customary International Humanitarian Law: A Contribution to the Understanding and Respect for the Rule of Law in Armed Conflict' (2005) 87(857) *International Review of the Red Cross* 175

Henckaerts, Jean-Marie, 'New Rules for the Protection of Cultural Property in Armed Conflict' (1999) 835 *International Review of the Red Cross* 593

Henderson, Ian, 'Civilian Intelligence Agencies and the Use of Armed Drones' (2010) 13 *Yearbook of International Humanitarian Law* 133

Hensley, Thomas, 'National Bias and the International Court of Justice' (1968) 12 *Midwest Journal of Political Science* 568, 568–9

Hoare, Marko Attila, 'A Case Study in Underachievement: The International Courts and Genocide in Bosnia-Herzegovina' (2011) 6(1) *Genocide Studies and Prevention* 81

Howe, Zoë, 'Can the 1954 Hague Convention Apply to Non-State Actors? A Study of Iraq and Libya' (2012) 47(2) *Texas International Law Journal* 403

Jochnick, Chris af and Roger Normand, 'The Legitimation of Violence: A Critical History of the Laws of War' (1994) 35 *Harvard International Law Journal* 49

Johnston, Peter and Claire Harris, 'Case Notes: SRYYY v Minister for Immigration and Multicultural and Indigenous Affairs: War Crimes and the *Refugee Convention*' (2007) 8(1) *Melbourne Journal of International Law* 108

Jonas, David S and Thomas N Saunders, 'The Object and Purpose of a Treaty: Three Interpretive Methods' (2010) 43 *Vanderbilt Journal of Transnational Law* 565

Kahn, Paul, 'Lessons for International Law From the Gulf War' (1992–1993) 45 *Stanford Law Review* 425

Kalle, Kirss, 'Role of the International Court of Justice: Example of the Genocide Case' (2007–2008) 3 *Acta Societatis Martensis* 143

Kalshoven, Frits, 'The Undertaking to Respect and Ensure Respect in All Circumstances: From Tiny Seed to Ripening Fruit' (1999) 2 *Yearbook of International Humanitarian Law* 3

Katzman, Rachel, 'The Non-Disclosure of Confidential Exculpatory Evidence and the *Lubanga* Proceedings: How the ICC Defence System Affects the Accused's Right to a Fair Trial' (2009) 8 (1) *Northwestern Journal of International Human Rights* 77

Kennedy, David, 'When Renewal Repeats: Thinking Against The Box' (2000) 32 *International Law And Politics* 335

Kennedy, Duncan, 'Form and Substance in Private Law Adjudication' (1976) 89 *Harvard Law Review* 1685

Kirby, Michael, 'War Crimes Prosecutions – An Australian Update' (1993) 10 *Australian Bar Review* 109

Koh, Harold Hongju, 'Why Do Nations Obey International Law' (1996–1997) 106 *Yale Law Journal* 2599

Koh, Harold Hongju, 'Transnational Legal Process' (1996) 75 *Nebraska Law Review* 181

Kohen, Marcelo G and Katherine Del Mar, 'The Kosovo Advisory Opinion and UNSCR 1244 (1999): A Declaration of "Independence from International Law"?' (2011) 24 (1) *Leiden Journal of International Law* 124

Korovin, IE, 'Respect for Sovereignty: An Unchanging Principle of Soviet Foreign Policy' (1956) *International Affairs* (Moscow) 11

Kretzmer, David, 'Rethinking the Application of IHL in Non-International Armed Conflicts' (2009) 42 *Israel Law Review* 8

Kuschnik, Bernhard, 'International Criminal Due Process in the Making: New Tendencies in the Proceedings before the ICC' (2009) 9 *International Criminal Law Review* 157

Lawland, Kathleen, 'Reviewing the Legality of New Weapons, Mean and Methods of Warfare' (2006) 88 (864) *International Review of the Red Cross* 925

Lohr, MF and S Gallotta, 'Legal Support in War: The Role of Military Lawyers' (2003) 4 *Chicago Journal of International Law* (2003) 465

Luban, David, 'Military Necessity and the Culture of Military Law' (2013) 26 *Leiden Journal of International Law* 315

Luban, David, 'A Theory of Crimes Against Humanity' (2004) 29 *Yale Journal of International Law* 85

Lubell, Noam, 'Challenges in Applying Human Rights Law to Armed Conflict' (2005) 87 *International Review of the Red Cross* 737

MacGregor, David, 'Bringing War Criminals to Justice in Australia: Upholding International Criminal Law and the Principle of Non-Refoulement' (2007) 32(3) *Alternative Law Journal* 154

Margalit, Alon, 'Did LOAC Take the Lead? Reassessing Israel's Targeted Killing of Salah Shehadeh and the Subsequent Calls for Criminal Accountability' (2012) 17 *Journal of Conflict & Security Law* 147

May, Larry, 'Targeted Killings and Proportionality in Law: Two Models' (2013) 11 *Journal of International Criminal Justice* 47

McCormack, Tim, 'The Contribution of the International Criminal Court to Increasing Respect for International Humanitarian Law' (2009) 27(1) *University of Tasmania Law Review* 22

McCormack, Tim, 'Sixty Years From Nuremberg: What Progress for International Criminal Law?' (2005) 1 *Jurnul Hukum Humaniter (Humanitarian Law Journal* – in Bahasa) 1 [the same article is also published (with the mutual agreement of both journals) in (2005) 5 *New Zealand Armed Forces Law Review* 1]

McCormack, Tim, 'What's in an Emblem?: Humanitarian Assistance Under Any Other Banner Would be as Comforting' (2000) 1 *Melbourne Journal of International Law* 175

McCormack, Tim, 'From Solferino to Sarajevo: A Continuing Role for International Humanitarian Law?' (1997) 21 *Melbourne University Law Review* 621

McCormack, Tim, 'Selective Reaction to Atrocity: War Crimes and the Development of International Criminal Law' (1997) 60 *Albany Law Review* 68

McCormack, Tim and S Robertson, 'Jurisdictional Aspects of the *Rome Statute* for a New International Criminal Court' (1999) 23 *Melbourne University Law Review* 635

Melzer, Nils, 'Keeping the Balance between Military Necessity and Humanity: A Response to Four Critiques on the ICRC's Interpretive Guidance on the Notion of Direct Participation in Hostilities' (2010) 42 *New York Journal of International Law and Politics* 831

Meron, Theodor, 'The Protection of Cultural Property in the Event of Armed Conflict Within the Case-Law of the International Criminal Tribunal for the Former Yugoslavia' (2005) 57(4) *Museum International* 41

Meyer, David, 'The 1954 Hague Cultural Property Convention and Its Emergence into Customary International Law' (1993) 11 *Boston University International Law Journal* 349

Milligan, Ashlyn, 'Targeting Cultural Property: The Role of International Law' (2008) 19 *Journal of Public and International Affairs* 91

Mitchell, Andrew, 'Genocide, Human Rights Implementation and the Relationship between International and Domestic Law: *Nulyarimma v Thompson*' (2000) 24 *Melbourne University Law Review* 15

Moore, Michael, 'Causing, Aiding, and the Superfluity of Accomplice Liability' (2008) 156 *University of Pennsylvania Law Review* 395

Nemes, Irene, 'Punishing Nazi War Criminals in Australia: Issues of Law and Morality' (1992) 4(2) *Current Issues in Criminal Justice* 141

O'Brien, William, 'The Meaning of "Military Necessity" in International Law' (1957) 1 *World Polity* 109

O'Keefe, Roger, 'Protection of Cultural Property Under International Criminal Law' (2010) 11 *Melbourne Journal of International Law* 1

Palwankar, Umesh, 'Measures Available to States for Fulfilling their Obligation to Ensure Respect for International Humanitarian Law' (1994) 298 *International Review of the Red Cross* 9

Paola, Gaeta, 'On What Conditions Can a State be Held Responsible for Genocide?' (2007) 18(4) *European Journal of International Law* 631

Peters, Anne, 'Does Kosovo Lie in the *Lotus-Land* of Freedom?' (2011) 24 (1) *Leiden Journal of International Law* 95

Petrovic, Jadranka, 'What Next for Endangered Cultural Treasures? The Timbuktu Crisis and the Responsibility to Protect' (2013) 11 *New Zealand Journal of Public and International Law* 381

Quntar, Al, 'Syrian Cultural Property in the Crossfire: Reality and Effectiveness of Protection Efforts' (2013) 1(4) *Journal of Eastern Mediterranean Archaeology and Heritage Studies* 348

Raimondo, Fabian O, 'The International Court of Justice as Guardian of the Unity of Humanitarian Law' (2007) 20 *Leiden Journal of International Law* 593

Rajkovic, Nikolas, 'On "Bad Law" and "Good Politics": The Politics of the ICJ *Genocide* Case and Its Interpretation' (2008) 21 *Leiden Journal of International Law* 885

Ranki, Vera, 'Holocaust History and the Law: 1985–1995' (1997) 3 *Law Text Culture* 53

Ratner, Steven, 'The Schizophrenias of International Criminal Law' (1998) 33(2) *Texas International Law Review* 237

Rottenstiener, Christa, 'The Denial of Humanitarian Assistance as a Crime Under International Law' (1999) 81(835) *International Review of the Red Cross* 555

SáCouto, Susana, 'Reflections on the Judgment of the International Court of Justice in Bosnia's Genocide Case against Serbia and Montenegro' (2007) 15 *Human Rights Brief* 2

Sassoli, Marco, 'State Responsibility for Violations of International Humanitarian Law' (2002) 846 *International Review of the Red Cross* 401

Saul, Ben, 'Prosecuting War Criminals at Balibo under Australian Law: The Killing of Five Journalists in East Timor by Indonesia' (2009) 31 *Sydney Law Review* 83

Saul, Ben, 'The International Crime of Genocide in Australian Law' (2000) 22 *Sydney Law Review* 527

Scheffer, David, 'The World Court's Fractured Ruling on Genocide' (2007) 2(2) *Genocide Studies and Prevention* 123

Schlag, Pierre, 'Rules and Standards' (1985–1986) 33 *UCLA Law Review* 379

Schmitt, Michael N, 'Investigating Violations of International Law in Armed Conflict' (2011) 2 *Harvard National Security Journal* 31

Schmitt, Michael, 'Military Necessity and Humanity in International Humanitarian Law: Preserving the Delicate Balance' (2009–2010) 50 *Virginia Journal of International Law* 795

Scott, Shirley, 'Why Wasn't Genocide A Crime in Australia?: Accounting for the Half-Century Delay in Australia Implementing the Genocide Convention' (2004) 10(2) *Australian Journal of Human Rights* 22

Singleterry, Douglas, '"Ethnic Cleansing" and Genocidal Intent: A Failure of Judicial Interpretation?' (2010) 5(1) *Genocide Studies and Prevention* 39

Sivakumaran, Sandesh, 'Re-Envisaging the International Law of Internal Armed Conflict' (2011) 22(1) *European Journal of International Law* 219

Slim, Hugo, 'Relief Agencies and Moral Standing in War: Principles of Neutrality, Impartiality and Solidarity' (1997) 7(4) *Development in Practice* 342

Sofaer, Abraham, 'International Law and Kosovo' (2000) 36 *Stanford Journal of International Law* 1

Solf, Waldemar, 'The Status of Combatants in non-International Armed Conflicts under Domestic Law and Transnational Practice' (1983) 33 *American University Law Review* 53

Stephens, Dale, 'Rules of Engagement and the Concept of Unit Self Defence' (1998) 45 *Naval Law Review* 126

Stoffels, Ruth Abril, 'Legal Regulation of Humanitarian Assistance in Armed Conflict: Achievements and Gaps' (2004) 86 (855) *International Review of the Red Cross* 515

Suh, Ro, 'Voting Behaviour of National Judges in International Courts' (1969) 63 *American Journal of International Law* 224

Terry, Fiona, 'The International Committee of the Red Cross in Afghanistan: Reasserting the Neutrality of Humanitarian Action' (2011) 93(881) *International Review of the Red Cross* 176

Tonkin, Hannah, 'Defensive Force under the Rome Statute' (2005) 6 *Melbourne Journal of International Law* 86

Triggs, Gillian, 'Implementation of the Rome Statute for the International Criminal Court: A Quiet Revolution in Australian Law' (2003) 25 *Sydney Law Review* 507

Triggs, Gillian, 'Australia's War Crimes Act: Justice Delayed or Denied?' (March, 1990) *Law Institute Journal* 153

Triggs, Gillian, 'Australia's War Crimes Trials: A Moral Necessity or Legal Minefield?' (1987) 16 *Melbourne University Law Review* 382

Trumbull, Charles, 'The Basis of Unit Self-Defence and Implications for the Use of Force' (2012–2013) 23 *Duke Journal of Comparative and International Law* 121

Trumbull, Charles P, 'The Victims of Victim Participation in International Criminal Proceedings' (2008) 29 *Michigan Journal of International Law* 777

Van den Wyngaert, Christine, 'Victims before International Criminal Courts: Some Views and Concerns of an ICC Trial Judge' (2011) 44 *Case Western Reserve Journal of International Law* 475

Varner, Elizabeth, 'The Art of Armed Conflicts: An Analysis of the United States' Legal Requirements Towards Cultural Property under the 1954 Hague Convention' (2011) 44 *Creighton Law Review* 1185

Vidmar, Jure, 'Remedial Secession in International Law: Theory and (Lack of) Practice' (2010) 6(1) *St Anthony's International Review* 37.

Voon, Tania, 'Closing the Gap between Legitimacy and Legality of Humanitarian Intervention: Lessons from East Timor and Kosovo' (2002–2003) 7 *UCLA Journal of International Law and Foreign Affairs* 31

Watkin, Kenneth, 'Assessing Proportionality: Moral Complexity and Legal Rules' (2005) 8 *Yearbook of International Humanitarian Law* 3

Watkin, Kenneth, 'Controlling the Use of Force: A Role for Human Rights Norms in Contemporary Armed Conflict' (2004) 98 *American Journal of International Law* 1

Weill, Sharon, 'The Targeted Killing of Salah Shehadeh: From Gaza to Madrid' (2009) 7 *Journal of International Criminal Justice* 617

Weller, Marc, 'Modesty Can Be A Virtue: Judicial Economy in the *Kosovo* Opinion?' (2011) 24 *Leiden Journal of International Law* 130

Wemmers, Jo-Anne, 'Victims' Rights and the International Criminal Court: Perceptions within the Court regarding the Victims' Right to Participate' (2010) 23 *Leiden Journal of International Law* 629

Wright, Jason, D, '"Excessive" Ambiguity: Analysing and Refining the Proportionality Standard' (2012) 94 *International Review of the Red Cross* 823

Yeo, Stanley, 'Blamable Causation' (2000) 24 *Criminal Law Journal* 144

Zappalà, Salvatore, 'The Rights of Victims v the Rights of the Accused' (2010) 8 *Journal of International Criminal Justice* 137

Other

American Association for the Advancement of Science (AAAS), Geospatial Technologies and Human Rights Project, Ancient History, Modern Destruction: Assessing the Current Status of Syria's World Heritage Sites Using High-Resolution Satellite Imagery www.aaas.org/page/ancient-history-modern-destruction-assessing-current-status ...

AAP, 'UN Urges Halt to Attacks on Syria's Cultural Sites', The Australian (online), 13 March 2014 www.theaustralian.com.au/in-depth/middle-east-in-turmoil/un-urges-halt-to-atta ...

ABC Radio National, 'War Criminals in Australia', Background Briefing, 18 October 2009 www.abc.net.au/rn/backgroundbriefing/stories/2009/2715237.htm

Arimatsu, Louise and Mohbuba Choudhury, 'The Legal Classification of the Armed Conflicts in Syria, Yemen and Libya' (March 2014) Chatham House www.chathamhouse.org/.../20140300ClassificationConflicts/ArimatsuCho ...

Assyrian International News Agency, 'Emergency Support for Syria's Cultural Heritage', 17 July 2014 www.penn.museum

Attorney-General's Department, Report of the Investigations of War Criminals in Australia (1993)

Attorney-General's Department, Report on the Operations of the War Crimes Act 1945 to June 1992 (1992)

Attorney-General's Department, Review of Commonwealth Criminal Law: Final Report (1991)

Attorney-General's Department, Special Investigations Unit – Annual Report 1989 (1990)

Australian Declaration attached to instrument of ratification for the *Rome Statute of the International Criminal Court* (Rome, 17 July 1998), 1 July 2002

'Australian Red Cross' Role in Syria and Iraq', Wednesday, 1 October 2014 www.redcross.org.au/news-syria-iraw-3-oct.aspx

Barnard, Anne, 'Syrian War Takes Heavy Toll at a Crossroad of Cultures', The New York Times (online), 16 April 2014

Bartels, Rogier, 'Prlić *et al.*: The Destruction of the Old Bridge of Mostar and Proportionality', European Journal of International Law Talk www.ejiltalk.org/wp-content/uploads/2013/07/

BBC News Middle East, 'Syria Profile', 7 October 2014 www.bbc.com/news/world-middle-east-14703856

Benvenisti, Eyal, Legal Opinion Submitted to the Turkel Commission, 'The State of Israel's Obligation to Examine and Investigate Violations of the Laws of War' www.turkelcommittee.com/files/wordocs/Benvenisti_opinion.pdf

'Briefing: Holding ISIS to Account' (16 October 2014) IRIN www.irinnews.org/report/ 100720/briefing-holding-isis-to-account

Chulov, Martin, 'Syria's Heritage in Ruins: Before-And-After Pictures', The Guardian (online), 27 January 2014 www.theguardian.com/world/2014/jan/26/syria-heritage-in-ruins-before-and-aft...

Cockburn, Patrick, 'ISIS Consolidates', LRB (online), 21 August 2014 www.lrb.co.uk/ v36/n16/patrick-cockburn/isis-consolidates

Colvin, Mark, 'Fears for Syria's Lost Heritage', PM on ABC News, 3 September 2012 www.abc.net.au/pm/content/2012/s3581988.htm

Commonwealth, Parliamentary Debates, Senate, 4 October 1945, 6464 (George McLeay, Leader of the Opposition)

Commonwealth, Parliamentary Debates, House of Representatives, 4 October 1945, 6510 (John Beasley, Minister for Defence)

Commonwealth, Parliamentary Debates, House of Representatives, 4 October 1945, 6511 (John Beasley, Minister for Defence)

Commonwealth, Parliamentary Debates, House of Representatives, 4 October 1945, 6511 (Archie Cameron)

Commonwealth, Parliamentary Debates, House of Representatives, 19 May 1949, 92 (Joseph Chifley, Prime Minister)

Commonwealth, Parliamentary Debates, House of Representatives, 30 June 1949, 1864 (Robert Menzies, Leader of Opposition)

Commonwealth, Parliamentary Debates, House of Representatives, 30 June 1949, 1865 (Henry Gullett)

Commonwealth, Parliamentary Debates, House of Representatives, 30 June 1949, 1865 (Herbert Evatt, Attorney-General and Minister for External Affairs)

Commonwealth, Parliamentary Debates, House of Representatives, 30 June 1949, 1865 (Robert Menzies, Leader of Opposition)

Commonwealth, Parliamentary Debates, House of Representatives, 30 June 1949, 1867 (Joseph Abbott)

Commonwealth, Parliamentary Debates, House of Representatives, 30 June 1949, 1871 (Archie Cameron)

Commonwealth, Parliamentary Debates, House of Representatives, 30 June 1949, 1872 (Robert Menzies, Leader of Opposition)

Commonwealth, Parliamentary Debates, House of Representatives, 30 June 1949, 1874 (Adair Blain)

Commonwealth, Parliamentary Debates, House of Representatives, 12 November 1957, 2749 (Gough Whitlam)

Commonwealth, Parliamentary Debates, House of Representatives, 12 November 1957, 2769 (Harold Holt)

Commonwealth, Parliamentary Debates, Senate, 5 December 1957, 1754–1755 (Reginald Wright)

Commonwealth, Parliamentary Debates, Senate, 5 December 1957, 1756 (Reginald Wright)

Commonwealth, Parliamentary Debates, House of Representatives, 22 March 1961, 449 (Sir Garfield Barwick, Acting Minister for External Affairs and Attorney General)

Commonwealth, Parliamentary Debates, Senate, 15 August 1974, 965 (Donald Willesee, Minister for Foreign Affairs)

Commonwealth, Parliamentary Debates, House of Representatives, 23 March 1988, 1227 (Lionel Bowen, Attorney-General)

Commonwealth, Parliamentary Debates, House of Representatives, 20 April 1988, 1831 (Duncan Kerr)

Commonwealth, Parliamentary Debates, House of Representatives, 20 April 1988, 1833 (Peter McGauran)

Commonwealth, Parliamentary Debates, Senate, 15 December 1988, 4246 (Robert Hill)

Commonwealth, Parliamentary Debates, Senate, 15 December 1988, 4250 (Robert Hill)

Commonwealth, Parliamentary Debates, Senate, 20 December 1988, 4572 (Michael Tate)

Commonwealth, Parliamentary Debates, House of Representatives, 12 February 1991, 380 (Gavan Duffy)

Commonwealth, Parliamentary Debates, House of Representatives, 19 November 2009, 12197 (Robert McClelland, Attorney-General)

Cotterrell, Lin, Human Rights and Poverty Reduction: Approaches to Human Rights in Humanitarian Crises (October 2005) The Overseas Development Institute www.odi.org.uk/sites/odi.org.uk/files/odi-assets/publications-opinion-files/4345.pdf

Council of Australian Governments, Report, Review of Counter Terrorism Legislation (2013) www.coagctreview.gov.au/Report/Pages/default.aspx

Cunliffe, Emma, Damage to the Soul: Syria's Cultural Heritage in Conflict, Report on the Damage to Cultural Property in Syria (Durham University and Global Heritage Fund, 16 May 2012)

Darke, Diana, 'How Syria's Ancient Treasures are being Smashed', BBC News Magazine (online) 9 July 2014, 2

Fincham, Derek, 'Looting at Ebla in Syria' (8 April 2013) Illicit Cultural Property http://illicitculturalproperty.com/author/webmaster/

Fincham, Derek, 'Documenting destruction in Syria from afar' (13 December 2012) Illicit Cultural Property http://illicitculturalproperty.com/documenting-destruction-in-syria-from-afar/

Fisk, Robert, 'Syria's Ancient Treasures Pulverised' The Independent, Sunday (online) 5 August 2012 www.independent.co.uk/voices/commentators/fisk/robert-fisk-syrias-ancient-tre ...

Frésard, Jean-Jacques, 'Roots of Behaviour in War; A Survey of the Literature' (ICRC, 2004) www.icrc.org/eng/resources/documents/misc/5zbggl.htm 105

Goldman, Robert and Brian Tittemore, 'Unprivileged Combatants and the Hostilities in Afghanistan: Their Status and Rights under International Humanitarian and Human Rights Law' (American Society of International Law: Task Force on Terrorism, 2002) www.asil.org/taskforce/goldman.pdf

Hansen, Fergus, 'Confronting Reality: Responding to War Criminals Living in Australia' (Policy Brief, Lowy Institute for International Policy, February 2009)

Hayashi, Nobuo, 'Basic Principles' www.militarynecessity.com/ .../routledge_loac_handbook_basic_princip...

Heritage for Peace www.heritageforpeace.org/

Huffer, Damien, 'Documenting the Damage: An Interview with Dr Simone Mühl' (3 October 2014) Saving Antiquities for Everyone www.savingantiquities.org/tag/cultural-heritage-3/

Human Rights Council, Report of the Committee of Independent Experts in International Humanitarian and Human Rights Law Established Pursuant to Council Resolution 13/9 A/HRC/16/24 (18 March 2011)

Human Rights and Equal Opportunity Commission, 'Australia's Compliance with the Convention against Torture and Other Cruel, Inhuman and Degrading Treatment or Punishment' (Sydney, April 2008)

ICRC, Under the Protection of the Palm: Wars of Dignity in the Pacific (2009)

ICRC, A Guide to the Legal Review of New Weapons, Means and Methods of Warfare (January 2006) www.icrc.org/eng/assets/files/other/icrc_002_0902.pdf

ICRC, Spared by the Spear: Traditional Somali Behaviour in Warfare (1997)

ICRC, 'Arabian Epics' (ICRC Cairo 1997)

Illicit Cultural Property http://illicitculturalproperty.com/

Independent National Security Legislation Monitor, Declassified Annual Report (2012) www.dpmc.gov.au/inslm/docs/INSLM_Annual_Report_20121220.pdf

Inquest into the Death of Brian Raymond Peters (Unreported, Coroner's Court of New South Wales, Magistrate Pinch, 16 November 2007)

Inter-American Commission on Human Rights, Report on Terrorism and Human Rights, OEA/Ser.L/V/II.116 Doc. 5 rev. 1 corr. (22 October 2002) www.cidh. oas.org/Terrorism/Eng/toc.htm

International Committee of the Red Cross's website www.icrc.org

International Committee of the Red Cross, The Relevance of IHL in the Context of Terrorism (2011) www.icrc.org/eng/resources/documents/misc/terrorism-ihl-210705.htm

International Court of Justice website www.icj-cij.org

International Criminal Tribunal for the Former Yugoslavia website www.icty.org

International Law Commission, 'Draft Code of Crimes against the Peace and Security of Mankind with Commentaries' (1996), reprinted in (1996) II(2) *Yearbook of the International Law Commission* 17

IRIN, 'Briefing: Holding ISIS to Account' www.irinnews.org/report/100720/briefing-holding-isis-to-account

Joint Standing Committee on Treaties, Parliament of the Commonwealth of Australia, Report 45: *The Statute of the International Criminal Court* (2002)

Jordash, Wayne, Fairness of Karadžic Trial in Question (4 October 2010) International Justice Tribune www.rnw.nl/international-justice/article/fairness-karadzic-trial-question

Ki-moon, Ban, United Nations Secretary-General, 'Crisis in Syria: Civil War, Global Threat' (25 June 2014) Huffington Post www.huffingtonpost.com/ban-kimoon/crisis-in-syria-civil-war_b_5529973.html

Koelbl, Susanne, 'Interview with UN Peace Envoy Brahimi: "Syria will Become another Somalia"', Spiegel Online International, 7 June 2014 www.spiegel.de/international/world/interview-with-former-un-peace-envoy-to-s ...

Legal and Constitutional References Committee, Senate, Humanity Diminished: The Crime of Genocide – Inquiry into the Anti-Genocide Bill 1999 (2000)

Library of Congress website, Military Legal Resources www.loc.gove/rr/frd/Military_Law

Liivoja, Rain, 'Divergent Approaches to Combatant's Privilege in Municipal Law', Paper presented at the Conference on Investigating Operational Incidents in a Military Context: Law, Justice, Politics, Australian Centre for Military & Security Law, Australian National University, Canberra, 29 September 2012)

Maigua, Patrick, 'UN Envoy: Syrian Crisis a Big Threat to World Peace and Security', United Nations Radio, Geneva www.multimedia.org/radio/english/2013/08/un-envoy-syrian-crisis-a-big-thre ...

Mashberg, Tom, 'Obama Asked to Protect Syrian Heritage Sites' The New York Times (online) 11 September 2013 www.nytimes.com

McCormack, Tim and Paramdeep B. Mtharu, 'Expected Civilian Damage and the Proportionality Equation', Asia Pacific Centre for Military Law, University of Melbourne Law School 2006 www.apcml.org/.../un_report_exp_civilian_damage_1106.pdf

Model Penal Code (American Law Institute, Tentative Draft No 1, 1953)

Nebehay, Stephanie, 'UN Documents New War Crimes in Syria for Future Prosecution' Reuters (online) 25 January 2014 www.reuters.com/article/2014/01/25/us-syria-crisis-warcrimes-idUSBREA0N1SV20140125

Perini, Silvia and Emma Cunliffe, Towards a Protection of the Syrian Cultural Heritage: A Summary of the International Responses (March 2011–March 2014) (Heritage for Peace, April 2014)

Press Conference on Heritage and Conflict in Iraq and Syria at the Metropolitan Museum of Art (22 September, 2014) World Monuments Fund www.wmf.org/journal/remarks-bonnie-burnham-president-world-monuments-fu...

Roorda, Sandra, 'Syria's Cultural Heritage in Danger: What Can We Do?' (21 October 2013) Cultural Heritage – Saving Antiquities for Everyone www.savingantiquities.org/tag/cultural-heritage-3/

'Russia, China Block Security Council Referral of Syria to International Criminal Court' (22 May 2014) United Nations www.un.org/apps/news/story.asp?NewsID=47860

Shaw, Martin, 'The International Court of Justice, Serbia, Bosnia, and Genocide' (28 Feb 2007) Open Democracy www.opendemocracy.net/node/4392/

Sinha, Sanskrity, 'Illicit Excavation in Syria Lethal to Ancient Heritage' IBTimes (online) 6 February 2014 www.ibtimes.co.uk/illicit-excavation-syria-lethal-ancient-heritage-warns-un-143...

Sissons, David, 'The Australian War Crimes Trials and Investigations (1942–1951)' 2006 www.ocf.berkeley.edu/~changmin/documents/Sissons%20Final%20War%20Crimes%20Text%2018-3-06.pdf

Smith, Laura, 'More than 191,000 Dead in Syria, UN Rights Chief Slams "Global Paralysis"' CNN (online) 15 October 2014 www.cnn/com/2014/08/22/world/meast/syria-conflict

Sokol, David, 'World Monuments Fund Releases 2014 Watch List', Architectural Record, 9 October 2013 http://archrecord.construction.com/news/2013/10/13/1009-World-Monuments-Fund-R...

'Syria Opposition Contradicts UN. Says Conflict not Sectarian', Naharnet (online) 22 December 2012 www.nasharnet.com/.../65685-syria-opposition-contradicts-u-n-says-conflict

'Syria Rebels Battle Army in Landmark Aleppo Mosque', The Daily Star (Lebanon) (online) 10 October 2012 www.dailystar.com.lb/News/Middle-East/2012/Oct-10/190895-syria-rebels-battle-army-in-landmark-aleppo-mosque.ashx#axzz29Cam5zsu

'Syrian Heritage' www.asor-syrianheritage.org

'Syrian Refugees Biggest Humanitarian Crisis', Middle East Star (online) 28 August 2014 www.c1000veld.nl/web/browse.php?u...b=5

'Syria's Six World Heritage Sites Placed on List of World Heritage in Danger' (20 June 2013) UNESCO World Heritage Centre http://whc.unesco.org/en/news/1038

Thompson, Edwina, Principled Pragmatism: NGO Engagement with Armed Actors (2008) World Vision International www.eisf.eu/resources/library/Principled pragmatism.pdf

UNESCO, 'Committee for the Protection of Cultural Property in the Event of Armed Conflict' established by the *1999 Protocol* www.unesco.org/new/en/culture/themes/armed-conflict-and-heritage/the-cimmi...

'UNESCO Director-General Condemns Military Presence and Destruction at World Heritage Sites in Syria', UNESCO, 20 February 2014 http://whc.unesco.org/en/news/1108

UNESCO Periodic Reports, 'Syria' www.unesco.org/new/en/safeguarding-syrian-cultural-heritage/

UNESCO Portal http://portal.unesco.org/en/ev.php

UNESCO World Heritage Centre http://whc.unesco.org/en/news/

UNESCO World Heritage Centre, 'World Heritage List' http://whc.unesco.org/en/list/

United Nations, 'Security Council Fails to Adopt Resolution on Syria', UN News Centre (19 July 2012) www.un.org/apps/news/story.asp?NewsID=42513#.U9sTsv7lpzk

United Nations Association of Australia Victoria Division, News, '"Stop the Destruction", UN Officials Urge in Plea to Save Syria's Cultural Heritage', 13 March 2014 www.unaavictoria.org.au/news

United Nations Human Rights, Independent International Commission of Inquiry on the Syrian Arab Republic www.ohchr.org/EN/HRBodies/HRC/IICISyria/Pages/AboutCoI.aspx

UNOSAT, Satellite Imagery Analysis to Assess Cultural Heritage Damage (UNITAR, Geneva, 22 December 2014) www.unitar.org/unosat-report-damage-cultural-heritage-sites-syria-calls-scaled...

UN Press Release, Security Council coverage, 'Referral of Syria to International Criminal Court Fails as Negative Votes Prevent Security Council from Adopting Draft Resolution', SC/11407 (22 May 2014) www.un.org/press/en/2014/sc11407.doc.htm

UNRWA, 'A War on Development: 2nd Report on the Impact of the Syrian Conflict', 30 October 2013 www.unrwa.org/newsroom/press-release/war-development-2nd-report-impact-...

US Department of Defense, Final Report to Congress on Conduct in Persian Gulf War (1992)

Watkin, Kenneth, 'Warriors without Rights? Combatants, Unprivileged Belligerents, and the Struggle over Legitimacy' (Programme on Humanitarian Policy and Conflict Research, 2005) www.hpcr.org/pdfs/OccasionalPaper2.pdf

Weiss, Michael, 'Trust Iran Only As Far As You Can Throw It' Foreign Policy (online) 23 June 2014 www.foreignpolicy.com/2014/06/.../trust-iran-only-as-far-as-you-can-throw-it

World Heritage Site www.worldheritagesite.org/forums/index.php?action=vthread&forum=8&topi...

Wynn-Pope, Phoebe, Evolution of the Protection of Civilians in Armed Conflict (February 2013) Oxfam Australia and Australian Civil-Military Centre www.oxfam.org.au/2013/05/research-for-protection/ and http://acmc.gov.au/in-search-of-common-ground-protection-of-civilians-in-armed-conflict/

Index

Introductory Note

References such as '178–9' indicate (not necessarily continuous) discussion of a topic across a range of pages. Wherever possible in the case of topics with many references, these have either been divided into sub-topics or only the most significant discussions of the topic are listed. Because the entire work is about 'international humanitarian law', the use of this term (and certain others which occur constantly throughout the book) as an entry point has been minimized. Information will be found under the corresponding detailed topics.